Why Do You Need This New Edition?

If you're wondering why you should buy this fifth edition of *Writing and Reading Across the Curriculum, Brief Edition,* here are 8 good reasons!

1. Over 40 brand-new readings span the disciplines and help stimulate your writing by offering new, engaging perspectives on all themes covered in the anthology.

2. To help you make the transition from the instruction of Part I to the anthology chapters in Part III, the fifth edition offers a brand-new section called "A Brief Take." This discussion of "tiger moms" plunges you into the controversy surrounding the op-ed and the book by a mother who denied her children playdates so that they could study relentlessly and master musical instruments.

3. The new anthology chapter "Have You Heard This? The Latest on Rumor" takes a close look at several fascinating rumors of recent decades and provides you with a number of approaches to analyzing these and other rumors—so that you can examine why they began, how they spread, and how they might be stopped.

4. This new edition offers a completely revised and reorganized chapter on analysis that gives you a thorough grounding in both the process of and rhetorical strategies for writing analyses.

5. The Analysis chapter includes a new, excellent student example, "The Case of the Missing Kidney: An Analysis of Rumor." You can pursue the current, fascinating topic of rumor creation and spread more fully in Chapter 7.

6. Roughly half of the anthology selections are new to the fifth edition. Nearly seventy percent of the reading selections for the chapter "The Changing Landscape of Work in the Twenty-First Century" are new to this edition. Also, roughly half of the readings in "Green Power" are new to this edition. Both chapters have been substantially reorganized into clusters of topical readings.

7. The remaining content chapter "New and Improved: Six Decades of Advertising," has also been updated, with several new print ads and TV commercials.

8. *VIDEO LINKS* allow readers to more fully explore aspects of the subject matter through videos readily available on YouTube and other sites. You will be directed to engaging interviews, dramatizations, animations, documentaries, news features, clips from feature films and TV shows, music, and more—all of which should deepen your understanding and enjoyment of the subject at hand.

PEARSON

Writing and Reading Across the Curriculum

 **B** RIEF EDITION

FIFTH EDITION

Laurence Behrens
University of California Santa Barbara

Leonard J. Rosen
Bentley University

Boston   Columbus   Indianapolis   New York   San Francisco
Upper Saddle River   Amsterdam   Cape Town   Dubai   London   Madrid
Milan   Munich   Paris   Montréal   Toronto   Delhi   Mexico City   São Paulo
Sydney   Hong Kong   Seoul   Singapore   Taipei   Tokyo

Senior Acquisitions Editor: Brad Potthoff
Senior Marketing Manager: Sandra McGuire
Senior Supplements Editor: Donna Campion
Production Manager: Savoula Amanatidis
Project Coordination, Text Design, and Electronic Page Makeup: Integra

Cover Design Manager: Wendy Ann Fredericks
Photo Researcher: Catherine Abelman
Senior Manufacturing Buyer: Roy L. Pickering, Jr.
Printer and Binder: R. R. Donnelley and Sons Company—Crawfordsville
Cover Printer: R. R. Donnelley and Sons Company—Crawfordsville

For permission to use copyrighted material, grateful acknowledgment is made to the copyright holders on pp. 399–400, which are hereby made part of this copyright page.

Library of Congress Control Number: (2012955514)

10 9 8 7 6 5 4 3 2 1— DOC —16 15 14 13

Student Edition
ISBN-10:   0-321-90636-5
ISBN-13: 978-0-321-90636-6

Instructor's Review Copy
ISBN-10:   0-321-89540-1
ISBN-13: 978-0-321-89540-0

www.pearsonhighered.com

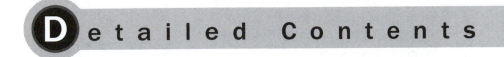

Detailed Contents

Part ▮▮▮ A Brief Take   137

Chapter 5 The Roar of the Tiger Mom   139

*"Here are some things my daughters, Sophia and Louisa, were never allowed to do,"
announces Yale law school professor Amy Chua in an op-ed titled "Why Chinese Mothers
Are Superior." Among her list of prohibitions: having a playdate, watching TV, playing
computer games, and getting any grade less than A. Chua's piece provoked a deluge of responses from readers and professional commentators, some outraged, some cheering her on.
Here is a sampling of some of those responses, part of what became a national debate over the
best way to raise children to become successful adults.*

Part ▮▮▮ An Anthology of Readings   169

Chapter 6 The Changing Landscape of Work in the
Twenty-First Century   171

*A graphic artist and two reporters survey the job prospects for recent college graduates.
Depending on your major, you'll find the comic funny (or not) and the news articles encouraging (or not).*

Chapter 8 Green Power   277

Preface for Instructors

Writing and Reading Across the Curriculum: Brief Edition was created for those who find the standard edition appealing and useful but who also find its length impractical. The present text offers five of the most popular anthology chapters, somewhat abridged, from the longer edition. The rhetoric section preceding the anthology of readings has been abbreviated to cover those writing types for which Writing and Reading Across the Curriculum (WRAC) is best known: the summary, the critique, the synthesis, and the analysis. The Brief Edition does not include the longer text's chapters on introductions, conclusions, and theses. Many instructors, however, already supplement their course reader with a handbook that provides ample coverage of these topics, as well as coverage of research and documentation.

In developing each successive edition of WRAC, we have retained the essential multidisciplinary character of the text, while providing ample new topics and individual readings to keep it fresh and timely. We take care to make sure that at least half of the book is completely new every time, both by extensively revising existing chapters and by creating new ones. While we have retained an emphasis on summary, critique, synthesis, and analysis, we continue to develop content on such issues as the process of writing and argumentation that addresses the issues and interests of today's classrooms.

WHAT'S NEW IN THIS EDITION?

Students will benefit from a variety of new content and features, including:

- New student model papers in the "Critique" and "Analysis" chapters.
- A completely revised and reorganized "Analysis" chapter.
- Over forty new readings in the book.
- Search-term referrals to relevant online text and video sources.
- A new Part II, "A Brief Take," consists of a mini-anthology practice chapter, featuring step-by-step exercises to help students transition from the rhetorical instruction of Part I to the more complex readings and writing assignments in the full-length anthology chapters of Part III.
- A new anthology chapter, "Have You Heard This? The Latest on Rumor," featuring numerous examples of rumors, together with theories about how and why rumors originate and spread.

- Major revisions to two returning chapters, "The Changing Landscape of Work in the Twenty-First Century" (nearly seventy percent new readings) and "Green Power" (roughly half new readings).

- An updated "Advertising" chapter with new print ads and TV commercials.

- A new section of "Video Links": referrals to online videos related to the subject matter of textual sources for virtually every chapter in the book.

WRAC IN THE DIGITAL AGE

WRAC increasingly draws upon online text and video resources to supplement the anthology. To access such resources, you will be directed to a Web site or to a search engine such as Google or Bing and asked to enter a particular set of search terms. And of course, by adjusting the search terms you gain access to an almost inexhaustible set of resources on the subject of the chapter. These resources will allow you to find related materials, conduct additional research, and enhance your understanding of the subject matter.

STRUCTURE

Like its predecessors, the fifth edition of *Writing and Reading Across the Curriculum, Brief Edition* is divided into a rhetoric and an anthology of readings. With this edition, however, the anthology of readings is further subdivided into two parts, the first of these serving as a kind of bridge between the rhetoric and the anthology. Part I introduces the strategies of summary, critique, synthesis, and analysis. We take students step-by-step through the process of writing papers based on source material, explaining and demonstrating how summaries, critiques, syntheses, and analyses can be generated from the kinds of readings students will encounter later in the book—and throughout their academic careers. Parts II and III consist of subject chapters drawn from both academic and professional disciplines. Each subject is representative of the kinds of topics typically studied during the course of an undergraduate education. We believe that students and teachers will discover connections among the thematic chapters of this edition that further enhance opportunities for writing, discussion, and inquiry.

CONTINUED FOCUS ON ARGUMENTATION

Part I of *WRAC, Brief Edition* is designed to prepare students for college-level assignments across the disciplines. The fifth edition continues the previous edition's strengthened emphasis on the writing process, and on argument in particular. In treating argument, we emphasize the following:

- **The Elements of Argument: Claim, Support, Assumption.** This section adapts the Toulmin approach to argument to the kinds of readings that students will encounter in Parts II and III of the text.
- **Developing and Organizing the Support for Your Arguments.** This section helps students to mine source materials for facts, expert opinions, and examples that will support their arguments.
- **Annotated Student Argument Paper.** A sample student paper highlights and discusses argumentative strategies that a student writer uses in drafting and developing a paper.

PART I: NEW APPARATUS, TOPICS, READINGS, AND STUDENT PAPERS

Chapter 2: Critical Reading and Critique

Chapter 2 features a new model critique based on Charles Krauthammer's "The Moon We Left Behind," an argument against the cancellation of the manned lunar program.

Chapter 3: Synthesis

The model argument synthesis in Chapter 3 has been revised to show a current example—airport security pat-downs—of how the issue of individual privacy versus public safety will follow students off campus, into the wider world.

Chapter 4: Analysis

Chapter 4, on analysis, has been almost completely reorganized and rewritten. The new model analysis in this chapter applies a classic theory of rumor propagation to a particular rumor that some years ago went "viral" on the Internet and raised fears of travelers in foreign lands being drugged and surgically deprived of their kidneys. Note: The subject of this model analysis—rumor—is the basis of a new full-length subject chapter in the anthology section in Part III.

PART II: NEW FEATURE: A BRIEF TAKE

Chapter 5: The Roar of the Tiger Mom

In this edition, we are delighted to offer an entirely new feature to *WRAC*: a mini-chapter designed to allow students to test their skills at summary, critique, synthesis, and analysis before immersing themselves in the full-length chapters of the anthology. As a transition from the rhetoric of Part I to the anthology section of Part III, this mini-chapter offers a look at the recent and intensely heated debate over "tiger moms" (that is, parents heavily invested in their child's academic and other achievements). The chapter consists of seven readings and is accompanied by a set of sequential writing exercises distinct from those in the chapters of Part III. We see working on this brief take as a kind of "warm-up" exercise for the more intensive intellectual activities involved in tackling the full-length chapters.

PART III: NEW THEMATIC CHAPTER

As in earlier editions, the anthology section of *WRAC* provides students with opportunities to practice the skills of summary, synthesis, critique, and analysis that they have learned in Part I. In addition to the new "A Brief Take," chapter, we have prepared a new thematic chapter for Part III of *WRAC, Brief Edition.*

Chapter 7: Have You Heard This? The Latest on Rumor

Almost everyone deplores rumors, yet almost everyone has helped start or spread them sometime in their lives. Our new chapter includes multiple perspectives on this uniquely and universally human phenomenon. The chapter is concerned with how rumors start, mutate, and spread; how they help us make sense of the world; why we believe them; how we attempt to counteract them. This chapter builds on the model student analysis in Chapter 4, which examines how the notorious missing-kidney rumor follows some of the basic rules of rumor propagation and adaptation to different locales.

PART III: REVISED THEMATIC CHAPTERS

Three anthology chapters are carried over from the previous edition. Many of the reading selections for each, however, are new to this edition.

Chapter 6: The Changing Landscape of Work in the Twenty-First Century

Retained from the previous edition, "The Changing Landscape of Work in the Twenty-First Century" continues to offer students a wealth of information and informed opinion on how the modern workplace differs markedly from the workplaces of their parents and grandparents. Emphasizing the promise and perils of the new economy, this chapter continues to draw from a number of disciplines: economics, sociology, public policy, business, and investigative journalism. Students will consider questions on the changing nature of work, the role of technology, and the security of jobs they intend to pursue. Because the data on employment and the trends emerging from this data are in constant flux, we have revised extensively to keep pace with these changes.

Chapter 8: Green Power

A growing body of evidence points to a global climate crisis caused by massive levels of greenhouse gases that are being ceaselessly spewed into the atmosphere by the burning of coal and oil. Reducing our dependence upon these fossil fuels involves developing renewable sources of clean energy. In this chapter, students will consider the views of scientists, environmentalists, businesspeople, members of a government task force, and reporters about the nature of the problem and about ways of addressing it. This chapter has been re-organized and includes five new readings, including a cluster on the viability of nuclear power in the wake of the nuclear accident at Fukushima after the 2011 earthquake and tsunami.

Chapter 9: New and Improved: Six Decades of Advertising

The centerpiece of this chapter continues to be a set of two portfolios of memorable advertising: sixteen full-page print ads and fifteen TV commercials. The print ads, which have appeared in popular American magazines since the mid-1940s, promote cigarettes, liquor and beer, automobiles, and beauty and cleaning products. The section on TV commercials refers students to historical and current gems of the genre viewable on YouTube. Like genetic markers, print advertisements and TV commercials are key indicators of our consumerism, our changing cultural values, and our less variable human psychology. Students will find this material both entertaining and well suited for practicing and honing their skills of analysis.

NEW FEATURE: VIDEO LINKS

Video Links for most chapters appear in a separate section at the end of the text. They allow readers to more fully explore aspects of the subject matter through videos readily available on YouTube and other sites. Students will be directed to engaging interviews, dramatizations, animations, documentaries, news features, clips from feature films and TV shows, music, and more—all of which should deepen their understanding and enjoyment of the subject at hand.

RESOURCES FOR TEACHERS AND STUDENTS

- The *Instructor's Manual* of WRAC provides sample syllabi and course calendars, chapter summaries, classroom ideas for writing assignments, introductions to each set of readings, and answers to review questions. ISBN: 0-321-89554-1.

- Pearson's *MyLab* Web site integrates the market-leading instruction, multimedia tutorials, and exercises for writing, grammar, and research that users have come to identify with the program, along with a new online composing space and new assessment tools. The result is a revolutionary application that offers a seamless and flexible teaching and learning environment built specifically for writers. Created by faculty and students across the country, the new Pearson *MyLab* provides help for writers in the context of their writing, with: instructor and peer commenting functionality; proven tutorials and exercises for writing, grammar, and research; an e-portfolio; an assignment-builder; a bibliography tool; tutoring services; and a gradebook and course management organization created specifically for writing classes.

ACKNOWLEDGMENTS

We have benefited over the years from the suggestions and insights of many teachers—and students—across the country. We would especially like to thank these reviewers of this edition: David Bordelon, Ocean County College; Michelle LaFrance, University of Massachusetts Dartmouth; Meg Matheny, Jefferson Community and Technical College, Southwest; Catherine Olson, Lone Star College-Tomall; Scott Vander Ploeg, Madisonville Community College; Jeff Pruchnic, Wayne State University; and Ellen Sorg, Owens Community College.

We would also like to thank the following reviewers for their help in the preparation of past editions: Angela Adams, Loyola University Chicago; James Allen, College of DuPage; Fabián Álvarez, Western Kentucky University; Chris Anson, North Carolina State University; Phillip Arrington, Eastern Michigan University; Anne Bailey, Southeastern Louisiana University; Carolyn Baker, San Antonio College; Bob Brannan, Johnson County Community College; Joy Bashore, Central Virginia Community College; Nancy Blattner, Southeast Missouri State University; Mary Bly, University of California, Davis; Laurel Bollinger, University of Alabama in Huntsville; Paul Buczkowski, Eastern Michigan University; Jennifer Bullis, Whatcom Community College; Paige Byam, Northern Kentucky University; Susan Callendar, Sinclair Community College; Anne Carr, Southeast Community College; Jeff Carroll, University of Hawaii; Joseph Rocky Colavito, Northwestern State University; Michael Colonneses, Methodist College; James A. Cornette, Christopher Newport University; Timothy Corrigan, Temple University; Kathryn J. Dawson, Ball State University; Cathy Powers Dice, University of Memphis; Kathleen Dooley, Tidewater Community College; Judith Eastman, Orange Coast College; David Elias, Eastern Kentucky University; Susan Boyd English, Kirkwood Community College; Kathy Evertz, University of Wyoming; Kathy Ford, Lake Land College; University of Wyoming; Wanda Fries, Somerset Community College; Bill Gholson, Southern Oregon University; Karen Gordon, Elgin Community College; Deborah Gutschera, College of DuPage; Lila M. Harper,

Central Washington University; M. Todd Harper, University of Louisville; Kip Harvigsen, Ricks College; Michael Hogan, Southeast Missouri State University; Sandra M. Jensen, Lane Community College; Anita Johnson, Whatcom Community College; Mark Jones, University of Florida; Daven M. Kari, Vanguard University; Jane Kaufman, University of Akron; Kerrie Kawasaki-Hull, Ohlone College; Rodney Keller, Ricks College; Walt Klarner, Johnson County Community College; Jeffery Klausman, Whatcom Community College; Alison Kuehner, Ohlone College; William B. Lalicker, West Chester University; Dawn Leonard, Charleston Southern University; Lindsay Lewan, Arapahoe Community College; Clifford L. Lewis, U Mass Lowell; Signee Lynch, Whatcom Community College; Jolie Martin; San Francisco State University; Krista L. May, Texas A&M University; Stella Nesanovich, McNeese State University; Kathy Mendt, Front Range Community College–Larimer Campus; RoseAnn Morgan, Middlesex County College; David Moton, Bakersfield College; Roark Mulligan, Christopher Newport University; Joan Mullin, University of Toledo; Susie Paul, Auburn University at Montgomery; Thomas Pfau, Bellevue Community College; Aaron Race, Southern Illinois University–Carbondale; Nancy Redmond, Long Beach City College; Deborah Reese, University of Texas at Arlington; Alison Reynolds, University of Florida; Priscilla Riggle, Bowling Green State University; Jeanette Riley, University of New Mexico; Robert Rongner, Whatcom Community College; Sarah C. Ross, Southeastern Louisiana University; Deborah L. Ruth, Owensboro Community & Technical College; Amy Rybak, Bowling Green State University; Raul Sanchez, University of Utah; Rebecca Shapiro, Westminster College; Mary Sheldon, Washburn University; Horacio Sierra, University of Florida; Philip Sipiora, University of Southern Florida; Joyce Smoot, Virginia Tech; Bonnie A. Spears, Chaffey College; Bonnie Startt, Tidewater Community College; R. E. Stratton, University of Alaska–Fairbanks; Katherine M. Thomas, Southeast Community College; Victor Villanueva, Washington State University; Deron Walker, California Baptist University; Jackie Wheeler, Arizona State University; Pat Stephens Williams, Southern Illinois University at Carbondale; Kristin Woolever, Northeastern University; and Mary R. Seel, Broome Community College.

We gratefully acknowledge the work of Michael Behrens, who made significant contributions to the "Argument Synthesis" chapter. The authors also wish to thank Robert Krut of the University of California, Santa Barbara Writing Program, for his invaluable contributions to the new "Rumor" chapter and to the revised "Green Power" and "Advertising" chapters. Finally, special thanks to Brad Pothoff, Suzanne Phelps Chambers, Paul Smith, Lisa Yakmalian, Jorgensen Fernandez, Martha Beyerlein, and Shannon Kobran for helping shepherd the manuscript through the editorial and production process. And our continued gratitude to Joe Opiela, longtime friend, supporter, and publisher.

LAURENCE BEHRENS
LEONARD J. ROSEN

A Note to the Student

Your sociology professor asks you to write a paper on attitudes toward the homeless population of an urban area near your campus. You are expected to consult books, articles, Web sites, and other online sources on the subject, and you are also encouraged to conduct surveys and interviews.

Your professor is making a number of assumptions about your capabilities. Among them:

- that you can research and assess the value of relevant sources;
- that you can comprehend college-level material, both print and digital;
- that you can use theories and principles learned from one set of sources as tools to investigate other sources (or events, people, places, or things);
- that you can synthesize separate but related sources;
- that you can intelligently respond to such material.

Your professors will expect you to demonstrate that you can read and understand not only textbooks, but also critical articles and books, primary sources, Internet sources, online academic databases, and other material related to a particular subject of study. An example: For a paper on the changing nature of the workforce in the twenty-first century, you would probably look to articles and Internet sources for the latest information. You'd be expected to assess the relevance of such sources to your topic and to draw from them the information and ideas you need. It's even possible that the final product of your research and reading wouldn't be a conventional paper at all, but rather a Web site alerting fellow students to job categories that experts think are expanding or disappearing.

You might, for a different class, be assigned a research paper on the films of director Wes Anderson. To get started, you might consult your film studies textbook, biographical sources on Anderson, and anthologies of criticism. Instructor and peer feedback on a first draft might lead you to articles in both popular magazines and scholarly journals; you might also consult relevant Web sites.

These two example assignments are very different, of course, but the skills you need to work with them are the same. You must be able to research relevant sources. You must be able to read and comprehend these sources. You must be able to perceive the relationships among several pieces of source material. And you must be able to apply your own critical judgments to these various materials.

Writing and Reading Across the Curriculum: Brief Edition provides you with the opportunity to practice the essential college-level skills we have just outlined and the forms of writing associated with them, namely:

- the *summary*
- the *critique*
- the *synthesis*
- the *analysis*

Each chapter of Parts II and III of this text represents a subject from a particular area of the academic curriculum: Sociology, Economics, Business, and Public Policy. These chapters illustrate the types of material you will study in your other courses.

Questions following the readings will allow you to practice typical college writing assignments. "Review Questions" help you recall key points of content. "Discussion and Writing Suggestions" ask you for personal, sometimes imaginative, responses to the readings. "Synthesis Activities" allow you to practice assignments of the type that are covered in detail in Part I of this book. For instance, you may be asked to *summarize* Jib Fowles's article on "Advertising's Fifteen Basic Appeals," or to *compare and contrast* Fowles's explanations with examples from your own experience with advertisements. Finally, "Research Activities" ask you to go beyond the readings in this text in order to conduct your own independent research on these subjects.

In this book, you'll find articles and essays written by literary critics, sociologists, psychologists, lawyers, political scientists, journalists, and specialists from other fields. Our aim is that you become familiar with the various subjects and styles of academic writing and that you come to appreciate the interrelatedness of knowledge. The novel you read in your literature course may be able to shed some light upon an assigned article for your economics course—and vice versa.

We hope, therefore, that your writing course will serve as a kind of bridge to your other courses and that, as a result of this work, you will become more skillful at perceiving relationships among diverse topics. Because it involves such critical and widely applicable skills, your writing course may well turn out to be one of the most valuable—and one of the most interesting—of your academic career.

Laurence Behrens
Leonard J. Rosen

P art

I

How to Write Summaries, Critiques, Syntheses, and Analyses

Summary

After completing this chapter, you will be able to:

LO 1.1 Explain what a summary is.

LO 1.2 Describe how prior knowledge and frame of reference can affect the objectivity of a summary.

LO 1.3 Identify the situations in which a summary would be useful.

LO 1.4 Apply systematic strategies as you read in order to prepare a summary.

LO 1.5 Write summaries of varying lengths by reading critically, dividing a passage into stages of thought, writing a thesis, and drafting.

LO 1.6 Determine the appropriate length for your summary.

LO 1.7 Avoid plagiarism by citing sources and using your own words and sentence structure.

WHAT IS A SUMMARY?

The best way to demonstrate that you understand the information and the ideas in any piece of writing is to compose an accurate and clearly written summary of that piece. By a *summary* we mean a *brief restatement, in your own words, of the content of a passage* (a group of paragraphs, a chapter, an article, a book). This restatement should focus on the *central idea* of the passage. The briefest of summaries (one or two sentences) will do no more than this. A longer, more complete summary will indicate, in condensed form, the main points in the passage that support or explain the central idea. It will reflect the order in which these points are presented and the emphasis given to them. It may even include some important examples from the passage. But it will not include minor details. It will not repeat points simply for the purpose of emphasis. And it will not contain any of your own opinions or conclusions. A good summary, therefore, has three central qualities: *brevity*, *completeness*, and *objectivity*.

CAN A SUMMARY BE OBJECTIVE?

Objectivity could be difficult to achieve in a summary. By definition, writing a summary requires you to select some aspects of the original and leave out others. Since deciding what to select and what to leave out calls for your personal judgment, your summary really is a work of interpretation. And, certainly, your interpretation of a passage may differ from another person's.

One factor affecting the nature and quality of your interpretation is your *prior knowledge* of the subject. For example, if you're attempting to summarize an anthropological article and you're a novice in that field, then your summary of the article will likely differ from that of your professor, who has spent twenty years studying this particular area and whose judgment about what is more or less significant is undoubtedly more reliable than your own. By the same token, your personal or professional *frame of reference* may also affect your interpretation. A union representative and a management representative attempting to summarize the latest management offer would probably come up with two very different accounts. Still, we believe that in most cases it's possible to produce a reasonably objective summary of a passage if you make a conscious, good-faith effort to be unbiased and to prevent your own feelings on the subject from coloring your account of the author's text.

USING THE SUMMARY

In some quarters, the summary has a bad reputation—and with reason. Summaries are often provided by writers as substitutes for analyses. As students, many of us have summarized books that we were supposed to *review critically*. All the same, the summary does have a place in respectable college work. First, writing a summary is an excellent way to understand what you read. This in itself is an important goal of academic study. If you don't understand your source material, chances are you won't be able to refer to it usefully in a paper. Summaries help you understand what you read because they force you to put the text into your own words. Practice with writing summaries also develops your general writing habits, because a good summary, like any other piece of good writing, is clear, coherent, and accurate.

Second, summaries are useful to your readers. Let's say you're writing a paper about the McCarthy era in the United States, and in part of that paper you want to discuss Arthur Miller's *The Crucible* as a dramatic treatment of the subject. A summary of the plot would be helpful to a reader who hasn't seen or read—or who doesn't remember—the play. Or perhaps you're writing a paper about the politics of recent American military interventions. If your reader isn't likely to be familiar with American actions in Kosovo and Afghanistan, it would be a good idea to summarize these events at some early point in the paper. In many cases (an exam, for instance), you can use a summary to demonstrate your knowledge of what your professor already knows; when writing a paper, you can use

WHERE DO WE FIND WRITTEN SUMMARIES?

Here are just a few of the types of writing that involve summary:

Academic Writing

- **Critique papers** summarize material in order to critique it.
- **Synthesis papers** summarize to show relationships between sources.
- **Analysis papers** summarize theoretical perspectives before applying them.
- **Research papers** require note taking that summarizes the content of source materials.
- **Literature reviews** summarize current research on a topic.
- **Argument papers** summarize evidence and opposing arguments.
- **Essay exams** demonstrate understanding of course materials through summary.

Workplace Writing

- **Policy briefs** condense complex public policy.
- **Business plans** summarize costs, relevant environmental impacts, and other important matters.
- **Memos, letters, and reports** summarize procedures, meetings, product assessments, expenditures, and more.
- **Medical charts** record patient data in summarized form.
- **Legal briefs** summarize relevant facts and arguments of cases.

a summary to inform your professor about some relatively unfamiliar source.

Third, summaries are required frequently in college-level writing. For example, on a psychology midterm, you may be asked to explain Carl Jung's theory of the collective unconscious and to show how it differs from Sigmund Freud's theory of the personal unconscious. You may have read about Jung's theory in your textbook or in a supplementary article, or your instructor may have outlined it in her lecture. You can best demonstrate your understanding of it by summarizing it. Then you'll proceed to contrast it with Freud's theory—which, of course, you must also summarize.

THE READING PROCESS

It may seem to you that being able to tell (or retell) in summary form exactly what a passage says is a skill that ought to be taken for granted in anyone who can read at high school level. Unfortunately, this is not so: For all kinds of reasons, people don't always read carefully. In fact, it's probably safe to say that usually they don't. Either they read so inattentively that they skip over words, phrases, or even whole sentences, or, if they do see the words in front of them, they see them without registering their significance.

When a reader fails to pick up the meaning and implications of a sentence or two, usually there's no real harm done. (An exception: You could lose credit on an exam or paper because you failed to read or to realize the significance of a crucial direction by your instructor.) But over longer stretches—the paragraph, the section, the article, or the chapter—inattentive or haphazard reading interferes with your goals as a reader: to perceive the shape of the argument, to grasp the central idea, to determine the main points that compose it, to relate the parts of the whole, and to note key examples. This kind of reading takes a lot more energy and determination than casual reading. But in the long run it's an energy-saving method because it enables you to retain the content of the material and to draw upon that content in your own responses. In other words, it allows you to develop an accurate and coherent written discussion that goes beyond summary.

CRITICAL READING FOR SUMMARY

- *Examine the context.* Note the credentials, occupation, and publications of the author. Identify the source in which the piece originally appeared. This information helps illuminate the author's perspective on the topic he or she is addressing.
- *Note the title and subtitle.* Some titles are straightforward; the meanings of others become clearer as you read. In either case, titles typically identify the topic being addressed and often reveal the author's attitude toward that topic.
- *Identify the main point.* Whether a piece of writing contains a thesis statement in the first few paragraphs or builds its main point without stating it up front, look at the entire piece to arrive at an understanding of the overall point being made.
- *Identify the subordinate points.* Notice the smaller subpoints that make up the main point, and make sure you understand how they relate to the main point. If a particular subpoint doesn't clearly relate to the main point you've identified, you may need to modify your understanding of the main point.
- *Break the reading into sections.* Notice which paragraphs make up a piece's introduction, body, and conclusion. Break up the body paragraphs into sections that address the writer's various subpoints.
- *Distinguish between points, examples, and counterarguments.* Critical reading requires careful attention to what a writer is *doing* as well as what he or she is *saying*. When a writer quotes someone else,

or relays an example of something, ask yourself why this is being done. What point is the example supporting? Is another source being quoted as support for a point or as a counterargument that the writer sets out to address?

- *Watch for transitions within and between paragraphs.* In order to follow the logic of a piece of writing, as well as to distinguish between points, examples, and counterarguments, pay attention to the transitional words and phrases writers use. Transitions function like road signs, preparing the reader for what's next.
- *Read actively and recursively.* Don't treat reading as a passive, linear progression through a text. Instead, read as though you are engaged in a dialogue with the writer: Ask questions of the text as you read, make notes in the margin, underline key ideas in pencil, put question or exclamation marks next to passages that confuse or excite you. Go back to earlier points once you finish a reading, stop during your reading to recap what's come so far, and move back and forth through a text.

HOW TO WRITE SUMMARIES

Every article you read will present its own challenge as you work to summarize it. As you'll discover, saying in a few words what has taken someone else a great many can be difficult. But like any other skill, the ability to summarize improves with practice. Here are a few pointers to get you started. They represent possible stages, or steps, in the process of writing a summary. These pointers are not meant to be ironclad rules; rather, they are designed to encourage habits of thinking that will allow you to vary your technique as the situation demands.

GUIDELINES FOR WRITING SUMMARIES

- *Read the passage carefully.* Determine its structure. Identify the author's purpose in writing. (This will help you distinguish between more important and less important information.) Make a note in the margin when you get confused or when you think something is important; highlight or underline points sparingly, if at all.
- *Reread.* This time divide the passage into sections or stages of thought. The author's use of paragraphing will often be a useful guide. *Label*, on the passage itself, each section or stage of thought. *Underline* key ideas and terms. Write notes in the margin.

(continued)

- *Write one-sentence summaries,* on a separate sheet of paper, of each stage of thought.
- *Write a thesis—a one- or two-sentence summary of the entire passage.* The thesis should express the central idea of the passage as you have determined it from the preceding steps. You may find it useful to follow the approach of most newspaper stories—naming the *what, who, why, where, when,* and *how* of the matter. For persuasive passages, summarize in a sentence the author's conclusion. For descriptive passages, indicate the subject of the description and its key feature(s). *Note:* In some cases, *a suitable thesis statement may already be in the original passage.* If so, you may want to quote it directly in your summary.
- *Write the first draft of your summary* by (1) combining the thesis with your list of one-sentence summaries or (2) combining the thesis with one-sentence summaries *plus* significant details from the passage. In either case, eliminate repetition and less important information. Disregard minor details or generalize them (e.g., Bill Clinton and George W. Bush might be generalized as "recent presidents"). Use as few words as possible to convey the main ideas.
- *Check your summary against the original passage,* and make whatever adjustments are necessary for accuracy and completeness.
- *Revise your summary,* inserting transitional words and phrases where necessary to ensure coherence. Check for style. *Avoid a series of short, choppy sentences.* Combine sentences for a smooth, logical flow of ideas. Check for grammatical correctness, punctuation, and spelling.

DEMONSTRATION: SUMMARY

To demonstrate these points at work, let's go through the process of summarizing a passage of expository material—that is, writing that is meant to inform and/or persuade. Read the following selection carefully. Try to identify its parts and understand how they work together to create an overall statement.

WILL YOUR JOB BE EXPORTED?

Alan S. Blinder

Alan S. Blinder is the Gordon S. Rentschler Memorial Professor of Economics at Princeton University. He has served as vice chairman of the Federal Reserve Board and was a member of President Clinton's original Council of Economic Advisers.

The great conservative political philosopher Edmund Burke, who probably would not have been a reader of *The American Prospect,* once observed,

"You can never plan the future by the past."* But when it comes to preparing the American workforce for the jobs of the future, we may be doing just that.

For about a quarter-century, demand for labor appears to have shifted toward the college-educated and away from high school graduates and dropouts. This shift, most economists believe, is the primary (though not the sole) reason for rising income inequality, and there is no end in sight. Economists refer to this phenomenon by an antiseptic name: skill-biased technical progress. In plain English, it means that the labor market has turned ferociously against the low skilled and the uneducated.

In a progressive society, such a worrisome social phenomenon might elicit some strong policy responses, such as more compensatory education, stepped-up efforts at retraining, reinforcement (rather than shredding) of the social safety net, and so on. You don't fight the market's valuation of skills; you try to mitigate its more deleterious effects. We did a bit of this in the United States in the 1990s, by raising the minimum wage and expanding the Earned Income Tax Credit.** Combined with tight labor markets, these measures improved things for the average worker. But in this decade, little or no mitigation has been attempted. Social Darwinism has come roaring back.†

With one big exception: We have expended considerable efforts to keep more young people in school longer (e.g., reducing high-school dropouts and sending more kids to college) and to improve the quality of schooling (e.g., via charter schools and No Child Left Behind‡). Success in these domains may have been modest, but not for lack of trying. You don't have to remind Americans that education is important; the need for educational reform is etched into the public consciousness. Indeed, many people view education as the silver bullet. On hearing the question "How do we best prepare the American workforce of the future?" many Americans react reflexively with: "Get more kids to study science and math, and send more of them to college."

---

*Edmund Burke (1729–1797) was a conservative British statesman, philosopher, and author. *The American Prospect*, in which "Will Your Job Be Exported?" first appeared in the November 2006 issue, describes itself as "an authoritative magazine of liberal ideas."

**The Earned Income Tax Credit, an antipoverty measure enacted by Congress in 1975 and revised in the 1980s and 1990s, provides a credit against federal income taxes for any filer who claims a dependent child.

†Social Darwinism, a largely discredited philosophy dating from the Victorian era and espoused by Herbert Spenser, asserts that Charles Darwin's observations on natural selection apply to human societies. Social Darwinists argue that the poor are less fit to survive than the wealthy and should, through a natural process of adaptation, be allowed to die out.

‡Charter schools are public schools with specialized missions to operate outside of regulations that some feel restrict creativity and performance in traditional school settings. The No Child Left Behind Act of 2001 (NCLB) mandates standards-based education for all schools receiving federal funding. Both the charter schools movement and NCLB can be understood as efforts to improve public education.

5   Which brings me to the future. As I argued in a recent article in *Foreign Affairs* magazine, the greatest problem for the next generation of American workers may not be lack of education, but rather "offshoring"—the movement of jobs overseas, especially to countries with much lower wages, such as India and China. Manufacturing jobs have been migrating overseas for decades. But the new wave of offshoring, of *service* jobs, is something different.

Traditionally, we think of service jobs as being largely immune to foreign competition. After all, you can't get your hair cut by a barber or your broken arm set by a doctor in a distant land. But stunning advances in communication technology, plus the emergence of a vast new labor pool in Asia and Eastern Europe, are changing that picture radically, subjecting millions of presumed-safe domestic service jobs to foreign competition. And it is not necessary actually to move jobs to low-wage countries in order to restrain wage increases; the mere threat of offshoring can put a damper on wages.

Service-sector offshoring is a minor phenomenon so far, Lou Dobbs notwithstanding; probably well under 1 percent of U.S. service jobs have been outsourced.* But I believe that service-sector offshoring will eventually exceed manufacturing-sector offshoring by a hefty margin—for three main reasons. The first is simple arithmetic: There are vastly more service jobs than manufacturing jobs in the United States (and in other rich countries). Second, the technological advances that have made service-sector offshoring possible will continue and accelerate, so the range of services that can be moved offshore will increase ineluctably. Third, the number of (e.g., Indian and Chinese) workers capable of performing service jobs offshore seems certain to grow, perhaps exponentially.

I do not mean to paint a bleak picture here. Ever since Adam Smith and David Ricardo, economists have explained and extolled the gains in living standards that derive from international trade.† Those arguments are just as valid for trade in services as for trade in goods. There really *are* net gains to the United States from expanding service-sector trade with India, China, and the rest. The offshoring problem is not about the adverse nature of what economists call the economy's eventual equilibrium. Rather, it is about the so-called transition—the ride from here to there. That ride, which could take a generation or more, may be bumpy. And during the long adjustment period, many U.S. wages could face downward pressure.

Thus far, only American manufacturing workers and a few low-end service workers (e.g., call-center operators) have been competing, at least

---

*Lou Dobbs, a conservative columnist and former political commentator for CNN, is well known for his anti-immigration views.

†Adam Smith (1723–1790), Scottish author of *An Inquiry into the Nature and Causes of the Wealth of Nations* (1776), established the foundations of modern economics. David Ricardo (1772–1823) was a British businessman, statesman, and economist who founded the classical school of economics and is best known for his studies of monetary policy.

potentially, with millions of people in faraway lands eager to work for what seems a pittance by U.S. standards. But offshoring is no longer limited to low-end service jobs. Computer code can be written overseas and e-mailed back to the United States. So can your tax return and lots of legal work, provided you do not insist on face-to-face contact with the accountant or lawyer. In writing and editing this article, I communicated with the editors and staff of *The American Prospect* only by telephone and e-mail. Why couldn't they (or I, for that matter) have been in India? The possibilities are, if not endless, at least vast.

10   What distinguishes the jobs that cannot be offshored from the ones that can? The crucial distinction is not—and this is the central point of this essay—the required levels of skill and education. These attributes have been critical to labor-market success in the past, but may be less so in the future. Instead, the new critical distinction may be that some services either require personal delivery (e.g., driving a taxi and brain surgery) or are seriously degraded when delivered electronically (e.g., college teaching—at least, I hope!), while other jobs (e.g., call centers and keyboard data entry) are not. Call the first category personal services and the second category impersonal services. With this terminology, I have three main points to make about preparing our workforce for the brave, new world of the future.

First, we need to think about, plan, and redesign our educational system with the crucial distinction between personal service jobs and impersonal service jobs in mind. Many of the impersonal service jobs will migrate offshore, but the personal service jobs will stay here.

Second, the line that divides personal services from impersonal services will move in only one direction over time, as technological progress makes it possible to deliver an ever-increasing array of services electronically.

Third, the novel distinction between personal and impersonal jobs is quite different from, and appears essentially unrelated to, the traditional distinction between jobs that do and do not require high levels of education.

For example, it is easy to offshore working in a call center, typing transcripts, writing computer code, and reading X-rays. The first two require little education; the last two require quite a lot. On the other hand, it is either impossible or very difficult to offshore janitorial services, fast-food restaurant service, college teaching, and open-heart surgery. Again, the first two occupations require little or no education, while the last two require a great deal. There seems to be little or no correlation between educational requirements (the old concern) and how "offshorable" jobs are (the new one).

15   If so, the implications could be startling. A generation from now, civil engineers (who must be physically present) may be in greater demand in the United States than computer engineers (who don't). Similarly, there might be more divorce lawyers (not offshorable) than tax lawyers (partly offshorable). More imaginatively, electricians might earn more than computer programmers. I am not predicting any of this; lots of things influence

relative demands and supplies for different types of labor. But it all seems within the realm of the possible as technology continues to enhance the offshorability of even highly skilled occupations. What does seem highly likely is that the relative demand for labor in the United States will shift away from impersonal services and toward personal services, and this shift will look quite different from the familiar story of skill-biased technical progress. So Burke's warning is worth heeding.

I am *not* suggesting that education will become a handicap in the job market of the future. On the contrary, to the extent that education raises productivity and that better-educated workers are more adaptable and/or more creative, a wage premium for higher education should remain. Thus, it still makes sense to send more of America's youth to college. But, over the next generation, the kind of education our young people receive may prove to be more important than how much education they receive. In that sense, a college degree may lose its exalted "silver bullet" status.

Looking back over the past 25 years, "stay in school longer" was excellent advice for success in the labor market. But looking forward over the next 25 years, more subtle occupational advice may be needed. "Prepare yourself for a high-end personal service occupation that is not offshorable" is a more nuanced message than "stay in school." But it may prove to be more useful. And many non-offshorable jobs—such as carpenters, electricians, and plumbers—do not require college education.

The hard question is how to make this more subtle advice concrete and actionable. The children entering America's educational system today, at age 5, will emerge into a very different labor market when they leave it. Given gestation periods of 13 to 17 years and more, educators and policymakers need to be thinking now about the kinds of training and skills that will best prepare these children for their future working lives. Specifically, it is essential to educate America's youth for the jobs that will actually be available in America 20 to 30 years from now, not for the jobs that will have moved offshore.

Some of the personal service jobs that will remain in the United States will be very high-end (doctors), others will be less glamorous though well paid (plumbers), and some will be "dead end" (janitor). We need to think long and hard about the types of skills that best prepare people to deliver high-end personal services, and how to teach those skills in our elementary and high schools. I am not an education specialist, but it strikes me that, for example, the central thrust of No Child Left Behind is pushing the nation in exactly the wrong direction. I am all for accountability. But the nation's school system will not build the creative, flexible, people-oriented workforce we will need in the future by drilling kids incessantly with rote preparation for standardized tests in the vain hope that they will perform as well as memory chips.

20   Starting in the elementary schools, we need to develop our youngsters' imaginations and people skills as well as their "reading, writing, and 'rithmetic." Remember that kindergarten grade for "works and plays well with others"? It may become increasingly important in a world of

personally delivered services. Such training probably needs to be continued and made more sophisticated in the secondary schools, where, for example, good communications skills need to be developed.

More vocational education is probably also in order. After all, nurses, carpenters, and plumbers are already scarce, and we'll likely need more of them in the future. Much vocational training now takes place in community colleges; and they, too, need to adapt their curricula to the job market of the future.

While it is probably still true that we should send more kids to college and increase the number who study science, math, and engineering, we need to focus on training more college students for the high-end jobs that are unlikely to move offshore, and on developing a creative workforce that will keep America incubating and developing new processes, new products, and entirely new industries. Offshoring is, after all, mostly about following and copying. America needs to lead and innovate instead, just as we have in the past.

Educational reform is not the whole story, of course. I suggested at the outset, for example, that we needed to repair our tattered social safety net and turn it into a retraining trampoline that bounces displaced workers back into productive employment. But many low-end personal service jobs cannot be turned into more attractive jobs simply by more training—think about janitors, fast-food workers, and nurse's aides, for example. Running a tight labor market would help such workers, as would a higher minimum wage, an expanded Earned Income Tax Credit, universal health insurance, and the like.

Moving up the skill ladder, employment is concentrated in the public or quasi-public sector in a number of service occupations. Teachers and health-care workers are two prominent examples. In such cases, government policy can influence wages and working conditions directly by upgrading the structure and pay of such jobs—developing more professional early-childhood teachers and fewer casual daycare workers for example—as long as the taxpayer is willing to foot the bill. Similarly, some service jobs such as registered nurses are in short supply mainly because we are not training enough qualified personnel. Here, too, public policy can help by widening the pipeline to allow more workers through. So there are a variety of policy levers that might do some good—if we are willing to pull them.

25   But all that said, education is still the right place to start. Indeed, it is much more than that because the educational system affects the entire population and because no other institution is nearly as important when it comes to preparing our youth for the world of work. As the first industrial revolution took hold, America radically transformed (and democratized) its educational system to meet the new demands of an industrial society. We may need to do something like that again. There is a great deal at stake here. If we get this one wrong, the next generation will pay dearly. But if we get it (close to) right, the gains from trade promise coming generations a prosperous future.

The somewhat inchoate challenge posed here—preparing more young Americans for personal service jobs—brings to mind one of my favorite Churchill quotations: "You can always count on Americans to do the right thing—after they've tried everything else." It is time to start trying.

Read, Reread, Highlight

Let's consider our recommended pointers for writing a summary.

As you reread the passage, note in the margins of the essay important points, shifts in thought, and questions you may have. Consider the essay's significance as a whole and its stages of thought. What does it say? How is it organized? How does each part of the passage fit into the whole? What do all these points add up to?

Here is how several paragraphs from the middle of Blinder's article might look after you have marked the main ideas by highlighting and by marginal notations.

Offshored service jobs will eclipse lost manufacturing jobs —3 reasons

Service-sector offshoring is a minor phenomenon so far, Lou Dobbs notwithstanding; probably well under 1 percent of U.S. service jobs have been outsourced. But I believe that service-sector offshoring will eventually exceed manufacturing-sector offshoring by a hefty margin—for three main reasons. The first is simple arithmetic: There are vastly more service jobs than manufacturing jobs in the United States (and in other rich countries). Second, the technological advances that have made service-sector offshoring possible will continue and accelerate, so the range of services that can be moved offshore will increase ineluctably. Third, the number of (e.g., Indian and Chinese) workers capable of performing service jobs offshore seems certain to grow, perhaps exponentially.

Long–term economy will be ok. Short–to–middle term will be "bumpy"

I do not mean to paint a bleak picture here. Ever since Adam Smith and David Ricardo, economists have explained and extolled the gains in living standards that derive from international trade. Those arguments are just as valid for trade in services as for trade in goods. There really are net gains to the United States from expanding service-sector trade with India, China, and the rest. The offshoring problem is not about the adverse nature of what economists call the economy's eventual equilibrium. Rather, it is about the so-called transition—the ride from here to there. That ride, which could take a generation or more, may be bumpy. And during the long adjustment period, many U.S. wages could face downward pressure.

Thus far, only American manufacturing workers and a few low-end service workers (e.g., call-center operators) have been competing, at least potentially, with millions of people in faraway lands eager to work for what seems a pittance by U.S. standards. But offshoring is no longer limited to low-end service jobs. Computer code can be written overseas and e-mailed back to the United States. So can your tax return and lots of legal work, provided you do not insist on face-to-face contact with the accountant or lawyer. In writing and editing this article, I communicated with the editors and staff of *The American Prospect* only by telephone and e-mail. Why couldn't they (or I, for that matter) have been in India? The possibilities are, if not endless, at least vast.

High-end jobs to be lost

What distinguishes the jobs that cannot be offshored from the ones that can? The crucial distinction is not—and this is the central point of this essay—the required levels of skill and education. These attributes have been critical to labor-market success in the past, but may be less so in the future. Instead, the new critical distinction may be that some services either require personal delivery (e.g., driving a taxi and brain surgery) or are seriously degraded when delivered electronically (e.g., college teaching—at least, I hope!), while other jobs (e.g., call centers and keyboard data entry) are not. Call the first category personal services and the second category impersonal services. With this terminology, I have three main points to make about preparing our workforce for the brave, new world of the future.

B's main point: Key distinction: Personal service jobs stay; impersonal jobs go

3 points re: prep of future workforce

First, we need to think about, plan, and redesign our educational system with the crucial distinction between personal service jobs and impersonal service jobs in mind. Many of the impersonal service jobs will migrate offshore, but the personal service jobs will stay here.

Movement: impersonal → personal

Second, the line that divides personal services from impersonal services will move in only one direction over time, as technological progress makes it possible to deliver an ever-increasing array of services electronically.

Level of ed. not related to future job security

Third, the novel distinction between personal and impersonal jobs is quite different from, and appears essentially unrelated to, the traditional distinction between jobs that do and do not require high levels of education.

Divide into Stages of Thought

When a selection doesn't contain sections with thematic headings, as is the case with "Will Your Job Be Exported?", how do you determine where one stage of thought ends and the next one begins? Assuming that what you have read is coherent and unified, this should not be difficult. (When a selection is unified, all of its parts pertain to the main subject; when a selection is coherent, the parts follow one another in logical order.) Look particularly for transitional sentences at the beginning of paragraphs. Such sentences generally work in one or both of two ways: (1) They summarize what has come before; (2) they set the stage for what is to follow.

Look at the sentences that open paragraphs 5 and 10: "Which brings me to the future" and "What distinguishes the jobs that cannot be offshored from the ones that can?" In both cases, Blinder makes a clear announcement. Grammatically speaking, "Which brings me to the future" is a fragment, not a sentence. Experienced writers will use fragments on occasion to good effect, as in this case. The fragment clearly has the sense of a complete thought: The pronoun "which" refers readers to the content of the preceding paragraphs, asking them to summarize that content and then, with the predicate "brings me to the future," to move forward into the next part of the article. Similarly, the question "What distinguishes the jobs that cannot be offshored from the ones that can?" implicitly asks readers to recall an important distinction just made (the definitions of offshorable and non-offshorable jobs) and then clearly moves readers forward to new, related content. As you can see, the openings of paragraphs 5 and 10 announce new sections in the article.

Each section of an article generally takes several paragraphs to develop. Between paragraphs, and almost certainly between sections of an article, you will usually find transitions that help you understand what you have just read and what you are about to read. For articles that have no subheadings, try writing your own section headings in the margins as you take notes. Blinder's article can be divided into five sections.

> **Section 1:** *Recent past: education of workers important*—For twenty-five years, the labor market has rewarded workers with higher levels of education (paragraphs 1–4).
>
> **Section 2:** *Future: ed level won't always matter—workers in service sector will lose jobs offshore*—Once thought immune to outsourcing, even highly trained service workers will lose jobs to overseas competition (paragraphs 5–9).
>
> **Section 3:** *Which service jobs at highest risk?* Personal service workers are safe; impersonal service workers, both highly educated and not, will see jobs offshored (paragraphs 10–15).
>
> **Section 4:** *Educating the future workforce*—Emphasizing the kind, not amount, of education will help to prepare workers for jobs of the future (paragraphs 16–22).

Section 5: *Needed policy reforms*—Government can improve conditions for low-end service workers and expand opportunities for higher-end service workers; start with education (paragraphs 23–26).

Write a Brief Summary of Each Stage of Thought

The purpose of this step is to wean yourself from the language of the original passage, so that you are not tied to it when writing the summary. Here are brief summaries, one for each stage of thought in "Will Your Job Be Exported?":

Section 1: Recent past: education of workers important (paragraphs 1–4).

For the past twenty-five years, the greater a worker's skill or level of education, the better and more stable the job.

Section 2: Future: ed level won't always matter—workers in service sector will lose jobs offshore (paragraphs 5–9).

Advances in technology have brought to the service sector the same pressures that forced so many manufacturing jobs offshore to China and India. The rate of offshoring in the service sector will accelerate and "eventually exceed" job losses in manufacturing, says Blinder, and jobs requiring both relatively little education (such as call-center staffing) and extensive education (such as software development) will be lost to workers overseas.

Section 3: Which service jobs at highest risk? (paragraphs 10–15).

While "personal services" workers (such as barbers and surgeons) will be relatively safe from offshoring because their work requires close physical proximity to customers, "impersonal services" workers (such as call-center operators and radiologists), regardless of their skill or education, will be at risk because their work can be completed remotely without loss of quality and then delivered via phone or computer. Blinder believes that "the relative demand for labor in the United States will [probably] shift away from impersonal services and toward personal services."

Section 4: Educating the future workforce (paragraphs 16–22).

Blinder advises young people to plan for "a high-end personal service occupation that is not offshorable." He also urges educators to prepare the future workforce by anticipating the needs of a personal services economy and redesigning classroom instruction and vocational training accordingly.

Section 5: Needed policy reforms (paragraphs 23–26).

Blinder urges the government to develop policies that will improve wages and conditions for low-wage personal service workers (such as janitors); to encourage more low-wage workers (such as daycare providers) to retrain and take on better jobs; and to increase opportunities for professional and vocational training in high-demand areas (such as nursing and carpentry).

Write a Thesis: A Brief Summary of the Entire Passage

The thesis is the most general statement of a summary (or any other type of academic writing). It is the statement that announces the paper's subject and the claim that you or—in the case of a summary—another author will be making about that subject. Every paragraph of a paper illuminates the thesis by providing supporting detail or explanation. The relationship of these paragraphs to the thesis is analogous to the relationship of the sentences within a paragraph to the topic sentence. Both the thesis and the topic sentences are general statements (the thesis being the more general) that are followed by systematically arranged details.

To ensure clarity for the reader, *the first sentence of your summary should begin with the author's thesis, regardless of where it appears in the article itself.* An author may locate her thesis at the beginning of her work, in which case the thesis operates as a general principle from which details of the presentation follow. This is called a *deductive* organization: thesis first, supporting details second. Alternatively, an author may locate his thesis at the end of the work, in which case the author begins with specific details and builds toward a more general conclusion, or thesis. This is called an *inductive* organization. And, as you might expect, an author might locate the thesis anywhere between beginning and end, at whatever point it seems best positioned.*

A thesis consists of a subject and an assertion about that subject. How can we go about fashioning an adequate thesis for a summary of Blinder's article? Probably no two versions of Blinder's thesis statement would be worded identically, but it is fair to say that any reasonable thesis will indicate that Blinder's subject is the future loss to offshoring of American jobs in the service sector— that part of the economy that delivers services to consumers, from low end (e.g., janitorial services) to high end (e.g., neurosurgery). How does Blinder view the situation? How secure will service jobs be if Blinder's distinction between personal and impersonal services is valid? Looking back over our section summaries, we find that Blinder insists on three points: (1) that education and skill matter less than they once did in determining job

---

*Blinder positions his thesis midway through his five-section article. He opens the selection by discussing the role of education in the labor market during the past twenty-five years (Section 1, pars. 1–4). He continues by summarizing an earlier article on the ways in which service jobs are following manufacturing jobs offshore (Section 2, pars. 5–9). He then presents a two-sentence thesis in answer to the question that opens paragraph 10: "What distinguishes the jobs that cannot be offshored from the ones that can?" The remainder of the article either develops this thesis (Section 3, pars. 10–15) or follows its implications for education (Section 4, pars. 16–22) and public policy (Section 5, pars. 23–26).

quality and security; (2) that the distinction between personal and impersonal services will increasingly determine which jobs remain and which are offshored; and (3) that the distinction between personal and impersonal has implications for the future of both education and public policy.

Does Blinder make a statement anywhere in this passage that pulls all this together? Examine paragraph 10 and you will find his thesis—two sentences that answer his question about which jobs will and will not be sent offshore: "The crucial distinction is not—and this is the central point of this essay—the required levels of skill and education.... Instead, the new critical distinction may be that some services either require personal delivery (e.g., driving a taxi and brain surgery) or are seriously degraded when delivered electronically (e.g., college teaching—at least, I hope!), while other jobs (e.g., call centers and keyboard data entry) are not."

You may have learned that a thesis statement must be expressed in a single sentence. We would offer a slight rewording of this generally sound advice and say that a thesis statement must be *expressible* in a single sentence. For reasons of emphasis or style, a writer might choose to distribute a thesis across two or more sentences. Certainly, the sense of Blinder's thesis can take the form of a single statement: "The critical distinction is X, not Y." For reasons largely of emphasis, he divides his thesis into two sentences—in fact, separating these sentences with another sentence that explains the first part of the thesis: "These attributes [that is, skill and education] have been critical to labor-market success in the past, but may be less so in the future."

Here is a one-sentence version of Blinder's two-sentence thesis:

> The quality and security of future jobs in America's service sector will be determined by how "offshorable" those jobs are.

Notice that the statement anticipates a summary of the *entire* article: both the discussion leading up to Blinder's thesis and his discussion after. To clarify for our readers the fact that this idea is Blinder's and not ours, we might qualify the thesis as follows:

> In "Will Your Job Be Exported?" economist Alan S. Blinder argues that the quality and security of future jobs in America's service sector will be determined by how "offshorable" those jobs are.

The first sentence of a summary is crucially important, for it orients readers by letting them know what to expect in the coming paragraphs. In the example above, the sentence refers directly to an article, its author, and the thesis for the upcoming summary. The author and title reference could also be indicated in the summary's title (if this were a freestanding summary), in which case their mention could be dropped from the thesis statement. And lest you become frustrated too quickly with how much effort it takes to come up with this crucial sentence, keep in mind that writing an acceptable thesis for a summary takes time. In this case, it took three drafts, roughly ten minutes, to compose a thesis and another few minutes of fine-tuning after a draft of the entire summary was completed. The thesis needed revision because the first draft was vague; the second draft was improved but too specific on a secondary point; the third draft was more complete but too general on a key point:

> **Draft 1:** We must begin now to train young people for high-quality personal service jobs.
>
> *(Vague. The question of why we should begin training isn't clear, nor is the phrase "high-quality personal service jobs." Define this term or make it more general.)*

> **Draft 2:** Alan S. Blinder argues that, unlike in the past, the quality and security of future American jobs will not be determined by skill level or education, but rather by how "offshorable" those jobs are.
>
> *(Better, but the reference to "skill level or education" is secondary to Blinder's main point about offshorable jobs.)*

> **Draft 3:** In "Will Your Job Be Exported?" economist Alan S. Blinder argues that the quality and security of future jobs will be determined by how "offshorable" those jobs are.
>
> *(Close — but not "all" jobs. Blinder specifies which types of jobs are "offshorable.")*

> **Final Draft:** In "Will Your Job Be Exported?" economist Alan S. Blinder argues that the quality and security of future jobs in America's service sector will be determined by how "offshorable" those jobs are.

Write the First Draft of the Summary

Let's consider two possible summaries of Blinder's article: (1) a short summary, combining a thesis with brief section summaries, and (2) a longer summary, combining thesis, brief section summaries, and some carefully chosen details. Again, keep in mind that you are reading final versions; each of the following summaries is the result of at least two full drafts. Highlighting indicates transitions added to smooth the flow of the summary.

Summary 1: Combine Thesis Sentence with Brief Section Summaries

> In "Will Your Job Be Exported?" economist Alan S. Blinder argues that the quality and security of future jobs in America's service sector will be determined by how "offshorable" those jobs are. For the past twenty-five years, the greater a worker's skill or level of education, the better and more stable the job. No longer. Advances in technology have brought to the service sector the same pressures that forced so many manufacturing jobs offshore to China and India. The rate of offshoring in the service sector will accelerate, and jobs requiring both relatively little education (such as call-center staffing) and extensive education (such as software development) will increasingly be lost to workers overseas.

These losses will "eventually exceed" losses in manufacturing, but not all services jobs are equally at risk. While "personal services" workers (such as barbers and surgeons) will be relatively safe from offshoring because their work requires close physical proximity to customers, "impersonal services" workers (such as call-center operators and radiologists), regardless of their skill or education, will be at risk because their work can be completed remotely without loss of quality and then delivered via phone or computer. "[T]he relative demand for labor in the United States will [probably] shift away from impersonal services and toward personal services."

Blinder recommends three courses of action: He advises young people to plan for "a high-end personal service occupation that is not offshorable." He urges educators to prepare the future workforce by anticipating the needs of a personal services economy and redesigning classroom instruction and vocational training accordingly. Finally, he urges the government to adopt policies that will improve existing personal services jobs by increasing wages for low-wage workers; retraining workers to take on better jobs; and increasing opportunities in high-demand, well-paid areas such as nursing and carpentry. Ultimately, Blinder wants America to prepare a new generation to "lead and innovate" in an economy that will continue exporting jobs that require "following and copying."

The Strategy of the Shorter Summary

This short summary consists essentially of a restatement of Blinder's thesis plus the section summaries, modified or expanded a little for stylistic purposes. You'll recall that Blinder locates his thesis midway through the article, in paragraph 10. But note that this model summary *begins* with a restatement of his thesis. Notice also the relative weight given to the section summaries within the model. Blinder's main point, his "critical distinction" between personal and impersonal services jobs, is summarized in paragraph 2 of the model. The other paragraphs combine summaries of relatively less important (that is, supporting or explanatory) material. Paragraph 1 combines summaries of the article's Sections 1 and 2; paragraph 3 combines summaries of Sections 4 and 5.

Between the thesis and the section summaries, notice the insertion of three (highlighted) transitions. The first—a fragment (*No longer*)—bridges the first paragraph's summaries of Sections 1 and 2 of Blinder's article. The second transition links a point Blinder makes in his Section 2 (*Losses in the service sector will "eventually exceed" losses in manufacturing*) with an introduction to the key point he will make in Section 3 (*Not all service jobs are equally at risk*). The third transition (*Blinder recommends three courses of action*) bridges the summary of Blinder's Section 3 to summaries of Sections 4 and 5. Each transition, then, links sections of the whole: Each casts the reader back to recall points just made; each casts the reader forward by announcing related points about to be made. Our model ends with a summary of Blinder's motivation for writing, the sense of which is implied by the section summaries but nowhere made explicit.

Summary 2: Combine Thesis Sentence, Section Summaries, and Carefully Chosen Details

The thesis and brief section summaries could also be used as the outline for a more detailed summary. However, most of the details in the passage won't be necessary in a summary. It isn't necessary even in a longer summary of this passage to discuss all of Blinder's examples of jobs that are more or less likely to be sent offshore. It would be appropriate, though, to mention one example of such a job; to review his reasons for thinking "that service-sector offshoring will eventually exceed manufacturing-sector offshoring by a hefty margin"; and to expand on his point that a college education in itself will no longer ensure job security.

None of these details appeared in the first summary; but in a longer summary, a few carefully selected details might be desirable for clarity. How do you decide which details to include? First, working with Blinder's point that one's job type (personal services vs. impersonal services) will matter more for future job quality and security than did the once highly regarded "silver bullet" of education, you may want to cite some of the most persuasive evidence supporting this idea. For example, you could explore why some highly paid physicians, such as radiologists, might find themselves competing for jobs with lower-paid physicians overseas. Further, your expanded summary might reflect the relative weight Blinder gives to education (seven paragraphs, the longest of the article's five sections).

You won't always know which details to include and which to exclude. Developing good judgment in comprehending and summarizing texts is largely a matter of reading skill and prior knowledge (see p. 4). Consider the analogy of the seasoned mechanic who can pinpoint an engine problem by simply listening to a characteristic sound that to a less experienced person is just noise. Or consider the chess player who can plot three separate winning strategies from a board position that to a novice looks like a hopeless jumble. In the same way, the more practiced a reader you are, the more knowledgeable you will become about the subject and the better able you will be to make critical distinctions between elements of greater and lesser importance. In the meantime, read as carefully as you can and use your own best judgment as to how to present your material.

Here's one version of a completed summary with carefully chosen details. Note that we have highlighted phrases and sentences added to the original, briefer summary.

> In "Will Your Job Be Exported?" economist Alan S. Blinder argues that the quality and security of future jobs in America's service sector will be determined by how "offshorable" those jobs are. For the past twenty-five years, the greater a worker's skill or level of education, the better and

more stable the job. Americans have long regarded education as the "silver bullet" that could propel motivated people to better jobs and a better life. No longer. Advances in technology have brought to the service sector the same pressures that forced so many manufacturing jobs offshore to China and India. The rate of offshoring in the service sector will accelerate, says Blinder, and jobs requiring both relatively little education (such as call-center staffing) and extensive education (such as software development) will increasingly be lost to workers overseas.

Blinder expects that job losses in the service sector will "eventually exceed" losses in manufacturing, for three reasons. Developed countries have more service jobs than manufacturing jobs; as technology speeds communications, more service jobs will be offshorable; and the numbers of qualified offshore workers is increasing. Service jobs lost to foreign competition may cause a "bumpy" period as the global economy sorts out what work gets done where, by whom. In time, as the global economy finds its "eventual equilibrium," offshoring will benefit the United States; but the consequences in the meantime may be painful for many.

That pain will not be shared equally by all service workers, however. While "personal service" workers (such as barbers and surgeons) will be relatively safe from offshoring because their work requires close physical proximity to customers, "impersonal service" workers (such as audio transcribers and radiologists), regardless of their skill or education, will be at risk because their work can be completed remotely without loss of quality and then delivered via phone or computer. In the coming decades, says Blinder, "the relative demand for labor in the United States will [probably] shift away from impersonal services and toward personal services." This shift will be influenced by the desire to keep good jobs in the United States while exporting jobs that require "following and copying." Highly trained computer coders will face the same pressures of outsourcing as relatively untrained call-center attendants. A tax attorney whose work requires no face-to-face interaction with clients may see her work migrate overseas, while a divorce attorney, who must interact with clients on a case-by-case basis, may face no such competition. Same educations, different outcomes: What determines their fates in a global economy is the nature of their work (that is, personal vs. impersonal), not their level of education.

Based on this analysis, Blinder recommends three courses of action: First, he advises young people to plan for "a high-end personal service occupation that is not offshorable." Many good jobs, such as carpentry and plumbing, will not require a college degree. Next, Blinder urges educators to prepare the future workforce by anticipating the needs of a personal services economy and redesigning classroom instruction and vocational training accordingly. These efforts should begin in elementary school and develop imagination and interpersonal skills rather than capacities for rote memorization. Finally, Blinder urges the government to develop policies that will improve wages and conditions for low-wage personal services workers (such as janitors); to encourage more low-wage workers (such as daycare providers) to retrain and take on better service jobs; and to increase opportunities for professional and vocational training for workers in high-demand services areas (such as nurses and electricians). Ultimately, Blinder wants America to prepare a new generation of workers who will "lead and innovate...just as we have in the past."

The Strategy of the Longer Summary

Compared to the first, briefer summary, this effort (70 percent longer than the first) includes Blinder's reasons for suggesting that job losses in the services sector will exceed losses in manufacturing. It emphasizes Blinder's point that job type (personal vs. impersonal services), not a worker's education level, will ensure job security. It includes Blinder's point that offshoring in the service sector is part of a larger global economy seeking "equilibrium." And it offers more on Blinder's thoughts concerning the education of future workers.

The final two of our suggested steps for writing summaries are (1) to check your summary against the original passage, making sure that you have included all the important ideas, and (2) to revise so that the summary reads smoothly and coherently. The structure of this summary generally reflects the structure of the original article—with one significant departure, as noted earlier. Blinder uses a modified inductive approach, stating his thesis midway through the article. The summary, however, states the thesis immediately, then proceeds deductively to develop that thesis.

HOW LONG SHOULD A SUMMARY BE?

The length of a summary depends both on the length of the original passage and on the use to which the summary will be put. If you are summarizing an entire article, a good rule of thumb is that your summary should be no longer than one-fourth the length of the original passage. Of course, if you were summarizing an entire chapter or even an entire book, it would have to be much shorter than that. The longer summary above is one-quarter the length of Alan Blinder's original. Although it shouldn't be very much longer, you have seen (pp. 22–24) that it could be quite a bit shorter.

The length as well as the content of the summary also depends on the *purpose* to which it will be put. Let's suppose you decided to use Blinder's piece in a paper that deals with the loss of manufacturing jobs in the United States and the rise of the service economy. In this case, in an effort to explain the complexities of the service economy to your readers, you might summarize *only* Blinder's core distinction between jobs in personal services and impersonal services, likely mentioning that jobs in the latter category are at risk of offshoring. If, instead, you were writing a paper in which you argued that the forces of globalization will eventually collapse the world's economies into a single, global economy, you would likely give less attention to

Blinder's distinction between personal and impersonal services. More to the point might be his observation that highly skilled, highly educated workers in the United States are now finding themselves competing with qualified, lower-wage workers in China and India. Thus, depending on your purpose, you would summarize either selected portions of a source or an entire source. We will see this process more fully demonstrated in the upcoming chapters on syntheses.

Exercise 1.1 ◯

Individual and Collaborative Summary Practice

Turn to Chapter 8 and read William Tucker's article "Why I Still Support Nuclear Power, Even After Fukushima." Follow the steps for writing summaries outlined above—read, underline, and divide into stages of thought. Write a one-or two-sentence summary of each stage of thought in Tucker's article. Then gather in groups of three or four classmates and compare your summary sentences. Discuss the differences in your sentences, and come to some consensus about the divisions in Tucker's stages of thought—and the ways in which to best sum them up.

As a group, write a one-or two-sentence thesis statement summing up the entire passage. You could go even further, and, using your individual summary sentences—or the versions of them your group revised—put together a brief summary of Tucker's essay. Model your work on the brief summary of Blinder's article, on pp. 17–18.

AVOIDING PLAGIARISM

Plagiarism is generally defined as the attempt to pass off the work of another as one's own. Whether born out of calculation or desperation, plagiarism is the least tolerated offense in the academic world. The fact that most plagiarism is unintentional—arising from an ignorance of the conventions rather than deceitfulness—makes no difference to many professors.

The ease of cutting and pasting whole blocks of text from Web sources into one's own paper makes it tempting for some to take the easy way out and avoid doing their own research and writing. But, apart from the serious ethical issues involved, the same technology that makes such acts possible also makes it possible for instructors to detect them. Software marketed to instructors allows them to conduct Web searches, using suspicious phrases as keywords. The results often provide irrefutable evidence of plagiarism.

Of course, plagiarism is not confined to students. Recent years have seen a number of high-profile cases—some of them reaching the front pages of newspapers—of well-known scholars who were shown to have copied passages from sources into their own book manuscripts, without proper attribution. In some cases, the scholars maintained that these appropriations were simply a matter of carelessness, that in the press and volume of work, they had lost track of which words were theirs and which were the words of their sources. But such excuses sounded hollow: These careless acts inevitably embarrassed the scholars professionally, tarnished their otherwise fine work and reputations, and disappointed their many admirers.

You can avoid plagiarism and charges of plagiarism by following the basic rules provided in the box at the end of the chapter.

Following is a passage from an article by Richard Rovere on Senator Joseph P. McCarthy, along with several student versions of the ideas represented.

> McCarthy never seemed to believe in himself or in anything he had said. He knew that Communists were not in charge of American foreign policy. He knew that they weren't running the United States Army. He knew that he had spent five years looking for Communists in the government and that—although some must certainly have been there, since Communists had turned up in practically every other major government in the world—he hadn't come up with even one.*

One student version of this passage reads:

> McCarthy never believed in himself or in anything he had said. He knew that Communists were not in charge of American foreign policy and weren't running the United States Army. He knew that he had spent five years looking for Communists in the government, and although there must certainly have been some there, since Communists were in practically every other major government in the world, he hadn't come up with even one.

Clearly, this is intentional plagiarism. The student has copied the original passage almost word for word.

Here is another version of the same passage:

> McCarthy knew that Communists were not running foreign policy or the Army. He also knew that although there must have been some Communists in the government, he hadn't found a single one, even though he had spent five years looking.

This student has attempted to put the ideas into her own words, but both the wording and the sentence structure are so heavily dependent on the original passage that even if it *were* cited, most professors would consider it plagiarism.

In the following version, the student has sufficiently changed the wording and sentence structure, and she uses a *signal phrase* (a phrase used to introduce a quotation or paraphrase, signaling to the reader that the words

---

*Richard Rovere, "The Most Gifted and Successful Demagogue This Country Has Ever Known," *New York Times Magazine*, 30 Apr. 1967.

to follow come from someone else) to properly credit the information to Rovere, so that there is no question of plagiarism:

> According to Richard Rovere, McCarthy was fully aware that Communists were running neither the government nor the Army. He also knew that he hadn't found a single Communist in government, even after a lengthy search (192).

And although this is not a matter of plagiarism, as noted above, it's essential to quote accurately. You are not permitted to change any part of a quotation or to omit any part of it without using brackets or ellipses.

RULES FOR AVOIDING PLAGIARISM

- Cite *all* quoted material and *all* summarized and paraphrased material, unless the information is common knowledge (e.g., the Civil War was fought from 1861 to 1865).
- Make sure that both the *wording* and the *sentence structure* of your summaries and paraphrases are substantially your own.

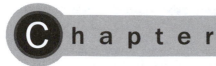

Critical Reading and Critique

After completing this chapter, you will be able to:

LO 2.1   Read critically to determine (1) how well an article, editorial, or chapter has succeeded in achieving its purpose and (2) how fully you agree with the author's points.

LO 2.2   Write a critique of an article, editorial, or chapter that expresses (1) how well the passage has succeeded in achieving its purpose and (2) how fully you agree with the author's points.

CRITICAL READING

When writing papers in college, you are often called on to respond critically to source materials. Critical reading requires the abilities to both summarize and evaluate a presentation. As you have seen in Chapter 1, a *summary* is a brief restatement in your own words of the content of a passage; an *evaluation* is a more ambitious undertaking. In your college work, you read to gain and *use* new information. But because sources are not equally valid or equally useful, you must learn to distinguish critically among them by evaluating them.

There is no ready-made formula for determining validity. Critical reading and its written equivalent—the *critique*—require discernment, sensitivity, imagination, knowledge of the subject, and, above all, willingness to become involved in what you read. These skills are developed only through repeated practice. But you must begin somewhere, so we recommend you start by posing two broad questions about passages, articles, and books that you read: (1) To what extent does the author succeed in his or her purpose? (2) To what extent do you agree with the author?

Question 1: To What Extent Does the Author Succeed in His or Her Purpose?

All critical reading *begins with an accurate summary.* Before attempting an evaluation, you must be able to locate an author's thesis and identify the selection's content and structure. You must understand the author's *purpose.* Authors write to inform, to persuade, and to entertain. A given piece may be primarily *informative* (a summary of the research on cloning), primarily *persuasive* (an argument on what the government should do to alleviate homelessness), or primarily *entertaining* (a play about the frustrations of young lovers). Or it may be all three (as in John Steinbeck's novel *The Grapes of Wrath*, about migrant workers during the Great Depression). Sometimes authors are not fully conscious of their purpose. Sometimes their purpose changes as they write. Also, multiple purposes can overlap: A piece of writing may need to inform the reader about an issue in order to make a persuasive point. But if the finished piece is coherent, it will have a primary reason for having been written, and it should be apparent that the author is attempting primarily to inform, persuade, or entertain a particular audience. To identify this primary reason—this purpose—is your first job as a critical reader. Your next job is to determine how successful the author has been in achieving this objective.

As a critical reader, you bring various criteria, or standards of judgment, to bear when you read pieces intended to inform, persuade, or entertain.

WHERE DO WE FIND WRITTEN CRITIQUES?

Here are just a few of the types of writing that involve critique:

Academic Writing

- **Research papers** critique sources in order to establish their usefulness.
- **Position papers** stake out a position by critiquing other positions.
- **Book reviews** combine summary with critique.
- **Essay exams** demonstrate understanding of course material by critiquing it.

Workplace Writing

- **Legal briefs and legal arguments** critique previous arguments made or anticipated by opposing counsel.
- **Business plans and proposals** critique other less cost-effective, cost-efficient, or reasonable approaches.
- **Policy briefs** communicate strengths and weaknesses of policies and legislation through critique.

Writing to Inform

A piece intended to inform will provide definitions, describe or report on a process, recount a story, give historical background, and/or provide facts and figures. An informational piece responds to questions such as:

What (or who) is _____?

How does _____ work?

What is the controversy or problem about?

What happened?

How and why did it happen?

What were the results?

What are the arguments for and against _____?

To the extent that an author answers these and related questions and that the answers are a matter of verifiable record (you could check for accuracy if you had the time and inclination), the selection is intended to inform. Having identified such an intention, you can organize your response by considering three other criteria: accuracy, significance, and fair interpretation of information.

Evaluating Informative Writing

Accuracy of Information   If you are going to use any of the information presented, you must be satisfied that it is trustworthy. One of your responsibilities as a critical reader, then, is to find out if the information is accurate. This means you should check facts against other sources. Government publications are often good resources for verifying facts about political legislation, population data, crime statistics, and the like. You can also search key terms in library databases and on the Web. Since material on the Web is essentially self-published, however, you must be especially vigilant in assessing its legitimacy. A wealth of useful information is now available on the Internet—as are distorted "facts," unsupported opinion, and hidden agendas.

Significance of Information   One useful question that you can put to a reading is "So what?" In the case of selections that attempt to inform, you may reasonably wonder whether the information makes a difference. What can the reader gain from this information? How is knowledge advanced by the publication of this material? Is the information of importance to you or to others in a particular audience? Why or why not?

Fair Interpretation of Information   At times you will read reports whose sole purpose is to relate raw data or information. In these cases, you will build your response on Question 1, introduced on page 29: To what extent does the author succeed in his or her purpose? More frequently, once an author has presented information, he or she will attempt to evaluate or interpret it—which is only reasonable, since information that has not been evaluated or interpreted is of little use. One of your tasks as a critical reader is to make a distinction between the author's presentation of facts and figures and his or her attempts to evaluate them. Watch for shifts from straightforward descriptions of factual information ("20 percent of the population") to assertions about what this information means ("a *mere* 20 percent of the population"), what its implications are, and so on. Pay attention to whether the logic with which the author connects interpretation with facts is sound. You may find that the information is valuable but the interpretation is not. Perhaps the author's conclusions are not justified. Could you offer a contrary explanation for the same facts? Does more information need to be gathered before firm conclusions can be drawn? Why?

Writing to Persuade

Writing is frequently intended to persuade—that is, to influence the reader's thinking. To make a persuasive case, the writer must begin with an assertion that is arguable, some statement about which reasonable people could disagree. Such an assertion, when it serves as the essential organizing principle of the article or book, is called a *thesis*. Here are two examples:

> Because they do not speak English, many children in this affluent land are being denied their fundamental right to equal educational opportunity.

> Bilingual education, which has been stridently promoted by a small group of activists with their own agenda, is detrimental to the very students it is supposed to serve.

Thesis statements such as these—and the subsequent assertions used to help support them—represent conclusions that authors have drawn as a result of researching and thinking about an issue. You go through the same process yourself when you write persuasive papers or critiques. And just as you are entitled to evaluate critically the assertions of authors you read, so your professors—and other students—are entitled to evaluate *your* assertions, whether they be written arguments or comments made in class discussion.

Keep in mind that writers organize arguments by arranging evidence to support one conclusion and to oppose (or dismiss) another. You can assess the validity of an argument and its conclusion by determining whether the author has (1) clearly defined key terms, (2) used information fairly, and (3) argued logically and not fallaciously (see pp. 36–40).

Informative and Persuasive Thesis Statements

With a partner from your class, identify at least one informative and one persuasive thesis statement from two passages of your own choosing. Photocopy these passages and highlight the statements you have selected.

As an alternative, and also working with a partner, write one informative and one persuasive thesis statement for *three* of the topics listed in the last paragraph of this exercise. For example, for the topic of prayer in schools, your informative thesis statement could read:

> Both advocates and opponents of school prayer frame their position as a matter of freedom.

Your persuasive thesis statement might be worded:

> As long as schools don't dictate what kinds of prayers students should say, then school prayer should be allowed and even encouraged.

Don't worry about taking a position that you agree with or feel you could support; this exercise doesn't require that you write an essay. The topics:

school prayer

gun control

immigration

stem cell research

grammar instruction in English class

violent lyrics in music

teaching computer skills in primary schools

curfews in college dormitories

course registration procedures

Evaluating Persuasive Writing

Read the argument that follows on the cancellation of the National Aeronautics and Space Administration's lunar program. We will illustrate our discussion on defining terms, using information fairly, and arguing logically by referring to Charles Krauthammer's argument, which appeared as an op-ed in the *Washington Post* on July 17, 2009. The model critique that follows these illustrations will be based on this same argument.

THE MOON WE LEFT BEHIND

Charles Krauthammer

Michael Crichton once wrote that if you told a physicist in 1899 that within a hundred years humankind would, among other wonders (nukes, commercial airlines), "travel to the moon, and then lose interest...the physicist would almost certainly pronounce you mad." In 2000, I quoted these lines expressing Crichton's incredulity at America's abandonment of the moon. It is now 2009 and the moon recedes ever further.

Next week marks the 40th anniversary of the first moon landing. We say we will return in 2020. But that promise was made by a previous president, and this president [Obama] has defined himself as the antimatter to George Bush. Moreover, for all of Barack Obama's Kennedyesque qualities, he has expressed none of Kennedy's enthusiasm for human space exploration.

So with the Apollo moon program long gone, and with Constellation,* its supposed successor, still little more than a hope, we remain in retreat from space. Astonishing. After countless millennia of gazing and dreaming, we finally got off the ground at Kitty Hawk in 1903. Within 66 years, a nanosecond in human history, we'd landed on the moon. Then five more landings, 10 more moonwalkers and, in the decades since, nothing.

To be more precise: almost 40 years spent in low Earth orbit studying, well, zero-G nausea and sundry cosmic mysteries. We've done it with the most beautiful, intricate, complicated—and ultimately, hopelessly impractical—machine ever built by man: the space shuttle. We turned this magnificent bird into a truck for hauling goods and people to a tinkertoy we call the international space station, itself created in a fit of post-Cold War internationalist absentmindedness as a place where people of differing nationality can sing "Kumbaya" while weightless.

5   The shuttle is now too dangerous, too fragile and too expensive. Seven more flights and then it is retired, going—like the Spruce Goose** and the Concorde†—into the Museum of Things Too Beautiful and Complicated to Survive.

America's manned space program is in shambles. Fourteen months from today, for the first time since 1962, the United States will be incapable not just of sending a man to the moon but of sending anyone into Earth orbit. We'll be totally grounded. We'll have to beg a ride from the Russians or perhaps even the Chinese.

"The Moon We Left Behind" by Charles Krauthammer from *The Washington Post*, © July 17, 2009, The Washington Post. All rights reserved. Used by permission and protected by the Copyright Laws of the United States. The printing, copying, redistribution, or retransmission of the Material without express written permission is prohibited. www.washingtonpost.com

*Constellation was a NASA human spaceflight program designed to develop post–space shuttle vehicles capable of traveling to the moon and perhaps to Mars. Authorized in 2005, the program was canceled by President Obama in 2010.

**Spruce Goose was the informal name bestowed by critics on the H4 Hercules, a heavy transport aircraft designed and built during World War II by the Hughes Aircraft Company. Built almost entirely of birch (not spruce) because of wartime restrictions on war materials, the aircraft boasted the largest height and wingspan of any aircraft in history. Only one prototype was built, and the aircraft made only one flight, on November 2, 1947. It is currently housed at the Evergreen Aviation Museum in McMinnville, Oregon.

†Admired for its elegant design as well as its speed, the Concorde was a supersonic passenger airliner built by a British-French consortium. It was first flown in 1969, entered service in 1976 (with regular flights to and from London, Paris, Washington, and New York), and was retired in 2003, a casualty of economic pressures. Only twenty Concordes were built.

So what, you say? Don't we have problems here on Earth? Oh, please. Poverty and disease and social ills will always be with us. If we'd waited for them to be rectified before venturing out, we'd still be living in caves.

Yes, we have a financial crisis. No one's asking for a crash Manhattan Project. All we need is sufficient funding from the hundreds of billions being showered from Washington—"stimulus" monies that, unlike Eisenhower's interstate highway system or Kennedy's Apollo program, will leave behind not a trace on our country or our consciousness—to build Constellation and get us back to Earth orbit and the moon a half-century after the original landing.

Why do it? It's not for practicality. We didn't go to the moon to spin off cooling suits and freeze-dried fruit. Any technological return is a bonus, not a reason. We go for the wonder and glory of it. Or, to put it less grandly, for its immense possibilities. We choose to do such things, said JFK, "not because they are easy, but because they are hard." And when you do such magnificently hard things—send sailing a Ferdinand Magellan or a Neil Armstrong—you open new human possibility in ways utterly unpredictable.

10   The greatest example? Who could have predicted that the moon voyages would create the most potent impetus to—and symbol of—environmental consciousness here on Earth: Earthrise, the now iconic Blue Planet photograph brought back by Apollo 8?

Ironically, that new consciousness about the uniqueness and fragility of Earth focused contemporary imagination away from space and back to Earth. We are now deep into that hyper-terrestrial phase, the age of iPod and Facebook, of social networking and eco-consciousness.

But look up from your BlackBerry one night. That is the moon. On it are exactly 12 sets of human footprints—untouched, unchanged, abandoned. For the first time in history, the moon is not just a mystery and a muse, but a nightly rebuke. A vigorous young president once summoned us to this new frontier, calling the voyage "the most hazardous and dangerous and greatest adventure on which man has ever embarked." And so we did it. We came. We saw. Then we retreated.

How could we?

Exercise 2.2

Critical Reading Practice

Look back at the Critical Reading for Summary box on pages 6–7 of Chapter 1. Use each of the guidelines listed there to examine the essay by Charles Krauthammer. Note in the margins of the selection—or on a separate sheet of paper—the essay's main point, subpoints, and use of examples.

Persuasive Strategies

Clearly Defined Terms   The validity of an argument depends to some degree on how carefully an author has defined key terms. Take the assertion, for example, that American society must be grounded in "family values." Just what do people who use this phrase mean by it? The validity of their argument depends on whether they and their readers agree on a definition of "family values"—as well as what it means to be "grounded in" family values. If an author writes that in the recent past, "America's elites accepted as a matter of course that a free society can sustain itself only through virtue and temperance in the people,"* readers need to know what exactly the author means by "elites" and by "virtue and temperance" before they can assess the validity of the argument. In such cases, the success of the argument—its ability to persuade—hinges on the definition of a term. So, in responding to an argument, be sure you (and the author) are clear on what exactly is being argued. Unless you are, no informed response is possible.

Note that in addition to their *denotative* meaning (their specific or literal meaning), many words carry a *connotative* meaning (their suggestive, associative, or emotional meaning). For example, the denotative meaning of "home" is simply the house or apartment where one lives. But the connotative meaning—with its associations of family, belongingness, refuge, safety, and familiarity—adds a significant emotional component to this literal meaning. (See more on connotation in "Emotionally Loaded Terms," pp. 36–37.)

In the course of his argument, Krauthammer writes of "America's abandonment of the moon" and of the fact that we have "retreated" from lunar exploration. Consider the words "abandon" and "retreat." What do these words mean to you? Look them up in a dictionary for precise definitions (note all possible meanings provided). In what contexts are we most likely to see these words used? What emotional meaning and significance do they generally carry? For example, what do we usually think of people who abandon a marriage or military units that retreat? To what extent does it appear to you that Krauthammer is using these words in accordance with one or more of their dictionary definitions, their denotations? To what extent does the force of his argument also depend upon the power of these words' connotative meanings?

When writing a paper, you will need to decide, like Krauthammer, which terms to define and which you can assume the reader will define in the same way you do. As the writer of a critique, you should identify and discuss any undefined or ambiguous term that might give rise to confusion.

Fair Use of Information   Information is used as evidence in support of arguments. When you encounter such evidence, ask yourself two questions: (1) "Is the information accurate and up to date?" At least a portion of an argument becomes invalid when the information used to support

---

*Charles Murray, "The Coming White Underclass," *Wall Street Journal*, 20 Oct. 1993.

it is wrong or stale. (2) "Has the author cited *representative* information?" The evidence used in an argument must be presented in a spirit of fair play. An author is less than ethical when he presents only the evidence favoring his own views even though he is well aware that contrary evidence exists. For instance, it would be dishonest to argue that an economic recession is imminent and to cite only indicators of economic downturn while ignoring and failing to cite contrary (positive) evidence.

"The Moon We Left Behind" is not an information-heavy essay. The success of the piece turns on the author's powers of persuasion, not on his use of facts and figures. Krauthammer does, however, offer some key facts relating to Project Apollo and the fact that President Obama was not inclined to back a NASA-operated lunar-landing program. And, in fact, Krauthammer's fears were confirmed in February 2010, about six months after he wrote "The Moon We Left Behind," when the president canceled NASA's plans for further manned space exploration flights in favor of government support for commercial space operations.

Logical Argumentation: Avoiding Logical Fallacies

At some point, you'll need to respond to the logic of the argument itself. To be convincing, an argument should be governed by principles of *logic*—clear and orderly thinking. This does *not* mean that an argument cannot be biased. A biased argument—that is, an argument weighted toward one point of view and against others, which is in fact the nature of argument—may be valid as long as it is logically sound.

Let's examine several types of faulty thinking and logical fallacies you will need to watch for.

Emotionally Loaded Terms   Writers sometimes attempt to sway readers by using emotionally charged words. Words with positive connotations (e.g., "family values") are intended to sway readers to the author's point of view; words with negative connotations (e.g., "paying the price") try to sway readers away from an opposing point of view. The fact that an author uses emotionally loaded terms does not necessarily invalidate an argument. Emotional appeals are perfectly legitimate and time-honored modes of persuasion. But in academic writing, which is grounded in logical argumentation, they should not be the *only* means of persuasion. You should be sensitive to *how* emotionally loaded terms are being used. In particular, are they being used deceptively or to hide the essential facts?

We've already noted Krauthammer's use of the emotionally loaded terms "abandonment" and "retreat" when referring to the end of the manned space program. Notice also his use of the term "Kumbaya" in the sentence declaring that the international space station was "created in a fit of post-Cold War internationalist absentmindedness as a place where people of differing nationality can sing 'Kumbaya' while weightless." "Kumbaya" is an African-American spiritual dating from the 1930s, often sung by scouts around campfires. Jeffrey Weiss reports on the dual connotations of this word: "The song was originally associated with human and spiritual unity, closeness and compassion, and it still is, but more recently it is also cited or alluded to in satirical, sarcastic or even cynical ways that suggest blind or false moralizing, hypocrisy, or naively optimistic views of the world and human nature."* Is Krauthammer drawing upon the emotional power of the original meaning or upon the more recent significance of this term? How does his particular use of "Kumbaya" strengthen (or weaken) his argument? What appears to be the difference in his mind between the value of the international space station and the value of returning to the moon? As someone evaluating the essay, you should be alert to this appeal to your emotions and then judge whether or not the appeal is fair and convincing. Above all, you should not let an emotional appeal blind you to shortcomings of logic, ambiguously defined terms, or a misuse of facts.

Ad Hominem Argument   In an *ad hominem* argument, the writer rejects opposing views by attacking the person(s) who holds them. By calling opponents names, an author avoids the issue. Consider this excerpt from a political speech:

> I could more easily accept my opponent's plan to increase revenues by collecting on delinquent tax bills if he had paid more than a hundred dollars in state taxes in each of the past three years. But the fact is, he's a millionaire with a millionaire's tax shelters. This man hasn't paid a wooden nickel for the state services he and his family depend on. So I ask you: Is *he* the one to be talking about taxes to *us*?

It could well be that the opponent has paid virtually no state taxes for three years; but this fact has nothing to do with, and is used as a ploy to divert attention from, the merits of a specific proposal for increasing revenues. The proposal is lost in the attack against the man himself, an attack that violates principles of logic. Writers (and speakers) should make their points by citing evidence in support of their views and by challenging contrary evidence.

In "The Moon We Left Behind," Krauthammer's only individual target is President Obama. While he does, at several points, unfavorably compare Obama to Kennedy, he does not do so in an *ad hominem* way. That is, he attacks Obama less for his personal qualities than for his policy decision to close down NASA's manned space program. At most, he laments that Obama "has expressed none of Kennedy's enthusiasm for human space exploration."

Faulty Cause and Effect   The fact that one event precedes another in time does not mean that the first event has caused the second. An example: Fish begin dying by the thousands in a lake near your hometown. An environmental group immediately cites chemical dumping by several manufacturing plants as the cause. But other causes are possible: A disease might have affected the

---

*Jeffery Weiss, "'Kumbaya': How did a sweet simple song become a mocking metaphor?" *Dallas Morning News*. 12 Nov. 2006.

TONE

Tone refers to the overall emotional effect produced by a writer's choice of language. Writers might use especially emphatic words to create a tone: A film reviewer might refer to a "magnificent performance," or a columnist might criticize "sleazeball politics."

These are extreme examples of tone; tone can also be more subtle, particularly if the writer makes a special effort *not* to inject emotion into the writing. As we indicated in the section on emotionally loaded terms, the fact that a writer's tone is highly emotional does not necessarily mean that the writer's argument is invalid. Conversely, a neutral tone does not ensure an argument's validity.

Many instructors discourage student writing that projects a highly emotional tone, considering it inappropriate for academic or preprofessional work. (One sure sign of emotion: the exclamation mark, which should be used sparingly.)

---

fish; the growth of algae might have contributed to the deaths; or acid rain might be a factor. The origins of an event are usually complex and are not always traceable to a single cause. So you must carefully examine cause-and-effect reasoning when you find a writer using it. In Latin, this fallacy is known as *post hoc, ergo propter hoc* ("after this, therefore because of this").

Toward the end of "The Moon We Left Behind," Krauthammer declares that having turned our "imagination away from space and back to Earth...[w]e are now deep into that hyper-terrestrial phase, the age of iPod and Facebook, of social networking and eco-consciousness." He appears here to be suggesting a pattern of cause and effect: that as a people, we are no longer looking outward but, rather, turning inward; and this shift in our attention and focus has resulted in—or at least is a significant cause of—the death of the manned space program. Questions for a critique might include the following: (1) To what extent do you agree with Krauthammer's premise that we live in an inward-looking, rather than an outward-looking, age and that it is fair to call our present historical period "the age of iPod and Facebook"? (2) To what extent do you agree that because we may live in such an age, the space program no longer enjoys broad public or political support?

Either/Or Reasoning   Either/or reasoning also results from an unwillingness to recognize complexity. If in analyzing a problem an author artificially restricts the range of possible solutions by offering only two courses of action, and then rejects the one that he opposes, he cannot logically argue that the remaining course of action, which he favors, is therefore the only one that makes sense. Usually, several other options (at least) are possible. For whatever reason, the author has chosen to overlook them. As an example, suppose you are reading a selection on genetic engineering in which the author builds an argument on the basis of the following:

> Research in gene splicing is at a crossroads: Either scientists will be carefully monitored by civil authorities and their efforts limited to acceptable applications, such as disease control; or, lacking regulatory guidelines, scientists will set their own ethical standards and begin programs in embryonic manipulation that, however well intended, exceed the proper limits of human knowledge.

Certainly, other possibilities for genetic engineering exist beyond the two mentioned here. But the author limits debate by establishing an either/or choice. Such a limitation is artificial and does not allow for complexity. As a critical reader, you need to be on the alert for reasoning based on restrictive, either/or alternatives.

Hasty Generalization   Writers are guilty of hasty generalization when they draw their conclusions from too little evidence or from unrepresentative evidence. To argue that scientists should not proceed with the Human Genome Project because a recent editorial urged that the project be abandoned is to make a hasty generalization. That lone editorial may be unrepresentative of the views of most individuals—both scientists and laypeople—who have studied and written about the matter. To argue that one should never obey authority because Stanley Milgram's Yale University experiments in the 1960s showed the dangers of obedience is to ignore the fact that Milgram's experiments were concerned primarily with obedience to *immoral* authority. The experimental situation was unrepresentative of most routine demands for obedience—for example, to obey a parental rule or to comply with a summons for jury duty—and a conclusion about the malevolence of all authority would be a hasty generalization.

False Analogy   Comparing one person, event, or issue to another may be illuminating, but it can also be confusing or misleading. Differences between the two may be more significant than their similarities, and conclusions drawn from one may not necessarily apply to the other. A candidate for governor or president who argues that her experience as CEO of a major business would make her effective in governing a state or the country is assuming an analogy between the business and the political/civic worlds that does not hold up to examination. Most businesses are hierarchical, or top down: When a CEO issues an order, he or she can expect it to be carried out without argument. But governors and presidents command only their own executive branches. They cannot issue orders to independent legislatures or courts (much less private citizens); they can only attempt to persuade. In this case, the implied analogy fails to convince the thoughtful reader or listener.

Begging the Question   To beg the question is to assume as proven fact the very thesis being argued. To assert, for example, that America does not need a new health care delivery system because America currently has the best health care in the world does not prove anything: It merely repeats the claim in different—and equally unproven—words. This fallacy is also known as *circular reasoning*.

Non Sequitur   *Non sequitur* is Latin for "it does not follow"; the term is used to describe a conclusion that does not logically follow from the premise. "Since minorities have made such great strides in the past few decades," a writer may argue, "we no longer need affirmative action programs." Aside from the fact that the premise itself is arguable (*have* minorities made such great strides?), it does not follow that because minorities *may* have made great strides, there is no further need for affirmative action programs.

Oversimplification   Be alert for writers who offer easy solutions to complicated problems. "America's economy will be strong again if we all 'buy American,'" a politician may argue. But the problems of America's economy are complex and cannot be solved by a slogan or a simple change in buying habits. Likewise, a writer who argues that we should ban genetic engineering assumes that simple solutions ("just say no") will be sufficient to deal with the complex moral dilemmas raised by this new technology.

Exercise 2.3

Understanding Logical Fallacies

Make a list of the nine logical fallacies discussed in the preceding section. Briefly define each one in your own words. Then, in a group of three or four classmates, review your definitions and the examples we've provided for each logical fallacy. Collaborate with your group to find or invent additional examples for each of the fallacies. Compare your examples with those generated by the other groups in your class.

Writing to Entertain

Authors write not only to inform and persuade, but also to entertain. One response to entertainment is a hearty laugh, but it is possible to entertain without encouraging laughter: A good book or play or poem may prompt you to reflect, grow wistful, become elated, get angry. Laughter is only one of many possible reactions. Like a response to an informative piece or an argument, your response to an essay, poem, story, play, novel, or film should be precisely stated and carefully developed. Ask yourself some of the following questions (you won't have space to explore all of them, but try to consider the most important ones):

- Did I care for the portrayal of a certain character?
- Did that character (or a group of characters united by occupation, age, ethnicity, etc.) seem overly sentimental, for example, or heroic?
- Did his adversaries seem too villainous or stupid?

- Were the situations believable?
- Was the action interesting or merely formulaic?
- Was the theme developed subtly or powerfully, or did the work come across as preachy or unconvincing?
- Did the action at the end of the work follow plausibly from what had come before? Was the language fresh and incisive or stale and predictable?

Explain as specifically as possible what elements of the work seemed effective or ineffective and why. Offer an overall assessment, elaborating on your views.

Question 2: To What Extent Do You Agree with the Author?

A critical evaluation consists of two parts. The first part, just discussed, assesses the accuracy and effectiveness of an argument in terms of the author's logic and use of evidence. The second part, discussed here, responds to the argument—that is, agrees or disagrees with it.

Identify Points of Agreement and Disagreement

Be precise in identifying where you agree and disagree with an author. State as clearly as possible what *you* believe, in relation to what the author believes, as presented in the piece. Whether you agree enthusiastically, agree with reservations, or disagree, you can organize your reactions in two parts:

- Summarize the author's position.
- State your own position and explain why you believe as you do. The elaboration, in effect, becomes an argument itself, and this is true regardless of the position you take.

Any opinion that you express is effective to the extent you support it by supplying evidence from your reading (which should be properly cited), your observation, or your personal experience. Without such evidence, opinions cannot be authoritative. "I thought the article on inflation was lousy." Or: "It was terrific." Why? "I just thought so, that's all." Such opinions have no value because the criticism is imprecise: The critic has taken neither the time to read the article carefully nor the time to carefully explore his or her own reactions.

Exercise 2.4

Exploring Your Viewpoints—in Three Paragraphs

Go to a Web site that presents short, persuasive essays on current social issues, such as reason.com, opinion-pages.org, drudgereport.com, or Speakout.com. Or go to an Internet search engine such as Google or Bing and type in a social issue together with the word "articles," "editorials," or "opinion," and see what you find. Locate a selection on a topic of interest that takes a clear, argumentative position. Print out the selection on which you choose to focus.

- Write one paragraph summarizing the author's key argument.
- Write two paragraphs articulating your agreement or disagreement with the author. (Devote each paragraph to a *single* point of agreement or disagreement.)

Be sure to explain why you think or feel the way you do and, wherever possible, cite relevant evidence—from your reading, experience, or observation.

Explore the Reasons for Agreement and Disagreement: Evaluate Assumptions

One way of elaborating your reactions to a reading is to explore the underlying *reasons* for agreement and disagreement. Your reactions are based largely on assumptions that you hold and how those assumptions compare with the author's. An *assumption* is a fundamental statement about the world and its operations that you take to be true. Often, a writer will express an assumption directly, as in this example:

> #1 One of government's most important functions is to raise and spend tax revenues on projects that improve the housing, medical, and nutritional needs of its citizens.

In this instance, the writer's claim is a direct expression of a fundamental belief about how the world, or some part of it, should work. The argumentative claim *is* the assumption. Just as often, an argument and its underlying assumption are not identical. In these cases, the assumption is some other statement that is implied by the argumentative claim—as in this example:

> #2 Human spaceflight is a waste of public money.

The logic of this second statement rests on an unstated assumption relating to the word *waste*. What, in this writer's view, is a *waste* of money? What is an effective or justified use? In order to agree or not with statement #2, a critical reader must know what assumption(s) it rests on. A good candidate for such an assumption would be statement #1. That is, a person who believes statement #1 about how governments ought to raise and spend money could well make statement #2. This may not be the only assumption underlying statement #2, but it could well be one of them.

Inferring and Implying Assumptions

Infer and *imply* are keywords relating to hidden, or unstated, assumptions; you should be clear on their meanings. A critical reader *infers* what is hidden in a statement and, through that inference, brings what is hidden into the open for examination. Thus, the critical reader infers from statement #2 on human spaceflight the writer's assumption (statement #1) on how governments should spend money. At the same time, the writer of statement #2 *implies* (hints at but does not state directly) an assumption about how governments should spend money. There will be times when writers make statements and are unaware of their own assumptions.

Assumptions provide the foundation on which entire presentations are built. You may find an author's assumptions invalid—that is, not supported by factual evidence. You may disagree with value-based assumptions underlying an author's position—for instance, what constitutes "good" or "correct" behavior. In both cases, you may well disagree with the conclusions that follow from these assumptions. Alternatively, when you find that your own assumptions are contradicted by actual experience, you may be forced to conclude that certain of your fundamental beliefs about the world and how it works were mistaken.

An Example of Hidden Assumptions from the World of Finance

An interesting example of an assumption fatally colliding with reality was revealed during a recent congressional investigation into the financial meltdown of late 2008, which was precipitated by the collapse of the home mortgage market—itself precipitated, many believed, by an insufficiently regulated banking and financial system run amuck. During his testimony before the House Oversight Committee in October of that year, former Federal Reserve chairman Alan Greenspan was grilled by committee chairman Henry Waxman (D-CA) about his "ideology"—essentially, an assumption or set of assumptions that become a governing principle. (In the following transcript, you can substitute the word "assumption" for "ideology.")

Greenspan responded, "I do have an ideology. My judgment is that free, competitive markets are by far the unrivaled way to organize economies. We have tried regulation; none meaningfully worked." Greenspan defined an ideology as "a conceptual framework [for] the way people deal with reality. Everyone has one. You have to. To exist, you need an ideology." And he pointed out that the assumptions on which he and the Federal Reserve operated were supported by "the best banking lawyers in the business...and an outside counsel of expert professionals to advise on regulatory matters."

Greenspan then admitted that in light of the economic disaster engulfing the nation, he had found a "flaw" in his ideology—that actual experience had violated some of his fundamental beliefs. The testimony continued:

> Chairman Waxman: You found a flaw?
>
> Mr. Greenspan: I found a flaw in the model that I perceived is the critical functioning structure that defines how the world works, so to speak.
>
> Chairman Waxman: In other words, you found that your view of the world, your ideology, was not right, it was not working.

> Mr. Greenspan: Precisely. That's precisely the reason I was shocked, because I had been going for 40 years or more with very considerable evidence that it was working exceptionally well.*

The lesson? All the research, expertise, and logical argumentation in the world will fail if the premise (assumption, ideology) on which it is based turns out to be "flawed."

How do you determine the validity of assumptions once you have identified them? In the absence of more-scientific criteria, you start by considering how well the author's assumptions stack up against your own experience, observations, reading, and values—while remaining honestly aware of the limits of your own personal knowledge.

Readers will want to examine the assumption at the heart of Krauthammer's essay: that continuing NASA's manned space program and, in particular, the program to return human beings to the moon, is a worthwhile enterprise. The writer of the critique that follows questions this assumption. But you may not: You may instead fully support such a program. That's your decision, perhaps made even *before* you read Krauthammer's essay, perhaps as a *result* of having read it. What you must do as a critical reader is to recognize assumptions, whether they are stated or not. You should spell them out and then accept or reject them. Ultimately, your agreement or disagreement with an author will rest on your agreement or disagreement with that author's assumptions.

CRITIQUE

In Chapter 1 we focused on summary—the condensed presentation of ideas from another source. Summary is fundamental to much of academic writing, because such writing relies so heavily on the works of others for the support of its claims. It's not going too far to say that summarizing is the critical thinking skill from which a majority of academic writing builds. However, most academic thinking and writing goes beyond summary. Generally, we use summary to restate our understanding of things we see or read. We then put that summary to use. In academic writing, one typical use of summary is as a prelude to critique.

A *critique* is a *formalized, critical reading of a passage.* It is also a personal response; but writing a critique is considerably more rigorous than saying that a movie is "great," or a book is "fascinating," or "I didn't like it." These are all responses, and, as such, they're a valid, even essential, part of your understanding of what you see and read. But such responses don't illuminate the subject—even for you—if you haven't explained how you arrived at your conclusions.

---

*United States. Cong. House Committee on Oversight and Government Reform. *The Financial Crisis and the Role of Federal Regulators.* 110th Cong., 2nd sess. Washington: GPO, 2008.

Your task in writing a critique is to turn your critical reading of a passage into a systematic evaluation in order to deepen your reader's (and your own) understanding of that passage. When you read a selection to critique, determine the following:

- What an author says
- How well the points are made
- What assumptions underlie the argument
- What issues are overlooked
- What implications can be drawn from such an analysis

When you write a critique, positive or negative, include the following:

- A fair and accurate summary of the passage
- Information and ideas from other sources (your reading or your personal experience and observations), if you think these are pertinent
- A statement of your agreement or disagreement with the author, backed by specific examples and clear logic
- A clear statement of your own assumptions

Remember that you bring to bear on any subject an entire set of assumptions about the world. Stated or not, these assumptions underlie every evaluative comment you make. You therefore have an obligation, both to the reader and to yourself, to clarify your standards by making your assumptions explicit. Not only do your readers stand to gain by your forthrightness, but you do as well. The process of writing a critical assessment forces you to examine your own knowledge, beliefs, and assumptions. Ultimately, the critique is a way of learning about yourself—yet another example of the ways in which writing is useful as a tool for critical thinking.

How to Write Critiques

You may find it useful to organize a critique into five sections: introduction, summary, assessment of the presentation (on its own terms), your response to the presentation, and conclusion.

The next box offers guidelines for writing critiques. These guidelines do not constitute a rigid formula. Most professional authors write critiques that do not follow the structure outlined here. Until you are more confident and practiced in writing critiques, however, we suggest you follow these guidelines. They are meant not to restrict you, but rather to provide a workable sequence for writing critiques until a more fully developed set of experiences and authorial instincts are available to guide you.

GUIDELINES FOR WRITING CRITIQUES

- **Introduce.** Introduce both the passage under analysis and the author. State the author's main argument and the point(s) you intend to make about it.

  Provide background material to help your readers understand the relevance or appeal of the passage. This background material might include one or more of the following: an explanation of why the subject is of current interest; a reference to a possible controversy surrounding the subject of the passage or the passage itself; biographical information about the author; an account of the circumstances under which the passage was written; a reference to the intended audience of the passage.

- **Summarize.** Summarize the author's main points, making sure to state the author's purpose for writing.

- **Assess the presentation.** Evaluate the validity of the author's presentation, distinct from your points of agreement or disagreement. Comment on the author's success in achieving his or her purpose, by reviewing three or four specific points. You might base your review on one or more of the following criteria:

  Is the information accurate?

  Is the information significant?

  Has the author defined terms clearly?

  Has the author used and interpreted information fairly?

  Has the author argued logically?

- **Respond to the presentation.** Now it is your turn to respond to the author's views. With which views do you agree? With which do you disagree? Discuss your reasons for agreement and disagreement, when possible tying these reasons to assumptions—both the author's and your own. Where necessary, draw on outside sources to support your ideas.

- **Conclude.** State your conclusions about the overall validity of the piece—your assessment of the author's success at achieving his or her aims and your reactions to the author's views. Remind the reader of the weaknesses and strengths of the passage.

DEMONSTRATION: CRITIQUE

The critique that follows is based on Charles Krauthammer's op-ed piece "The Moon We Left Behind" (pp. 32–34), which we have already begun to examine. In this formal critique, you will see that it is possible to agree with an author's main point, at least provisionally, yet disagree with other elements of the argument. Critiquing a different selection, you could just as easily accept the author's facts and figures but reject the conclusion he draws from them. As long as you carefully articulate the author's assumptions and your own, explaining in some detail your agreement and disagreement, the critique is yours to take in whatever direction you see fit.

Let's summarize the preceding sections by returning to the core questions that guide critical reading. You will see how, when applied to Charles Krauthammer's argument, they help to set up a critique.

To What Extent Does the Author Succeed in His or Her Purpose?

To answer this question, you will need to know the author's purpose. Krauthammer wrote "The Moon We Left Behind" to persuade his audience that manned space flight must be supported. He makes his case in three ways: (1) He attacks the Obama administration's decision to "retreat" from the moon—i.e., to end NASA's manned space program; (2) he argues for the continuation of this program; and (3) he rebuts criticisms of the program. He aims to achieve this purpose by unfavorably comparing President Obama to President Kennedy, who challenged the nation to put a man on the moon within a decade; by arguing that we should return to the moon for "the wonder and glory of it"; and by challenging the claims that (a) we need first to fix the problems on earth and that (b) we can't afford such a program. One of the main tasks of the writer of a critique of this article is to explain the extent to which Krauthammer has achieved his purpose.

To What Extent Do You Agree with the Author? Evaluate Assumptions

Krauthammer's argument rests upon two assumptions: (1) It is an essential characteristic of humankind to explore—and going to the moon was a great and worthwhile example of exploration; and (2) inspiring deeds are worth our expense and sacrifice—and thus continuing NASA's manned program and returning to the moon is worth our time, effort, and money. One who critiques Krauthammer's op-ed piece must determine the extent to which she or he shares these assumptions. The writer of the model critique does, in fact, share Krauthammer's first assumption, while expressing doubt about the second.

One must also determine the persuasiveness of Krauthammer's arguments for returning to the moon, as well as the persuasiveness of his counterarguments to those who claim this program is too impractical and too expensive. The writer of the model critique believes that Krauthammer's arguments are generally persuasive, even (in the conclusion) judging them "compelling." On the other hand, the critique ends on a neutral note—taking into account the problems with Krauthammer's arguments.

Remember that you don't need to agree with an author to believe that he or she has succeeded in his or her purpose. You may well admire how cogently and forcefully an author has argued, without necessarily accepting her position. Conversely, you may agree with a particular author, while acknowledging that he has not made a very strong case—and perhaps has even made a flawed one—for his point of view. For example, you may heartily approve of the point Krauthammer is making—that the United States should return to the moon. At the same time, you may find problematic the substance of his arguments and/or his strategy for arguing, particularly the dismissive manner in which he refers to the U.S. efforts in space over the last forty years:

> To be more precise: almost 40 years spent in low Earth orbit studying, well, zero-G nausea and sundry cosmic mysteries. We've done it with the most beautiful, intricate, complicated—and ultimately, hopelessly impractical—machine ever built by man: the space shuttle. We turned this magnificent bird into a truck for hauling goods and people to a tinkertoy we call the international space station....

Perhaps you support Krauthammer's position but find his sarcasm distasteful. That said, these two major questions for critical analysis (whether or not the author has been successful in his purpose and the extent to which you agree with the author's assumptions and arguments) are related. You will typically conclude that an author whose arguments have failed to persuade you has not succeeded in her purpose.

The selections you are likely to critique will be those, like Krauthammer's, that argue a specific position. Indeed, every argument you read is an invitation to agree or disagree. It remains only for you to speak up and justify your own position.

MODEL CRITIQUE

Harlan 1

Andrew Harlan

Professor Rose Humphreys

Writing 2

11 January 2011

A Critique of Charles Krauthammer's

"The Moon We Left Behind"

In his 1961 State of the Union address, President John F. Kennedy issued a stirring challenge: "that this nation should commit itself to achieving the goal, before this decade is out, of landing a man on the

Moon and returning him safely to the Earth." At the time, Kennedy's proposal seemed like science fiction. Even the scientists and engineers of the National Aeronautics and Space Administration (NASA) who were tasked with the job didn't know how to meet Kennedy's goal. Spurred, however, partly by a unified national purpose and partly by competition with the Soviet Union, which had beaten the United States into space with the first artificial satellite in 1957, the Apollo program to land men on the moon was launched. On July 20, 1969 Kennedy's challenge was met when Apollo 11 astronauts Neil Armstrong and Buzz Aldrin landed their lunar module on the Sea of Tranquility.

During the next few years, five more Apollo flights landed on ②
the moon. In all, twelve Americans walked on the lunar surface; some even rode on a 4-wheeled "Rover," a kind of lunar dune buggy. But in December 1972 the Apollo program was cancelled. Since that time, some 40 years ago, humans have frequently returned to space, but none have returned to the moon. In February 2010 President Obama ended NASA's moon program, transferring responsibility for manned space exploration to private industry and re-focusing the government's resources on technological development and innovation. The administration had signaled its intentions earlier, in 2009. In July of that year, in an apparent attempt to rouse public opinion against the President's revised priorities for space exploration, Charles Krauthammer wrote "The Moon We Left Behind." It is these revised priorities that are the focus of his op-ed piece, a lament for the end of lunar exploration and a powerful, if flawed, critique of the administration's decision.

Trained as a doctor and a psychiatrist, Charles Krauthammer is a ③
prominent conservative columnist who has won the Pulitzer Prize for his political commentary. Krauthammer begins and ends his op-ed with expressions of dismay and anger at "America's abandonment of the moon." He unfavorably compares the current president, Barack Obama, with the "vigorous young" John F. Kennedy, in terms of their support for manned space exploration. It is inconceivable to Krauthammer that a program

that achieved such technical glories and fired the imaginations of millions in so short a span of time has fallen into such decline.

(4)   Krauthammer anticipates the objections to his plea to keep
America competitive in manned space exploration and to return to the
moon. We have problems enough on earth, critics will argue. His answer:
If we waited to solve these perennial problems before continuing
human progress, "we'd still be living in caves." Concerning the expense
of continuing the space program, Krauthammer argues that a fraction
of the funds being "showered" on the government's stimulus programs
(some $1 trillion) would be sufficient to support a viable space program.
And as for practicality, he dismisses the idea that we need a practical reason to return to the moon. "We go," he argues, "for the wonder
and glory of it. Or, to put it less grandly, for its immense possibilities."
Ultimately, Krauthammer urges us to turn away from our mundane pre-
occupations and look up at the moon where humans once walked. How
could Americans have gone so far, he asks, only to retreat?

(5)   In this opinion piece, Charles Krauthammer offers a powerful,
inspiring defense of the American manned space program; and it's
hard not to agree with him that our voyages to the moon captured
the imagination and admiration of the world and set a new standard
for scientific and technical achievement. Ever since that historic day
in July 1969, people have been asking, "If we can land a man on the
moon, why can't we [fill in your favorite social or political challenge]?"
In a way, the fact that going to the moon was not especially practical
made the achievement even more admirable: we went not for gain, but
rather to explore the unknown, to show what human beings, working
cooperatively and exercising their powers of reason and their genius
in design and engineering, can accomplish when sufficiently challenged. "We go," Krauthammer reminds us, "for the wonder and glory
of it...for its immense possibilities."

(6)   And what's wrong with that? For a relatively brief historical moment, Americans, and indeed the peoples of the world, came together

in pride and anticipation as Apollo 11 sped toward the moon and, days later, as the lunar module descended to the surface. People collectively held their breaths after an oxygen tank explosion disabled Apollo 13 on the way to the moon and as the astronauts and Mission Control guided the spacecraft to a safe return. A renewed moon program might similarly help to reduce divisions among people—or at least among Americans—and highlight the reality that we are all residents of the same planet, with more common interests (such as protecting the environment) than is often apparent from our perennial conflicts. Krauthammer's praise of lunar exploration and its benefits is so stirring that many who do not accept his conclusions may share his disappointment and indignation at its demise.

"The Moon We Left Behind" may actually underestimate the practical aspects of moon travel. "Any technological return," Krauthammer writes, "is a bonus, not a reason." But so many valuable bonuses have emerged from space flight and space exploration that the practical offshoots of lunar exploration may in fact be a valid reason to return to the moon. For instance, the technology developed from the special requirements of space travel has found application in health and medicine (breast cancer detection, laser angioplasty), industrial productivity and manufacturing technology, public safety (radiation hazard detectors, emergency rescue cutters), and transportation (studless winter tires, advanced lubricants, aids to school bus design) ("NASA Spinoffs"). A renewed moon program would also be practical in providing a huge employment stimulus to the economy. According to the NASA Langley Research Center, "At its peak, the Apollo program employed 400,000 people and required the support of over 20,000 industrial firms and universities" ("Apollo Program"). Returning to the moon would create comparable numbers of jobs in aerospace engineering, computer engineering, biology, general engineering, and meteorology, along with hosts of support jobs, from accounting to food service to office automation specialists ("NASA Occupations").

Harlan 5

8.   Krauthammer's emotional call may be stirring, but he dismisses too quickly some of the practical arguments against a renewed moon program. He appears to assume a degree of political will and public support for further lunar exploration that simply does not exist today. First, public support may be lacking—for legitimate reasons. It is not as if with a renewed lunar program we would be pushing boundaries and exploring the unknown: we would not be *going* to the moon; we would be *returning* to the moon. A significant percentage of the public, after considering the matter, may reasonably conclude: "Been there, done that." They may think, correctly or not, that we should set our sights elsewhere rather than collecting more moon rocks or taking additional stunning photographs from the lunar surface. Whatever practical benefits can be derived from going to the moon, many (if not all) have already been achieved. It would not be at all unreasonable for the public, even a public that supports NASA funding, to say, "Let's move on to other goals."

9.   Second, Krauthammer's argument that poverty and disease and social ills will always be with us is politically flawed. This country faces financial pressures more serious than those at any other time since the Great Depression; and real, painful choices are being made by federal, state, and local officials about how to spend diminished tax dollars. The "vigorous young" JFK, launching the moon program during a time of expansion and prosperity, faced no such restrictions. Krauthammer's dismissal of ongoing poverty and other social ills is not likely to persuade elected representatives who are shuttering libraries, closing fire stations, ending unemployment benefits, and curtailing medical services. Nor will a public that is enduring these cuts be impressed by Krauthammer's call to "wonder and glory." Accurately or not, the public is likely to see the matter in terms of choices between a re-funded lunar program (nice, but optional) and renewed jobless benefits (essential). Not many politicians, in such distressed times, would be willing to go

on record by voting for "nice" over "essential"—not if they wanted to keep their jobs.

Finally, it's surprising—and philosophically inconsistent—for a conservative like Krauthammer, who believes in a smaller, less free-spending government, to be complaining about the withdrawal of massive government support for a renewed moon program. After all, the government hasn't banned moon travel; it has simply turned over such projects to private industry. If lunar exploration and other space flights appear commercially viable, there's nothing to prevent private companies and corporations from pursuing their own programs.

In "The Moon We Left Behind," Charles Krauthammer stirs the emotions with his call for the United States to return to the moon; and, in terms of practical spinoffs, such a return could benefit this country in many ways. Krauthammer's argument is compelling, even if he too easily discounts the financial and political problems that will pose real obstacles to a renewed lunar program. Ultimately, what one thinks of Krauthammer's call to renew moon exploration depends on how one defines the human enterprise and the purpose of collective agreement and collective effort—what we call "government." To what extent should this purpose be to solve problems in the here and now? To what extent should it be to inquire and to push against the boundaries for the sake of discovery and exploration, to learn more about who we are and about the nature of our universe? There have always been competing demands on national budgets and more than enough problems to justify spending every tax dollar on problems of poverty, social justice, crime, education, national security, and the like. Krauthammer argues that if we are to remain true to our spirit of inquiry, we cannot ignore the investigation of space, because scientific and technological progress is also a human responsibility. He argues that we can—indeed, we must—do both: look to our needs here at home and also dream and explore. But the public may not find his argument convincing.

Harlan 7

Works Cited

"Apollo Program." *Apollo Program HSF*. National Aeronautics and Space
    Administration, 2 July 2009. Web. 16 Sept. 2010.

Harwood, William. "Obama Kills Moon Program, Endorses Commercial
    Space." *Spaceflight Now*. Spaceflight Now, 1 Feb. 2010. Web. 13
    Sept. 2010.

Kennedy, John F. "Rice University Speech." 12 Sept. 1962. *Public
    Papers of the Presidents of the United States*. Vol. 1., 1962. 669–
    70. Print.

---. "Special Message to the Congress on Urgent National Needs." *John
    F. Kennedy Presidential Library and Museum*. John F. Kennedy
    Presidential Library and Museum, 25 May 1961. Web. 14 Sept.
    2010.

Krauthammer, Charles. "The Moon We Left Behind." *Washington Post* 17
    July 2009: A17. Print.

"NASA Occupations." *Nasajobsoccupations*. National Aeronautics and
    Space Administration, 28 July 2009. Web. 12 Sept. 2010.

"NASA Spinoffs: Bringing Space Down to Earth." *The Ultimate Space
    Place*. National Aeronautics and Space Administration, 2 Feb.
    2004. Web. 18 Sept. 2010.

Exercise 2.5

Informal Critique of the Model Critique

Before reading our analysis of this model critique, write your own informal
response to it. What are its strengths and weaknesses? To what extent does the
critique follow the general Guidelines for Writing Critiques that we outlined
on page 46? To the extent that it varies from the guidelines, speculate on why.
Jot down ideas for a critique that takes a different approach to Krauthammer's
op-ed.

The Strategy of the Critique

- Paragraphs 1 and 2 of the model critique introduce the topic. They
  provide a context by way of a historical review of America's lunar-
  exploration program from 1962 to 1972, leading up to the president's

CRITICAL READING FOR CRITIQUE

- *Use the tips from Critical Reading for Summary on pages 6–7.* Remember to examine the context; note the title and subtitle; identify the main point; identify the subpoints; break the reading into sections; distinguish between points, examples, and counterarguments; watch for transitions within and between paragraphs; and read actively.
- *Establish the writer's primary purpose in writing.* Is the piece meant primarily to inform, persuade, or entertain?
- *Evaluate informative writing. Use these criteria (among others):*

  Accuracy of information

  Significance of information

  Fair interpretation of information
- *Evaluate persuasive writing. Use these criteria (among others):*

  Clear definition of terms

  Fair use and interpretation of information

  Logical reasoning
- *Evaluate writing that entertains. Use these criteria (among others):*

  Interesting characters

  Believable action, plot, and situations

  Communication of theme

  Use of language
- *Decide whether you agree or disagree with the writer's ideas, position, or message.* Once you have determined the extent to which an author has achieved his or her purpose, clarify your position in relation to the writer's.

decision to scrub plans for a return to the moon. The two-paragraph introduction also provides a context for Krauthammer's—and the world's—admiration for the stunning achievement of the Apollo program. The second paragraph ends with the thesis of the critique, the writer's overall assessment of Krauthammer's essay.

- Paragraphs 3–4 introduce Krauthammer and summarize his arguments.
  - Paragraph 3 provides biographical information about Krauthammer and describes his disappointment and indignation at "America's abandonment of the moon."
  - Paragraph 4 treats Krauthammer's anticipated objections to the continuation of the manned space program and rebuttals to these objections.

- Paragraphs 5, 6, and 7 support Krauthammer's argument.
  - ○ Paragraphs 5 and 6 begin the writer's evaluation, focusing on the reasons why Krauthammer finds so much to admire in the lunar-exploration program. Most notably: It was a stunning technological achievement that brought the people of the world together (if only briefly). The writer shares this admiration.
  - ○ Paragraph 7 indirectly supports Krauthammer by pointing out that even though he downplays the practical benefits of lunar exploration, the space program has yielded numerous practical technological spinoffs.

- Paragraphs 8–10 focus on the problems with Krauthammer's argument.
  - ○ In paragraph 8, the writer points out that there is little public support for returning to the moon, a goal that many people will see as already accomplished and impractical for the immediate future.
  - ○ Paragraph 9 argues that Krauthammer underestimates the degree to which an electorate worried about skyrocketing deficits and high unemployment would object to taxpayer dollars being used to finance huge government spending on a renewed lunar program.
  - ○ Paragraph 10 points out how surprising it is that a conservative such as Krauthammer would advocate a government-financed manned space program when the same goal could be accomplished by private enterprise.

- Paragraph 11 concludes the critique, summing up the chief strengths and weaknesses of Krauthammer's argument and pointing out that readers' positions will be determined by their views on the "human enterprise" and the purpose of government. How do we balance our "human responsibility" for the expansion of knowledge and technology with the competing claims of education, poverty, crime, and national security?

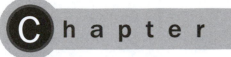

Chapter 3

Synthesis

After completing this chapter, you will be able to:

LO 3.1   View synthesis as a discussion that draws upon an inferred relationship between or among sources.

LO 3.2   Identify the situations in which a synthesis would be useful.

LO 3.3   Use your purpose to guide your use of sources in a synthesis.

LO 3.4   Distinguish between explanatory and argument syntheses.

LO 3.5   Use the guidelines for writing syntheses.

LO 3.6   Write an explanatory synthesis that builds on your purpose, thesis, carefully chosen sources, and a clear plan.

LO 3.7   Apply the elements of argument (claim, support, and assumption) to the writing of argument synthesis.

LO 3.8   Recognize the limits of argument when writing on controversial subjects.

LO 3.9   As you prepare to write an argument synthesis, consider your purpose, create your thesis, research your sources, and devise a logical plan of development.

LO 3.10 Use various organizational strategies to construct your argument synthesis.

LO 3.11 Avoid common fallacies.

LO 3.12 Use comparison-and-contrast, where appropriate, to develop your argument synthesis.

WHAT IS A SYNTHESIS?

A *synthesis* is a written discussion that draws on two or more sources. It follows that your ability to write syntheses depends on your ability to infer relationships among sources such as these:

- Essays
- Fiction

57

- Interviews
- Articles
- Lectures
- Visual media

This process is nothing new for you because you infer relationships all the time—say, between something you've read in the newspaper and something you've seen for yourself, or between the teaching styles of your favorite and least favorite instructors. In fact, if you've written research papers, you've already written syntheses.

In a *synthesis*, you make explicit the relationships that you have inferred among separate sources.

Summary and Critique as a Basis for Synthesis

The skills you've already learned and practiced in the previous chapter will be vital in writing syntheses. Before you're in a position to draw relationships between two or more sources, you must understand what those sources say; you must be able to *summarize* those sources. Readers will frequently benefit from at least partial summaries of sources in your synthesis essays. At the same time, you must go beyond summary to make judgments—judgments based on your *critical reading* of your sources: what conclusions you've drawn about the quality and validity of these sources, whether you agree or disagree with the points made in your sources, and why you agree or disagree.

Inference as a Basis for Synthesis: Moving Beyond Summary and Critique

In a synthesis, you go beyond the critique of individual sources to determine the relationships among them. Is the information in source B, for example, an extended illustration of the generalizations in source A? Would it be useful to compare and contrast source C with source B? Having read and considered sources A, B, and C, can you infer something else—in other words, D (not a source, but your own idea)?

Because a synthesis is based on two or more sources, you will need to be selective when choosing information from each. It would be neither possible nor desirable, for instance, to discuss in a ten-page paper on the American Civil War every point that the authors of two books make about their subject. What you as a writer must do is select from each source the ideas and information that best allow you to achieve your purpose.

PURPOSE

Your purpose in reading source materials and then drawing on them to write your own material is often reflected in the wording of an assignment. For instance, consider the following assignments on the Civil War:

American History: Evaluate the author's treatment of the origins of the Civil War.

Economics: Argue the following proposition, in light of your readings: "The Civil War was fought not for reasons of moral principle but for reasons of economic necessity."

Government: Prepare a report on the effects of the Civil War on Southern politics at the state level between 1870 and 1917. Focus on one state.

Mass Communications: Discuss how the use of photography during the Civil War may have affected the perceptions of the war by Northerners living in industrial cities.

WHERE DO WE FIND WRITTEN SYNTHESES?

Here are just a few of the types of writing that involve synthesis:

Academic Writing

- **Analysis papers** synthesize and apply several related theoretical approaches.
- **Research papers** synthesize multiple sources.
- **Argument papers** synthesize different points into a coherent claim or position.
- **Essay exams** demonstrate understanding of course material through comparing and contrasting theories, viewpoints, or approaches in a particular field.

Workplace Writing

- **Newspaper and magazine articles** synthesize primary and secondary sources.
- **Position papers and policy briefs** compare and contrast solutions for solving problems.
- **Business plans** synthesize ideas and proposals into one coherent plan.
- **Memos and letters** synthesize multiple ideas, events, and proposals into concise form.
- **Web sites** synthesize information from various sources to present in Web pages and related links.

Literature: Select two Southern writers of the twentieth century whose work you believe was influenced by the divisive effects of the Civil War. Discuss the ways this influence is apparent in a novel or a group of short stories written by each author. The works should not be *about* the Civil War.

Applied Technology: Compare and contrast the technology of warfare available in the 1860s with the technology available a century earlier.

Each of these assignments creates a particular purpose for writing. Having located sources relevant to your topic, you would select for possible use in a paper only the parts of those sources that helped you in fulfilling this purpose. And how you used those parts—how you related them to other material from other sources—would also depend on your purpose.

Example: Same Sources, Different Uses

If you were working on the government assignment, you might draw on the same source as a student working on the literature assignment by referring to Robert Penn Warren's novel *All the King's Men*, about Louisiana politics in the early part of the twentieth century. But because the purposes of the two assignments are different, you and the other student would make different uses of the source. The parts or aspects of the novel that you find worthy of detailed analysis might be mentioned only in passing—or not at all—by the other student.

USING YOUR SOURCES

Your purpose determines not only what parts of your sources you will use, but also how you will relate those parts to one another. Since the very essence of synthesis is the combining of information and ideas, you must have some basis on which to combine them. *Some relationships among the material in your sources must make them worth synthesizing.* It follows that the better able you are to discover such relationships, the better able you will be to use your sources in writing syntheses. Notice that the mass communications assignment requires you to draw a *cause-and-effect* relationship between photographs of the war and Northerners' perceptions of the war. The applied technology assignment requires you to *compare and contrast* state-of-the-art weapons technology in the eighteenth and nineteenth centuries. The economics assignment requires you to *argue* a proposition. In each case, *your purpose will determine how you relate your source materials to one another.*

Consider some other examples. You may be asked on an exam question or in the instructions for a paper to *describe* two or three approaches to prison reform during the past decade. You may be asked to *compare and contrast* one country's approach to imprisonment with another's. You may be asked to *develop an argument* of your own on this subject, based on your reading. Sometimes (when you are not given a specific assignment) you determine your own purpose: You are interested in exploring a particular subject; you are interested in making a case for one approach or another. In any event, your purpose shapes your essay. Your purpose determines which sources you research, which ones you use, which parts of them you use, at which points in your paper you use them, and in what manner you relate them to one another.

TYPES OF SYNTHESES: EXPLANATORY AND ARGUMENT

In this chapter, we categorize syntheses into two main types: *explanatory* and *argument*. The easiest way to recognize the difference between the two types may be to consider the difference between a news article and an editorial on the same subject. For the most part, we'd say that the main purpose of the news article is to convey *information* and that the main purpose of the editorial is to convey *opinion* or *interpretation*. Of course, this distinction is much too simplified: News articles often convey opinion or bias, sometimes subtly, sometimes openly; and editorials often convey unbiased information along with opinion. But as a practical matter, we can generally agree on the distinction between a news article that primarily conveys information and an editorial that primarily conveys opinion. You should be able to observe this distinction in the selections shown here as "Explanation" and "Argument."

Explanation: News Article from the *New York Times*

WHILE WARNING ABOUT FAT, U.S. PUSHES CHEESE SALES

By Michael Moss
November 6, 2010

Domino's Pizza was hurting early last year. Domestic sales had fallen, and a survey of big pizza chain customers left the company tied for the worst tasting pies.

Then help arrived from an organization called Dairy Management. It teamed up with Domino's to develop a new line of pizzas with 40 percent more cheese, and proceeded to devise and pay for a $12 million marketing campaign.

Consumers devoured the cheesier pizza, and sales soared by double digits. "This partnership is clearly working," Brandon Solano, the Domino's vice president for brand innovation, said in a statement to *The New York Times*.

But as healthy as this pizza has been for Domino's, one slice contains as much as two-thirds of a day's maximum recommended amount of saturated fat, which has been linked to heart disease and is high in calories.

5   And Dairy Management, which has made cheese its cause, is not a private business consultant. It is a marketing creation of the United States Department of Agriculture—the same agency at the center of a federal anti-obesity drive that discourages over-consumption of some of the very foods Dairy Management is vigorously promoting....

Argument: Editorial from the *Boston Globe*

GOT TOO MUCH CHEESE?

By Derrick Z. Jackson
November 9, 2010

...The chief executive of Dairy Management, Thomas Gallagher,...declined to be interviewed by the [*New York*] *Times*, but in a column last year in a trade publication, he wrote, "More cheese on pizza equals more cheese sales. In fact, if every pizza included one more ounce of cheese, we would see an additional 250 million pounds of cheese annually."

Emboldened by its success with cheese, Dairy Management is now reportedly working on bamboozling the public that chocolate milk is a sports recovery drink and persuading children to eat green beans by slathering them with cheese.

A year ago, at a joint press conference held by the USDA, the National Dairy Council and the National Football League to promote exercise, Gallagher said, "Child nutrition, particularly in schools, has been a cornerstone of the National Dairy Council for nearly a century. The program centers on youth taking the lead in changing the school environment."

The truth makes this a galling proclamation. Despite all the nutrition initiatives launched by the Obama administration, the cornerstone of federal policy continues to clog the nation's arteries, making a mockery of programs boasting how youth can take the lead. What is a cornerstone for the USDA is a gravestone for nutrition.

We'll say, for the sake of convenience, that the news article *explains* the contradictory messages on nutrition that the federal government is communicating and that the editorial *argues* that the contradiction is damaging. This important distinction between explanation and argument extends beyond the news to other materials you might consult while doing research. Consider a second set of passages:

What Are Genetically Modified (GM) Foods?

GENETICALLY MODIFIED FOODS AND ORGANISMS

The United States Department of Energy
November 5, 2008

Combining genes from different organisms is known as recombinant DNA technology, and the resulting organism is said to be "genetically modified," "genetically engineered," or "transgenic." GM products (current or those in development) include medicines and vaccines, foods and food ingredients, feeds, and fibers.

Locating genes for important traits—such as those conferring insect resistance or desired nutrients—is one of the most limiting steps in the process. However, genome sequencing and discovery programs for hundreds of organisms are generating detailed maps along with data-analyzing technologies to understand and use them.

In 2006, 252 million acres of transgenic crops were planted in 22 countries by 10.3 million farmers. The majority of these crops were herbicide- and insect-resistant soybeans, corn, cotton, canola, and alfalfa. Other crops grown commercially or field-tested are a sweet potato resistant to a virus that could decimate most of the African harvest, rice with increased iron and vitamins that may alleviate chronic malnutrition in Asian countries, and a variety of plants able to survive weather extremes.

On the horizon are bananas that produce human vaccines against infectious diseases such as hepatitis B; fish that mature more quickly; cows that are resistant to bovine spongiform encephalopathy (mad cow disease); fruit and nut trees that yield years earlier, and plants that produce new plastics with unique properties.

WHY A GM FREEZE?

The GM Freeze Campaign
November 11, 2010

Genetic modification in food and farming raises many fundamental environmental, social, health and ethical concerns. There is increasing evidence of contamination of conventional crops and wild plants, and potential damage to wildlife. The effects on human health of eating these foods remain uncertain and some scientists are calling for much more rigorous safety testing. It is clear that further research into all these issues is vital. Furthermore the public has not been properly involved in decision making processes, despite strong public support for the precautionary approach to GM in the [United Kingdom] and the [European Union].

Much more time is needed to assess the need for and implications of using genetic modification in food and farming, in particular the increasing control of corporations who rely on patents to secure their future markets.

Both of these passages deal with the topic of genetically modified (GM) foods. The first is excerpted from a largely informational Web site published by the U.S. Department of Energy, which oversees the Human Genome Project, the government's ongoing effort to map gene sequences and apply that knowledge. We say the DOE account is "largely informational" because readers can find a great deal of information here about genetically modified foods. At the same time, however, the DOE explanation is subtly biased in favor of genetic modification: Note the absence of any language raising questions about the ethics or safety of GM foods; note also the use of terms such as "desired nutrients" and "insect resistance," with their positive connotations. The DOE examples show GM foods in a favorable light, and the passage as a whole assumes the value and importance of genetic manipulation.

As we see in the second passage, however, that assumption is not shared by all. Excerpted from a Web site advocating a freeze on genetically modified crops, the second passage primarily argues against the ethics and safety of such manipulation, calling for more study before modified crops are released widely into the environment. At the same time, the selection provides potentially important explanatory materials: (1) the claim that there is "increasing evidence of contamination of conventional crops and wild plants, and potential damage to wildlife"; (2) the claim that corporations control GM crops, and potentially the food supply, through patents. We can easily and quickly confirm these claims through research; if confirmed, the information—which is nested in a primarily argumentative piece—could prove useful in a paper on GM foods.

So while it is fair to say that most writing can be broadly categorized as explanatory or argumentative, understand that in practice, many of the materials you read will be a mix: *primarily* one or the other but not altogether one or the other. It will be your job as an alert, critical reader to determine when authors are explaining or arguing—sometimes in the same sentence.

For instance, you might read the following in a magazine article: "The use of goats to manufacture anticlotting proteins for humans in their milk sets a dangerous precedent." Perhaps you did not know that scientists have genetically manipulated goats (by inserting human genes) to create medicines. That much of the statement is factual. It is explanatory. Whether or not this fact "sets a dangerous precedent" is an argument. You could agree or not with the argument, but your views would not change the fact about the genetic manipulation of farm animals. Even within a single sentence, then, you must be alert to distinguishing between explanation and argument.

HOW TO WRITE SYNTHESES

Although writing syntheses can't be reduced to a lockstep method, it should help you to follow the guidelines listed in the box below.

GUIDELINES FOR WRITING SYNTHESES

- *Consider your purpose in writing*. What are you trying to accomplish in your paper? How will this purpose shape the way you approach your sources?
- *Select and carefully read your sources* according to your purpose. Then reread the passages, mentally summarizing each. Identify those aspects or parts of your sources that will help you fulfill your purpose. When rereading, *label* or *underline* the sources' main ideas, key terms, and any details you want to use in the synthesis.
- *Take notes on your reading.* In addition to labeling or underlining key points in the readings, you might write brief one- or two-sentence summaries of each source. This will help you in formulating your thesis statement and in choosing and organizing your sources later.
- *Formulate a thesis.* Your thesis is the main idea that you want to present in your synthesis. It should be expressed as a complete sentence. You might do some predrafting about the ideas discussed in the readings in order to help you work out a thesis. If you've written one-sentence summaries of the readings, looking over the summaries will help you to brainstorm connections between readings and to devise a thesis.

  When you write your synthesis drafts, you will need to consider where your thesis fits in your paper. Sometimes the thesis is the first sentence, but more often it is *the final sentence of the first paragraph.* If you are writing an *inductively arranged* synthesis (see p. 79), the thesis sentence may not appear until the final paragraphs.
- *Decide how you will use your source material.* How will the information and the ideas in the passages help you fulfill your purpose?
- *Develop an organizational plan,* according to your thesis. How will you arrange your material? It is not necessary to prepare a formal outline. But you should have some plan that will indicate the order in which you will present your material and the relationships among your sources.

(continued)

- *Draft the topic sentences for the main sections.* This is an optional step, but you may find it a helpful transition from organizational plan to first draft.
- *Write the first draft* of your synthesis, following your organizational plan. Be flexible with your plan, however. Frequently, you will use an outline to get started. As you write, you may discover new ideas and make room for them by adjusting the outline. When this happens, reread your work frequently, making sure that your thesis still accounts for what follows and that what follows still logically supports your thesis.
- *Document your sources.* You must do this by crediting sources within the body of the synthesis—citing the author's last name and the page number from which the point was taken—and then providing full citation information in a list of "Works Cited" at the end. Don't open yourself to charges of plagiarism! (See pp. 25–27.)
- *Revise your synthesis,* inserting transitional words and phrases where necessary. Make sure that the synthesis reads smoothly, logically, and clearly from beginning to end. Check for grammatical correctness, punctuation, and spelling.

Note: The writing of syntheses is a recursive process, and you should accept a certain amount of backtracking and reformulating as inevitable. For instance, in developing an organizational plan (Step 6 of the procedure), you may discover a gap in your presentation that will send you scrambling for another source—back to Step 2. You may find that formulating a thesis and making inferences among sources occur simultaneously; indeed, inferences are often made before a thesis is formulated. Our recommendations for writing syntheses will give you a structure that will get you started. But be flexible in your approach; expect discontinuity and, if possible, be assured that through backtracking and reformulating, you will produce a coherent, well-crafted paper.

THE ARGUMENT SYNTHESIS

An argument is an attempt to persuade a reader or listener that a particular and debatable claim is true. Writers argue in order to establish facts, to make statements of value, and to recommend policies. For instance, answering the question *Why do soldiers sometimes commit atrocities in wartime?* would involve making an argument. To develop this argument, researchers might conduct experiments, interview experts, collect historical evidence, and examine and interpret data. The researchers might then present their findings at professional conferences and in journals and books. The extent to which readers (or listeners) accept these findings will depend on the quality of the supporting evidence and the care with which the researchers have argued their case. What we are calling an *argument synthesis* draws upon evidence from a variety of sources in an attempt to persuade others of the truth or validity of a debatable claim.

By contrast, the explanatory synthesis, as we have seen, is fairly modest in purpose. It emphasizes the sources themselves—not the writer's use of sources—to persuade others. The writer of an explanatory synthesis aims to inform, not persuade. Here, for example, is a thesis devised for an explanatory synthesis on the ubiquity of cell phones in contemporary life:

> Cell phones make it possible for us to be always within reach, though many people would prefer *not* to be always within reach.

This thesis summarizes two viewpoints about the impact of cell phones on contemporary life, arguing neither for nor against either viewpoint.

An argument thesis, however, is *persuasive* in purpose. A writer working with the same source material might conceive and support an opposing thesis:

> Cell phones have ruined our ability to be isolated, to be willfully *out of touch* with the rest of the world.

So the thesis for an argument synthesis is a claim about which reasonable people could disagree. It is a claim with which—given the right arguments— your audience might be persuaded to agree. The strategy of your argument synthesis is therefore to find and use convincing *support* for your *claim.*

The Elements of Argument: Claim, Support, and Assumption

One way of looking at an argument is to see it as an interplay of three essential elements: claim, support, and assumption. A *claim* is a proposition or conclusion that you are trying to prove. You prove this claim by using *support* in the form of fact, statistics, or expert opinion. Linking your supporting evidence to your claim is your *assumption* about the subject. This assumption (as we've discussed in Chapter 2), also called a *warrant*, is an underlying belief or principle about some aspect of the world and how it operates. By their nature, assumptions (which are often unstated) tend to be more general than either claims or supporting evidence.

Here are the essential elements of an argument advocating parental restriction of television viewing for high school students:

Claim

> High school students should be restricted to no more than two hours of TV viewing per day.

Support

> An important new study and the testimony of educational specialists reveal that students who watch more than two hours of TV a night have, on average, lower grades than those who watch less TV.

Assumption

> Excessive TV viewing adversely affects academic performance.

As another example, here's an argumentative claim on the topic of computer-mediated communication (CMC)—a term sociologists use to describe online contacts among friends and family:

> CMC threatens to undermine human intimacy, connection, and ultimately community.

Here are the other elements of this argument:

Support

- People are spending increasing amounts of time in cyberspace: In 1998, the average Internet user spent over four hours per week online, a figure that more than tripled in the last decade.
- College health officials report that excessive Internet use threatens many college students' academic and psychological well-being.
- New kinds of relationships fostered on the Internet often pose challenges to preexisting relationships.

Assumptions

- The communication skills used and the connections formed during Internet contact fundamentally differ from those used and formed during face-to-face contact.
- "Real" connection and a sense of community are sustained by face-to-face contact, not by Internet interactions.

For the most part, arguments should be constructed logically so that assumptions link evidence (supporting facts, statistics, and expert opinions) to claims. As we'll see, however, logic is only one component of effective arguments.

Exercise 3.1

Practicing Claim, Support, and Assumption

Devise two sets of claims, support, and assumptions. First, in response to the example above on computer-mediated communication and relationships, write a one-sentence claim addressing the positive impact (or potentially positive impact) of CMC on relationships—whether you personally agree with the claim or not. Then list the supporting statements on which such a claim might rest, and the assumption that underlies them. Second, write a claim that states your own position on any debatable topic you choose. Again, devise statements of support and relevant assumptions.

DEMONSTRATION: DEVELOPING AN ARGUMENT SYNTHESIS—BALANCING PRIVACY AND SAFETY IN THE WAKE OF VIRGINIA TECH

To demonstrate how to plan and draft an argument synthesis, let's suppose you are taking a course on Law and Society or Political Science or (from the Philosophy Department) Theories of Justice, and you find yourself considering the competing claims of privacy and public safety. The tension between these two highly prized values burst anew into public consciousness in 2007 after a mentally disturbed student at the Virginia Polytechnic Institute shot to death thirty-two fellow students and faculty members and injured seventeen more. Unfortunately, this incident was only the latest in a long history of mass killings at American schools.* It was later revealed that the shooter had a documented history of mental instability, but because of privacy rules, this information was not made available to university officials. Many people demanded to know why the information had not been shared with campus police or other officials so that Virginia Tech could have taken measures to protect members of the university community. Didn't the safety of those who were injured or killed outweigh the privacy of the shooter? At what point, if any, *does* the right to privacy outweigh the right to safety? What *should* the university have done before the killing started? Should federal and state laws on privacy be changed or even abandoned in the wake of this and other similar incidents?

Suppose, in preparing to write a paper on balancing privacy and safety, you located (among others) the following sources:

- *Mass Shootings at Virginia Tech, April 16, 2007: Report of the Review Panel Presented to Governor Kaine, Commonwealth of Virginia*, August 2007 (a report)
- "Colleges Are Watching Troubled Students" (a newspaper article)
- The Family Educational Rights and Privacy Act (FERPA), Sec. 1232g (a federal statute)

Carefully read these sources (which follow), noting the kinds of evidence—facts, expert opinions, and statistics—you could draw on to develop an *argument synthesis*. Some of these passages are excerpts only; in preparing your paper, you would draw on the entire articles, reports, and book chapters from which these passages were taken. And you would draw on more sources than these in your search for supporting materials (as the writer of the model synthesis has done; see pp. 83–91). But these seven sources provide a good introduction to the subject. Our discussion of how these passages can form the basis of an argument synthesis resumes on page 78.

---

*In 1966, a student at the University of Texas at Austin, shooting from the campus clock tower, killed 14 people and wounded 31. In 2006 a man shot and killed five girls at an Amish school in Lancaster, Pennsylvania.

MASS SHOOTINGS AT VIRGINIA TECH, APRIL 16, 2007

Report of the Review Panel
Presented to Governor Kaine, Commonwealth of Virginia,
August 2007

The following passage leads off the official report of the Virginia Tech shootings by the panel appointed by Virginia Governor Tim Kaine to investigate the incident. The mission of the panel was "to provide an independent, thorough, and objective incident review of this tragic event, including a review of educational laws, policies and institutions, the public safety and health care procedures and responses, and the mental health delivery system." Panel members included the chair, Colonel Gerald Massenghill, former Virginia state police superintendent; Tom Ridge, former director of Homeland Security and former governor of Pennsylvania; Gordon Davies; Dr. Roger L. Depue; Dr. Aradhana A. "Bela" Sood; Judge Diane Strickland; and Carol L. Ellis. The panel's Web site may be found at http://www.vtreviewpanel.org/panel_info/.

Summary of Key Findings

On April 16, 2007, Seung Hui Cho, an angry and disturbed student, shot to death 32 students and faculty of Virginia Tech, wounded 17 more, and then killed himself.

The incident horrified not only Virginians, but people across the United States and throughout the world.

Tim Kaine, Governor of the Commonwealth of Virginia, immediately appointed a panel to review the events leading up to this tragedy; the handling of the incidents by public safety officials, emergency services providers, and the university; and the services subsequently provided to families, survivors, caregivers, and the community.

The Virginia Tech Review Panel reviewed several separate but related issues in assessing events leading to the mass shootings and their aftermath:

- The life and mental health history of Seung Hui Cho, from early childhood until the weeks before April 16.

- Federal and state laws concerning the privacy of health and education records.

- Cho's purchase of guns and related gun control issues.

- The double homicide at West Ambler Johnston (WAJ) residence hall and the mass shootings at Norris Hall, including the responses of Virginia Tech leadership and the actions of law enforcement officers and emergency responders.

- Emergency medical care immediately following the shootings, both onsite at Virginia Tech and in cooperating hospitals.

- The work of the Office of the Chief Medical Examiner of Virginia.

- The services provided for surviving victims of the shootings and others injured, the families and loved ones of those killed and injured, members of the university community, and caregivers.

5   The panel conducted over 200 interviews and reviewed thousands of pages of records, and reports the following major findings:

1. Cho exhibited signs of mental health problems during his childhood. His middle and high schools responded well to these signs and, with his parents' involvement, provided services to address his issues. He also received private psychiatric treatment and counseling for selective mutism and depression.

   In 1999, after the Columbine shootings, Cho's middle school teachers observed suicidal and homicidal ideations in his writings and recommended psychiatric counseling, which he received. It was at this point that he received medication for a short time. Although Cho's parents were aware that he was troubled at this time, they state they did not specifically know that he thought about homicide shortly after the 1999 Columbine school shootings.

2. During Cho's junior year at Virginia Tech, numerous incidents occurred that were clear warnings of mental instability. Although various individuals and departments within the university knew about each of these incidents, the university did not intervene effectively. No one knew all the information and no one connected all the dots.

3. University officials in the office of Judicial Affairs, Cook Counseling Center, campus police, the Dean of Students, and others explained their failures to communicate with one another or with Cho's parents by noting their belief that such communications are prohibited by the federal laws governing the privacy of health and education records. In reality, federal laws and their state counterparts afford ample leeway to share information in potentially dangerous situations.

4. The Cook Counseling Center and the university's Care Team failed to provide needed support and services to Cho during a period in late 2005 and early 2006. The system failed for lack of resources, incorrect interpretation of privacy laws, and passivity. Records of Cho's minimal treatment at Virginia Tech's Cook Counseling Center are missing.

5. Virginia's mental health laws are flawed and services for mental health users are inadequate. Lack of sufficient resources results in gaps in the mental health system including short term crisis stabilization and comprehensive outpatient services. The involuntary commitment process is challenged by unrealistic time constraints, lack of critical psychiatric data and collateral information, and barriers (perceived or real) to open communications among key professionals.

6. There is widespread confusion about what federal and state privacy laws allow. Also, the federal laws governing records of health care provided in educational settings are not entirely compatible with those governing other health records.

7. Cho purchased two guns in violation of federal law. The fact that in 2005 Cho had been judged to be a danger to himself and ordered to outpatient treatment made him ineligible to purchase a gun under federal law.

8. Virginia is one of only 22 states that report any information about mental health to a federal database used to conduct background checks on would-be gun purchasers. But Virginia law did not clearly require that persons such as Cho—who had been ordered into out-patient treatment but not committed to an institution—be reported to the database. Governor Kaine's executive order to report all persons involuntarily committed for outpatient treatment has temporarily addressed this ambiguity in state law. But a change is needed in the Code of Virginia as well.

9. Some Virginia colleges and universities are uncertain about what they are permitted to do regarding the possession of firearms on campus.

10. On April 16, 2007, the Virginia Tech and Blacksburg police departments responded quickly to the report of shootings at West Ambler Johnston residence hall, as did the Virginia Tech and Blacksburg rescue squads. Their responses were well coordinated.

11. The Virginia Tech police may have erred in prematurely concluding that their initial lead in the double homicide was a good one, or at least in conveying that impression to university officials while continuing their investigation. They did not take sufficient action to deal with what might happen if the initial lead proved erroneous. The police reported to the university emergency Policy Group that the "person of interest" probably was no longer on campus.

12. The VTPD erred in not requesting that the Policy Group issue a campus-wide notification that two persons had been killed and that all students and staff should be cautious and alert.

13. Senior university administrators, acting as the emergency Policy Group, failed to issue an all-campus notification about the WAJ killings until almost 2 hours had elapsed. University practice may have conflicted with written policies.

14. The presence of large numbers of police at WAJ led to a rapid response to the first 9-1-1 call that shooting had begun at Norris Hall.

15. Cho's motives for the WAJ or Norris Hall shootings are unknown to the police or the panel. Cho's writings and videotaped pronouncements do not explain why he struck when and where he did.

16. The police response at Norris Hall was prompt and effective, as was triage and evacuation of the wounded. Evacuation of others in the building could have been implemented with more care.

17. Emergency medical care immediately following the shootings was provided very effectively and timely both onsite and at the hospitals, although providers from different agencies had some difficulty

communicating with one another. Communication of accurate information to hospitals standing by to receive the wounded and injured was
somewhat deficient early on. An emergency operations center at Virginia
Tech could have improved communications.

18. The Office of the Chief Medical Examiner properly discharged the
    technical aspects of its responsibility (primarily autopsies and iden-
    tification of the deceased). Communication with families was poorly
    handled.
19. State systems for rapidly deploying trained professional staff to help
    families get information, crisis intervention, and referrals to a wide
    range of resources did not work.
20. The university established a family assistance center at The Inn at
    Virginia Tech, but it fell short in helping families and others for two
    reasons: lack of leadership and lack of coordination among service
    providers. University volunteers stepped in but were not trained or
    able to answer many questions and guide families to the resources
    they needed.
21. In order to advance public safety and meet public needs, Virginia's
    colleges and universities need to work together as a coordinated sys-
    tem of state-supported institutions.

As reflected in the body of the report, the panel has made more
than 70 recommendations directed to colleges, universities, mental health
providers, law enforcement officials, emergency service providers, lawmakers, and other public officials in Virginia and elsewhere.

COLLEGES ARE WATCHING TROUBLED STUDENTS

Jeffrey McMurray

During the year following the Virginia Tech shootings, many colleges and universities took a hard look at their policies on student privacy and their procedures for
monitoring and sharing information about troubled students. This article, by the
Associated Press, was first published on March 28, 2008. AP writer Sue Lindsay
contributed to this report.

On the agenda: A student who got into a shouting match with a faculty member. Another who harassed a female classmate. Someone found sleeping in a
car. And a student who posted a threat against a professor on Facebook.

In a practice adopted at one college after another since the massacre at
Virginia Tech, a University of Kentucky committee of deans, administrators, campus police and mental health officials has begun meeting regularly to discuss a watch list of troubled students and decide whether they
need professional help or should be sent packing.

These "threat assessment groups" are aimed at heading off the kind of bloodshed seen at Virginia Tech a year ago and at Northern Illinois University last month.

"You've got to be way ahead of the game, so to speak, expect what may be coming. If you're able to identify behaviors early on and get these people assistance, it avoids disruptions in the classrooms and potential violence," said Maj. Joe Monroe, interim police chief at Kentucky.

5   The Kentucky panel, called Students of Concern, held its first meeting last week and will convene at least twice a month to talk about students whose strange or disturbing behavior has come to their attention.

Such committees represent a change in thinking among U.S. college officials, who for a long time were reluctant to share information about students' mental health for fear of violating privacy laws.

"If a student is a danger to himself or others, all the privacy concerns go out the window," said Patricia Terrell, vice president of student affairs, who created the panel.

Terrell shared details of the four discussed cases with The Associated Press on the condition that all names and other identifying information be left out.

Among other things, the panel can order a student into counseling or bar him or her from entering a particular building or talking to a certain person. It can also order a judicial hearing that can lead to suspension or expulsion if the student's offense was a violation of the law or school policy.

10   Although the four cases discussed last week were the ones administrators deemed as needing the most urgent attention, a database listing 26 other student cases has been created, providing fodder for future meetings.

Students are encouraged during their freshman orientation to report suspicious behavior to the dean of students, and university employees all the way down to janitors and cafeteria workers are instructed to tell their supervisors if they see anything.

Virtually every corner of campus is represented in the group's closed-door meetings, including dorm life, academics, counseling, mental health and police.

"If you look back at the Virginia Tech situation, the aftermath, there were several people who knew that student had problems, but because of privacy and different issues, they didn't talk to others about it," said Lee Todd, UK president.

High schools have been doing this sort of thing for years because of shootings, but only since Virginia Tech, when a disturbed student gunman killed 32 people and committed suicide, have colleges begun to follow suit, said Mike Dorn, executive director of Safe Havens International, a leading campus safety firm.

15   "They didn't think it was a real threat to them," Dorn said.

Virginia Tech has added a threat assessment team since the massacre there. Boston University, the University of Utah, the University of Illinois–Chicago and numerous others also have such groups, said Gwendolyn Dungy, executive director of the National Association of Student Personnel Administrators.

Bryan Cloyd, a Virginia Tech accounting professor whose daughter Austin was killed in the rampage, welcomed the stepped-up efforts to monitor troubled students but stressed he doesn't want to turn every college campus into a "police state."

"We can't afford to overreact," Cloyd said, but "we also can't afford to underreact."

Seung-Hui Cho, the Virginia Tech gunman, was ruled a danger to himself in a court hearing in 2005 that resulted from a roommate's call to police after Cho mentioned suicide in an e-mail. He was held overnight at a mental health center off campus and was ordered into outpatient treatment, but he received no follow-up services, despite his sullen, withdrawn behavior and his twisted, violence-filled writings.

20 Mary Bolin-Reece, director of counseling and testing at Kentucky, attends the threat assessment group's meetings but cannot share what she knows or, in most cases, even whether a student has been undergoing counseling. But participants can share information on other possible red flags.

"We always look at, 'Is there a change in the baseline?'" Bolin-Reece said. "The student had previously gotten very good grades, and then there was a drop-off. Something has happened. Is there some shift in their ability to function? If a student is coming to the attention of various parties around the university, we begin to be able to connect the dots."

The University of Kentucky has not had a murder on campus since 1984. Still, the threat-assessment effort has the strong backing of Carol Graham of Fort Carson, Colo., whose son Kevin was a Kentucky student when he committed suicide before leaving for an ROTC summer camp in 2003.

"UK is such a huge university," Graham said. "It's important to know there's a safety net—that people are looking out for each other. With Kevin, his professors thought he was perfect. He'd be an A student. But the people around him were noticing differences."

As for the four cases taken up by the committee: The student who got into an argument with a faculty member—and had also seen a major dip in grades and exhibited poor hygiene—was ordered to meet with the dean of students.

25 The one accused of harassment was referred to a judicial hearing, during which he was expelled from university housing. The student who made the Facebook threat was given a warning. In the case of the student sleeping in a car, a committee member was dispatched to check on the person. No further details were released.

THE FAMILY EDUCATIONAL RIGHTS AND PRIVACY ACT
(FERPA)

United States Code
Title 20. Education
CHAPTER 31. General Provisions Concerning Education
§ 1232g. Family Educational and Privacy Rights

Following are excerpts from the *Family Educational Rights and Privacy Act (FERPA)*, the federal law enacted in 1974 that governs restrictions on the release of student educational records. FERPA provides for the withholding of federal funds to educational institutions that violate its provisions, and it is the federal guarantor of the privacy rights of post-secondary students.

(1) (A) No funds shall be made available under any applicable program to any educational agency or institution which has a policy of denying, or which effectively prevents, the parents of students who are or have been in attendance at a school of such agency or at such institution, as the case may be, the right to inspect and review the education records of their children. If any material or document in the education record of a student includes information on more than one student, the parents of one of such students shall have the right to inspect and review only such part of such material or document as relates to such student or to be informed of the specific information contained in such part of such material. Each educational agency or institution shall establish appropriate procedures for the granting of a request by parents for access to the education records of their children within a reasonable period of time, but in no case more than forty-five days after the request has been made....

　　(C) The first sentence of subparagraph (A) shall not operate to make available to students in institutions of postsecondary education the following materials:

　　(i)　financial records of the parents of the student or any information contained therein;

　　(ii)　confidential letters and statements of recommendation, which were placed in the education records prior to January 1, 1975, if such letters or statements are not used for purposes other than those for which they were specifically intended;

　　(iii)　if the student has signed a waiver of the student's right of access under this subsection in accordance with subparagraph (D), confidential recommendations—

　　　　(I)　respecting admission to any educational agency or institution,

　　　　(II)　respecting an application for employment, and

　　　　(III)　respecting the receipt of an honor or honorary recognition.

(B) The term "education records" does not include—

  (i) records of instructional, supervisory, and administrative personnel and educational personnel ancillary thereto which are in the sole possession of the maker thereof and which are not accessible or revealed to any other person except a substitute;

  (ii) records maintained by a law enforcement unit of the educational agency or institution that were created by that law enforcement unit for the purpose of law enforcement;

  (iii) in the case of persons who are employed by an educational agency or institution but who are not in attendance at such agency or institution, records made and maintained in the normal course of business which relate exclusively to such person in that person's capacity as an employee and are not available for use for any other purpose; or

  (iv) records on a student who is eighteen years of age or older, or is attending an institution of postsecondary education, which are made or maintained by a physician, psychiatrist, psychologist, or other recognized professional or paraprofessional acting in his professional or paraprofessional capacity, or assisting in that capacity, and which are made, maintained, or used only in connection with the provision of treatment to the student, and are not available to anyone other than persons providing such treatment, except that such records can be personally reviewed by a physician or other appropriate professional of the student's choice....

(h) Certain disciplinary action information allowable. Nothing in this section shall prohibit an educational agency or institution from—

  (1) including appropriate information in the education record of any student concerning disciplinary action taken against such student for conduct that posed a significant risk to the safety or well-being of that student, other students, or other members of the school community; or

  (2) disclosing such information to teachers and school officials, including teachers and school officials in other schools, who have legitimate educational interests in the behavior of the student.

Exercise 3.2

Critical Reading for Synthesis

Having read the selections relating to privacy and safety, pages 70–77, write a one-sentence summary of each. On the same page, list two or three topics that you think are common to several of the selections. Beneath each topic, list the authors who have something to say on that topic and briefly note what they have to say. Finally, for each topic, jot down what *you* have to say. Now regard your effort: With each topic you have created a discussion point suitable for inclusion in a paper. (Of course, until you determine the claim of such a paper, you won't know to what end you might put the discussion.) Write a paragraph or two in which you introduce the topic and then conduct a brief conversation among the interested parties (including yourself).

Consider Your Purpose

Your specific purpose in writing an argument synthesis is crucial. What exactly you want to do will affect your claim and how you organize the evidence. Your purpose may be clear to you before you begin research, or it may not emerge until after you have completed your research. Of course, the sooner your purpose is clear to you, the fewer wasted motions you will make. On the other hand, the more you approach research as an exploratory process, the likelier that your conclusions will emerge from the sources themselves rather than from preconceived ideas. Each new writing project will have its own rhythm in this regard. Be flexible in your approach: Through some combination of preconceived structures and invigorating discoveries, you will find your way to the source materials that will yield a promising paper.

Let's say that while reading these seven (and additional) sources on the debate about campus safety and student privacy, you share the outrage of many who blamed the university (and the federal privacy laws on which it relied) for not using the available information in a way that might have spared the lives of those who died. Perhaps you also blame the legislators who wrote the privacy laws, for being more concerned about the confidentiality of the mental health records of the individual person than with the safety of the larger college population. Perhaps, you conclude, society has gone too far in valuing privacy more than it appears to value safety.

On the other hand, in your own role as a student, perhaps you share the high value placed on the privacy of sensitive information about yourself. After all, one of the functions of higher education is to foster students' independence as they make the transition from adolescence to adulthood. You can understand that many students like yourself might not want their parents or others to know details about academic records or disciplinary measures, much less information about therapy sought and undertaken at school. Historically, in the decades since the university officially stood *in loco parentis*—in place of parents—students have struggled hard to win the same civil liberties and rights (including the right to privacy) as their elders.

Further, you may wonder whether federal privacy laws do in fact forbid the sharing of information about potentially dangerous students when the health and safety of others are at stake. A little research may begin to confirm your doubts whether Virginia Tech officials were really as helpless as they claimed they were.

Your purpose in writing, then, emerges from these kinds of responses to the source materials you find.

Making a Claim: Formulate a Thesis

As we indicated in this chapter, one useful way of approaching an argument is to see it as making a *claim*. A claim is a proposition, a conclusion you have made, that you are trying to prove or demonstrate. If your purpose is to argue that we should work to ensure campus safety without enacting restrictive laws that overturn the hard-won privacy rights of students, then that claim (generally expressed in one-sentence form as a *thesis*) is at the heart of your argument. You will draw support from your sources as you argue logically for your claim.

Not every piece of information in a source is useful for supporting a claim. You must read with care and select the opinions, facts, and statistics that best advance your position. You may even find yourself drawing support from sources that make claims entirely different from your own. For example, in researching the subject of student privacy and campus safety, you may come across editorials arguing that in the wake of the Virginia Tech shootings, student privacy rights should be greatly restricted. Perhaps you will find information in these sources to help support your own contrary arguments.

You might use one source as part of a *counterargument*—an argument opposing your own—so that you can demonstrate its weaknesses and, in the process, strengthen your own claim. On the other hand, the author of one of your sources may be so convincing in supporting a claim that you adopt it yourself, either partially or entirely. The point is that *the argument is in your hands.* You must devise it yourself and use your sources in ways that will support the claim you present in your thesis.

You may not want to divulge your thesis until the end of the paper, thereby drawing the reader along toward your conclusion, allowing the thesis to flow naturally out of the argument and the evidence on which it is based. If you do this, you are working *inductively.* Or you may wish to be more direct and (after an introduction) *begin* with your thesis, following the thesis statement with evidence and reasoning to support it. If you do this, you are working *deductively.* In academic papers, deductive arguments are far more common than inductive ones.

Based on your reactions to reading sources—and perhaps also on your own inclinations as a student—you may find yourself essentially in sympathy with the approach to privacy taken by one of the schools covered in your sources, M.I.T. At the same time, you may feel that M.I.T.'s position does not demonstrate sufficient concern for campus safety and that Cornell's position, on the other hand, restricts student privacy too much. Perhaps most important, you conclude that we don't need to change the law because, if correctly interpreted, the law already incorporates a good balance between privacy and safety. After a few tries, you develop this thesis:

> In responding to the Virginia Tech killings, we should resist rolling back federal rules protecting student privacy; for as long as college officials effectively respond to signs of trouble, these rules already provide a workable balance between privacy and public safety.

Decide How You Will Use Your Source Material

Your claim commits you to (1) arguing that student privacy should remain protected, and (2) demonstrating that federal law already strikes a balance between privacy and public safety. The sources (some provided here, some located elsewhere) offer information and ideas—evidence—that will allow you to support your claim. The excerpt from the official report on the Virginia Tech shootings reveals a finding that school officials failed to correctly interpret federal privacy rules and failed to "intervene effectively." The article "Virginia Tech Massacre Has Altered Campus Mental Health Systems" outlines some of the ways that campuses around the country have instituted policy changes regarding troubled students and privacy in the wake of Virginia Tech. And the excerpt from the Family Educational Rights and Privacy Act (FERPA), the federal law, reveals that restrictions on revealing students' confidential information have a crucial exception for "the safety or well-being of ... students, or other members of the school community." (These and several other sources not included in this chapter will be cited in the model argument paper.)

Develop an Organizational Plan

Having established your overall purpose and your claim, having developed a thesis (which may change as you write and revise the paper), and having decided how to draw upon your source materials, how do you logically organize your paper? In many cases, a well-written thesis will suggest an organization. Thus, the first part of your paper will deal with the debate over rolling back student privacy. The second part will argue that as long as educational institutions behave proactively—that is, as long as they actively seek to help troubled students and foster campus safety—existing federal rules already preserve a balance between privacy and safety. Sorting through your material and categorizing it by topic and subtopic, you might compose the following outline:

> I. Introduction. Recap Va. Tech shooting. College officials, citing privacy rules, did not act on available info about shooter with history of mental problems.

II. Federal rules on privacy. Subsequent debate over balance between privacy and campus safety. Pendulum now moving back toward safety. *Thesis.*

III. Developments in student privacy in recent decades.
   A. Doctrine of *in loco parentis* defines college-student relationship.
   B. Movement away from *in loco parentis* begins in 1960s, in context not only of student rights but also broader civil rights struggles of the period.
   C. FERPA, enacted 1974, establishes new federal rules protecting student privacy.

IV. Arguments *against* student privacy.
   A. In wake of Virginia Tech, many blame FERPA protections and college officials, believing privacy rights have been taken too far, putting campus community at risk.
   B. Cornell rolls back some FERPA privacy rights.

V. Arguments *for* student privacy.
   A. M.I.T. strongly defends right to privacy.
   B. Problem is not federal law but incorrect interpretation of federal law. FERPA provides health and safety exceptions. Virginia Tech officials erred in citing FERPA for not sharing info about shooter earlier.
   C. Univ. of Kentucky offers good balance between competing claims of privacy and safety.
      1. watch lists of troubled students
      2. threat assessment groups
      3. open communication among university officials

VI. Conclusion.
   A. Virginia Tech incident was an instance of a legal issue students will encounter in the broader world: rights of the individual vs. rights of the larger group.
   B. Virginia Tech incident was tragic but should not cause us to overturn hard-won privacy rights.
   C. We should support a more proactive approach to student mental health problems and improve communication between departments.

Formulate an Argument Strategy

The argument that emerges through this outline will build not only on evidence drawn from sources but also on the writer's assumptions. Consider the bare-bones logic of the argument:

Laws protecting student privacy serve a good purpose. (*assumption*)

If properly interpreted and implemented, federal law as currently written is sufficient both to protect student privacy and to ensure campus safety. (*support*)

We should not change federal law to overturn or restrict student privacy rights. (*claim*)

The crucial point about which reasonable people will disagree is the *assumption* that laws protecting student privacy serve a good purpose. Those who wish to restrict the information made available to parents are likely to agree with this assumption. Those who favor a policy that allows college officials to inform parents of problems without their children's permission are likely to disagree.

Writers can accept or partially accept an opposing assumption by making a *concession*, in the process establishing themselves as reasonable and willing to compromise (see pp. 99–100). David Harrison does exactly this in the following model synthesis when he summarizes the policies of the University of Kentucky. By raising objections to his own position and conceding some validity to them, he blunts the effectiveness of *counterarguments*. Thus, Harrison concedes the absolute requirement for campus safety, but he argues that this requirement can be satisfied as long as campus officials correctly interpret existing federal law and implement proactive procedures aimed at dealing more effectively with troubled students.

The *claim* of the argument about privacy versus safety is primarily a claim about *policy*, about actions that should (or should not) be taken. An argument can also concern a claim about *facts* (Does X exist? How can we define X? Does X lead to Y?), a claim about *value* (What is X worth?), or a claim about *cause and effect* (Why did X happen?).

The present argument rests to some degree on a dispute about cause and effect. No one disputes that the primary cause of this tragedy was that a disturbed student was not stopped before he killed people. But many have disputed the secondary cause: Did the massacre happen, in part, because federal law prevented officials from sharing crucial information about the disturbed student? Or did it happen, in part, because university officials failed to interpret correctly what they could and could not do under the law? As you read the following paper, observe how these opposing views are woven into the argument.

Draft and Revise Your Synthesis

The final draft of an argument synthesis, based on the outline above, follows. Thesis, transitions, and topic sentences are highlighted; Modern Language Association (MLA) documentation style is used throughout (except in the citing of federal law).

A cautionary note: When writing syntheses, it is all too easy to become careless in properly crediting your sources. Before drafting your paper, always review "Rules for Avoiding Plagiarism" at the end of Chapter 1.

MODEL ARGUMENT SYNTHESIS

David Harrison

Professor Shanker

Law and Society I

21 February 2011

Balancing Privacy and Safety in the Wake of Virginia Tech

On April 16, 2007, Seung Hui Cho, a mentally ill student at Virginia Polytechnic Institute, shot to death 32 fellow students and faculty members, and injured 17 others, before killing himself. It was the worst mass shooting in U.S. history, and the fact that it took place on a college campus lent a special horror to the event. In the days after the tragedy, several facts about Seung Hui Cho came to light. According to the official Virginia State Panel report on the killings, Cho had exhibited signs of mental disturbance, including "suicidal and homicidal ideations" dating back to high school. And during Cho's junior year at Virginia Tech, numerous incidents occurred that provided clear warnings of Cho's mental instability and violent impulses (Virginia Tech Review 1). University administrators, faculty, and officials were aware of these incidents but failed to intervene to prevent the impending tragedy.

In the search for answers, attention quickly focused on federal rules governing student privacy that Virginia Tech officials said prevented them from communicating effectively with each other or with Cho's parents regarding his troubles. These rules, the officials argued, prohibit the sharing of information concerning students' mental health with parents or other students. The publicity about such restrictions revived an ongoing debate over university policies that balance student privacy against campus safety. In the wake of the Virginia Tech tragedy, the pendulum seems to have swung in favor of safety. In April 2008, Virginia Governor Tim Kaine signed into law a measure requiring colleges to alert parents when dependent students may be a danger to themselves or to others ("Virginia Tech Massacre" 1). Peter Lake, an educator at Stetson University College of Law, predicted that in the wake of Virginia Tech, "people will go in a direction of safety over privacy" (qtd. in Bernstein, "Mother").

Harrison 2

(3)   The shootings at Virginia Tech demonstrate, in the most horrifying way, the need for secure college campuses. Nevertheless, privacy remains a crucial right to most Americans—including college students, many of whom for the first time are exercising their prerogatives as adults. Many students who pose no threat to anyone will, and should, object strenuously to university administrators peering into and making judgments about their private lives. Some might be unwilling to seek professional therapy if they know that the records of their counseling sessions might be released to their parents or to other students. In responding to the Virginia Tech killings, we should resist rolling back federal rules protecting student privacy; for as long as college officials effectively respond to signs of trouble, these rules already provide a workable balance between privacy and public safety.

(4)   In these days of Facebook and reality TV, the notion of privacy rights, particularly for young people, may seem quaint. In fact, a top lawyer for the search engine Google claimed that in the Internet age, young people just don't care about privacy the way they once did (Cohen A17). Whatever the changing views of privacy in a wired world, the issue of student privacy rights is a serious legal matter that must be seen in the context of the student-college relationship. This relationship has its historical roots in the doctrine of *in loco parentis*, Latin for "in the place of the parents." Generally, this doctrine is understood to mean that the college stands in place of the student's parent or guardian. The college therefore has "a duty to protect the safety, morals, and welfare of their students, just as parents are expected to protect their children" (Pollet).

(5)   Writing of life at the University of Michigan before the 1960s, one historian observes that "*in loco parentis* comprised an elaborate structure of written rules and quiet understandings enforced in the trenches by housemothers [who] governed much of the what, where, when, and whom of students' lives, especially women: what to wear to dinner, what time to be home, where, when, and for how long they might receive visitors" (Tobin).

During the 1960s court decisions began to chip away at the doctrine of *in loco parentis*. These rulings illustrate that the students' rights movement during that era was an integral part of a broader contemporary social movement for civil rights and liberties. In *Dixon v. Alabama State Board of Education*, Alabama State College invoked *in loco parentis* to defend its decision to expel six African-American students without due process for participating in a lunchroom counter sit-in. Eventually, a federal appeals court rejected the school's claim to unrestrained power, ruling that students' constitutional rights did not end once they stepped onto campus (Weigel).

(6)

Students were not just fighting for the right to hold hands in dorm rooms; they were also asserting their rights as the vanguard of a social revolution. As Stetson law professor Robert Bickel notes: "The fall of *in loco parentis* in the 1960s correlated exactly with the rise of student economic power and the rise of student civil rights" (qtd. in Weigel).

(7)

The students' rights movement received a further boost with the Family Educational Rights and Privacy Act (FERPA), signed into law by President Ford in 1974. FERPA barred schools from releasing educational records—including mental health records—without the student's permission. The Act provides some important exceptions: educational records *can* be released in the case of health and safety emergencies or if the student is declared a dependent on his or her parents' tax returns (*Family*).

(8)

In the wake of Virginia Tech, however, many observers pointed the finger of blame at federal restrictions on sharing available mental health information. Also held responsible were the school's officials, who admitted knowing of Cho's mental instability but claimed that FERPA prevented them from doing anything about it. The State of Virginia official report on the killings notes as follows:

(9)

> University officials...explained their failures to communicate with one another or with Cho's parents by noting their belief that such communications are prohibited by the federal laws governing the privacy of health and education records. (Virginia Tech Review 2)

(10)   Observers were quick to declare the system broken. "Laws Limit Schools Even after Alarms," trumpeted a headline in the *Philadelphia Inquirer* (Gammage and Burling). Commentators attacked federal privacy law, charging that the pendulum had swung too far away from campus safety. Judging from this letter to the editor of the *Wall Street Journal*, many agreed wholeheartedly: "Parents have a right to know if their child has a serious problem, and they need to know the progress of their child's schoolwork, especially if they are paying the cost of the education. Anything less than this is criminal" (Guerriero).

(11)   As part of this public clamor, some schools have enacted policies that effectively curtail student privacy in favor of campus safety. For example: after Virginia Tech, Cornell University began assuming that students were dependents of their parents. Exploiting what the *Wall Street Journal* termed a "rarely used legal exception" in FERPA allows Cornell to provide parents with confidential information without students' permission (Bernstein, "Bucking" A9).

(12)   Conversely, the Massachusetts Institute of Technology lies at the opposite end of the spectrum from Cornell in its staunch defense of student privacy. M.I.T. has stuck to its position even in the wake of Virginia Tech, demanding that the mother of a missing M.I.T. student obtain a subpoena in order to access his dorm room and e-mail records. That student was later found dead, an apparent suicide (Bernstein, "Mother"). Even in the face of lawsuits, M.I.T. remains committed to its stance. Its chancellor explained the school's position this way:

> Privacy is important.... Different students will do different things they absolutely don't want their parents to know about.... Students expect this kind of safe place where they can address their difficulties, try out lifestyles, and be independent of their parents (qtd. in Bernstein, "Mother").

(13)   One can easily understand how parents would be outraged by the M.I.T. position. No parent would willingly let his or her child enter an

environment where that child's safety cannot be assured. Just as the first priority for any government is to protect its citizens, the first priority of an educational institution must be to keep its students safe. But does this responsibility justify rolling back student privacy rights or returning to a more traditional interpretation of *in loco parentis* in the relationship between a university and its students? No, for the simple reason that the choice is a false one.

As long as federal privacy laws are properly interpreted and implemented, they do nothing to endanger campus safety. The problem at Virginia Tech was not the federal government's policy; it was the university's own practices based on a faulty interpretation of that policy. The breakdown began with the failure of Virginia Tech officials to understand federal privacy laws. Interpreted correctly, these laws would *not* have prohibited officials from notifying appropriate authorities of Cho's problems. The Virginia Tech Review Panel report was very clear on this point: "[F]ederal laws and their state counterparts afford ample leeway to share information in potentially dangerous situations" (2). FERPA does, in fact, provide for a "health and safety emergencies" exception; educational records *can* be released without the student's consent "in connection with an emergency, [to] appropriate persons if the knowledge of such information is necessary to protect the health or safety of the student or other person..." (232g (b) (1) (g-h)). But Virginia Tech administrators did not invoke this important exception to FERPA's privacy rules. [Nor did they inform students of Cho's initial murder of two students, according to the Department of Education—an action that might have averted the thirty other murders (Potter).]

An editorial in the *Christian Science Monitor* suggested several other steps that the university could legally have taken, including informing Cho's parents that he had been briefly committed to a mental health facility, a fact that was public information. The editorial concluded, scornfully, that "federal law, at least, does recognize a balance between privacy and public safety, even when colleges can't, or won't" ("Perilous").

14

15

(16)   To be fair, such confusion about FERPA's contingencies appears widespread among college officials. For this reason, the U.S. Department of Education's revised privacy regulations, announced in March 2008 and intended to "clarify" when schools may release student records, are welcome and necessary. But simply reassuring anxious university officials that they won't lose federal funds for revealing confidential student records won't be enough to ensure campus safety. We need far more effective intervention for troubled students than the kind provided by Virginia Tech, which the Virginia Tech Review Panel blasted for its "lack of resources" and "passivity" (2). Yet effective interventions can be difficult to coordinate, and the consequences of inaction are sadly familiar. Three years after the Virginia Tech shootings, a student sued the University of California Regents because administrators at UCLA had allegedly failed to address the troubling behaviors of another student who later slashed and nearly killed her (Gordon).

(17)   Schools like the University of Kentucky offer a positive example of intervention, demonstrating that colleges can adopt a robust approach to student mental health without infringing on privacy rights. At Kentucky, "threat assessment groups" meet regularly to discuss a "watch list" of troubled students and decide what to do about them (McMurray). These committees emphasize proactiveness and communication—elements that were sorely missing at Virginia Tech. The approach represents a prudent middle ground between the extreme positions of M.I.T. and Cornell.

(18)   This middle ground takes full account of student privacy rights. For example, the University of Kentucky's director of counseling attends the threat assessment group's meetings but draws a clear line at what information she shares—for instance, whether or not a student has been undergoing counseling. Instead, the group looks for other potential red flags, such as a sharp drop-off in grades or difficulty functioning in the campus environment (McMurray). This open communication between university officials will presumably also help with delicate judgments— whether, for example, a student's violent story written for a creative

Harrison 7

writing class is an indication of mental instability or simply an early work by the next Stephen King ("Virginia Tech Massacre" 1).

The debate over rights to individual privacy versus public safety is sure to follow students into the wider world because that debate is one instance of a larger issue. The Fourth Amendment protects citizens "against unreasonable searches and seizures." But for more than two centuries, what constitutes *unreasonable* has been vigorously debated in the courts. Such arguments are not likely to end any time soon—on or off college campuses. Consider the recent public controversy over the installation of full body scanners at U.S. airports and intrusive pat-downs of travelers, measures taken by the U.S. Department of Homeland Security to foil terrorist threats. Predictably, many protested what they considered an assault on personal privacy, complaining that the scanners revealed body parts otherwise hidden by clothing and that the pat-downs amounted to sexual groping. On September 1, 2010, a civil liberties group even filed a lawsuit to block deployment of the scanners (Electronic). But many others vigorously defended the Homeland Security measures as essential to ensuring public safety. According to a *Washington Post*-ABC News poll, "Nearly two-thirds of Americans support the new full-body security-screening machines at the country's airports, as most say they put higher priority on combating terrorism than protecting personal privacy" (Cohen and Halsey).

What happened at Virginia Tech was a tragedy. Few of us can appreciate the grief of the parents of the shooting victims at Virginia Tech, parents who trusted that their children would be safe and who were devastated when that faith was betrayed. To these parents, the words of the M.I.T. chancellor quoted earlier—platitudes about students "try[ing] out lifestyles" or "address[ing] their difficulties"—must sound hollow. But we must guard against allowing a few isolated incidents, however tragic, to restrict the rights of millions of students, the vast majority of whom graduate college safely and without incident. Schools must not use Virginia Tech as a pretext to bring back the bad old days of resident assistants snooping on the private lives of students and infringing on their privacy. That step is the first down a slippery slope of dictating morality. Both the federal

19

20

courts and Congress have rejected that approach and for good reason have established the importance of privacy rights on campus. These rights must be preserved.

(21)   The Virginia Tech shooting does not demonstrate a failure of current policy, but rather a breakdown in the enforcement of policy. In its wake, universities have undertaken important modifications to their procedures. We should support changes that involve a more proactive approach to student mental health and improvements in communication between departments, such as those at the University of Kentucky. Such measures will not only bring confidential help to the troubled students who need it, they will also improve the safety of the larger college community. At the same time, these measures will preserve hard-won privacy rights on campus.

Works Cited

Bernstein, Elizabeth. "Bucking Privacy Concerns, Cornell Acts as
        Watchdog." *Wall Street Journal* 27 Dec. 2007: A1+. *LexisNexis.*
        Web. 10 Feb. 2011.

—. "A Mother Takes On MIT." *Wall Street Journal* 20 Sept. 2007: A1.
        LexisNexis. Web. 10 Feb. 2011.

Cohen, Adam. "One Friend Facebook Hasn't Made Yet: Privacy Rights."
        New York Times 18 Feb. 2008: A1+. *Academic Search Complete.*
        Web. 9 Feb. 2011.

Cohen, Jon, and Ashley Halsey III. "Poll: Nearly Two-Thirds of
        Americans Support Full-Body Scanners at Airports." *Washington
        Post.* The Washington Post Co., 23 Nov. 2010. Web. 17 Feb. 2011.

Electronic Privacy Information Center v. Dept. of Homeland Security.
        No. 10-1157. D.C. Cir. of the US. Sept 1, 2010. *epic.org.* Electronic
        Privacy Information Center, 1 Sept. 2010. Web. 15 Feb. 2011.

Harrison 10

Family Educational Rights and Privacy Act (FERPA). 20 U.S.C. §1232g
(b) (1) (g–h) (2006). Print.

Gammage, Jeff, and Stacy Burling. "Laws Limit Schools Even after
Alarms." *Philadelphia Inquirer* 19 Apr. 2007: A1. *Academic Search
Complete.* Web. 10 Feb. 2011.

Gordon, Larry. "Campus Stabbing Victim Sues UC Regents." *Los Angeles
Times* 8 Dec. 2010. *LexisNexis.* Web. 13 Feb. 2011.

Guerriero, Dom. Letter. *Wall Street Journal* 7 Jan. 2008. *LexisNexis.* Web.
11 Feb. 2011.

McMurray, Jeffrey. "Colleges Are Watching Troubled Students." *AP Online.*
Associated Press, 28 Mar. 2008. Web. 11 Feb. 2011.

"Perilous Privacy at Virginia Tech." Editorial. *Christian Science Monitor* 4
Sept. 2007: 8. *Academic Search Complete.* Web. 10 Feb. 2011.

Pollet, Susan J. "Is 'In Loco Parentis' at the College Level a Dead
Doctrine?" *New York Law Journal* 288 (2002): 4. Print.

Potter, Dena. "Feds: Va. Tech Broke Law in '07 Shooting Response."
Washington Post. The Washington Post Co., 10 Dec. 2010. Web. 12
Feb. 2011.

Tobin, James. "The Day 'In Loco Parentis' Died." *Michigan Today.* U of
Michigan, Nov. 2007. Web. 10 Feb. 2011.

U.S. Constitution: Fourth Amendment. *Findlaw.com.* Thomson Reuters,
n.d. Web. 16 Feb. 2011.

"Virginia Tech Massacre Has Altered Campus Mental Health Systems."
Los Angeles Times 14 Apr. 2008: A1+. *LexisNexis.* Web. 8 Feb.
2011.

Virginia Tech Review Panel. *Mass Shootings at Virginia Tech, April
16, 2007: Report of the Virginia Tech Review Panel Presented to
Timothy M. Kaine, Governor, Commonwealth of Virginia.* Arlington,
VA: n.p., 2007. Print.

Weigel, David. "Welcome to the Fun-Free University: The Return of *In
Loco Parentis* Is Killing Student Freedom." *Reasononline.* Reason
Magazine, Oct. 2004. Web. 7 Feb. 2011.

The Strategy of the Argument Synthesis

In his argument synthesis, Harrison attempts to support a *claim*—one that favors laws protecting student privacy while at the same time helping to ensure campus safety—by offering *support* in the form of facts (what campuses such as the University of Kentucky are doing, what Virginia Tech officials did and failed to do) and opinions (testimony of persons on both sides of the issue). However, because Harrison's claim rests on an *assumption* about the value of student privacy laws, its effectiveness depends partially on the extent to which we, as readers, agree with this assumption. (See our discussion of assumptions in Chapter 2, pp. 42–44.) An assumption (sometimes called a warrant) is a generalization or principle about how the world works or should work—a fundamental statement of belief about facts or values. In this case, the underlying assumption is that college students, as emerging adults and as citizens with civil rights, are entitled to keep their educational records private. Harrison makes this assumption explicit. Though you are under no obligation to do so, stating assumptions explicitly will clarify your arguments to readers.

Assumptions are often deeply rooted in people's psyches, sometimes derived from lifelong experiences and observations and not easily changed, even by the most logical of arguments. People who lose loved ones in incidents such as Virginia Tech, or people who believe that the right to safety of the larger campus community outweighs the right of individual student privacy, are not likely to accept the assumption underlying this paper, nor are they likely to accept the support provided by Harrison. But readers with no firm opinion might well be persuaded and could come to agree with him that existing federal law protecting student privacy is sufficient to protect campus safety, provided that campus officials act responsibly.

A discussion of the model argument's paragraphs, along with the argument strategy for each, follows. Note that the paper devotes one paragraph to developing each section of the outline on pages 80–81. Note also that Harrison avoids plagiarism by the careful attribution and quotation of sources.

- **Paragraph 1:** Harrison summarizes the key events of the Virginia Tech killings and establishes that Cho's mental instability was previously known to university officials.

  Argument strategy: Opening with the bare facts of the massacre, Harrison proceeds to lay the basis for the reaction against privacy rules that will be described in the paragraphs to follow. To some extent, Harrison encourages the reader to share the outrage of many in the general public that university officials failed to act to prevent the killings before they started.

- **Paragraph 2:** Harrison now explains the federal rules governing student privacy and discusses the public backlash against such rules and the new law signed by the governor of Virginia restricting privacy at colleges within the state.

Argument strategy: This paragraph highlights the debate over student privacy—and in particular the sometimes conflicting demands of student privacy and campus safety that will be central to the rest of the paper. Harrison cites both fact (the new Virginia law) and opinion (the quotation by Peter Lake) to develop this paragraph.

- **Paragraph 3:** Harrison further clarifies the two sides of the apparent conflict between privacy and safety, maintaining that both represent important social values but concluding with a thesis that argues for not restricting privacy.

  Argument strategy: For the first time, Harrison reveals his own position on the issue. He starts the paragraph by conceding the need for secure campuses but begins to make the case for privacy (for example, without privacy rules, students might be reluctant to enter therapy). In his thesis, he emphasizes that the demands of both privacy and safety can be satisfied because existing federal rules incorporate the necessary balance.

- **Paragraphs 4–7:** These paragraphs constitute the next section of the paper (see outline, pp. 80–81), covering the developments in student privacy over the past few decades. Paragraphs 4 and 5 cover the doctrine of *in loco parentis*; paragraph 6 discusses how court decisions such as *Dixon v. Alabama State Board of Education* began to erode this doctrine.

  Argument strategy: This section of the paper establishes the situation that existed on college campuses before the 1960s—and that presumably would exist again were privacy laws to be rolled back. By linking the erosion of the *in loco parentis* doctrine to the civil rights struggle, Harrison attempts to bestow upon pre-1960s college students (especially women), who were "parented" by college administrators, something of the *ethos* of African-Americans fighting for full citizenship during the civil rights era. Essentially, Harrison is making an analogy between the two groups—one that readers may or may not accept.

- **Paragraph 8:** This paragraph on FERPA constitutes the final part of the section of the paper dealing with the evolution of student privacy since before the 1960s. Harrison explains what FERPA is and introduces an exception to its privacy rules that will be more fully developed later in the paper.

  Argument strategy: FERPA is the federal law central to the debate over the balance between privacy and safety, so Harrison introduces it here as the culmination of a series of developments that weakened *in loco parentis* and guaranteed a certain level of student privacy. But since Harrison in his thesis argues that federal law on student privacy already establishes a balance between privacy and safety, he ends the paragraph by referring to the "health and safety" exception, an exception that will become important later in his argument.

- **Paragraphs 9–11:** These paragraphs constitute the section of the paper that covers the arguments *against* student privacy. Paragraph 9 discusses public reaction against both FERPA and Virginia Tech officials, who were accused of being more concerned with privacy than with safety. Paragraph 10 cites antiprivacy sentiments expressed in newspapers. Paragraph 11 explains how, in the wake of Virginia Tech, schools such as Cornell have enacted new policies restricting student privacy.

  Argument strategy: Harrison sufficiently respects the sentiments of those whose position he opposes to deal at some length with the counterarguments to his thesis. He quotes the official report on the mass shootings, to establish that Virginia Tech officials believed that they were acting according to the law. He quotes the writer of an angry letter about parents' right to know, without attempting to rebut its arguments. In outlining the newly restrictive Cornell policies on privacy, Harrison also establishes what he considers an extreme reaction to the massacres: essentially gutting student privacy rules. He is therefore setting up one position on the debate that he will later contrast with other positions—those of M.I.T. and the University of Kentucky.

- **Paragraphs 12–16:** These paragraphs constitute the section of the paper devoted to arguments *for* student privacy. Paragraphs 12 and 13 discuss the M.I.T. position on privacy, as expressed by its chancellor. Paragraph 14 refocuses on FERPA and quotes language to demonstrate that existing federal law provides a health and safety exception to the enforcement of privacy rules. Paragraph 15 quotes an editorial supporting this interpretation of FERPA. Paragraph 16 concedes the existence of confusion about federal rules and makes the transition to an argument about the need for more-effective action by campus officials to prevent tragedies such as the one at Virginia Tech.

  Argument strategy: Because these paragraphs express Harrison's position, as embedded in his thesis, this is the longest segment of the discussion. Paragraphs 12 and 13 discuss the M.I.T. position on student privacy, which (given that school's failure to accommodate even prudent demands for safety) Harrison believes is too extreme. Notice the transition at the end of paragraph 13. Conceding that colleges have a responsibility to keep students safe, Harrison poses a question: Does the goal of keeping students safe justify the rolling back of privacy rights? In a pivotal sentence, he responds, "No, for the simple reason that the choice is a false one." Paragraph 14 develops this response and presents the heart of Harrison's argument. Recalling the health and safety exception introduced in paragraph 8, Harrison now explains *why* the choice is false: He quotes the exact language of FERPA to establish that the problem at Virginia Tech was due not to federal law that prevented campus officials from protecting students, but rather to campus officials who *misunderstood* the law.

Paragraph 15 amplifies Harrison's argument, with a reference to an editorial in the *Christian Science Monitor*. Paragraph 16 marks a transition, within this section, to a position (developed in paragraphs 17 and 18) that Harrison believes represents a sensible stance in the debate over campus safety and student privacy. He bolsters his case by citing here, as elsewhere in the paper, the official report on the Virginia Tech killings. The report, prepared by an expert panel that devoted months to investigating the incident, carries considerable weight as evidence in this argument.

- **Paragraphs 17–18:** These paragraphs continue the arguments in favor of Harrison's position. They focus on new policies in practice at the University of Kentucky that offer a "prudent middle ground" in the debate.

  Argument strategy: Having discussed schools such as Cornell and M.I.T., where the reaction to the Virginia Tech killings was inadequate or unsatisfactory, Harrison now outlines a set of policies and procedures in place at the University of Kentucky since April 2007. Following the transition at the end of paragraph 16 on the need for more-effective intervention on the part of campus officials, Harrison explains how Kentucky established a promising form of such intervention: watch lists of troubled students, threat assessment groups, and more-open communication among university officials. Thus, Harrison positions what is happening at the University of Kentucky— as opposed to rollbacks of federal rules—as the most effective way of preventing future killings like those at Virginia Tech. Kentucky therefore becomes a crucial example for Harrison of how to strike a good balance between the demands of student privacy and campus safety.

- **Paragraphs 19–21:** In his conclusion, Harrison both broadens the context of his discussion about Virginia Tech and reiterates points made in the body of the paper. In paragraph 19, he turns from the shooting to the broader world, suggesting that the tension between the individual's right to privacy and the public's right to safety is not unique to college campuses. In paragraph 20, he agrees that what happened at Virginia Tech was a tragedy but maintains that an isolated incident should not become an excuse for rolling back student privacy rights and bringing back "the bad old days" when campus officials took an active, and intrusive, interest in students' private lives. In paragraph 21, Harrison reiterates the position stated in his thesis: that the problem at Virginia Tech was not a restrictive federal policy that handcuffed administrators, but rather a breakdown in enforcement. He concludes on the hopeful note that new policies established since Virginia Tech will both protect student privacy and improve campus safety.

Argument strategy: The last three paragraphs, the conclusion, provide Harrison with an opportunity both to extend his thinking beyond a single case and to reemphasize his main points. In paragraph 19, he moves beyond the world of college and broadens the reach of his argument. The final two paragraphs to some degree parallel the structure of the thesis itself. In paragraph 20, Harrison makes a final appeal against rolling back student privacy rights. This appeal parallels the first clause of the thesis ("In responding to the Virginia Tech killings, we should resist rolling back federal rules protecting student privacy"). In paragraph 21, Harrison focuses not on federal law itself, but rather on the kind of measures adopted by schools such as the University of Kentucky that go beyond mere compliance with federal law—and thereby demonstrate the validity of part two of Harrison's thesis ("…as long as college officials effectively respond to signs of trouble, these rules already provide a workable balance between privacy and public safety"). Harrison thus ends a paper on a grim subject with a note that provides some measure of optimism and that attempts to reconcile proponents on both sides of this emotional debate.

Another approach to an argument synthesis based on the same and additional sources could argue (along with some of the sources quoted in the model paper) that safety as a social value should never be outweighed by the right to privacy. Such a position could draw support from other practices in contemporary society—searches at airports, for example—illustrating that most people are willing to give up a certain measure of privacy, as well as convenience, in the interest of the safety of the community. Whatever your approach to a subject, in first *critically examining* the various sources and then *synthesizing* them to support a position about which you feel strongly, you are engaging in the kind of critical thinking that is essential to success in a good deal of academic and professional work.

DEVELOPING AND ORGANIZING THE SUPPORT FOR YOUR ARGUMENTS

Experienced writers seem to have an intuitive sense of how to develop and present supporting evidence for their claims; this sense is developed through much hard work and practice. Less-experienced writers wonder what to say first, and having decided on that, wonder what to say next. There is no single method of presentation. But the techniques of even the most experienced writers often boil down to a few tried and tested arrangements.

As we've seen in the model synthesis in this chapter, the key to devising effective arguments is to find and use those kinds of support that most persuasively strengthen your claim. Some writers categorize support into two broad types: *evidence* and *motivational appeals.* Evidence—in the form of facts, statistics, and expert testimony—helps make the appeal to reason. Motivational appeals—appeals grounded in emotion and upon the authority of the speaker—are employed to get people to change their minds, to agree with the writer or speaker, or to decide upon a plan of action.

Following are the most common strategies for using and organizing support for your claims.

Summarize, Paraphrase, and Quote Supporting Evidence

In most of the papers and reports you will write in college and in the professional world, evidence and motivational appeals derive from your summarizing, paraphrasing, and quoting of material in sources that either have been provided to you or that you have independently researched. For example, in paragraph 9 of the model argument synthesis, Harrison uses a long quotation from the Virginia Tech Review Panel report to make the point that college officials believed they were prohibited by federal privacy law from communicating with one another about disturbed students like Cho. You will find another long quotation later in the synthesis and a number of brief quotations woven into sentences throughout. In addition, you will find summaries and paraphrases. In each case, Harrison is careful to cite the source.

Provide Various Types of Evidence and Motivational Appeals

Keep in mind that you can use appeals to both reason and emotion. The appeal to reason is based on evidence that consists of a combination of *facts* and *expert testimony*. The sources by Tobin and Weigel, for example, offer facts about the evolution over the past few decades of the *in loco parentis* doctrine. Bernstein and McMurray interview college administrators at Cornell, M.I.T., and the University of Kentucky, who explain the changing policies at those institutions. The model synthesis makes an appeal to emotion by engaging the reader's self-interest: If campuses are to be made more secure from the acts of mentally disturbed persons, then college officials should take a proactive approach to monitoring and intervention.

Use Climactic Order

Climactic order is the arrangement of examples or evidence in order of anticipated impact on the reader, least to greatest. Organize by climactic order when you plan to offer a number of categories or elements of support for your claim. Recognize that some elements will be more important—and likely more persuasive—than others. The basic principle here is that you should *save the most important evidence for the end*, because whatever you say last is what readers are likely to remember best. A secondary principle is that whatever you say first is what they are *next* most likely to remember. Therefore, when you have several reasons to offer in support of your claim, an effective argument strategy is to present the second most important, then one or more additional reasons, and finally the most important reason. Paragraphs 7 to 11 of the model synthesis do exactly this.

Use Logical or Conventional Order

Using a logical or conventional order involves using as a template a preestablished pattern or plan for arguing your case.

- One common pattern is describing or arguing a *problem/solution*. Using this pattern, you begin with an introduction in which you typically define the problem, perhaps explain its origins, then offer one or more solutions, then conclude.

- Another common pattern presents *two sides of a controversy*. Using this pattern, you introduce the controversy and (in an argument synthesis) your own point of view or claim; then you explain the other side's arguments, providing reasons why your point of view should prevail.

- A third common pattern is *comparison-and-contrast*. This pattern is so important that we will discuss it separately in the next section.

The order in which you present elements of an argument is sometimes dictated by the conventions of the discipline in which you are writing. For example, lab reports and experiments in the sciences and social sciences often follow this pattern: *Opening* or *Introduction*, *Methods and Materials* (of the experiment or study), *Results*, *Discussion*. Legal arguments often follow the so-called IRAC format: *Issue*, *Rule*, *Application*, *Conclusion*.

Present and Respond to Counterarguments

When developing arguments on a controversial topic, you can effectively use *counterargument* to help support your claims. When you use counterargument, you present an argument *against* your claim and then show that this argument is weak or flawed. The advantage of this technique is that you demonstrate that you are aware of the other side of the argument and that you are prepared to answer it.

Here is how a counterargument is typically developed:

I. Introduction and claim

II. Main opposing argument

III. Refutation of opposing argument

IV. Main positive argument

DEVELOPING AND ORGANIZING SUPPORT FOR YOUR ARGUMENTS

- *Summarize, paraphrase, and quote supporting evidence.* Draw on the facts, ideas, and language in your sources.
- *Provide various types of evidence and motivational appeal.*
- *Use climactic order.* Save the most important evidence in support of your argument for the *end*, where it will have the most impact. Use the next most important evidence *first*.
- *Use logical or conventional order.* Use a form of organization appropriate to the topic, such as problem/solution; sides of a controversy; comparison/contrast; or a form of organization appropriate to the academic or professional discipline, such as a report of an experiment or a business plan.
- *Present and respond to counterarguments.* Anticipate and evaluate arguments against your position.
- *Use concession.* Concede that one or more arguments against your position have some validity; reassert, nonetheless, that your argument is the stronger one.

Use Concession

Concession is a variation of counterargument. As in counterargument, you present an opposing viewpoint, but instead of dismissing that position, you *concede* that it has some validity and even some appeal, although your own position is the more reasonable one. This concession bolsters your standing as a fair-minded person who is not blind to the virtues of the other side. In the model synthesis, Harrison acknowledges the grief and sense of betrayal of the parents of the students who were killed. He concedes that parents have a right to expect that "the first priority of an educational institution must be to keep its students safe." But he insists that this goal of achieving campus safety can be accomplished without rolling back hard-won privacy rights.

Here is an outline for a typical concession argument:

I. Introduction and claim

II. Important opposing argument

III. Concession that this argument has some validity

IV. Positive argument(s) that acknowledge the counterargument and (possibly) incorporate some elements of it

Sometimes when you are developing a counterargument or concession argument, you may become convinced of the validity of the opposing point of view and change your own views. Don't be afraid of this happening.

Writing is a tool for learning. To change your mind because of new evidence is a sign of flexibility and maturity, and your writing can only be the better for it.

THE COMPARISON-AND-CONTRAST SYNTHESIS

A particularly important type of argument synthesis is built on patterns of comparison and contrast. Techniques of comparison and contrast enable you to examine two subjects (or sources) in terms of one another. When you compare, you consider *similarities*. When you contrast, you consider *differences*. By comparing and contrasting, you perform a multifaceted analysis that often suggests subtleties that otherwise might not have come to your (or your reader's) attention.

To organize a comparison-and-contrast argument, you must carefully read sources in order to discover *significant criteria for analysis*. A *criterion* is a specific point to which both of your authors refer and about which they may agree or disagree. (For example, in a comparative report on compact cars, criteria for *comparison and contrast* might be road handling, fuel economy, and comfort of ride.) The best criteria are those that allow you not only to account for obvious similarities and differences—those concerning the main aspects of your sources or subjects—but also to plumb deeper, exploring subtle yet significant comparisons and contrasts among details or subcomponents, which you can then relate to your overall thesis.

Note that comparison-and-contrast is frequently not an end in itself, but serves some larger purpose. Thus, a comparison-and-contrast synthesis may be a component of a paper that is essentially a critique, an explanatory synthesis, an argument synthesis, or an analysis.

Organizing Comparison-and-Contrast Syntheses

Two basic approaches to organizing a comparison-and-contrast synthesis are organization by *source* and organization by *criteria.*

Organizing by Source or Subject

You can organize a comparative synthesis by first summarizing each of your sources or subjects and then discussing the significant similarities and differences between them. Having read the summaries and become familiar with the distinguishing features of each source, your readers will most likely be able to appreciate the more obvious similarities and differences. In the discussion, your task is to consider both the obvious and the subtle comparisons and contrasts, focusing on the most significant—that is, on those that most clearly support your thesis.

Organization by source or subject works best with passages that can be briefly summarized. If the summary of your source or subject becomes too long, your readers might have forgotten the points you made in the first summary when they are reading the second. A comparison-and-contrast synthesis organized by source or subject might proceed like this:

I. Introduce the paper; lead to thesis.

II. Summarize source/subject A by discussing its significant features.

III. Summarize source/subject B by discussing its significant features.

IV. Discuss in a paragraph (or two) the significant points of comparison and contrast between sources or subjects A and B. Alternatively, begin the comparison-contrast in Section III as you introduce source/subject B.

V. Conclude with a paragraph in which you summarize your points and, perhaps, raise and respond to pertinent questions.

Organizing by Criteria

Instead of summarizing entire sources one at a time with the intention of comparing them later, you could discuss two sources simultaneously, examining the views of each author point by point (criterion by criterion), comparing and contrasting these views in the process. The criterion approach is best used when you have a number of points to discuss or when passages or subjects are long and/or complex. A comparison-and-contrast synthesis organized by criteria might look like this:

I. Introduce the paper; lead to thesis.

II. Criterion 1
   A. Discuss what author 1 says about this point. Or present situation 1 in light of this point.
   B. Discuss what author 2 says about this point, comparing and contrasting 2's treatment of the point with 1's. Or present situation 2 in light of this point and explain its differences from situation 1.

III. Criterion 2
   A. Discuss what author 1 says about this point. Or present situation 1 in light of this point.
   B. Discuss what author 2 says about this point, comparing and contrasting 2's treatment of the point with 1's. Or present situation 2 in light of this point and explain its differences from situation 1.

And proceed so on, criterion by criterion, until you have completed your discussion. Be sure to arrange criteria with a clear method; knowing how the discussion of one criterion leads to the next will ensure smooth transitions throughout your paper. End by summarizing your key points and perhaps raising and responding to pertinent questions.

However you organize your comparison-and-contrast synthesis, keep in mind that comparing and contrasting are not ends in themselves. Your discussion should point to a conclusion, an answer to the question "So what—why bother to compare and contrast in the first place?" If your discussion is part of a larger synthesis, point to and support the larger claim. If you write a stand-alone comparison-and-contrast synthesis, though, you must by the final paragraph answer the "Why bother?" question. The model comparison-and-contrast synthesis that follows does exactly this.

Exercise 3.3 ◯

Comparing and Contrasting

Review the model argument synthesis (pp. 83–91) for elements of comparison and contrast—specifically those paragraphs concerning how Cornell University, M.I.T., and the University of Kentucky balance student privacy with the parental right to know about the health and welfare of their children.

1. From these paragraphs in the model paper, extract raw information concerning the positions of the three schools on the issue of student privacy, and then craft your own brief comparison-and-contrast synthesis. Identify criteria for comparison and contrast, and discuss the positions of each school in relation to these criteria. *Note:* For this exercise, do not concern yourself with parenthetical citation (that is, with identifying your source materials).

2. Write a paragraph or two that traces the development of comparison-and-contrast throughout the model paper. Having discussed the *how* and *where* of this development, discuss the *why*. Answer this question: Why has the writer used comparison-and-contrast? (Hint: It is not an end in itself.) To what use is it put?

A Case for Comparison-and-Contrast: World War I and World War II

Let's see how the principles of comparison-and-contrast can be applied to a response to a final examination question in a course on modern history. Imagine that having attended classes involving lecture and discussion, and having read excerpts from John Keegan's *The First World War* and Tony Judt's *Postwar: A History of Europe Since 1945*, you were presented with this examination question:

> Based on your reading to date, compare and contrast the two world wars in light of any four or five criteria you think significant. Once you have called careful attention to both similarities and differences, conclude

with an observation. What have you learned? What can your compara-tive analysis teach us?

Comparison-and-Contrast Organized by Criteria

Here is a plan for a response, essentially a comparison-and-contrast synthe-sis, organized by *criteria* and beginning with the thesis—and the *claim.*

> *Thesis:* In terms of the impact on cities and civilian populations, the military aspects of the two wars in Europe, and their aftermaths, the differences be-tween World War I and World War II considerably outweigh the similarities.
>
> I. Introduction. World Wars I and II were the most devastating conflicts in history. *Thesis.*
>
> II. Summary of main similarities: causes, countries involved, battle-grounds, global scope.
>
> III. First major difference: Physical impact of war.
>   A. WWI was fought mainly in rural battlegrounds.
>   B. In WWII cities were destroyed.
>
> IV. Second major difference: Effect on civilians.
>   A. WWI fighting primarily involved soldiers.
>   B. WWII involved not only military, but also massive noncombatant casualties: Civilian populations were displaced, forced into slave labor, and exterminated.
>
> V. Third major difference: Combat operations.
>   A. World War I, in its long middle phase, was characterized by trench warfare.
>   B. During the middle phase of World War II, there was no major mili-tary action in Nazi-occupied Western Europe.
>
> VI. Fourth major difference: Aftermath.
>   A. Harsh war terms imposed on defeated Germany contributed sig-nificantly to the rise of Hitler and World War II.
>   B. Victorious allies helped rebuild West Germany after World War II but allowed Soviets to take over Eastern Europe.
>
> VII. Conclusion. Since the end of World War II, wars have been far smaller in scope and destructiveness, and warfare has expanded to involve stateless combatants committed to acts of terror.

The following model exam response, a comparison-and-contrast synthesis organized by criteria, is written according to the preceding plan. (Thesis and topic sentences are highlighted.)

MODEL EXAM RESPONSE

(1)   World War I (1914–1918) and World War II (1939–1945) were the most catastrophic and destructive conflicts in human history. For those who believed in the steady but inevitable progress of civilization, it was impossible to imagine that two wars in the first half of the twentieth century could reach levels of barbarity and horror that would outstrip those of any previous era. Historians estimate that more than 22 million people, soldiers and civilians, died in World War I; they estimate that between 40 and 50 million died in World War II. In many ways, these two conflicts were similar: They were fought on many of the same European and Russian battlegrounds, with more or less the same countries on opposing sides. Even many of the same people were involved: Winston Churchill and Adolf Hitler figured in both wars. And the main outcome in each case was the same: total defeat for Germany. However, in terms of the impact on cities and civilian populations, the military aspects of the two wars in Europe, and their aftermaths, the differences between World Wars I and II considerably outweigh the similarities.

(2)   The similarities are clear enough. In fact, many historians regard World War II as a continuation--after an intermission of about twenty years--of World War I. One of the main causes of each war was Germany's dissatisfaction and frustration with what it perceived as its diminished place in the world. Hitler launched World War II partly out of revenge for Germany's humiliating defeat in World War I. In each conflict, Germany and its allies (the Central Powers in WWI, the Axis in WWII) went to war against France, Great Britain, Russia (the Soviet Union in WWII), and eventually, the United States. Though neither conflict included literally the entire world, the participation of countries not only in Europe but also in the Middle East, the Far East, and the Western Hemisphere made both conflicts global in scope. And as indicated earlier, the number of casualties in each war was unprecedented in history, partly because modern technology had enabled the creation of deadlier weapons--including tanks, heavy artillery, and aircraft--than had ever before been used in warfare.

Despite these similarities, the differences between the two world wars are considerably more significant. One of the most noticeable differences was the physical impact of each war in Europe and in Russia--the western and eastern fronts. The physical destruction of World War I was confined largely to the battlefield. The combat took place almost entirely in the rural areas of Europe and Russia. No major cities were destroyed in the first war; cathedrals, museums, government buildings, urban houses and apartments were left untouched. During the second war, in contrast, almost no city or town of any size emerged unscathed. Rotterdam, Warsaw, London, Minsk, and--when the Allies began their counterattack--almost every major city in Germany and Japan, including Berlin and Tokyo, were flattened. Of course, the physical devastation of the cities created millions of refugees, a phenomenon never experienced in World War I.

The fact that World War II was fought in the cities as well as on the battlefields meant that the second war had a much greater impact on civilians than did the first war. With few exceptions, the civilians in Europe during WWI were not driven from their homes, forced into slave labor, starved, tortured, or systematically exterminated. But all of these crimes happened routinely during WWII. The Nazi occupation of Europe meant that the civilian populations of France, Belgium, Norway, the Netherlands, and other conquered lands--along with the industries, railroads, and farms of these countries--were put into the service of the Third Reich. Millions of people from conquered Europe, those who were not sent directly to the death camps, were forcibly transported to Germany and put to work in support of the war effort.

During both wars, the Germans were fighting on two fronts: the western front in Europe and the eastern front in Russia. But while both wars were characterized by intense military activity during their initial and final phases, the middle and longest phases--at least in Europe--differed considerably. The middle phase of the First World War was characterized by trench warfare, a relatively static form of military activity in which fronts seldom moved, or moved only a few hundred yards at a time, even after major battles. By contrast, in the years between the German conquest of most of Europe by early 1941 and the Allied invasion of Normandy in mid-1944, there was no major fighting in Nazi-occupied Western Europe. (The land battles then shifted to North Africa and the Soviet Union.)

(6)   And of course, the two world wars differed in their aftermaths. The most significant consequence of World War I was that the humiliating and costly war reparations imposed on the defeated Germany by the terms of the 1919 Treaty of Versailles made possible the rise of Hitler and thus led directly to World War II. In contrast, after the end of the Second World War in 1945, the Allies helped rebuild West Germany (the portion of a divided Germany that it controlled), transformed the new country into a democracy, and helped make it one of the most thriving economies of the world. But perhaps the most significant difference in the aftermath of each war involved Russia. That country, in a considerably weakened state, pulled out of World War I a year before hostilities ended so that it could consolidate its 1917 Revolution. Russia then withdrew into itself and took no significant part in European affairs until the Nazi invasion of the Soviet Union in 1941. In contrast, it was the Red Army in World War II that was most responsible for the crushing defeat of Germany. In recognition of its efforts and of its enormous sacrifices, the Allies allowed the Soviet Union to take control of the countries of Eastern Europe after the war, leading to fifty years of totalitarian rule--and the Cold War.

(7)   While the two world wars that devastated much of Europe were similar in that, at least according to some historians, they were the same war interrupted by two decades, and similar in that combatants killed more efficiently than armies throughout history ever had, the differences between the wars were significant. In terms of the physical impact of the fighting, the impact on civilians, the action on the battlefield at mid-war, and the aftermaths, World Wars I and II differed in ways that matter to us decades later. The wars in Iraq, Afghanistan,

and Bosnia have involved an alliance of nations pitted against single nations; but we have not seen, since the two world wars, grand alliances moving vast armies across continents. The destruction implied by such action is almost unthinkable today. Warfare is changing, and "stateless" combatants like Hamas and Al Qaeda wreak destruction of their own. But we may never again see, one hopes, the devastation that follows when multiple nations on opposing sides of a conflict throw millions of soldiers--and civilians--into harm's way.

The Strategy of the Exam Response

The general strategy of this argument is an organization by *criteria*. The writer argues that although the two world wars exhibited some similarities, the differences between the two conflicts were more significant. Note that the writer's thesis doesn't merely state these significant differences; it also presents them in a way that anticipates both the content and the structure of the response to follow.

In argument terms, the *claim* the writer makes is the conclusion that the two global conflicts were significantly different, if superficially similar. The *assumption* is that key differences and similarities are clarified by employing specific criteria: the impact of the wars upon cities and civilian populations and the consequences of the Allied victories. The *support* comes in the form of historical facts regarding the levels of casualties, the scope of destruction, the theaters of conflict, the events following the conclusions of the wars, and so on.

- **Paragraph 1:** The writer begins by commenting on the unprecedented level of destruction of World Wars I and II and concludes with the thesis summarizing the key similarities and differences.
- **Paragraph 2:** The writer summarizes the key similarities in the two wars: the wars' causes, their combatants, their global scope, and the level of destructiveness made possible by modern weaponry.
- **Paragraph 3:** The writer discusses the first of the key differences: the battlegrounds of World War I were largely rural; the battlegrounds of World War II included cities that were targeted and destroyed.
- **Paragraph 4:** The writer discusses the second of the key differences: the impact on civilians. In World War I, civilians were generally spared from the direct effects of combat; in World War II, civilians were targeted by the Nazis for systematic displacement and destruction.

- **Paragraph 5:** The writer discusses the third key difference: Combat operations during the middle phase of World War I were characterized by static trench warfare. During World War II, in contrast, there were no major combat operations in Nazi-occupied Western Europe during the middle phase of the conflict.

- **Paragraph 6:** The writer focuses on the fourth key difference: the aftermath of the two wars. After World War I, the victors imposed harsh conditions on a defeated Germany, leading to the rise of Hitler and the Second World War. After World War II, the Allies helped Germany rebuild and thrive. However, the Soviet victory in 1945 led to its postwar domination of Eastern Europe.

- **Paragraph 7:** In the conclusion, the writer sums up the key similarities and differences just covered and makes additional comments about the course of more-recent wars since World War II. In this way, the writer responds to the questions posed at the end of the assignment: "What have you learned? What can your comparative analysis teach us?"

Avoid Common Fallacies in Developing and Using Support

In Chapter 2, in the section on critical reading, we considered criteria that, as a reader, you may use for evaluating informative and persuasive writing (see pp. 29–31). We discussed how you can assess the accuracy, the significance, and the author's interpretation of the information presented. We also considered the importance in good argument of clearly defined key terms and avoiding the pitfalls of emotionally loaded language. Finally, we saw how to recognize such logical fallacies as either/or reasoning, faulty cause-and-effect reasoning, hasty generalization, and false analogy. As a writer, no less than as a critical reader, you need to be aware of these common problems and how to avoid them.

Be aware, also, of your responsibility to cite source materials appropriately. When you quote a source, double- and triple-check that you have done so accurately. When you summarize or paraphrase, take care to use your own language and sentence structures (though you can, of course, also quote within these forms). When you refer to someone else's idea—even if you are not quoting, summarizing, or paraphrasing it—give the source credit. By being ethical about the use of sources, you uphold the highest standards of the academic community.

THE EXPLANATORY SYNTHESIS

Some of the papers you write in college will be more or less explanatory (as opposed to argumentative) in nature. An explanation helps readers understand a topic. Writers explain when they divide a subject into its component parts and present them to the reader in a clear and orderly fashion. Explanations may entail descriptions that re-create in words some object, place, emotion, event, sequence of events, or state of affairs. As a student reporter, you may need to explain an event—to relate when, where, and how it took place. In a science lab, you would observe the conditions and results of an experiment and record them for review by others. In a political science course, you might review research on a particular subject—say, the complexities underlying the debate over gay marriage— and then present the results of your research to your professor and the members of your class.

Your job in writing an explanatory synthesis—or in writing the explanatory portion of an argument synthesis—is not to argue a particular point, but rather *to present the facts in a reasonably objective manner.* Explanatory papers, like other academic papers, should be based on a thesis. But the purpose of a thesis in an explanatory paper is less to advance a particular opinion than it is to focus the various facts contained in the paper.

The explanatory synthesis is fairly modest in purpose. It emphasizes the materials in the sources, not the writer's interpretation of them. Because your reader is not always in a position to read your sources, this kind of synthesis, if done well, can be very informative. But the main characteristic of the explanatory synthesis is that it is designed more to *inform* than to *persuade.* As the writer of an explanatory synthesis, you remain for the most part a detached observer.

Model Explanatory Synthesis

Let's demonstrate the difference between an argument synthesis and an explanatory synthesis on the same subject. This is the same kind of demonstration we offered early in this chapter (see section "Types of Synthesis: Explanatory and Argument") in the contrast between a news article and an editorial on the same topic: the nutritional value of cheese. One source is primarily explanatory; the other is strongly argumentative. Following is a new, highly excerpted version of the argument synthesis on balancing privacy rights and safety with the argument components removed and the explanatory components reinforced. The writer is now, in effect, simply reporting on the debate rather than commenting upon it or offering his opinions and recommendations. He is now writing an explanatory synthesis.

Much of the content (including the parts represented by ellipses) remains the same as in the argument synthesis— which illustrates the fact that explanation often plays a pivotal role in making arguments. We highlight the sentences and attributive phrases (such as "officials hope"), as well as the revamped the thesis, that help convert this paper from an argument synthesis to an explanatory synthesis.

EXPLANATORY SYNTHESIS

(Thesis and topic sentences are highlighted.)

Privacy vs. Safety in the Wake of Virginia Tech

1 On April 16, 2007, Seung Hui Cho, a mentally ill student at Virginia Polytechnic Institute, shot to death 32 fellow students and faculty members, and injured 17 others, before killing himself. It was the worst mass shooting in U.S. history, and the fact that it took place on a college campus lent a special horror to the event....

2 The shootings at Virginia Tech demonstrate, in the most horrifying way, the need for secure college campuses. Nevertheless, privacy remains a crucial right to most Americans—including college students, many of whom for the first time are exercising their prerogatives as adults. Many students who pose no threat to anyone will object strenuously to university administrators peering into and making judgments about their private lives. Some might be unwilling to seek professional therapy if they knew that the records of their counseling sessions might be released to their parents or to other students. As they struggled to understand what had gone wrong at Virginia Tech, college officials, mental health professionals, lawmakers, and others attempted to develop new policies and procedures that would help prevent another such incident and also balance the demands of student privacy and campus safety.

3 In these days of *Facebook* and reality TV, the notion of privacy rights, particularly for young people, may seem quaint....

4 One can easily understand how parents would be outraged by the MIT position. No parent would willingly let his or her child enter an environment where that child's safety cannot be assured. Just as the first priority for any government is to protect its citizens, the first priority of an educational institution must be to keep its students safe. But how, exactly, to keep students safe, college officials concede, is a complicated matter.

5 One of the "key findings" of the Virginia Tech Review Panel was that federal privacy laws, properly interpreted and implemented, do nothing to endanger campus safety. "In reality," the panel concluded, "federal laws and their state counterparts afford ample leeway to share information in

potentially dangerous situations (Virginia Tech Review 2). So the problem at Virginia Tech, according to the panel, was not the federal government's policy; it was the university's own practices based on a faculty interpretation of that policy. The breakdown began with the failure of Virginia Tech officials to understand federal privacy laws....

This open communication between university officials presumably will also help with delicate judgments—whether, for example, a student's violent story written for a creative writing class is an indication of mental instability or simply an early work by the next Stephen King ("Virginia Tech Massacre" 1). ⑥

The tragic events at Virginia Tech have spurred renewed debate over the often competing claims of student privacy and campus safety. During the course of this debate universities have undertaken important modifications in their procedures. These new policies involve a more proactive approach to student mental health and improvements in communication between departments, such as those at the University of Kentucky. Such measures, officials hope, will not only bring confidential help to the troubled students who need it, they will also improve the safety of the larger college community. At the same time, they expect that these measures will preserve hard-won privacy rights on campus. ⑦

The Strategy of the Explanatory Synthesis

In developing this explanatory synthesis, the writer uses much of the same wording—that is, the same facts and claims—that appears in the argument synthesis. But the writer keeps his own opinions to himself. Note especially the new thesis: the original argument thesis that takes a strong position ("we should resist rolling back federal rules") has been replaced by an explanatory thesis reflecting a more neutral stance ("college officials ... and others attempted to develop new policies and procedures"). Note also such attributive phrases as "they expect that," which serve to relocate strongly held views away from the writer and credit them to others. As for the conclusion, note that the emphasis remains on explaining, not on finding fault or giving credit.

SUMMARY

In this chapter we've considered two main types of synthesis: the *explanatory synthesis* and the *argument synthesis*. Although for ease of comprehension we've placed these in separate categories, the types are not mutually exclusive. Both argument syntheses and explanatory syntheses often involve elements of one another. Which type of synthesis you choose will depend on your *purpose* and the method that you decide is best suited to achieve this purpose.

If your main purpose is to help your audience understand a particular subject, and in particular to help them understand the essential elements or significance of this subject, then you will be composing an explanatory synthesis. If your main purpose, on the other hand, is to persuade your audience to agree with your viewpoint on a subject, or to change their minds, or to decide on a particular course of action, then you will be composing an argument synthesis. If one effective technique for making your case is to establish similarities and differences between your subject and another one, then you will compose a comparison-and-contrast synthesis—which may well be only *part* of a larger synthesis.

In planning and drafting these syntheses, you can draw on a variety of strategies: supporting your claims by summarizing, paraphrasing, and quoting from your sources; and choosing from among strategies such as climactic or conventional order, counterargument, and concession the approach that will best help you to achieve your purpose.

The strategies of synthesis you've practiced in this chapter will be important in composing a research paper. The research paper involves all of the skills in preparing summary, critique, and synthesis that we've discussed thus far, the main difference being that you won't find the sources needed to write the paper in this particular text. We'll discuss approaches to locating and critically evaluating sources, selecting material from among them to provide support for your claims, and, finally, documenting your sources in standard professional formats.

We turn now to analysis, which is another important strategy for academic thinking and writing. Chapter 4, "Analysis," will introduce you to a strategy that, like synthesis, draws upon all the strategies you've been practicing as you move through *Writing and Reading Across the Curriculum*.

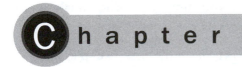

Chapter 4

Analysis

After completing this chapter, you will be able to:

LO 4.1   Establish the principle, the definition, or the personal perspective on which to base an analysis.

LO 4.2   Write an analysis considering purpose, using an analytical principle, formulating a thesis, and developing a plan.

WHAT IS AN ANALYSIS?

An *analysis* is a type of argument in which you study the parts of something—a physical object, a work of art, a person or group of people, an event, or a scientific, economic, or sociological phenomenon—to understand how it works, what it means, or why it might be significant. The writer of an analysis uses an analytical tool: a *principle* or *definition* on the basis of which the subject of study can be divided into parts and examined.

Here are excerpts from two analyses of the movie version of L. Frank Baum's *The Wizard of Oz*:

> At the dawn of adolescence, the very time she should start to distance herself from Aunt Em and Uncle Henry, the surrogate parents who raised her on their Kansas farm, Dorothy Gale experiences a hurtful reawakening of her fear that these loved ones will be rudely ripped from her, especially her Aunt (Em—M for Mother!).*

> [*The Wizard of Oz*] was originally written as a political allegory about grass-roots protest. It may seem harder to believe than Emerald City, but the Tin Woodsman is the industrial worker, the Scarecrow [is] the struggling farmer, and the Wizard is the president, who is powerful only as long as he succeeds in deceiving the people.†

---

*Harvey Greenberg, *The Movies on Your Mind* (New York: Dutton, 1975).
†Peter Dreier, "Oz Was Almost Reality," *Cleveland Plain Dealer* 3 Sept. 1989.

As these paragraphs suggest, what you discover through analysis depends entirely on the principle or definition you use to make your insights. Is *The Wizard of Oz* the story of a girl's psychological development, or is it a story about politics? The answer is *both*. In the first example, the psychiatrist Harvey Greenberg applies the principles of his profession and, not surprisingly, sees *The Wizard of Oz* in psychological terms. In the second example, a newspaper reporter applies the political theories of Karl Marx and, again not surprisingly, discovers a story about politics.

Different as they are, these analyses share an important quality: Each is the result of a specific principle or definition used as a tool to divide an object into parts in order to see what it means and how it works. The writer's choice of analytical tool simultaneously creates and limits the possibilities for analysis. Thus, working with the principles of Freud, Harvey Greenberg

WHERE DO WE FIND WRITTEN ANALYSES?

Here are just a few of the types of writing that involve analysis:

Academic Writing

- **Experimental and lab reports** analyze the meaning or implications of the study results in the Discussion section.
- **Research papers** analyze information in sources or apply theories to material being reported.
- **Process analyses** break down the steps or stages involved in completing a process.
- **Literary analyses** examine characterization, plot, imagery, or other elements in works of literature.
- **Essay exams** demonstrate understanding of course material by analyzing data using course concepts.

Workplace Writing

- **Grant proposals** analyze the issues you seek funding for, in order to address them.
- **Reviews of the arts** employ dramatic or literary analysis to assess artistic works.
- **Business plans** break down and analyze capital outlays, expenditures, profits, materials, and the like.
- **Medical charts** record analytical thinking and writing in relation to patient symptoms and possible options.
- **Legal briefs** break down and analyze facts of cases and elements of legal precedents, and apply legal rulings and precedents to new situations.
- **Case studies** describe and analyze the particulars of a specific medical, social service, advertising, or business case.

sees *The Wizard of Oz* in psychological, not political, terms; working with the theories of Karl Marx, Peter Dreier understands the movie in terms of the economic relationships among the characters. It's as if the writer of an analysis who adopts one analytical tool puts on a pair of glasses and sees an object in a specific way. Another writer, using a different tool (and a different pair of glasses), sees the object differently.

You might protest: Are there as many analyses of *The Wizard of Oz* as there are people to read the book or to see the movie? Yes, or at least as many analyses as there are analytical tools. This does not mean that all analyses are equally valid or useful. Each writer must convince the reader, using the power of her or his argument. In creating an analytical discussion, the writer must organize a series of related insights using the analytical tool to examine first one part and then another part of the object being studied. To read Harvey Greenberg's essay on *The Wizard of Oz* is to find paragraph after paragraph of related insights—first about Aunt Em, then the Wicked Witch, then Toto, and then the Wizard. All these insights point to Greenberg's single conclusion: that "Dorothy's 'trip' is a marvelous metaphor for the psychological journey every adolescent must make." Without Greenberg's analysis, we would probably not have thought about the movie as a psychological journey. This is precisely the power of an analysis: its ability to reveal objects or events in ways we would not otherwise have considered.

The writer's challenge is to convince readers that (1) the analytical tool being applied is legitimate and well matched to the object being studied; and (2) the analytical tool is being used systematically and insightfully to divide the object into parts and to make a coherent, meaningful statement about these parts and the object as a whole.

HOW TO WRITE ANALYSES

Let's consider a more extended example of analysis, one that approaches excessive TV watching as a type of addiction. This analytical passage illustrates the two defining features of the analysis: a statement of an analytical principle or definition and the use of that principle or definition in closely examining an object, behavior, or event. As you read, try to identify these features. An exercise with questions for discussion follows the passage.

THE PLUG-IN DRUG

Marie Winn

This analysis of television viewing as an addictive behavior appeared originally in Marie Winn's book *The Plug-In Drug: Television, Computers, and Family Life (2002)*. A writer and media critic, Winn has been interested in the effects of television on both individuals and the larger culture. In this passage, she carefully defines the term *addiction* and then applies it systematically to the behavior under study.

The word "addiction" is often used loosely and wryly in conversation. People will refer to themselves as "mystery-book addicts" or "cookie addicts." E. B. White wrote of his annual surge of interest in gardening: "We are hooked and are making an attempt to kick the habit." Yet nobody really believes that reading mysteries or ordering seeds by catalogue is serious enough to be compared with addictions to heroin or alcohol. In these cases the word "addiction" is used jokingly to denote a tendency to overindulge in some pleasurable activity.

People often refer to being "hooked on TV." Does this, too, fall into the lighthearted category of cookie eating and other pleasures that people pursue with unusual intensity? Or is there a kind of television viewing that falls into the more serious category of destructive addiction?

Not unlike drugs or alcohol, the television experience allows the participant to blot out the real world and enter into a pleasurable and passive mental state. To be sure, other experiences, notably reading, also provide a temporary respite from reality. But it's much easier to stop reading and return to reality than to stop watching television. The entry into another world offered by reading includes an easily accessible return ticket. The entry via television does not. In this way television viewing, for those vulnerable to addiction, is more like drinking or taking drugs—once you start it's hard to stop.

Just as alcoholics are only vaguely aware of their addiction, feeling that they control their drinking more than they really do ("I can cut it out any time I want—I just like to have three or four drinks before dinner"), many people overestimate their control over television watching. Even as they put off other activities to spend hour after hour watching television, they feel they could easily resume living in a different, less passive style. But somehow or other while the television set is present in their homes, it just stays on. With television's easy gratifications available, those other activities seem to take too much effort.

5   A heavy viewer (a college English instructor) observes:

> I find television almost irresistible. When the set is on, I cannot ignore it. I can't turn it off. I feel sapped, will-less, enervated. As I reach out to turn off the set, the strength goes out of my arms. So I sit there for hours and hours.

Self-confessed television addicts often feel they "ought" to do other things—but the fact that they don't read and don't plant their garden or sew or crochet or play games or have conversations means that those activities are no longer as desirable as television viewing. In a way, the lives of heavy viewers are as unbalanced by their television "habit" as drug addicts' or alcoholics' lives. They are living in a holding pattern, as it were, passing up the activities that lead to growth or development or a sense of accomplishment. This is one reason people talk about their television viewing so ruefully, so apologetically. They are aware that it is an unproductive experience, that by any human measure almost any other endeavor is more worthwhile.

It is the adverse effect of television viewing on the lives of so many people that makes it feel like a serious addiction. The television habit distorts the sense of time. It renders other experiences vague and curiously unreal while taking on a greater reality for itself. It weakens relationships by reducing and sometimes eliminating normal opportunities for talking, for communicating.

And yet television does not satisfy, else why would the viewer continue to watch hour after hour, day after day? "The measure of health," wrote the psychiatrist Lawrence Kubie, "is flexibility...and especially the freedom to cease when sated." But heavy television viewers can never be sated with their television experiences. These do not provide the true nourishment that satiation requires, and thus they find that they cannot stop watching.

Exercise 4.1

Reading Critically: Winn

In an analysis, an author first presents the analytical principle in full and then systematically applies parts of the principle to the object or phenomenon under study. In her brief analysis of television viewing, Marie Winn pursues an alternative, though equally effective, strategy by *distributing* parts of her analytical principle across the essay. Locate where Winn defines key elements of addiction. Locate where she uses each element as an analytical lens to examine television viewing as a form of addiction.

What function does ¶ 4 play in the analysis?

In the first two paragraphs, how does Winn create a funnel-like effect that draws readers into the heart of her analysis?

Recall a few television programs that genuinely moved you, educated you, humored you, or stirred you to worthwhile reflection or action. To what extent does Winn's analysis describe your positive experiences as a television viewer? (Consider how Winn might argue that from within an addicted state, a person may feel humored, moved, or educated but is in fact—from a sober outsider's point of view—deluded.) If Winn's analysis of television viewing as an addiction does *not* account for your experience, does it follow that her analysis is flawed? Explain.

Locate and Apply an Analytic Tool

The general purpose of all analysis is to enhance one's understanding of the subject under consideration. A good analysis provides a valuable—if sometimes unusual or unexpected—point of view, a way of *seeing*, a way of *interpreting* some phenomenon, person, event, policy, or pattern of behavior that otherwise may appear random or unexplainable. How well the analysis achieves its purpose depends upon the suitability to the subject and the precision of the analytical tools selected and upon the skill with which the writer (or speaker) applies these tools. Each reader must determine for her- or himself whether the analysis enhances understanding or—in the opposite case—is merely confusing or irrelevant. To what extent does it enhance your understanding of *The Wizard of Oz* to view the story in psychological terms? In political terms? To what extent does it enhance your understanding of excessive TV watching to view such behavior as an addiction?

When you are faced with writing an analysis, consider these two general strategies:

- Locate an analytic tool—a principle or definition that makes a general statement about the way something works.

- Systematically apply this principle or definition to the subject under consideration.

Let's more fully consider each of these strategies.

Locate an Analytic Tool

In approaching her subject, Marie Winn finds in the definition of "addiction" a useful principle for making sense of the way some people watch TV. The word "addiction," she notes, "is used jokingly to denote a tendency to overindulge in some pleasurable activity." The question she decides to tackle is whether, in the case of watching TV, such overindulgence is harmless, or whether it is destructive, and thus constitutes an addiction.

Make yourself aware, as both writer and reader, of a tool's strengths and limitations. Pose these questions of the analytical principle and definitions you use:

- Are they accurate?
- Are they well accepted?
- Do you accept them?
- How successfully do they account for or throw light upon the phenomenon under consideration?
- What are the arguments against them?
- What are their limitations?

Since every principle of definition used in an analysis is the end product of an argument, you are entitled—even obligated—to challenge it. If the analytical tool is flawed, the analysis that follows from it will necessarily be flawed.

Some, for example, would question whether addiction is a useful concept to apply to television viewing. First, we usually think of addiction as applying only to substances such as alcohol, nicotine, or drugs (whether legal or illegal). Second, many people think that the word "addiction" carries inappropriate moral connotations: We disapprove of addicts and think that they have only themselves to blame for their condition. For a time, the American

Psychiatric Association dropped the word "addiction" from its definitive guide to psychological disorders, the *Diagnostic and Statistical Manual of Mental Disorders* (DSM), in favor of the more neutral term "dependence." (The latest edition of the DSM has returned to the term "addiction.")

On the other hand, "addiction"—also known as "impulse control disorder"—has long been applied to behavior as well as to substances. People are said to be addicted to gambling, to shopping, to eating, to sex, even to hoarding newspapers. The editors of the new DSM are likely to add Internet addiction to the list of impulse control disorders. The term even has national implications: Many argue that this country must break its "addiction" to oil. Thus, there is considerable precedent for Winn to argue that excessive TV watching constitutes an addiction.

Apply the Analytic Tool

Having suggested that TV watching may be an addiction, Winn uses established psychological criteria* to identify the chief components of addictive behavior. She then applies each one of them to the behavior under consideration. In doing so, she presents her case that TV is a "plug-in drug"; and her readers are free to evaluate the success and persuasiveness of her analysis.

In the body of her analysis, Winn systematically applies the component elements of addiction to TV watching. She does this by identifying the major components of addiction and applying them to television watching. Users:

1. Turn away from the real world.
2. Overestimate how much control they have over their addiction.
3. Lead unbalanced lives and turn away from social activities.
4. Develop a distorted sense of time.
5. Are never satisfied with their use.

Analysis Across the Curriculum

The principle that you select can be a theory as encompassing as the statement that *myths are the enemy of truth*. It can be as modest as the definition of a term such as *addiction* or *comfort*. As you move from one subject area to

---

*For example, the Web site AddictionsandRecovery.org, drawing upon the *Diagnostic and Statistical Manual of Mental Disorders* (DSM) criteria, identifies seven components of substance addiction. A person who answers yes to three of the following questions meets the medical definition of addiction: **Tolerance** (increased use of drugs or alcohol increased over time); **Withdrawal** (adverse physical or emotional reactions to not using); **Difficulty controlling your use** (using more than you would like); **Negative consequences** (using even though use negatively affects mood, self-esteem, health, job, or family); **Neglecting or postponing activities** (putting off or reducing social, recreational, work in order to use); **Spending significant time or emotional energy** (spending significant time obtaining, using, concealing, planning, recovering from, or thinking about use); **Desire to cut down**.

another, the principles and definitions you use for analysis will change, as these assignments illustrate:

Sociology: Write a paper in which you place yourself in American society by locating both your absolute position and relative rank on each single criterion of social stratification used by Lenski and Lenski. For each criterion, state whether you have attained your social position by yourself or have "inherited" that status from your parents.

Literature: Apply principles of Jungian psychology to Hawthorne's "Young Goodman Brown." In your reading of the story, apply Jung's principles of the *shadow, persona*, and *anima.*

Physics: Use Newton's second law ($F = ma$) to analyze the acceleration of a fixed pulley from which two weights hang: m_1 (.45 kg) and m_2 (.90 kg). Explain in a paragraph the principle of Newton's law and your method of applying it to solve the problem. Assume your reader is not comfortable with mathematical explanations: Do not use equations in your paragraph.

Finance: Using Guilford C. Babcock's "Concept of Sustainable Growth" (*Financial Analysis* 26 [May–June 1970]: 108–114), analyze the stock price appreciation of the XYZ Corporation, figures for which are attached.

The analytical tools to be applied in these assignments must be appropriate to the discipline. Writing in response to the sociology assignment, you would use sociological principles developed by Lenski and Lenski. In your literature class, you would use principles of Jungian psychology; in physics, Newton's second law; and in finance, a particular writer's concept of "sustainable growth." But whatever discipline you are working in, the first part of your analysis will clearly state which (and whose) principles and definitions you are applying. For audiences unfamiliar with these principles, you will need to explain them; if you anticipate objections to their use, you will need to argue that they are legitimate principles capable of helping you conduct the analysis.

Formulate a Thesis

Like any other thesis, the thesis of an analysis compresses into a single sentence the main idea of your presentation. Some authors omit an explicit thesis statement, preferring to leave the thesis implied. Underlying Winn's analysis, for example, is an implied thesis: "By applying my multipart definition, we can understand television viewing as an addiction." Other authors may take two or perhaps even more sentences to articulate their thesis. But stated or implied, one sentence or more, your thesis must be clearly formulated at least in your own mind if your analysis is to hold together.

GUIDELINES FOR WRITING ANALYSES

Unless you are asked to follow a specialized format, especially in the sciences or the social sciences, you can present your analysis as a paper by following the guidelines below. As you move from one class to another, from discipline to discipline, the principles and definitions you use as the basis for your analyses will change, but the following basic components of analysis will remain the same.

- *Create a context for your analysis.* Introduce and summarize for readers the object, event, or behavior to be analyzed. Present a strong case for why an analysis is needed: Give yourself a motivation to write, and give readers a motivation to read. Consider setting out a problem, puzzle, or question to be investigated.
- *Locate an analytic tool—a principle or definition that will form the basis of your analysis.* Plan to devote an early part of your analysis to arguing for the validity of this principle or definition if your audience is not likely to understand it or if they are likely to think that the principle or definition is not valuable.
- *Analyze your topic by applying your selected analytic tool to the topic's component elements.* Systematically apply elements of the analytic tool to parts of the activity or object under study. You can do this by posing specific questions, based on your analytic principle or definition, about the object or phenomenon. Discuss what you find, part by part (organized perhaps by question), in clearly defined subsections of the paper.
- *Conclude by stating clearly what is significant about your analysis.* When considering your analytical paper as a whole, what new or interesting insights have you made concerning the object under study? To what extent has your application of the definition or principle helped you to explain how the object works, what it might mean, or why it is significant?

The analysis itself, as we have indicated, is a two-part argument. The first part states and establishes your use of a certain principle or definition that serves as your analytic tool. The second part applies specific parts or components of the principle or definition to the topic at hand.

Develop an Organizational Plan

You will benefit enormously in the writing of a first draft if you plan out the logic of your analysis. Turn key elements of your analytical principle or definition into questions, and then develop the paragraph-by-paragraph logic of the paper.

Turning Key Elements of a Principle or a Definition into Questions

Prepare for an analysis by phrasing questions based on the definition or principle you are going to apply, and then directing those questions to the activity or object to be studied. The method is straightforward:

- State as clearly as possible the principle or definition to be applied.
- Divide the principle or definition into its parts.
- Using each part, form a question.

For example, Marie Winn develops a multipart definition of addiction, each part of which is readily turned into a question that she directs at a specific behavior: television viewing. Her analysis of television viewing can be understood as *responses* to each of her analytical questions. Note that in her brief analysis, Winn does not first define addiction and then analyze television viewing. Rather, *as* she defines aspects of addiction, she analyzes television viewing.

Developing the Paragraph-by-Paragraph Logic of Your Paper

The following paragraph from Marie Winn's analysis illustrates the typical logic of a paragraph in an analytical paper:

> Self-confessed television addicts often feel they "ought" to do other things—but the fact that they don't read and don't plant their garden or sew or crochet or play games or have conversations means that those activities are no longer as desirable as television viewing. In a way, the lives of heavy viewers are as unbalanced by their television "habit" as drug addicts' or alcoholics' lives. They are living in a holding pattern, as it were, passing up the activities that lead to growth or development or a sense of accomplishment. This is one reason people talk about their television viewing so ruefully, so apologetically. They are aware that it is an unproductive experience, that by any human measure almost any other endeavor is more worthwhile.

We see in this paragraph the typical logic of an analysis:

- *The writer introduces a specific analytical tool.* Winn refers to one of the established components of addiction: The addictive behavior crowds out and takes precedence over other, more fruitful activities.
- *The writer applies this analytical tool to the object being examined.* Winn points out that people who spend their time watching television "don't read and don't plant their garden or sew or crochet or play games or have conversations...."
- *The writer uses the tool to identify and then examine the significance of some aspect of the subject under discussion.* Having

applied the analytic tool to the subject of television viewing, Winn generalizes about the significance of what is revealed: "This is one reason people talk about their television viewing so ruefully, so apologetically. They are aware that it is an unproductive experience, that by any human measure almost any other endeavor is worthwhile."

An analytic paper takes shape when a writer creates a series of such paragraphs, links them with an overall logic, and draws a general conclusion concerning what was learned through the analysis. Here is the logical organization of Marie Winn's analysis:

- **Paragraph 1:** Introduces the word "addiction" and indicates how the term is generally used.
- **Paragraph 2:** Suggests that television watching might be viewed as a "destructive addiction."
- **Paragraph 3:** Discusses the first component of the definition of addiction: an experience that "allows the participant to blot out the real world and enter into a pleasurable and passive mental state." Applies this first component to television viewing.
- **Paragraphs 4 and 5:** Discusses the second component of addiction—the participant has an illusion of control—and applies this to the experience of television viewing.
- **Paragraph 6:** Discusses the third component of addiction—because it requires so much time and emotional energy, the addictive behavior crowds out other, more productive or socially desirable activities—and applies this to the experience of television viewing.
- **Paragraph 7:** Discusses the fourth component of addiction—the negative consequences arising from the behavior—and applies this to the experience of television viewing.
- **Paragraph 8:** Discusses the fifth component of addiction—the participant is never satisfied because the experience is essentially empty—and applies this to the experience of television viewing. Note that in this paragraph, Winn brings in for support a relevant quotation by the psychiatrist Lawrence Kubie.

Draft and Revise Your Analysis

You will usually need at least two drafts to produce a paper that presents your idea clearly. The biggest changes in your paper will typically come between your first and second drafts. No paper that you write, analysis or otherwise, will be complete until you revise and refine your single compelling idea—in the case of analysis, your analytical conclusion about what the object, event, or behavior being examined means or how it is significant. You revise and refine by evaluating your first draft, bringing to it many of the same questions you pose when evaluating any piece of writing:

- Are the facts accurate?
- Are my opinions supported by evidence?
- Are the opinions of others authoritative?
- Are my assumptions clearly stated?
- Are key terms clearly defined?
- Is the presentation logical?
- Are all parts of the presentation well developed?
- Are significant opposing points of view presented?

Address these same questions to the first draft of your analysis, and you will have solid information to guide your revision.

Write an Analysis, Not a Summary

The most common error made in writing analyses—an error that is *fatal* to the form—is to present readers with a summary only. For analyses to succeed, you must *apply* a principle or definition and reach a conclusion about the object, event, or behavior you are examining. By definition, a summary (see Chapter 1) includes none of your own conclusions. Summary is naturally a part of analysis; you will need to summarize the object or activity being examined and, depending on the audience's needs, summarize the principle or definition being applied. But in an analysis, you must take the next step and share insights that suggest the meaning or significance of some object, event, or behavior.

Make Your Analysis Systematic

Analyses should give the reader the sense of a systematic, purposeful examination. Marie Winn's analysis illustrates the point: She sets out specific elements of addictive behavior in separate paragraphs and then uses each, within its paragraph, to analyze television viewing. Winn is systematic in her method, and we are never in doubt about her purpose.

Imagine another analysis in which a writer lays out four elements of a definition and then applies only two, without explaining the logic for omitting the others. Or imagine an analysis in which the writer offers a principle for analysis but directs it to only a half or a third of the object being discussed, without providing a rationale for doing so. In both cases the writer fails to deliver on a promise basic to analyses: Once a principle or definition is presented, it should be thoroughly and systematically applied.

Answer the "So What?" Question

An analysis should make readers *want* to read it. It should give readers a sense of getting to the heart of the matter, that what is important in the object or activity under analysis is being laid bare and discussed in revealing ways. If when rereading the first draft of your analysis, you cannot imagine readers saying, "I never thought of ＿＿＿＿＿ this way," then something may be seriously wrong. Reread closely to determine why the paper might leave readers flat and exhausted, as opposed to feeling that they have gained new and important insights. Closely reexamine your own motivations for writing. Have *you* learned anything significant through the analysis? If not, neither will readers, and they will turn away. If you have gained important insights through your analysis, communicate them clearly. At some point, pull together your related insights and say, in effect, "Here's how it all adds up."

CRITICAL READING FOR ANALYSIS

- *Read to get a sense of the whole in relation to its parts.* Whether you are clarifying for yourself a principle or a definition to be used in an analysis, or you are reading a text that you will analyze, understand how parts function to create the whole. If a definition or principle consists of parts, use them to organize sections of your analysis. If your goal is to analyze a text, be aware of its structure: Note the title and subtitle; identify the main point and subordinate points and where they are located; break the material into sections.

- *Read to discover relationships within the object being analyzed.* Watch for patterns. When you find them, be alert, for they create an occasion to analyze, to use a principle or definition as a guide in discussing what the patterns may mean.

  In fiction, a pattern might involve responses of characters to events or to each other, the recurrence of certain words or phrasings, images, themes, or turns of plot (to name a few examples).

  In poetry, a pattern might involve rhyme schemes, rhythm, imagery, figurative or literal language, and more.

The challenge to you as a reader is first to see a pattern (perhaps using a guiding principle or definition to do so) and then to locate other instances of that pattern. Reading carefully in this way prepares you to conduct an analysis.

Attribute Sources Appropriately

In an analysis, you often work with just a few sources and apply insights from them to some object or phenomenon you want to understand more thoroughly. Because you are not synthesizing large quantities of data, and because the strength of an analysis derives mostly from *your* application of a principle or definition, the opportunities for not appropriately citing sources are diminished. However, take special care to cite and quote, as necessary, those sources that you draw upon throughout the analysis.

When *Your* Perspective Guides the Analysis

In some cases, a writer's analysis of a phenomenon or a work of art may not result from anything as structured as a principle or a definition. It may instead follow from the writer's cultural or personal outlook, perspective, or interests. Imagine reading a story or observing the lines of a new building and being asked to analyze it—based not on someone else's definition or principle, but on your own. Your analysis of the story might largely be determined by your preference for fast pacing; intrepid, resourceful heroes; and pitiless, black-hearted villains. Among the principles you might use in analyzing the building are your admiration for curved exterior surfaces and the imaginative use of glass.

Like analyses based on principles or definitions, analyses based on one's personal perspective probe the parts of things to understand how they work and what they mean. They are likewise carefully structured, examining one part of a phenomenon at a time. The essential purpose of the analysis, to *reveal*, remains unchanged. This goal distinguishes the analysis from the critique, whose main purpose is to *evaluate* and *assess validity.*

An intriguing example of how shifts in personal perspective over time may affect one's analysis of a particular phenomenon is offered by Terri Martin Hekker. In 1977, Hekker wrote an op-ed for the *New York Times*, viewing traditional marriage from a perspective very different from that of contemporary feminists, who, she felt, valued self-fulfillment through work more than their roles as traditional housewives:

> I come from a long line of women...who never knew they were un-fulfilled. I can't testify that they were happy, but they *were* cheerful.... They took pride in a clean, comfortable home and satisfaction in serving a good meal because no one had explained to them that the only work worth doing is that for which you get paid.

Hekker's view of the importance of what she calls "housewifery"—the role of the traditional American wife and mother—derived from her own personal standards and ideals, which themselves derived from a cultural perspective that she admitted were no longer in fashion in the late 1970s.

Almost thirty years later (2006), Hekker's perspective had dramatically shifted. Her shattering experiences in the wake of her unexpected divorce had changed her view—and as a result, her analysis—of the status, value, and prospects of the traditional wife:

> Like most loyal wives of our generation, we'd contemplated eventual widowhood but never thought we'd end up divorced.... If I had it to do over again, I'd still marry the man I married and have my children.... But I would have used the years after my youngest started school to further my education. I could have amassed two doctorates using the time and energy I gave myself to charitable and community causes and been better able to support myself.*

Hekker's new analysis of the role of the traditional wife derives from her changed perspective, based on her own experience and the similar experiences of a number of her divorced friends.

If you find yourself writing an analysis guided by your own insights, not by someone else's, then you owe your reader a clear explanation of your guiding principles and the definitions by which you will probe the subject under study. Continue using the Guidelines for Writing Analyses (see p. 121), modifying this advice as you think fit to accommodate your own personal outlook, perspective, or interests. Above all, remember to structure your analysis with care. Proceed systematically and emerge with a clear statement about what the subject means, how it works, or why it might be significant.

DEMONSTRATION: ANALYSIS

Linda Shanker wrote the following paper as a first-semester sophomore in response to this assignment from her sociology professor:

> Read Robert H. Knapp's "A Psychology of Rumor" in your course anthology [*see Chapter 7 for excerpt from Knapp*]. Use some of Knapp's observations about rumor to examine a particular rumor that you have read about in your reading during the first few weeks of this course. Write for readers much like yourself: freshmen or sophomores who have taken one course in sociology. Your object in this paper is to draw upon Knapp to shed light on how the particular rumor you select spread so widely and so rapidly.

---

*"Modern Love, Paradise Lost" by Terri Martin Hekker from *The New York Times*, January 1, 2006 © 2006 The New York Times. All rights reserved. Used by permission and protected by the Copyright laws of the United States. The printing, copying, redistribution, or retransmission of this Content without express written permission is prohibited. www.nytimes.com

MODEL ANALYSIS

Linda Shanker

Social Psychology 1

UCLA

17 November 2010

The Case of the Missing Kidney: An Analysis of Rumor

> Rumor! What evil can surpass her speed?
>
> In movement she grows mighty, and achieves
>
> strength and dominion as she swifter flies...
>
> [F]oul, whispering lips, and ears, that catch
>
> at all...
>
> She can cling
>
> to vile invention and malignant wrong,
>
> or mingle with her word some tidings true.
>
> —Virgil, *The Aeneid* (Book IV, Ch. 8)

(1)   The phenomenon of rumor has been an object of fascination since ancient times. In his epic poem *The Aeneid*, Virgil noted some insidious truths about rumors: they spread quickly—especially in our own day, by means of phones, TV, e-mail, and Twitter; they can grow in strength and come to dominate conversation with vicious lies; and they are often mixed with a small portion of truth, a toxic combination that provides the rumor with some degree of credibility. In more recent years, sociologists and psychologists have studied various aspects of rumors: why they are such a common feature of any society, how they tie in to our individual and group views of the world, how and why they spread, why people believe them, and finally, how they can be prevented and contained.

(2)   One of the most important studies is Robert H. Knapp's "A Psychology of Rumor," published in 1944. Knapp's article appeared during World War II (during which he was in charge of rumor control for the Massachusetts Committee of Public Safety), and many of his examples are drawn from rumors that sprang up during that conflict; but his analysis of

why rumors form and how they work remains just as relevant today. First, Knapp defines rumor as an unverified statement offered about some topic in the hope that others will believe it (22). He proceeds to classify rumors into three basic types: the *pipe-dream or wish rumor,* based on what we would like to happen; the *bogie rumor,* based on our fears and anxieties; and the *wedge-driving or aggression rumor,* based on "dividing groups and destroying loyalties" (23–24). He notes that rumors do not spread randomly through the population, but rather through certain "sub-groups and factions" who are most susceptible to believing them. Rumors spread particularly fast, he notes, when these groups do not trust officials to tell them the truth. Most important, he maintains, "rumors express the underlying hopes, fears, and hostilities of the group" (27).

Not all rumors gain traction, of course, and Knapp goes on to outline the qualities that make for successful rumors. For example, a good rumor must be "short, simple, and salient." It must be a good story. Qualities that make for a good story include "a humorous twist...striking and aesthetic detail...simplification of plot and circumstances...[and] exaggeration" (29). Knapp explains how the same rumor can take various forms, each individually suited to the groups among which it is circulating: "[n]ames, numbers, and places are typically the most unstable components of any rumor." Successful rumors adapt themselves to the particular circumstances, anxieties, prejudices of the group, and the details change according to the "tide of current swings in public opinion and interest" (30).

Knapp's insights are valuable in helping us to understand why some contemporary rumors have been so frightening and yet so effective, for instance, the rumor of the missing kidney. One version of this story, current in 1992, is recounted by Robert Dingwall, a sociologist at the University of Nottingham in England:

> A woman friend of another customer had a 17-year-old
> son who went to a night club in Nottingham, called
> the Black Orchid, one Friday evening. He did not come

Shanker 3

home, so she called the police, who were not very inter-

ested because they thought that he had probably picked

up a girl and gone home with her. He did not come

back all weekend, but rang his mother from a call box

on Monday, saying he was unwell. She drove out to pick

him up and found him slumped on the floor of the call

box. He said that he had passed out after a drink in the

club and remembered nothing of the weekend. There was

a neat, fresh scar on his abdomen. She took him to the

Queen's Medical Centre, the main emergency hospital in

the city, where the doctors found that he had had a kid-

ney removed. The police were called again and showed

much more interest. A senior officer spoke to the mother

and said that there was a secret surveillance operation

going on in this club and others in the same regional

chain in other East Midlands cities because they had

had several cases of the same kind and they thought

that the organs were being removed for sale by an Asian

surgeon. (181)

(5)   It is not clear where this rumor originated, though at around this
time the missing kidney story had served as the basis of a *Law and Order*
episode in 1992 and a Hollywood movie, *The Harvest*, released in 1992. In
any event, within a few months the rumor had spread throughout Britain,
with the name of the night club and other details varying according to
the city where it was circulating. The following year, the story was trans-
planted to Mexico; a year later it was set in India. In the Indian version,
the operation was performed on an English woman traveling alone who
went to a New Delhi hospital to have an appendectomy. Upon returning to
England, she still felt ill, and after she was hospitalized, it was discovered
that her appendix was still there but that her kidney had been removed.
In subsequent years the rumor spread to the United States, with versions
of the story set in Philadelphia, New Orleans, Houston, and Las Vegas. In

1997, the following message, addressed "Dear Friends," was posted on an
Internet message board:

> I wish to warn you about a new crime ring that is tar-
> geting business travelers. This ring is well organized,
> well funded, has very skilled personnel, and is currently
> in most major cities and recently very active in New
> Orleans. The crime begins when a business traveler goes
> to a lounge for a drink at the end of the work day. A
> person in the bar walks up as they sit alone and offers
> to buy them a drink. The last thing the traveler remem-
> bers until they wake up in a hotel room bath tub, their
> body submerged to their neck in ice, is sipping that
> drink. There is a note taped to the wall instructing them
> not to move and to call 911. A phone is on a small table
> next to the bathtub for them to call. The business trav-
> eler calls 911 who have become quite familiar with this
> crime. The business traveler is instructed by the
> 911 operator to very slowly and carefully reach behind
> them and feel if there is a tube protruding from their
> lower back. The business traveler finds the tube and
> answers, "Yes." The 911 operator tells them to remain
> still, having already sent paramedics to help. The opera-
> tor knows that both of the business traveler's kidneys
> have been harvested. This is not a scam or out of a
> science fiction novel, it is real. It is documented and
> confirmable. If you travel or someone close to you
> travels, please be careful. ("You've Got to Be")

Subsequent posts on this message board supposedly confirmed this story   ⑥
("Sadly, this is very true"), adding different details.

Is there any truth to this rumor? None, whatsoever—not in any   ⑦
of its forms. Police and other authorities in various cities have posted
strenuous denials of the story in the newspapers, on official Web sites,

and in internal correspondence, as have The National Business Travel Association, the American Gem Trade Association, and the Sherwin Williams Co. ("'Stolen' Kidney Myth Circulating"). As reported in the rumor-reporting website Snopes.com, "the National Kidney Foundation has asked any individual who claims to have had his or her kidneys illegally removed to step forward and contact them. So far no one's showed up." The persistence and power of the missing kidney rumor can be more fully understood if we apply four of Knapp's principles of rumor formation and circulation to this particular urban legend: his notion of the "bogie"; the "striking" details that help authenticate a "good story" and that change as the rumor migrates to different populations; the ways a rumor can ride swings of public opinion; and the mingling of falsehood with truth.

(8)   The kidney rumor is first and foremost the perfect example of Knapp's bogie rumor, the rumor that draws its power from our fears and anxieties. One source of anxiety is being alone in a strange place. (Recall the scary folk tales about children lost in the forest, soon to encounter a witch.) These dreaded kidney removals almost always occur when the victim is away from home, out of town or even out of the country. Most of us enjoy traveling, but we may also feel somewhat uneasy in unfamiliar cities. We're not comfortably on our own turf, so we don't quite know our way around; we don't know what to expect of the local population; we don't feel entirely safe, or at least, we feel that some of the locals may resent us and take advantage of us. We can relate to the 17-year-old in the Nottingham nightclub, to the young English woman alone in New Delhi, to the business traveler having a drink in a New Orleans lounge.

(9)   Of course, our worry about being alone in an unfamiliar city is nothing compared to our anxiety about being cut open. Even under the best of circumstances (such as to save our lives), no one looks forward to surgery. The prospect of being drugged, taken to an unknown facility, and having members of a crime ring remove one of our organs without our

knowledge or consent—as apparently happened to the various subjects
of this rumor—would be our worst nightmare. It's little wonder that this
particular "bogie" man has such a powerful grip on our hearts.

Our anxiety about the terrible things that may happen to us in a ⑩
strange place may be heightened because of the fear that our fate is just
punishment for the bad things that we have done. In the Nottingham
version of the rumor, the victim "had probably picked up a girl and gone
home with her" (Dingwall 181). Another version of the story features "an
older man picked up by an attractive woman" (Dingwall 182). Still another
version of the story is set in Las Vegas, "Sin City, the place where Bad
Things Happen to the Unwary (especially the 'unwary' who were seen as
deservedly having brought it upon themselves, married men intent upon
getting up to some play-for-pay hanky panky" ("You've Got to Be"). As
Dingwall notes of this anxiety about a deserved fate, "[t]he moral is obvious: young people ought to be careful about night clubs, or more generally, about any activity which takes them out of a circle of family and
friends" (183).

In addition to being a classic bogie rumor, Knapp would suggest ⑪
that the missing kidney rumor persists because its "striking and aesthetic
detail[s]," while false, have the ring of truth and vary from one version
to another, making for a "good story" wherever the rumor spreads. Notice
that the story includes the particular names of the bar or nightclub, the
medical facility, the hotel; it describes the size and shape of the scar;
and it summarizes the instructions of the 911 operator to see if there is a
tube protruding from the victim's back. (The detail about the bathtub full
of ice and the advice to "call 911" was added to the story around 1995.)
As Knapp observes, "[n]ames, numbers, and places are typically the most
unstable components of any rumor" (30), and so the particular cities in
which the kidney operations are alleged to have been performed, as well
as the particular locations within those cities, changed as the rumor
spread. Another changing detail concerns the chief villains of this story.
Knapp notes that rumors adapt themselves to the particular anxieties and

prejudices of the group. Many groups hate or distrust foreigners and so we find different ethnic or racial "villains" named in different cities. In the Nottingham version of the story, the operation is performed by an "Asian surgeon." The English woman's kidney was removed by an Indian doctor. In another version of the story, a Kurdish victim of the kidney operation was lured to Britain "with the promise of a job by a Turkish businessman" ("You've Got to Be").

(12)   Third, Knapp observes that successful rumors "ride the tide of current swings in public opinion and interest" (30). From news reports as well as medical and police TV dramas, many people are aware that there is a great demand for organ transplants and that such demand, combined with a short supply, has given rise to a black market for illegally obtained organs. When we combine this awareness with stories that appear to provide convincing detail about the medical procedure involved (the "neat fresh scar," the tube, the name of the hospital), it is not surprising that many people accept this rumor as truth without question. One Internet correspondent, who affirmed that "Yes, this does happen" (her sister-in-law supposedly worked with a woman whose son's neighbor was a victim of the operation), noted that the only "good" thing about this situation was that those who performed the procedure were medically trained, used sterile equipment, made "exact and clean" incisions ("You've Got to Be"), and in general took measures to avoid complications that might lead to the death of the patient.

(13)   Finally, this rumor gains credibility because, as Virgil noted, rumor "mingle[s] with her word some tidings true." Although no documented case has turned up of a kidney being removed without the victim's knowledge and consent, there have been cases of people lured into selling their kidneys and later filing charges because they came to regret their decisions or were unhappy with the size of their payment ("You Got to Be").

(14)   Rumors can destroy reputations, foster distrust of government and other social institutions, and create fear and anxiety about perceived threats from particular groups of outsiders. Writing in the 1940s about rumors hatched during the war years, Knapp developed a powerful theory

Shanker 8

that helps us understand the persistence of rumors sixty years later. The rumor of the missing kidney, like any rumor, functions much like a mirror held up to society: it reveals anxiety and susceptibility to made-up but seemingly plausible "facts" related to contemporary social concerns. By helping us to understand the deeper structure of rumors, Knapp's theories can help free us from the "domination" and the "Foul, whispering lips" that Virgil observed so accurately 2,000 years ago.

Shanker 9

Works Cited

Dingwall, Robert. "Contemporary Legends, Rumors, and Collective Behavior: Some Neglected Resources for Medical Technology." *Sociology of Health and Illness* 23.2 (2001): 180–202. Print.

Knapp, Robert H. "A Psychology of Rumor." *Public Opinion Quarterly* 8.1 (1944): 22–37. Print.

"'Stolen' Kidney Myth Circulating: Organ Donation Hurt by Story of Kidney Heist." *UNOS*. United Network for Organ Sharing Newsroom Archive, 20 Aug. 1999. Web. 13 June 2010.

Virgil. *The Aeneid*. Trans. Theodore C. Williams. Perseus 4.0. *Perseus Digital Library*. Web. 17 Oct. 2010.

"You've Got to Be Kidneying." *Snopes.com*. Snopes, 12 Mar. 2008. Web. 12 June 2010.

Exercise 4.2

Informal Analysis of the Model Analysis

Before reading our analysis of this model analysis, write your own informal response. What are its strengths and weaknesses? To what extent does it follow the general Guidelines for Writing Analyses that we outlined on page 121? What function does each paragraph serve in the analysis as a whole?

THE STRATEGY OF THE ANALYSIS

- **Paragraph 1** creates a context for the analysis by introducing the phenomenon of rumor, indicating that it has been an object of fascination and study from ancient times (the poet Virgil is quoted) to the present.

- **Paragraphs 2 and 3** introduce the key principle that will be used to analyze the selected rumor, as explained by Robert H. Knapp in his article "A Psychology of Rumor." The principle includes Knapp's definition of rumor, his classification of rumors into three types, and the qualities that make for a successful rumor.

- **Paragraph 4** begins by indicating how Knapp's principles can be used to help us understand how rumor works, and then presents one particular manifestation of the rumor to be analyzed, the rumor of the missing kidney. Much of the paragraph consists of an extended quotation describing one of the original versions of the rumor, set in Nottingham, England.

- **Paragraph 5** describes how the missing kidney rumor metamorphosed and spread, first throughout England, and then to other countries, including Mexico, India, and the United States. A second extended quotation describes a version of the rumor set in New Orleans.

- **Paragraph 6** explains that the missing kidney rumor has no factual basis, but that its persistence and power can be accounted for by applying Knapp's principles. The final sentence of this paragraph is the thesis of the analysis.

- **Paragraph 7** applies the first of Knapp's principles to the missing kidney rumor: It is a bogie rumor that "draws its power from our fears and anxieties." One such fear is that of being alone in an unfamiliar environment.

- **Paragraph 8** continues to apply Knapp's principle of the bogie rumor, this time focusing on our fears about being unwillingly operated on.

- **Paragraph 9** discusses another aspect of the bogie rumor, the fear that what happens to us is a form of punishment for our own poor choices or immoral actions.

- **Paragraph 10** deals with a second of Knapp's principles, that the "facts" in rumors are constantly changing: names, places, and other details change as the rumor spreads from one city to another, but the reference to specific details lends the rumor a veneer of authenticity.

- **Paragraph 11** deals with a third of Knapp's principles: that successful rumors are often based on topics of current public interest—in this case, organ transplants and that, once again, a surface aura of facts makes the rumor appear credible.

- **Paragraph 12** returns to Virgil (cited in paragraph 1), who notes that successful rumors also appear credible because they often mix truth with fiction.

- **Paragraph 13** concluding the analysis, indicates why it is important to analyze rumor: Shedding light on how and why rumors such as this one spread may help us to counteract rumors' destructive effects.

A Brief Take

Chapter 5   **The Roar of the Tiger Mom**

IN THIS SECTION, you'll practice the skills you've learned in summary, critique, synthesis, and analysis. This "brief take" chapter on "tiger moms" is—as its name suggests—shorter than the four chapters that make up the main part of the anthology (Part III of this book), and it features a more limited number of writing assignments. The assignments are sequenced so that the early ones, such as those of summary and critique, can be incorporated into the more complex later ones, for example, analysis and argument synthesis.

After reading the articles you'll be asked to do some prewriting activities—drawing up lists of topics covered in the articles and establishing connections among topics from one reading to another. Then you'll be prompted to write summaries, critiques, syntheses, and analyses based on the articles, drawing upon the results of your prewriting activities and upon our suggestions for developing and organizing your papers.

This kind of practice will help firm up the skills you've learned in Part I and prepare you both for the lengthier reading and writing assignments of Part III and for the assignments of your other courses.

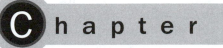

Chapter 5

The Roar of the Tiger Mom

"Chinese Mothers Are Superior" announced an op-ed in the *Wall Street Journal* in January 2011. That piece by Yale Law School professor Amy Chua and the book from which it was drawn, *The Battle Hymn of the Tiger Mother*, ignited a furious national debate over parenting methods. The online edition of the *Journal* records over 8,800 responses to the initial op-ed in which Chua lists the activities she does not allow her children to do (including attend a sleepover, watch TV or play computer games, or get any grade less than A). In the piece, Chua also describes her efforts to motivate her children to excellence (by calling one child "garbage," rejecting an amateurish birthday card as unworthy, and driving her 7-year-old to tears after she is unable, after hours of practice, to perfectly execute a complex piano piece). A cover story in *Time* magazine reports that when Chua appeared on the *Today* show, "the usually sunny host Meredith Viera could hardly contain her contempt as she read aloud a sample of viewer comments: 'She's a monster'; 'The way she raised her kids is outrageous'; 'Where is the love, the acceptance?'"

But Chua's ideas and methods resonated with many readers. At a time when American students are ranked seventeenth in the world in reading, twenty-third in science, and thirty-first in math, can the country settle for anything less than excellence? Can American citizens hope to compete with China and other rising economies in the global marketplace if they find academic mediocrity acceptable? And on the personal level, are parents helping their children if they accept anything less than the best, if they strive, in "Western" manner, not to damage their children's unearned self-esteem and to protect them from the consequences of failure?

And yet—what are the psychological consequences of the "Chinese" parenting methods advocated by Chua? To what extent should we allow children a childhood that is filled with play and exploration, not rigid goals? What is Chua's goal beyond strictly defined academic excellence? Does academic excellence correspond with success in one's profession? With one's broader happiness in life? Does a relentless focus on academic excellence in any way limit developing social skills?

These issues are the subject of the readings that follow. You'll be asked to consider such questions as you prepare several writing assignments. These assignments will culminate in an argument synthesis, a paper that will draw upon what you have already written for the summary, the critique, the explanatory synthesis, and the analysis.

Preceding the reading selections is a group of activities that will help prepare you for the writing assignments to come. The writing assignments themselves follow the readings.

READ; PREPARE TO WRITE

As you read these selections, prepare for the assignments by marking up the texts: Write notes to yourself in the margins and comment on what the authors have said.

And to prepare for the more ambitious of the assignments that follow—the explanatory and argument syntheses—consider drawing up a topic list of your sources as you read. For each topic about which two or more authors have something to say, jot down notes and page references. Here's an example entry:

Shaming/threatening children who underperform

Amy Chua: Sophia incident ("garbage") (p. 143); Lulu incidents ("Little White Donkey") (p. 145)

Hanna Rosin: birthday card; rejection of Chua's approach (p. 147)

Elizabeth Kolbert: Kolbert's sons' reaction to the Sophia episode (p. 158)

Such a topic list, keyed to your sources, will spare you the frustration of reading eight or nine sources and flipping through them later, saying, "Now where did I read that?" In the sample entry, we see four authors speaking to the wisdom of shaming or threatening underperforming children. At this early point, you don't need to know how you might write a paper based on this or any other topic. But a robust list with multiple topics and accurate notes for each lays the groundwork for your own discussion later and puts you in a good position to write a synthesis.

As it happens, the sample entry above should come in handy when you're preparing to write your own explanatory and argument syntheses on the subject of tiger moms. Creating a topic list with multiple entries will take you a bit more time as you read, but it will save you time as you write.

GROUP ASSIGNMENT #1: MAKE A TOPIC LIST

Working in groups of three or four, create a topic list for the selections in this chapter, making sure to jot down notes and page references for each. Here are some entries to get you started; find other topics common to two or more sources.

- overriding importance of children excelling academically—and musically
- importance for children in not wasting time (according to Chua) on nonacademic activities
- importance of practice and hard work for a child's sense of achievement and self-esteem
- effects of relentless academic focus on a child's creativity and/or social skills
- factors contributing to American competitiveness (or decline) in a global economy

GROUP ASSIGNMENT #2: CREATE A TOPIC WEB

Working in groups of three or four, create a network, or web, of connections among selected topics. That is, determine which topics relate or "speak" to other topics.

Articulate these connections in a series of different webs, understanding that not all topics will be connected to each web. For example, draw a line from one topic (say, the overriding importance of children excelling academically) to another (say, factors contributing to American competitiveness in a global economy). How are these topics related? As a group, generate as many topic webs as possible and, for each, as many connections as possible. At the conclusion of the session, you'll have in hand not only the fruits of Assignment #1, multiple authors discussing common topics, but you'll also have a potential connection *among* topics—basically, the necessary raw material for writing your syntheses.

Note that one synthesis—a single paper—couldn't possibly refer to every topic, or every connection among topics, that you have found. Your skill in preparing and writing a synthesis depends on your ability to *identify* closely related topics and to make and develop a claim that links and is supported by these topics.

The readings on "tiger moms" follow. After the readings, you will find a series of linked assignments that will lead you to write some combination of summary, critique, analysis, explanatory synthesis, and argument synthesis.

WHY CHINESE MOTHERS ARE SUPERIOR

Amy Chua

Amy Chua, a professor at Yale Law School, is the author of *The World on Fire: How Exporting Free Market Democracy Breeds Ethnic Hatred and Global Instability* (2002), *Day of Empire: How Hyperpowers Rise to Global Dominance—and Why They Fall* (2007), and *Battle Hymn of the Tiger Mother* (2011), from which the following selection was excerpted as an op-ed in the *Wall Street Journal* on January 8, 2011. The title "Why Chinese Mothers are Superior" was written by the editors of the *Journal*, not by Chua, most likely in an attempt (a successful one) to attract attention and encourage controversy.

A lot of people wonder how Chinese parents raise such stereotypically successful kids. They wonder what these parents do to produce so many math whizzes and music prodigies, what it's like inside the family, and whether they could do it too. Well, I can tell them, because I've done it. Here are some things my daughters, Sophia and Louisa, were never allowed to do:

- attend a sleepover
- have a playdate
- be in a school play
- complain about not being in a school play
- watch TV or play computer games
- choose their own extracurricular activities
- get any grade less than an A
- not be the No. 1 student in every subject except gym and drama
- play any instrument other than the piano or violin
- not play the piano or violin.

I'm using the term "Chinese mother" loosely. I know some Korean, Indian, Jamaican, Irish and Ghanaian parents who qualify too. Conversely, I know some mothers of Chinese heritage, almost always born in the West, who are not Chinese mothers, by choice or otherwise. I'm also using the term "Western parents" loosely. Western parents come in all varieties.

All the same, even when Western parents think they're being strict, they usually don't come close to being Chinese mothers. For example, my Western friends who consider themselves strict make their children practice their instruments 30 minutes every day. An hour at most. For a Chinese mother, the first hour is the easy part. It's hours two and three that get tough.

Despite our squeamishness about cultural stereotypes, there are tons of studies out there showing marked and quantifiable differences between Chinese and Westerners when it comes to parenting. In one study of 50 Western American mothers and 48 Chinese immigrant mothers, almost 70% of the Western mothers said either that "stressing academic success is not good for children" or that "parents need to foster the idea that learning is fun." By contrast, roughly 0% of the Chinese mothers felt the same way. Instead, the vast majority of the Chinese mothers said that they believe their children can be "the best" students, that "academic achievement reflects successful parenting," and that if children did not excel at school then there was "a problem" and parents "were not doing their job." Other studies indicate that compared to Western parents, Chinese parents spend approximately 10 times as long every day drilling academic activities with their children. By contrast, Western kids are more likely to participate in sports teams.

5   ⌈What Chinese parents understand is that nothing is fun until you're good at it.⌋ To get good at anything you have to work, and children on their own never want to work, which is why it is crucial to override their preferences. This often requires fortitude on the part of the parents because the child will resist; things are always hardest at the beginning, which is where Western parents tend to give up. But if done properly, the Chinese strategy produces a virtuous circle. Tenacious practice, practice, practice is crucial for excellence; rote repetition is underrated in America. Once a child starts to excel at something—whether it's math, piano, pitching or ballet—he or she gets praise, admiration and satisfaction. This builds confidence and makes the once not-fun activity fun. This in turn makes it easier for the parent to get the child to work even more.

Chinese parents can get away with things that Western parents can't. Once when I was young—maybe more than once—when I was extremely disrespectful to my mother, my father angrily called me "garbage" in our native Hokkien dialect. It worked really well. I felt terrible and deeply ashamed of what I had done. But it didn't damage my self-esteem or anything like that. I knew exactly how highly he thought of me. I didn't actually think I was worthless or feel like a piece of garbage.

As an adult, I once did the same thing to Sophia, calling her garbage in English when she acted extremely disrespectfully toward me. When I mentioned that I had done this at a dinner party, I was immediately ostracized. One guest named Marcy got so upset she broke down in tears and had to leave early. My friend Susan, the host, tried to rehabilitate me with the remaining guests.

The fact is that Chinese parents can do things that would seem unimaginable—even legally actionable—to Westerners. Chinese mothers can say to their daughters, "Hey fatty—lose some weight." By contrast, Western parents have to tiptoe around the issue, talking in terms of "health" and never ever mentioning the f-word, and their kids still end up in therapy for eating disorders and negative self-image. (I also once heard a Western father toast his adult daughter by calling her "beautiful and incredibly competent." She later told me that made her feel like garbage.)

Chinese parents can order their kids to get straight As. Western parents can only ask their kids to try their best. Chinese parents can say, "You're lazy. All your classmates are getting ahead of you." By contrast, Western parents have to struggle with their own conflicted feelings about achievement, and try to persuade themselves that they're not disappointed about how their kids turned out.

10   I've thought long and hard about how Chinese parents can get away with what they do. I think there are three big differences between the Chinese and Western parental mind-sets.

First, I've noticed that Western parents are extremely anxious about their children's self-esteem. They worry about how their children will feel if they fail at something, and they constantly try to reassure their children about how good they are notwithstanding a mediocre performance on a test or at a recital. In other words, Western parents are concerned about their children's psyches. Chinese parents aren't. They assume strength, not fragility, and as a result they behave very differently.

For example, if a child comes home with an A-minus on a test, a Western parent will most likely praise the child. The Chinese mother will gasp in horror and ask what went wrong. If the child comes home with a B on the test, some Western parents will still praise the child. Other Western parents will sit their child down and express disapproval, but they will be careful not to make their child feel inadequate or insecure, and they will not call their child "stupid," "worthless" or "a disgrace." Privately, the Western parents may worry that their child does not test well or have aptitude in the subject or that there is something wrong with the curriculum and possibly the whole school. If the child's grades do not improve, they may eventually schedule a meeting with the school principal to challenge the way the subject is being taught or to call into question the teacher's credentials.

If a Chinese child gets a B—which would never happen—there would first be a screaming, hair-tearing explosion. The devastated Chinese mother would then get dozens, maybe hundreds of practice tests and work through them with her child for as long as it takes to get the grade up to an A.

Chinese parents demand perfect grades because they believe that their child can get them. If their child doesn't get them, the Chinese parent assumes it's because the child didn't work hard enough. That's why the solution to substandard performance is always to excoriate, punish and shame the child. The Chinese parent believes that their child will be strong enough to take the shaming and to improve from it. (And when Chinese kids do excel, there is plenty of ego-inflating parental praise lavished in the privacy of the home.)

15   Second, Chinese parents believe that their kids owe them everything. The reason for this is a little unclear, but it's probably a combination of Confucian filial piety and the fact that the parents have sacrificed and done so much for their children. (And it's true that Chinese mothers get in the

trenches, putting in long grueling hours personally tutoring, training, interrogating and spying on their kids.) Anyway, the understanding is that Chinese children must spend their lives repaying their parents by obeying them and making them proud.

By contrast, I don't think most Westerners have the same view of children being permanently indebted to their parents. My husband, Jed, actually has the opposite view. "Children don't choose their parents," he once said to me. "They don't even choose to be born. It's parents who foist life on their kids, so it's the parents' responsibility to provide for them. Kids don't owe their parents anything. Their duty will be to their own kids." This strikes me as a terrible deal for the Western parent.

Third, Chinese parents believe that they know what is best for their children and therefore override all of their children's own desires and preferences. That's why Chinese daughters can't have boyfriends in high school and why Chinese kids can't go to sleepaway camp. It's also why no Chinese kid would ever dare say to their mother, "I got a part in the school play! I'm Villager Number Six. I'll have to stay after school for rehearsal every day from 3:00 to 7:00, and I'll also need a ride on weekends." God help any Chinese kid who tried that one.

Don't get me wrong: It's not that Chinese parents don't care about their children. Just the opposite. They would give up anything for their children. It's just an entirely different parenting model.

Here's a story in favor of coercion, Chinese-style. Lulu was about 7, still playing two instruments, and working on a piano piece called "The Little White Donkey" by the French composer Jacques Ibert. The piece is really cute—you can just imagine a little donkey ambling along a country road with its master—but it's also incredibly difficult for young players because the two hands have to keep schizophrenically different rhythms.

20   Lulu couldn't do it. We worked on it nonstop for a week, drilling each of her hands separately, over and over. But whenever we tried putting the hands together, one always morphed into the other, and everything fell apart. Finally, the day before her lesson, Lulu announced in exasperation that she was giving up and stomped off.

"Get back to the piano now," I ordered.
"You can't make me."
"Oh yes, I can."

Back at the piano, Lulu made me pay. She punched, thrashed and kicked. She grabbed the music score and tore it to shreds. I taped the score back together and encased it in a plastic shield so that it could never be destroyed again. Then I hauled Lulu's dollhouse to the car and told her I'd donate it to the Salvation Army piece by piece if she didn't have "The Little White Donkey" perfect by the next day. When Lulu said, "I thought you were going to the Salvation Army, why are you still here?" I threatened her with no lunch, no dinner, no Christmas or Hanukkah presents, no birthday parties for two, three, four years. When she still kept playing it wrong,

I told her she was purposely working herself into a frenzy because she was secretly afraid she couldn't do it. I told her to stop being lazy, cowardly, self-indulgent and pathetic.

25   Jed took me aside. He told me to stop insulting Lulu—which I wasn't even doing, I was just motivating her—and that he didn't think threatening Lulu was helpful. Also, he said, maybe Lulu really just couldn't do the technique—perhaps she didn't have the coordination yet—had I considered that possibility?

"You just don't believe in her," I accused.

"That's ridiculous," Jed said scornfully. "Of course I do."

"Sophia could play the piece when she was this age."

"But Lulu and Sophia are different people," Jed pointed out.

30   "Oh no, not this," I said, rolling my eyes. "Everyone is special in their special own way," I mimicked sarcastically. "Even losers are special in their own special way. Well don't worry, you don't have to lift a finger. I'm willing to put in as long as it takes, and I'm happy to be the one hated. And you can be the one they adore because you make them pancakes and take them to Yankees games."

I rolled up my sleeves and went back to Lulu. I used every weapon and tactic I could think of. We worked right through dinner into the night, and I wouldn't let Lulu get up, not for water, not even to go to the bathroom. The house became a war zone, and I lost my voice yelling, but still there seemed to be only negative progress, and even I began to have doubts.

Then, out of the blue, Lulu did it. Her hands suddenly came together—her right and left hands each doing their own imperturbable thing—just like that.

Lulu realized it the same time I did. I held my breath. She tried it tentatively again. Then she played it more confidently and faster, and still the rhythm held. A moment later, she was beaming.

"Mommy, look—it's easy!" After that, she wanted to play the piece over and over and wouldn't leave the piano. That night, she came to sleep in my bed, and we snuggled and hugged, cracking each other up. When she performed "The Little White Donkey" at a recital a few weeks later, parents came up to me and said, "What a perfect piece for Lulu—it's so spunky and so *her*."

35   Even Jed gave me credit for that one⌐ Western parents worry a lot about their children's self-esteem. But as a parent, one of the worst things you can do for your child's self-esteem is to let them give up⌐ On the flip side, there's nothing better for building confidence than learning you can do something you thought you couldn't.

There are all these new books out there portraying Asian mothers as scheming, callous, overdriven people indifferent to their kids' true interests. For their part, many Chinese secretly believe that they care more about their children and are willing to sacrifice much more for them than Westerners, who seem perfectly content to let their children turn out badly.

[I think it's a misunderstanding on both sides. All decent parents want to do what's best for their children. The Chinese just have a totally different idea of how to do that.]

Western parents try to respect their children's individuality, encouraging them to pursue their true passions, supporting their choices, and providing positive reinforcement and a nurturing environment. By contrast, the Chinese believe that the best way to protect their children is by preparing them for the future, letting them see what they're capable of, and arming them with skills, work habits and inner confidence that no one can ever take away.

MOTHER INFERIOR?

Hanna Rosin

Hanna Rosin is a contributing editor at the *Atlantic* and is working on a book based on her recent *Atlantic* cover story, "The End of Men." "Mother Inferior?" first appeared in the *Wall Street Journal* on January 15, 2011.

The other day I was playing a game called "Kids on Stage" with my 2-year-old. I had to act out "tiger," so I got down on all fours and roared. He laughed, so I roared even louder, which only made him laugh more. Eventually he came up to me, patted my head and said "kitty kat" with benevolent condescension. This perfectly sums up my status in the animal pack of mothers defined by Amy Chua's *Battle Hymn of the Tiger Mother*. There are the fierce tigers who churn out child prodigies, and then there are the pussycats who waste their afternoons playing useless board games and get bested by their own toddlers.

In pretty much every way, I am the weak-willed, pathetic Western parent that Ms. Chua describes. My children go on playdates and sleepovers; in fact I wish they would go on more of them. When they give me lopsided, hastily drawn birthday cards, I praise them as if they were Matisse, sometimes with tears in my eyes. (Ms. Chua threw back one quickly scribbled birthday card, saying "I reject this," and told her daughters they could do better.) My middle son is skilled at precisely the two extracurricular activities Ms. Chua most mocks: He just got a minor part in the school play as a fisherman, and he is a master of the drums, the instrument that she claims leads directly to using drugs (I'm not sure if she is joking or not).

I would be thrilled, of course, if my eldest child made it to Carnegie Hall at 14, which is the great crescendo of the Chua family story (although I would make sure to tell my other two children that they were fabulous in other ways!). But the chances that I would threaten to burn all her stuffed animals unless she played a piano piece perfectly, or to donate her favorite doll house to the Salvation Army piece by piece, as Ms. Chua did with her daughter, are exactly zero. It's not merely that such vigilant attention to how my daughter spends every minute of her afternoon is time-consuming and exhausting; after all, it takes time to play "Kids on Stage" and to drive to drum lessons, too. It's more that I don't have it in me. I just don't have the demented drive to pull it off.

Many American parents will read *Battle Hymn of the Tiger Mother* and feel somewhat defensive and regretful. *Well, I do make my Johnny practice his guitar twice a week! Or, Look, I have this nice discipline chart on my refrigerator with frowny faces for when he's rude at dinner!* But I don't feel all that defensive. In fact, I think Ms. Chua has the diagnosis of American childhood exactly backward. What privileged American children need is not more skills and rules and math drills. They need to lighten up and roam free, to express themselves in ways not dictated by their upright, over-invested parents. Like Ms. Chua, many American parents suffer from the delusion that, with careful enough control, a child can be made perfect. Ms. Chua does it with Suzuki piano books and insults, while many of my friends do it with organic baby food and playrooms filled with fully curated wooden toys. In both cases, the result is the same: an excess of children who are dutiful proto-adults, always responsible and good, incapable of proper childhood rebellion.

5   In the days since Ms. Chua's book has come out, the media have brought up horror stories of child prodigies gone bad, including this 16-year-old who stabbed her mother to death after complaining that her Chinese immigrant parents held her to impossibly high standards. Most prodigy stories, I imagine, involve more complicated emotions. (The Amy Chua of the book, by the way, is more seductive than the distilled media version. She is remarkably self-aware. "The truth is, I'm not good at enjoying life," she writes, and she never hesitates to tell stories that she knows make her look beastly. It's worth noting that, in TV and radio interviews about the book, she's been trending more pussycat).

I have a good friend who was raised by a Chinese-style mother, although her parents were actually German. Her mother pushed her to practice the violin for eight hours a day, and she rarely saw other people her age. Now she is my age, and she does not hate her mother or even resent her. She is grateful to her mother for instilling in her a drive and focus that she otherwise would have lacked. What she does hate is music, because it carries for her associations of loneliness and torture. She hasn't picked up the violin in a decade, and these days, she says, classical music leaves her cold. It's not an uncommon sentiment among prodigies: "I hate tennis," Andre Agassi says on the first page of his autobiography, "Open," "hate it with a dark and secret passion, and always have."

The oddest part of Ms. Chua's parenting prescription is that it exists wholly apart from any passion or innate talent. The Chua women rarely express pure love of music; instead they express joy at having mastered it. Ms. Chua writes that she listened to CDs of Itzhak Perlman to figure out "why he sounded so good." This conception of child prodigies is not just Chinese. It is the extreme expression of the modern egalitarian notion of genius, as described by Malcolm Gladwell in *Outliers*. Anyone can be a genius, if they just put in 10,000 hours of practice! It doesn't matter if they can carry a tune or have especially limber fingers. They don't even have to like music.

But why not wait for your children to show some small spark of talent or interest in an activity before you force them to work at it for hours a day? What would be so bad if they followed their own interests and became an expert flutist, or a soccer star or even a master tightrope walker? What's so special about the violin and the piano?

Ms. Chua's most compelling argument is that happiness comes from mastery. "What Chinese parents understand is that nothing is fun until you're good at it." There is some truth to this, of course. But there is no reason to believe that calling your child "lazy" or "stupid" or "worthless" is a better way to motivate her to be good than some other more gentle but persistent mode. There is a vast world between perfection and loserdom. With her own children, Ms. Chua does not just want them to be good at what they do; she wants them to be better than everyone else.

10 "Children on their own never want to work," Ms. Chua writes, but in my experience this is not at all true. Left to their own devices, many children of this generation still have giant superegos and a mad drive to succeed. They want to run faster than their siblings, be smarter than their classmates and save the world from environmental disaster. In my household, it's a struggle to get my children to steal a cookie from the cookie jar without immediately confessing.

Before I had children, I worried about all the wrong things. I was raised by (immigrant) parents who did not have a lot of money, and so I spent my childhood roaming the streets of Queens looking for an open handball court. My children, by contrast, have been raised by relatively well-off parents who can afford to send them to good schools and drum lessons. I wanted them to be coddled and never to experience hardship. But childhood, like life, doesn't work that way. Privilege does not shield a child from being painfully shy or awkward around peers or generally ostracized. There are a thousand ways a child's life can be difficult, and it's a parent's job to help them navigate through them.

Because Ms. Chua really likes bullet points, I will offer some of my own:

- Success will not make you happy.
- Happiness is the great human quest.
- Children have to find happiness themselves.
- It is better to have a happy, moderately successful child than a miserable high-achiever.

"Western parents," Ms. Chua writes, "have to struggle with their own conflicted feelings about achievement and try and persuade themselves that they're not disappointed in how their kids turned out." With that, she really has our number. At the present moment in Western parenting, we believe that our children are special and entitled, but we do not have the guts or the tools to make that reality true for them. This explains, I think, a large part of the fascination with Ms. Chua's book.

But *Battle Hymn of the Tiger Mother* will lead us down the wrong path. The answer is not to aim for more effective child-perfecting techniques; it is to give up altogether on trying to perfect our children. Now I look upon those aimless days wandering the streets of Queens with fondness, because my life since then, starting the moment I entered a competitive high school, has been one ladder rung after another.

15   In her book, Ms. Chua refers, with some disdain, to her mother-in-law's belief that childhood should be full of "spontaneity, freedom, discovery and experience." My mother-in-law believes that, too, and she is especially gifted at facilitating it with whatever tools are at hand: a cardboard box, some pots and pans, torn envelopes. One afternoon I watched her play with my then-2-year old daughter for hours with some elephant toothpick holders and Play-Doh. I suppose that I could quantify what my daughter learned in those few hours: the letter E, the meaning of "pachyderm," who Hannibal was and how to love her grandmother 2% more. But the real point is that they earned themselves knee scabs marching across those imaginary Alps, and pretty soon it was time for a nap.

AMY CHUA IS A WIMP

David Brooks

David Brooks is a columnist for the *New York Times* and a commentator on the PBS *News Hour* and National Public Radio. He has written for the *Wall Street Journal* and the *Washington Times* and has been an editor for *The Weekly Standard, The Atlantic,* and *Newsweek. His books include the anthology* Backward and Upward: The New Conservative Writing *(1996), a book of cultural commentary,* Bobos in Paradise: The New Upper Class and How They Got There *(2000), and* On Paradise Drive: How We Live Now (And Always Have) in the Future Tense *(2004). This article appeared in the New York Times on January 17, 2011.*

Sometime early last week, a large slice of educated America decided that Amy Chua is a menace to society. Chua, as you probably know, is the Yale professor who has written a bracing critique of what she considers the weak, cuddling American parenting style.

Chua didn't let her own girls go out on play dates or sleepovers. She didn't let them watch TV or play video games or take part in garbage activities like crafts. Once, one of her daughters came in second to a Korean kid in a math competition, so Chua made the girl do 2,000 math problems a night until she regained her supremacy. Once, her daughters gave her birthday cards of insufficient quality. Chua rejected them and demanded new cards. Once, she threatened to burn all of one of her daughter's stuffed animals unless she played a piece of music perfectly.

As a result, Chua's daughters get straight As and have won a series of musical competitions.

In her book, *Battle Hymn of the Tiger Mother*, Chua delivers a broadside against American parenting even as she mocks herself for her own extreme "Chinese" style. She says American parents lack authority and produce entitled children who aren't forced to live up to their abilities.

5   The furious denunciations began flooding my in-box a week ago. Chua plays into America's fear of national decline. Here's a Chinese parent working really hard (and, by the way, there are a billion more of her) and her kids are going to crush ours. Furthermore (and this Chua doesn't appreciate), she is not really rebelling against American-style parenting; she is the logical extension of the prevailing elite practices. She does everything over-pressuring upper-middle-class parents are doing. She's just hard core.

Her critics echoed the familiar themes. Her kids can't possibly be happy or truly creative. They'll grow up skilled and compliant but without the audacity to be great. She's destroying their love for music. There's a reason Asian-American women between the ages of 15 and 24 have such high suicide rates.

I have the opposite problem with Chua. I believe she's coddling her children. She's protecting them from the most intellectually demanding activities because she doesn't understand what's cognitively difficult and what isn't.

Practicing a piece of music for four hours requires focused attention, but it is nowhere near as cognitively demanding as a sleepover with 14-year-old girls. Managing status rivalries, negotiating group dynamics, understanding social norms, navigating the distinction between self and group—these and other social tests impose cognitive demands that blow away any intense tutoring session or a class at Yale.

Yet mastering these arduous skills is at the very essence of achievement. Most people work in groups. We do this because groups are much more efficient at solving problems than individuals (swimmers are often motivated to have their best times as part of relay teams, not in individual events). Moreover, the performance of a group does not correlate well with the average I.Q. of the group or even with the I.Q.'s of the smartest members.

10   Researchers at the Massachusetts Institute of Technology and Carnegie Mellon have found that groups have a high collective intelligence when

members of a group are good at reading each others' emotions—when they take turns speaking, when the inputs from each member are managed fluidly, when they detect each others' inclinations and strengths.

Participating in a well-functioning group is really hard. It requires the ability to trust people outside your kinship circle, read intonations and moods, understand how the psychological pieces each person brings to the room can and cannot fit together.

This skill set is not taught formally, but it is imparted through arduous experiences. These are exactly the kinds of difficult experiences Chua shelters her children from by making them rush home to hit the homework table.

Chua would do better to see the classroom as a cognitive break from the truly arduous tests of childhood. Where do they learn how to manage people? Where do they learn to construct and manipulate metaphors? Where do they learn to perceive details of a scene the way a hunter reads a landscape? Where do they learn how to detect their own shortcomings? Where do they learn how to put themselves in others' minds and anticipate others' reactions?

These and a million other skills are imparted by the informal maturity process and are not developed if formal learning monopolizes a child's time.

15   So I'm not against the way Chua pushes her daughters. And I loved her book as a courageous and thought-provoking read. It's also more supple than her critics let on. I just wish she wasn't so soft and indulgent. I wish she recognized that in some important ways the school cafeteria is more intellectually demanding than the library. And I hope her daughters grow up to write their own books, and maybe learn the skills to better anticipate how theirs will be received.

In the Eye of the Tiger

Meghan Daum

Meghan Daum is a columnist for the *Los Angeles Times*, where this piece first appeared on January 20, 2011. Her work has also appeared in the *New Yorker*, *Harper's*, *GQ*, and the *Village Voice*. Daum has also published a novel, *The Quality of Life Report* (2004), a collection of essays, *My Misspent Youth* (2001), and a memoir, *Life Would Be Perfect if I Lived in That House* (2010).

Amy Chua, a Yale law professor and mother of two, was unknown to most of the world until two weeks ago. On Jan. 8, the *Wall Street Journal* published an excerpt from her then-forthcoming, now-bestselling book, *Battle Hymn of the Tiger Mother*. Part memoir and part manifesto, the excerpt was titled "Why Chinese Mothers Are Superior" and led with a list of activities and behaviors that Chua's two daughters, now teen-agers, have never been allowed to engage in. These include "attend a sleepover," "have a play date," "be in a school play," "complain about not being in a school play" and "get anything less than an A."

That wasn't all. Chua's stratospherically demanding parenting tech-nique, a carryover from her own Chinese immigrant parents, required playing violin or piano and practicing several hours a day, even if that meant rising before dawn. In a particularly harrowing passage, Chua forces her 7-year-old into learning a difficult piano piece. When the child screamed and kicked and tore up the music score, Chua hauled the girl's dollhouse to the car and threatened to donate it to the Salvation Army.

"I told her she was purposely working herself into a frenzy because she was secretly afraid she couldn't do it," Chua writes. "I told her to stop being lazy, cowardly, self-indulgent and pathetic." She also denied the girl a bathroom break as they worked on the piece well into the evening.

Needless to say, the excerpt went viral. Though many readers were ap-palled by her methods, others praised her for bucking the trend of parents wanting to be their kids' best friend.

5 But Chua, who's reportedly received death threats, now appears to be trying to soften her message. At Vroman's Bookstore in Pasadena on Tuesday night, she was in defense mode and even a bit flustered, saying repeatedly that the excerpt had been misleading and that the book, which "poured" out of her over eight weeks, was meant to be funny in places. But even as she backed away from the deadpan, inflammatory tone of the book—and chose to read from the ending so we could see she'd changed her ways—Chua stood her ground about the effectiveness (if not neces-sarily the superiority) of her parenting philosophy.

"We talk about giving our kids freedom," she said, "but the way to be free is to be able to get a good job and have the opportunities that come from hard work."

I can't argue with that. And, yes, I feel her pain that the *Wall Street Journal* went for the most incendiary stuff in "Tiger Mother" and topped it with a headline she didn't write. But once I read the book—this can be done, cover to cover, in a few hours—it became painfully clear that Chua's image problem isn't really due to her mothering style. It's due to her in-ability as a writer to handle the provocative tone of her book, particularly the ostensibly self-parodying aspects. (I think the dollhouse bit was an attempt to make fun of herself.) Where in real life she might be endearingly wacky, she comes across in the book as possibly crazy. For all her control-ling impulses, as a writer she lacks the wit, pacing and emotional honesty to effectively control her own material.

Which is a shame really, because Chua has important things to say. Her book raises necessary questions about how permissive parenting affects not just children but society. She talks unflinchingly about the anxieties of the immigrant experience and the way the attendant work ethic feeds the myth that Asians are simply genetically smarter than Westerners.

In the end, though, I have to wonder if her lack of sensitivity to the tone and impact of her words doesn't in fact deliver a judgment about the very upbringing she espouses.

10   Chua's parenting method might garner perfect grades and test scores and multiple Harvard degrees (which she has, thank you very much). But maybe what gets sacrificed along the way is the ability to genuinely laugh at yourself, to recognize the absurd and to weave it into your existence—in other words, to hone the tools necessary for effectively seeing yourself in full, so that you can make others understand where you're coming from.

That's less a skill that can be learned than a gift that can come from only one source: the experience of failure. Surely no kid should be denied that.

★ TIGER MOM VS. TIGER MAILROOM

Patrick Goldstein

Patrick Goldstein writes "The Big Picture," a *Los Angeles Times* column dealing with the film industry. This article first appeared in the *Times* on February 6, 2011.

It's hard to go anywhere these days, especially if you're a parent with young kids, where the conversation doesn't eventually turn to Amy Chua's red-hot child-rearing memoir, *Battle Hymn of the Tiger Mother*. It offers a provocative depiction of Chinese-style extreme parenting—her daughters are not allowed to watch TV, have playdates or get any grade below an A, all as preparation for success in life, beginning with getting into an Ivy League school, like their Tiger Mom, who went to Harvard and now teaches at Yale Law School.

But of all the heated reaction to Chua's parenting strategy, none was as compelling as what former Harvard President Larry Summers had to say when he discussed parenting with Chua at the recent World Economic Forum in Davos, Switzerland. Summers made a striking point, arguing that the two Harvard students who'd had the most transformative impact on the world in the past 25 years were Bill Gates and Mark Zuckerberg, yet neither had, ahem, graduated from college. If they had been brought up by a Tiger Mom, Summers imagined, she would've been bitterly disappointed.

I have no beef with Chua's parenting code, which hardly seems any more extreme than the neurotic ambitions of mothers and fathers I'm exposed to living on the Westside of Los Angeles. But if Chua wants a radically different perspective on the relationship between higher education and career achievement, she should spend some time in Hollywood, a place that's been run for nearly a century by men who never made it through or even to college. The original moguls were famously uneducated, often having started as peddlers and furriers before finding their perches atop the studio dream factories. But even today, the industry is still dominated by titanic figures, both on the creative and on the business side, who never got anywhere near Harvard Yard.

A short list of the industry leaders who never finished or even attended college would include Steve Jobs, David Geffen, Steven Spielberg, Jeffrey Katzenberg, James Cameron, Clint Eastwood, Barry Diller, Ron Meyer, Peter Jackson, Harvey Weinstein, Scott Rudin and Quentin Tarantino. Some of this is clearly a generational thing, since everyone on that list is over 40. On the other hand, the younger new-media icons seem as likely to be degree-free as their Hollywood brethren, whether it's Zuckerberg or the founders of Twitter, who didn't graduate from college either. (Though it's true that Zuckerberg might not have even thought of Facebook if he hadn't been in the sexually charged freshman swirl at Harvard.)

Common Thread

5   But in showbiz, you learn by doing. If there is a common denominator to all of those success stories, it's that they were all men in a hurry, impatient with book learning, which could only take them so far in the rough-and-tumble world of Hollywood. Ron Meyer, a founder of Creative Artists Agency and now president of Universal Studios, dropped out of high school, served in the Marines and proudly notes on his résumé that his first job was as a messenger boy for the Paul Kohner Agency.

"The truth is that if you have a particular talent and the will to succeed, you don't really need a great education," Meyer told me last week. "In showbiz, your real college experience is working in a talent agency mail-room. That's the one place where you can get the most complete understanding of the arena you're playing in and how to deal with the complicated situations you'll come across in your career."

There are plenty of successful lawyers and MBAs in Hollywood, but the raw spirit of can-do invention and inspiration will take people further than the ability to read a complex profit and loss statement. Years ago, Geffen, who dropped out of night school at Brooklyn College before eventually landing a job in the William Morris mail-room, once told me that his early success was rooted in the ability to develop relationships. "It's not about where you went to college or how good-looking you are or whether you could play football—it's about whether you can create a relationship."

To produce a film or create a TV show or found a company requires the same kind of raw entrepreneurial zeal that it must have taken the '49ers who came west in search of gold. "You often feel like you're surrounded by a do-it-yourself ethic, almost a pioneer spirit," says Michael De Luca, producer of *The Social Network*, who dropped out of NYU four credits short of graduation to take a job at New Line Cinema, where he rose to become head of production. "All those successful guys you're talking about—they had an intense desire to create something big, new and different. They didn't need to wait around for the instruction manual."

In David Rensin's wonderful oral history *The Mailroom: Hollywood History From the Bottom Up,* survivors of the Mike Ovitz-era CAA experience tell war stories about how, as mail-room flunkies, they had to replenish Ovitz's candy dishes, stock his jars with raw cashews and fill his water jar with Evian. It seemed like hellish drudgery but, as the agents recalled, it prepared you for all the craziness of later Hollywood life, where multimillion-dollar movie star deals could fall a part if someone's exercise trainer or makeup specialist wasn't provided.

Do the Hustle

10 Even today, people in Hollywood are far more impressed by, say, your knack for finding new talent than by what your grades were like. "Show business is all about instinct and intuition," says Sam Gores, head of the Paradigm Agency, who went to acting school but never to college, having joined a meat-cutters' union by the time he was 18. "To succeed, you need to have a strong point of view and a lot of confidence. Sometimes being the most well-informed person in your circle can almost get in your way."

In show business, charm, hustle and guile are the aces in the deck. When New York Times columnist David Brooks was dissecting Chua's book recently, he argued that "managing status rivalries, negotiating group dynamics, understanding social norms, navigating the distinction between self and group" imposed the kind of cognitive demands that far exceed what's required of students in a class at Yale. He probably picked that up reading a fancy sociology text, but it was a letter-perfect description of the skill set for a gifted filmmaker, agent or producer.

In Hollywood, whether you were a C student or *summa cum laude,* it's a level playing field. "When you're working on a movie set, you've got 50 film profesors to learn from, from the sound man to the cinematographer," says producer David Permut, who dropped out of UCLA to work for Roger Corman. "I've never needed a résumé in my whole career. All you need a 110-page script that some one is dying to make and you're in business."

AMERICA'S TOP PARENT

Elizabeth Kolbert

Elizabeth Kolbert is a staff writer for the *New Yorker,* where this article first appeared on January 20, 2011. Kolbert has also written for the *New York Times* and is the author of *Field Notes from a Catastrophe: Man and Nature and Climate Change* (2006).

"Call me garbage."

The other day, I was having dinner with my family when the subject of Amy Chua's new book, *Battle Hymn of the Tiger Mother* (Penguin Press; $25.95), came up. My twelve-year-old twins had been read an excerpt from the book by their teacher, a well-known provocateur. He had been sent a link to the excerpt by another teacher, who had received it from her sister, who had been e-mailed it by a friend, and, well, you get the point. The excerpt, which had appeared in the *Wall Street Journal* under the headline "WHY CHINESE MOTHERS ARE SUPERIOR," was, and still is, an Internet sensation—as one blogger put it, the "Andromeda Strain of viral memes." Within days, more than five thousand comments had been posted, and "Tiger Mother" vaulted to No. 4 on Amazon's list of best-sellers. Chua appeared on NPR's "All Things Considered" and on NBC's "Nightly News" and "Today" show. Her book was the topic of two columns in last week's Sunday *Times*, and, under the racially neutral headline "IS EXTREME PARENTING EFFECTIVE?," the subject of a formal debate on the paper's Web site.

Thanks to this media blitz, the basic outlines of *Tiger Mother*'s story are by now familiar. Chua, the daughter of Chinese immigrants, is a Yale Law School professor. She is married to another Yale law professor and has two daughters, whom she drives relentlessly. Chua's rules for the girls include: no sleepovers, no playdates, no grade lower than an A on report cards, no choosing your own extracurricular activities, and no ranking lower than No. 1 in any subject. (An exception to this last directive is made for gym and drama.)

In Chua's binary world, there are just two kinds of mother. There are "Chinese mothers," who, she allows, do not necessarily have to be Chinese. "I'm using the term 'Chinese mothers' loosely," she writes. Then, there are "Western" mothers. Western mothers think they are being strict when they insist that their children practice their instruments for half an hour a day. For Chinese mothers, "the first hour is the easy part." Chua chooses the instruments that her daughters will play—piano for the older one, Sophia; violin for the younger, Lulu—and stands over them as they practice for three, four, sometimes five hours at a stretch. The least the girls are expected to do is make it to Carnegie Hall. Amazingly enough, Sophia does. Chua's daughters are so successful—once, it's true, Sophia came in second on a multiplication test (to a Korean boy), but Chua made sure this never happened again—that they confirm her thesis: Western mothers are losers. I'm using the term "losers" loosely.

5   Chua has said that one of the points of the book is "making fun of myself," but plainly what she was hoping for was to outrage. Whole chapters of "Tiger Mother"—admittedly, many chapters are only four or five pages long—are given over to incidents like that of the rejected smiley face.

"I don't want this," she tells Lulu, throwing back at her a handmade birthday card. "I want a better one."

In another chapter, Chua threatens to take Lulu's doll house to the Salvation Army and, when that doesn't work, to deny her lunch, dinner, and birthday parties for "two, three, four years" because she cannot master a piece called "The Little White Donkey." The kid is seven years old. In a third chapter, Chua tells Sophia she is "garbage." Chua's own father has called her "garbage," and she finds it a highly effective parenting technique.

Chua relates this at a dinner party, and one of the guests supposedly gets so upset that she breaks down in tears. The hostess tries to patch things up by suggesting that Chua is speaking figuratively.

"You didn't actually call Sophia garbage," the hostess offers.

"Yes, I did," Chua says.

10   When the dinner-party episode was read in class, my sons found it hilarious, which is why they were taunting me. "Call me garbage," one of the twins said again. "I dare you."

"O.K.," I said, trying, for once, to be a good mother. "You're garbage."

If Chua's tale has any significance—and it may not—it is as an allegory. Chua refers to herself as a Tiger because according to the Chinese zodiac she was born in the Year of the Tiger. Tiger people are "powerful, authoritative, and magnetic," she informs us, just as tigers that walk on four legs inspire "fear and respect." The "tiger economies" of Asia aren't mentioned in the book, but they growl menacingly in the background.

It's just about impossible to pick up a newspaper these days—though who actually *picks up* a newspaper anymore?—without finding a story about the rise of the East. The headlines are variations on a theme: "SOLAR PANEL MAKER MOVES WORK TO CHINA"; "CHINA DRAWING HIGH-TECH RESEARCH FROM U.S."; "IBM CUTTING 5,000 SERVICE JOBS; MOVING WORK TO INDIA." What began as an outflow of manufacturing jobs has spread way beyond car parts and electronics to include information technology, legal advice, even journalism. (This piece could have been written much more cost-effectively by a team in Bangalore and, who knows, maybe next month it will be.)

On our good days, we tell ourselves that our kids will be all right. The new, global economy, we observe, puts a premium on flexibility and creativity. And who is better prepared for such a future than little Abby (or Zachary), downloading her wacky videos onto YouTube while she texts her friends, messes with Photoshop, and listens to her iPod?

15   "Yes, you can brute-force any kid to learn to play the piano—just precisely like his or her billion neighbors" is how one of the comments on the *Wall Street Journal's* Web site put it. "But you'll never get a Jimi Hendrix that way."

On our bad days, we wonder whether this way of thinking is, as Chua might say, garbage. Last month, the results of the most recent Programme for International Student Assessment, or PISA, tests were announced. It was the first time that Chinese students had participated, and children from Shanghai ranked first in every single area. Students from the United States, meanwhile, came in seventeenth in reading, twenty-third in science, and an especially demoralizing thirty-first in math. This last ranking put American kids not just behind the Chinese, the Koreans, and the Singaporeans but also after the French, the Austrians, the Hungarians, the Slovenians, the Estonians, and the Poles.

"I know skeptics will want to argue with the results, but we consider them to be accurate and reliable," Arne Duncan, the U.S. Secretary of Education, told the *Times.* "The United States came in twenty-third or twenty-fourth in most subjects. We can quibble, or we can face the brutal truth that we're being out-educated."

Why is this? How is it that the richest country in the world can't teach kids to read or to multiply fractions? Taken as a parable, Chua's cartoonish narrative about browbeating her daughters acquires a certain disquieting force. Americans have been told always to encourage their kids. This, the theory goes, will improve their self-esteem, and this, in turn, will help them learn.

After a generation or so of applying this theory, we have the results. Just about the only category in which American students outperform the competition is self-regard. Researchers at the Brookings Institution, in one of their frequent studies of education policy, compared students' assessments of their abilities in math with their scores on a standardized test. Nearly forty per cent of American eighth graders agreed "a lot" with the statement "I usually do well in mathematics," even though only seven per cent of American students actually got enough correct answers on the test to qualify as advanced. Among Singaporean students, eighteen per cent said they usually did well in math; forty-four per cent qualified as advanced. As the Brookings researchers pointed out, even the least self-confident Singaporean students, on average, outscored the most self-confident Americans. You can say it's sad that kids in Singapore are so beaten down that they can't appreciate their own accomplishments. But you've got to give them this: at least they get the math right.

20   Our problems as a country cannot, of course, be reduced to our problems as educators or as parents. Nonetheless, there is an uncomfortable analogy. For some time now, the U.S. has, in effect, been drawing crappy, smiley-face birthday cards and calling them wonderful. It's made us feel a bit better about ourselves without improving the basic situation. As the cover story on China's ascent in this month's *Foreign Policy* sums things up: "American Decline: This Time It's Real."

It's hard to believe that Chua's book would be causing quite as much stir without the geopolitical subtext. (Picture the reaction to a similar tale told by a Hungarian or an Austrian über-mom.) At the same time, lots of people have clearly taken "Tiger Mother" personally.

Of the zillions of comments that have been posted on the Web, many of the most passionate are from scandalized "Western" mothers and fathers, or, as one blogger dubbed them, "Manatee dads." Some have gone as far as to suggest that Chua be arrested for child abuse. At least as emotional are the posts from Asians and Asian-Americans.

"Parents like Amy Chua are the reason why Asian-Americans like me are in therapy," Betty Ming Liu, who teaches journalism at N.Y.U., wrote on her blog.

"What's even more damning is her perpetuation of the media stereotypes of Asian-Americans," Frank Chi, a political consultant, wrote in the Boston *Globe's* opinion blog.

25   "Having lived through a version of the Chinese Parenting Experience, and having been surrounded since birth with hundreds of CPE graduates, I couldn't not say something," a contributor to the Web site Shanghaiist wrote after the *Wall Street Journal* excerpt appeared. "The article actually made me feel physically ill."

Chua's response to some of the unkind things said about her—she has reported getting death threats—has been to backpedal. "RETREAT OF THE 'TIGER MOTHER'" was the headline of one *Times* article. (It, too, quickly jumped to the top of the paper's "most e-mailed" list.) Chua has said that it was not her plan to write a parenting manual: "My actual book is not a how-to guide." Somehow or other, her publisher seems to be among those who missed this. The back cover spells out, in black and red type, "How to Be a Tiger Mother."

According to Chua, her "actual book" is a memoir. Memoir is, or at least is supposed to be, a demanding genre. It requires that the author not just narrate his or her life but reflect on it. By her own description, Chua is not a probing person. Of her years studying at Harvard Law School, she writes:

> I didn't care about the rights of criminals the way others did, and I froze whenever a professor called on me. I also wasn't naturally skeptical and questioning; I just wanted to write down everything the professor said and memorize it.

Battle Hymn of the Tiger Mother exhibits much the same lack of interest in critical thinking. It's breezily written, at times entertaining, and devoid of anything approaching introspection. Imagine your most self-congratulatory friend holding forth for two hours about her kids' triumphs, and you've more or less got the narrative. The only thing that keeps it together is Chua's cheerful faith that whatever happened to her or her daughters is interesting just because it happened to happen to them. In addition to all the schlepping back and forth to auditions, there are two chapters on Chua's dogs (Samoyeds named Coco and Pushkin), three pages of practice notes that she left behind for Lulu when she could not be there to berate her in person, and a complete list of the places that she had visited with her kids by the time they were twelve and nine:

> London, Paris, Nice, Rome, Venice, Milan, Amsterdam, The Hague, Barcelona, Madrid, Málaga, Liechtenstein, Monaco, Munich, Dublin, Brussels, Bruges, Strasbourg, Beijing, Shanghai, Tokyo, Hong Kong, Manila, Istanbul, Mexico City, Cancún, Buenos Aires, Santiago, Rio de Janeiro, São Paulo, La Paz, Sucre, Cochabamba, Jamaica, Tangier, Fez, Johannesburg, Cape Town, and the Rock of Gibraltar.

Chua's husband is not Chinese, in either sense of the word. He makes occasional appearances in the book to try—ineffectually, it seems—to shield the girls. Chua has said that she wrote more about their arguments, but her husband didn't like those passages, so they've been cut. Perhaps had more of his voice been included it would have provided some grit and at least the semblance of engagement. As it is, though, it's just her. "I'm happy to be the one hated," she tells her husband at one point, and apparently she means it.

30   Parenting is hard. As anyone who has gone through the process and had enough leisure (and still functioning brain cells) to reflect on it knows, a lot of it is a crapshoot. Things go wrong that you have no control over, and, on occasion, things also go right, and you have no control over those, either. The experience is scary and exhilarating and often humiliating, not because you're disappointed in your kids, necessarily, but because you're disappointed in yourself.

Some things do go wrong in Chua's memoir. Her mother-in-law dies; her younger sister develops leukemia. These events get roughly the same amount of space as Coco and Pushkin, and yet they are, on their own terms, moving. More central to the story line is a screaming fit in a Moscow restaurant during which a glass is thrown. The upshot of the crisis is that Lulu is allowed to take up tennis, which Chua then proceeds to micromanage.

Chua clearly wants to end her book by claiming that she has changed. She knows enough about the conventions of memoir-writing to understand that some kind of transformation is generally required. But she can't bring herself to do it. And so in the final pages she invokes the Founding Fathers. They, too, she tells her daughters, would not have approved of sleepovers.

IN DEFENSE OF BEING A KID

James Bernard Murphy

James Bernard Murphy is a professor of government at Dartmouth College, where he teaches the philosophy of law, ethics, and education, subjects on which he has written extensively. The following piece first appeared as an op-ed in the *Wall Street Journal* on February 9, 2011.

Amy Chua, the "tiger mother," is clearly hitting a nerve—especially among the anxious class (it used to be called the upper class), which understands how much skill and discipline are necessary for success in the new economy.

What Ms. Chua and her critics agree on is that childhood is all about preparation for adulthood. Ms. Chua claims that her parenting methods will produce ambitious, successful and happy adults—while her critics argue that her methods will produce neurotic, self-absorbed and unhappy ones.

It took economist Larry Summers, in a debate with Ms. Chua at the World Economic Forum in Davos, to point out that part of the point of childhood is childhood itself. Childhood takes up a quarter of one's life, Mr. Summers observed, and it would be nice if children enjoyed it.

Bravo, Larry.

5   Children are not merely adults in training. They are also people with distinctive powers and joys. A happy childhood is measured not only by the standards of adult success, but also by the enjoyment of the gifts given to children alone.

What are the unique blessings of childhood?

First is the gift of moral innocence: Young children are liberated from the burdens of the knowledge of the full extent of human evil—a knowledge that casts a pall over adult life. Childhood innocence permits children to trust others fully. How wonderful to live (even briefly) with such confidence in human goodness. Childhood innocence teaches us what the world ought to be.

Second is the gift of openness to the future. We adults are hamstrung by our own plans and expectations. Children alone are free to welcome the most improbable new adventures.

Third, children are liberated from the grim economy of time. Children become so absorbed in fantasy play and projects that they lose all sense of time. For them, time is not scarce and thus cannot be wasted.

10   Finally, we parents are so focused on adult superiority that we forget that most of us produced our best art, asked our deepest philosophical questions, and most readily mastered new gadgets when we were mere children.

Tragically, there is a real conflict within childhood between preparation for adulthood and the enjoyment of the gifts of youth. Preparation for adulthood requires the adoption of adult prudence, discipline and planning that undermine the spontaneous adventure of childhood.

[Parents are deeply conflicted about how to balance these two basic demands: raising good little ladies and gentlemen, while also permitting children to escape into the irresponsible joys of Neverland.]

Our wisest sages also disagree fundamentally about the nature of childhood. The ancient Greek philosopher Aristotle famously declared that "no child is happy" on the grounds that children are incapable of the complex moral and intellectual activities that constitute a flourishing life. Aristotle said that when we describe a child as happy, what we mean is that he or she is anticipating the achievements of adult life. For him, the only good thing about childhood is that we leave it behind.

By contrast, Jesus frequently praised children, welcomed their company, and even commanded adults to emulate them: "Unless you become like a little child, you shall not enter the kingdom of God."

15   Tom Sawyer enjoyed a childhood of nearly pure adventure with minimal preparation for adult life. The 19th-century philosopher John Stuart Mill, by contrast, barely survived a "tiger father" who enforced a regime of ruthless discipline and learning that would make Ms. Chua blanche.

Most of us would like Tom's childhood followed by Mill's adulthood. But as parents we are stuck with trying to balance the paradoxical demands of both preparing our children for adulthood and protecting them from it.

As the current dustup shows, many parents today would benefit hugely by taking a reflective time-out from teaching our children to discover how much we might learn from them.

SUMMARY

Following the guidelines in Chapter 1, particularly the Guidelines for Writing Summaries box (pp. 7–8), summarize "Chinese Mothers are Superior" by Amy Chua. In preparation for writing the summary, review the model summary (pp. 20–21) and consult the advice on note-taking (pp. 14–15).

As an alternative, summarize one of the other selections in this chapter. The article by Kolbert would also be a good subject for summary.

CRITIQUE

Following the guidelines in Chapter 2, particularly the Guidelines for Writing Critiques box (p. 46), write a critique of "Chinese Mothers are Superior." The early part of the critique should draw upon the summary of Chua that you prepared for the previous assignment. In preparation for writing the critique, review the model critique (pp. 48–54).

You've probably already noticed that most of the articles following Chua are to some extent critiques of either "Why Chinese Mothers Are Superior" or the book from which this selection was drawn, *Battle Hymn of the Tiger Mother*. Some authors argue with her basic premise, some support it, though perhaps with reservations, and others discuss related issues such as the preparedness of America's youth to compete with their counterparts in China. In developing your own critique, you're free to draw upon these other authors; but you should also stake out your own position based upon your own observations and experience and your own understanding of the issues Chua discusses. Doing so will help ensure that your critique isn't merely a compendium of other authors' observations and arguments.

Begin preparing for the critique by reflecting on your own observations and experiences in relation to Chua's main assumption (expressed in the two sentences that open ¶ 5): "What Chinese parents understand is that nothing is fun until you're good at it. To get good at anything you have to work, and children on their own never want to work, which is why it is crucial to override their preferences." Ask yourself:

- To what extent do you agree that "nothing is fun until you're good at it"? Do your own experiences and the experiences of your friends and relatives bear out this assumption? What have you read that supports or refutes it?

- Do you agree that "children on their own never want to work"? Cite examples in support or to the contrary.

- Consider the proposition that it is crucial for parents to override children's natural disinclination to work, in light of your own experiences, observations, and reading.

Throughout Chua's op-ed, you'll encounter controversial statements such as this one, along with anecdotes about the ways she has driven her children, sometimes mercilessly, in pursuit of her standards of excellence and success. And you'll find numerous comparisons between "Chinese" and "Western" approaches to child rearing. Your assessment of these statements should provide a rich source of material for your own critique.

Here's a suggested organizational plan for your critique:

1. An introduction, setting the issue in context

2. A summary of Chua's op-ed (a brief version of your response to the summary assignment above)

3. An evaluation of Chua's piece for clarity, logic, and/or fairness (the Question #1 topics in Chapter 2, p. 29)

4. An account of your own agreement or disagreement with Chua's argument (the Question #2 topics in Chapter 2, pp. 41–44)

5. A conclusion

In preparing your critique, follow the advice in Chapter 2, see particularly the Guidelines for Writing Critiques box (p. 46), along with the hints in Chapter 1 on incorporating summaries into your own writing.

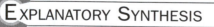

EXPLANATORY SYNTHESIS

Based on the readings in this chapter, write an explanatory synthesis that you might use in a broader argument on the subject of varying approaches to child rearing and preparing children to be competitive in the workplace of the future. The synthesis should each consist of three to five well-developed paragraphs on the following topics: (1) an account of the controversy over

Chua's op-ed and the book from which it was drawn; (2) an account of the two different approaches to parenting represented by the "Chinese" and "Western" models; and (3) an account of the different approaches to preparing children to be competitive in the current and future marketplace. Follow the guidelines in Chapter 3, particularly the Guidelines for Writing Syntheses box (pp. 65–66).

Key requirements for the explanatory synthesis:

- Craft a thesis for your paper, a single statement that will guide the writing of the paragraphs of explanation that follow.

- Begin each paragraph of explanation that follows the explanatory thesis with a clear topic sentence.

- Refer in each paragraph of explanation to *at least two* different sources. Set up the references carefully, using an appropriate citation format, most likely MLA (see the "Quick Index" at the end of this text).

- In developing your explanatory synthesis, draw on facts, examples, statistics, and expert opinions from your sources.

ANALYSIS

Select a principle or definition discussed in one of the readings in "The Roar of the Tiger Mom" and apply this principle or definition to either (1) a particular situation of which you have personal knowledge or (2) a situation that you have learned about in the course of your reading. Follow the guidelines in Chapter 4, particularly the Guidelines for Writing Analyses box (p. 121); review also the model analysis (pp. 128–135).

First, review the topic list you created in Group Assignment #1 after reading the selections in this chapter. At least one of the items on the list may point the way to an analytic principle that resonates with you. If so, follow through by locating a particular quotation that articulates this principle. Here are some examples of such quotations from the readings:

- "But as a parent, one of the worst things you can do for your child's self-esteem is to let them give up. On the flip side, there's nothing better for building confidence than learning you can do something you thought you couldn't." (Chua, p. 146)

- "What privileged American children need is not more skills and rules and math drills. They need to lighten up and roam free, to express themselves in ways not dictated by their uptight, over-invested parents." (Rosin, p. 148)

- "Managing status rivalries, negotiating group dynamics, understanding social norms, navigating the distinction between self and group—these and other social tests impose cognitive demands that blow away any intense tutoring session or a class at Yale." (Brooks, p. 151).

- "For some time now, the U.S. has, in effect, been drawing crappy, smiley-face birthday cards and calling them wonderful." (Kolbert, p. 159)

- "A happy childhood is measured not only by standards of adult success, but also by the enjoyment of the gifts given to children alone." (Murphy, p. 162)

Consider using the following structure for your analysis:

1. An introductory paragraph that sets a context for the topic and presents the claim you intend to support in the analysis that follows. Your claim (your thesis) distills the conclusions you've drawn from your analysis. Your claim may appear at the end of the introductory paragraph (or introductory section).

2. A paragraph or two introducing the analytic tool or principle you intend to use and discussing its key components. Suppose you decided to use Brooks' quotation as an analytic principle. You would need to explain what he means by one or more of these skills: "[m]anaging status rivalries," "negotiating group dynamics," "understanding social norms," and "navigating the distinction between self and group." You would also need to explain how successfully managing such social tests imposes "cognitive demands that blow away any intense tutoring session or a class at Yale." Note, however, that you're not required to establish that one set of tasks is *more* difficult or important than the other. It may be sufficient for your purpose to establish simply that the social skills are at least *as* important as the academic skills. Once you establish this analytic principle, you can proceed with the analysis.

3. A paragraph or two describing the situation that you will analyze—drawn from your own personal experience or observation or from your reading.

4. Several paragraphs (this is the heart of your analysis) in which you systematically apply the key components of the principle you have selected to the situation you have described. Staying with Brooks, you would apply such key components as managing status rivalries, negotiating group dynamics, and so on to the situation you have described. As you apply these key components each in turn, in separate paragraphs or groupings of paragraphs, you would discuss why such skills are, if not *more* difficult than undergoing a demanding class or tutoring session, then at least *as valuable* for success in later life as academic skills.

5. A conclusion in which you argue that, based on the insights gained through your analysis, the experience or situation in question can now be understood more deeply.

Argument

> Write an argument synthesis based upon the selections in "The Roar of
> the Tiger Mom." You may find it useful to draw upon the products of
> your earlier assignments in this section on summary, critique, explanatory
> synthesis, and analysis. Follow the guidelines in Chapter 3, particularly
> the Guidelines for Writing Synthesis box; review also the model argument
> synthesis (pp. 83–91).

In planning your synthesis, review the master list of topics and notes that you
and your classmates generated for Group Assignment #1 above (p. 141), and
draw upon what the authors of the passages have written about these topics in
developing your outline. Devise a claim, a thesis that distills your argument to a
sentence or two. Plan to support your claim with facts, opinions, and statistics
from the passages.

Note that one synthesis—a single paper—could not possibly refer to every topic, or every connection among authors, that you have found. The craft
of preparing and writing a synthesis depends on your ability to *select* closely
related topics and then to make and develop a claim that links and can be supported by them. You don't have to refer to *all* of the selections in this chapter
while developing your paper; but you will likely want to refer to most. You may
even want to research additional sources.

In formulating arguments on a controversial issue—for example, immigration, abortion, the size of government, or capital punishment—the immediate
temptation is to adopt one strong (and uncompromising) position or to adopt its
counterpart on the opposite side. Many commentators on Chua's book or op-ed
tend to divide themselves into pro-Chua or anti-Chua camps: she's either dead
right about her approach to parenting or she's dead wrong. Arguments supporting such polarized positions may be forceful, even eloquent, but seldom persuade
those predisposed to the opposite point of view.

After considering all the facts and the assertions, strive yourself for a more
nuanced approach. This doesn't necessarily mean adopting a straight-down-the-
middle/split-the-difference position, which is likely to persuade no one. It does
mean acknowledging opposing arguments and dealing with them in good faith.
(See "Present and Respond to Counterarguments" in Chapter 3, p. 98.) It does
mean considering the issue afresh, thinking about the implications of the problems
and the possible solutions, and coming up with your own insights, your own
distinctive take on the subject. Such thought, such nuance, should be reflected in
your thesis.

Without writing your thesis for you, we'll suppose for the sake of example that
the subject of your argument synthesis concerns how the debate over Chua's ideas
clarifies how parents can best help their children to succeed as they prepare for adulthood. An arguable claim on the subject would likely state which approach to child

rearing, in your opinion, would best prepare children. Here's one way of structuring such an argument synthesis:

- An introductory paragraph that sets a context for the topic—in the example above, the debate over Chua's op-ed and the best pathway to success—and presents the claim you intend to support in the argument that follows. Your claim (that is, your argumentative thesis) may appear at the end of this paragraph (or introductory section).

- A paragraph or two summarizing Chua's ideas. This section may be an abbreviated version of the summary you wrote earlier.

- One to three paragraphs discussing some of the commentary on Chua's ideas, organized by topic, rather than author. That is, identify two or three main categories of response to Chua—favorable, unfavorable, and neutral—and take up each category in turn. You may have created topic webs for these categories when preparing to write. See Group Assignments #1 and #2.

- A paragraph or two discussing your own assessment of the best pathway (or pathways) to success, supported in part by the comments of some of the authors in this chapter. Relate this assessment to ideas contained within the articles by Chua and her critics. For this section you may want to draw upon your responses to the earlier analysis or critique assignments. You may even elect to consult additional sources on the subject (for example, Chua's op-ed in the online edition of the *Wall Street Journal* is followed by almost nine thousand reader comments).

- A counterargument section, in which you concede the validity of positions on the subject different from your own and acknowledge the ideas of authors in this section with whom you disagree.

- A "nevertheless" section, in which you respond to the counterarguments and reaffirm your own position.

- A paragraph or two of conclusion.

Where you place the various elements of this argument synthesis will be your decision as writer. Which sources to use and what logic to present in defense of your claim is also yours to decide. See pages 80–81 for help in thinking about structuring and supporting your argument.

A Note on Incorporating Quotations and Paraphrases   Identify the sources you intend to use for your synthesis. Working with a phrase, sentence, or brief passage from each to write sentences that you can use to advance your argument. Some of these sentences should demonstrate the use of ellipsis marks and brackets. Paraphrase passages, as needed, and incorporate these as well into your papers.

Part **III**

An Anthology of
Readings

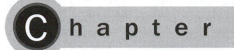

Chapter 6

The Changing Landscape of Work in the Twenty-First Century

You attend college for many reasons, but perhaps none is so compelling as the hope and expectation that higher education offers a passport to a better future, a future based on meaningful employment and financial independence—especially in an uncertain economy.

As fate would have it, you will enter the American workforce at a particularly dynamic and (most would acknowledge) stressful time. The recent "Great Recession" (January 2007–June 2009) continues to roil the economy. But long before the recession took hold, the twin forces of globalization and computer-driven technology began to alter the workplace of your future. If the wisdom of the analysts and economists collected in this chapter could be reduced to a single statement of advice, it would be this: Think strategically about your future working life.

As you begin, some recent history can provide perspective. In the second half of the twentieth century, since the end of World War II, the labor market rewarded the educated, conferring on those who attended college an "education premium." Even as the forces of globalization reshaped the American economy and workers began losing manufacturing jobs to competitors offshore in China and India, college-educated workers were generally spared major career disruptions. Today, higher education no longer promises such protection. The relentless search for cheap labor and plentiful raw materials, together with advances in technology, have opened the information-based service economy to foreign competition. Increasingly, the American college-educated workforce will face the same relentless pressures that decades ago unsettled the automotive and manufacturing sectors. Employers are already offshoring computer coding, certain types of accounting, and medical consultation (the reading of X-rays, MRIs, CT scans, and such)—services that require extensive training. Experts predict that more American jobs will be lost to foreign competition and fewer will entail a lifelong commitment between employer and employee. What are the implications of these developments for you and your intended career? Will they affect the courses you take, the major (and minors) you choose, the summer jobs and internships you pursue? Could you investigate *now* how to anticipate and avoid major disruptions to your working life tomorrow?

This chapter provides an opportunity to learn what economists, policy analysts, sociologists, educators, statisticians, and journalists are forecasting about the world of work in the twenty-first century. You'll find ten selections presented in four components, beginning with *Prospects for Graduates*. Jenna Brager's "A Post-College Flow Chart of Misery and Pain" might cut a little close to the bone for those pursuing a humanities degree. Next, reporter Catherine Rampell takes a snapshot of job prospects for graduates in May 2011, concluding that "Many with New College Degree Find Job Market Humbling." But writing just six months later, Lacey Johnson reports that the "Job Outlook for College Graduates Is Slowly Improving."

The second component of readings, *Data on the Job Market*, opens with a recent report showing that when it comes time for graduating seniors to find a job, "Not All College Degrees Are Created Equal." Next you'll find the U.S. Bureau of Labor Statistics summary of its employment projections for 2010–2020. This summary and the accompanying tables point you to vast online resources for determining which sectors of the economy are adding jobs and which are eliminating jobs.

What you do with this information as you chart a course of study is up to you; and what you decide will affect your sense of yourself—if, that is, you accept the premise of sociologist Richard Sennett, writing on *Work and Identity*. In this third component of the chapter, Sennett relates the story of a man whose talents for business allowed him to succeed in modern corporate life but at the cost of "corroding" his character. The selection will provoke you to consider how your job choices may affect your sense of self.

The final component of selections addresses *Trends Affecting Work*. Here, you will read what an economist, a former hedge-fund manager, and reporters predict about coming changes in the workforce. Next, former presidential advisor Alan Blinder traces the migration of service jobs (even those requiring a college degree) away from American shores. The chapter concludes with two writers who predict winners and losers in the evolving workplace. Former hedge-fund manager Andy Kessler asks "Is Your Job an Endangered Species?" Finally, economist and Nobel laureate Paul Krugman questions the widely assumed link between a college degree and job security.

The workplace you'll be entering is doubly uncertain as it struggles to emerge from a long recession and morphs due to global and technological forces that will continue to play out in the years to come. As you search for employment now and in the near future, the selections in this chapter may help inform your choices.

PROSPECTS FOR GRADUATES

That perfect job: It's out there, you hope—even in these distressed times. And now, you're taking the first steps to get it. In part, isn't this why you've come to college—to acquire skills that will lead to satisfying, well-paid work? You know the economy is uncertain, and you're more than curious: Just what are the job prospects these days for new college graduates?

This first component of readings will help to provide some answers. We begin with a provocative teaser—"A Post-College Flow Chart of Misery and Pain" by Jenna Brager, who writes a weekly webcomic for curmudgeon-comic.com. In this satiric look at job possibilities for humanities majors, Brager raises an important question: If the job market is so tough for humanities majors, why would anyone study the humanities? People do, of course—for many reasons, not always related to employability. This graphic first appeared on the shareable.com Web site and in its online book *Share or Die: Youth in Recession.*

Rounding out the "Prospects" component are two selections on job prospects for recent graduates. Writing for the *New York Times* on May 18, 2011, economics reporter Catherine Rampell concludes that "Many with New College Degree Find Job Market Humbling." Just six months later, Lacey Johnson reports in the *Chronicle of Higher Education* (November 17, 2011) that the "Job Outlook for College Graduates [is] Slowly Improving." Notwithstanding this brightening picture, the job market remains in flux. After reading these selections, you may want to update what you've learned by running a quick Internet search on "job prospects for college students."

A Post-College Flow Chart of Misery and Pain

Jenna Brager

MANY WITH NEW COLLEGE DEGREE FIND THE JOB MARKET HUMBLING

Catherine Rampell

The individual stories are familiar. The chemistry major tending bar. The classics major answering phones. The Italian studies major sweeping aisles at Wal-Mart.

Now evidence is emerging that the damage wrought by the sour economy is more widespread than just a few careers led astray or postponed. Even for college graduates—the people who were most protected from the slings and arrows of recession—the outlook is rather bleak.

Employment rates for new college graduates have fallen sharply in the last two years, as have starting salaries for those who can find work. What's more, only half of the jobs landed by these new graduates even require a college degree, reviving debates about whether higher education is "worth it" after all.

"I have friends with the same degree as me, from a worse school, but because of who they knew or when they happened to graduate, they're in much better jobs," said Kyle Bishop, 23, a 2009 graduate of the University of Pittsburgh who has spent the last two years waiting tables, delivering beer, working at a bookstore and entering data. "It's more about luck than anything else."

5   The median starting salary for students graduating from four-year colleges in 2009 and 2010 was $27,000, down from $30,000 for those who entered the work force in 2006 to 2008, according to a study released on Wednesday by the John J. Heldrich Center for Workforce Development at Rutgers University. That is a decline of 10 percent, even before taking inflation into account.

Of course, these are the lucky ones—the graduates who found a job. Among the members of the class of 2010, just 56 percent had held at least one job by this spring, when the survey was conducted. That compares with 90 percent of graduates from the classes of 2006 and 2007. (Some have gone for further education or opted out of the labor force, while many are still pounding the pavement.)

Even these figures understate the damage done to these workers' careers. Many have taken jobs that do not make use of their skills; about only half of recent college graduates said that their first job required a college degree.

The choice of major is quite important. Certain majors had better luck finding a job that required a college degree, according to an analysis by

Andrew M. Sum, an economist at Northeastern University, of 2009 Labor Department data for college graduates under 25.

Young graduates who majored in education and teaching or engineering were most likely to find a job requiring a college degree, while area studies majors—those who majored in Latin American studies, for example—and humanities majors were least likely to do so. Among all recent education graduates, 71.1 percent were in jobs that required a college degree; of all area studies majors, the share was 44.7 percent.

10   An analysis by the *New York Times* of Labor Department data about college graduates aged 25 to 34 found that the number of these workers employed in food service, restaurants and bars had risen 17 percent in 2009 from 2008, though the sample size was small. There were similar or bigger employment increases at gas stations and fuel dealers, food and alcohol stores, and taxi and limousine services.

This may be a waste of a college degree, but it also displaces the less-educated workers who would normally take these jobs.

"The less schooling you had, the more likely you were to get thrown out of the labor market altogether," said Mr. Sum, noting that unemployment rates for high school graduates and dropouts are always much higher than those for college graduates. "There is complete displacement all the way down."

Meanwhile, college graduates are having trouble paying off student loan debt, which is at a median of $20,000 for graduates of classes 2006 to 2010.

Mr. Bishop, the Pittsburgh graduate, said he is "terrified" of the effects his starter jobs might have on his ultimate career, which he hopes to be in publishing or writing. "It looks bad to have all these short-term jobs on your résumé, but you do have to pay the bills," he said, adding that right now his student loan debt was over $70,000.

15   Many graduates will probably take on more student debt. More than 60 percent of those who graduated in the last five years say they will need more formal education to be successful.

"I knew there weren't going to be many job prospects for me until I got my Ph.D.," said Travis Patterson, 23, a 2010 graduate of California State University, Fullerton. He is working as an administrative assistant for a property management company and studying psychology in graduate school. While it may not have anything to do with his degree, "it helps pay my rent and tuition, and that's what matters."

Going back to school does offer the possibility of joining the labor force when the economy is better. Unemployment rates are also generally lower for people with advanced schooling.

Those who do not go back to school may be on a lower-paying trajectory for years. They start at a lower salary, and they may begin their careers with employers that pay less on average or have less room for growth.

"Their salary history follows them wherever they go," said Carl Van Horn, a labor economist at Rutgers. "It's like a parrot on your shoulder, traveling with you everywhere, constantly telling you 'No, you can't make that much money.' "

20   And while young people who have weathered a tough job market may shy from risks during their careers, the best way to nullify an unlucky graduation date is to change jobs when you can, says Till von Wachter, an economist at Columbia.

"If you don't move within five years of graduating, for some reason you get stuck where you are. That's just an empirical finding," Mr. von Wachter said. "By your late 20s, you're often married, and have a family and have a house. You stop the active pattern of moving jobs."

JOB OUTLOOK FOR COLLEGE GRADUATES IS SLOWLY IMPROVING

Lacey Johnson

The job outlook for college students is expected to improve by a modest 4 percent this academic year [2011–2012], according to a major annual survey of employers released on Thursday. This is the second year in a row that the hiring of new graduates is predicted to increase, following drops of 35 percent to 40 percent in 2008. Bachelor's degree graduates should see the most hiring, with a 7-percent increase in available jobs.

Many employers overestimated their hiring growth last year, anticipating a 10-percent increase in new bachelor's degree hires; but this year's data appear to be "a little deeper" and show "a more consistent pattern of growth," says the survey, which is administered by the Collegiate Employment Research Institute at Michigan State University.

Between baby boomers retiring, the exhaustion of today's work force, and employers' need to revitalize their skill base, "this trend will only accelerate over the next decade," wrote Phil Gardner, director of the institute, in the latest report. "All these factors are nudging the college labor market out of the doldrums, ahead of other segments of the labor market."

Of the more than 3,300 employers surveyed, nearly 40 percent said they planned to hire graduates from all fields of study, regardless of their major. And, despite overall growth, one-third had decided to cut back on hiring.

5   Some industries look more promising than others, according to the report. Accounting, engineering, finance, and supply chain are all expected to do well, while state and local agencies are less likely to hire, because of budget cuts. The strongest job sector was agriculture/food processing, predicted to grow by 14 percent this year. Marketing, advertising, and public relations were also expecting to see strong hiring growth.

One of the most employable degrees continues to be in computer science— a field that will have more available positions than qualified graduates. The opposite is true in most other occupations, and competition will stay fierce, says the study.

While more graduates may be employed, it is unlikely that they will be earning more money than their predecessors; 70 percent of employers said they had no intention of raising salaries for new workers.

The results of this year's survey showed consistency across economic sector, organizational size, academic major, location, and are "basically boring," wrote Mr. Gardner. "But you know what? Boring is good." This kind of stability means the upcoming job market may "have legs," he said.

Review Questions

1. Summarize Jenna Brager's "A Post-College Flow Chart of Misery and Pain."

2. According to Rampell's article in the *New York Times*, how have graduates in 2010 fared in comparison with those graduating in the preceding four years?

3. According to Rampell, what are the dangers of having a low-paying "starter job"?

4. As discussed in Rampell, how can those landing a job in a challenging market improve their (initially low) salaries?

5. What data does Johnson point to in justifying the title of her article in the *Chronicle of Higher Education*: "Job Outlook for College Graduates Is Slowly Improving"?

Discussion and Writing Suggestions

1. The topic of marginal job prospects for college graduates is no laughing matter. Yet Brager's "A Post-College Flow Chart of Misery and Pain" brings a smile. Why? What is the role of humor in Brager's "flow chart"? Reread your summary of Brager. Which format—prose or graphic—do you find more compelling? Why? How does the graphic convey Brager's observations on job prospects in way that (1) your summary and (2) Catherine Rampell's article in the *New York Times* (especially ¶s 9–10) do not?

2. Johnson reports in mid-November 2011 that the hiring of college graduates will accelerate regardless of their field of study. Writing six months earlier, Rampell reports that the employment outlook for graduates "is rather bleak." Both writers cite authoritative sources, and both write for reputable papers. As a prospective job seeker, what do you make of the conflicting reports: Are you left hopeful, dejected, confused? As someone who may draw on these sources for a paper, how would you plan to use such conflicting evidence?

3. Brager premises her "Flow Chart" on a trend obvious to many who major in the humanities: Finding a job can be difficult when you haven't learned an immediately applicable skill such as accounting or engineering. Rampell draws on sources reporting the same phenomenon. Why, then, do you think that students continue to major in the humanities?

4. Rampell and Johnson cite conflicting data regarding job opportunities for students graduating college. Will you take either of their reports into account in choosing a major? Do you expect to conduct research on postcollege employment prospects relating to your major? Explain.

DATA ON THE JOB MARKET

What do we know about thousands of possible occupations—how much they pay, the ten-year prospects, the kind of education and training needed to land you that interview, what's involved in the job, the working conditions you'll experience? You don't have to guess at the answers, because clear, reliable information is out there. In the second component of this chapter, we take a close look at some of that information.

First, you'll examine unemployment and wage statistics associated with different academic majors, in tables from a report by the Georgetown University Center for Education and the Workforce. The report's coauthors, Anthony Carnevale, Ban Cheah, and Jeff Strohl, sum up their findings in the title "Not all College Degrees Are Created Equal." If such is the case, what effect (if any) will this data have on your choice of major?

Information about almost every possible type of occupation is readily available online, courtesy of the Bureau of Labor Statistics, a division of the U.S. Department of Labor. Every two years, the BLS releases ten-year employment projections as part of a "60-year tradition of providing information to individuals who are making education and training choices, entering the job market, or changing careers." What follows is a summary of the BLS data published as a news release on February 1, 2012. At the end of this summary, look for ten online tables sure to interest anyone contemplating a job search. For instance, one table reveals which industries over the next ten years have the potential for the largest growth, both in total job numbers and in wages.

COLLEGE MAJORS, UNEMPLOYMENT AND EARNINGS:
NOT ALL COLLEGE DEGREES ARE CREATED EQUAL

Anthony P. Carnevale, Ban Cheah, and Jeff Strohl

The question, as we slowly dig out from under the wreckage left by the Great Recession, is unavoidable: "Is college worth it?" Our answer: "Yes, extensive research, ours included, finds that a college degree is still worth it." A Bachelor's degree is one of the best weapons a job seeker can wield in the fight for employment and earnings. And staying on campus to earn a graduate degree provides safe shelter from the immediate economic storm, and will pay off with greater employability and earnings once the graduate enters the labor market. Unemployment for students with new Bachelor's degrees is an unacceptable 8.9 percent, but it's a catastrophic 22.9 percent for job seekers with a recent high school diploma—and an almost unthinkable 31.5 percent for recent high school dropouts.

Here is a look at several factors that current and future college students should consider as they choose their courses:

The risk of unemployment among recent college graduates depends on their major. The unemployment rate for recent graduates is highest in Architecture (13.9 percent) because of the collapse of the construction and home building industry in the recession. Unemployment rates are generally higher in non-technical majors, such as the Arts (11.1 percent), Humanities and Liberal Arts (9.4 percent), Social Science (8.9 percent) and Law and Public Policy (8.1 percent).

Unemployment in majors related to computers and mathematics vary widely depending on the technical and scientific content of the major. Employers are still hiring technical computer specialists who can write software and invent new applications. But for information specialists who use software to manipulate, mine, and disseminate information, hiring slows down in recessions. We can see the difference in unemployment between people who invent computer technology as opposed to people who use computer technology. The unemployment rate for recent college graduates in Information Systems has spiked to 11.7 percent, while the rates for majors in Computer Science and Mathematics are 7.8 percent and 6.0 percent, respectively.

Computer majors are likely to bounce back strongly as the recovery proceeds. For example, the unemployment rate for recent college graduates who major in information systems is a hefty 11.7 percent, but only 5.4 percent for experienced workers who major in Information Systems.

5   **The Education, Healthcare, Business and Professional Services industries have been the most stable employers for recent college graduates.** Unemployment rates are relatively low (5.4 percent) for recent college students who majored in Healthcare and Education because these majors are attached to stable or growing industry sectors. Recent graduates in Psychology and Social Work have relatively low unemployment rates (7.3 percent) nearly half work in Healthcare and Education. The same is true for unemployment among recent college graduates who majored in the Life and Physical Sciences (7.7 percent). More than 60 percent of these recent college graduates who are working have landed in the Healthcare, Professional Contracting Businesses or Education sectors.

Business majors have low unemployment rates (7.4 percent) with the exception of those who specialize in Hospitality Management (9.1 percent), which is hampered by the ongoing slump in Travel and Tourism. Similarly, recent graduates in Engineering do relatively well (7.5 percent unemployment), except for Civil and Mechanical Engineers who are still suffering from the deep dive in manufacturing and construction activity.

Majors that are more closely aligned with particular occupations and industries tend to experience lower unemployment rates. Majors such as Healthcare, Education and those related to technical occupations tend to have lower unemployment rates than more general majors, like Humanities and Liberal Arts, where graduates are broadly dispersed across occupations and industries. Unemployment rates for recent graduates in Healthcare and Education are 5.4 percent compared to 9.4 percent for people who majored in Humanities and the Liberal Arts. More than three out of four people who major in Education work in the Education industry while no more than 20 percent of Liberal Arts graduates are concentrated in any single industry.

At the same time, majors that are closely aligned with occupations and industries can misfire. For example, tying oneself to a particular major can be a problem if the associated occupations or industries collapse. Unemployment rates for recent college graduates who majored in Architecture start high at 13.9 percent and, due to its strong alignment with the collapse in construction and housing, unemployment remains high even for experienced college graduates at 9.2 percent.

As the recovery proceeds and recent college graduates gain access to work, especially in their major fields, their unemployment rates will drop substantially. Employment patterns among experienced workers who have been out of college for a while suggest that recent graduates will fare better as the recovery continues. With the exception of majors in Architecture, International Business and Theater Arts, more experienced workers have substantially lower unemployment rates and higher earnings than recent college graduates.

10   **Graduate degrees make a quantum difference in employment prospects across all majors.** Sometimes, when unemployment is high, the best strategy to increase future employability is to go to graduate school. The unemployment rate for people with graduate degrees is 3 percent compared with a 5 percent unemployment rate for those with a BA (recent college graduates and experienced workers holding a Bachelor's degree). With the exception of majors in the arts and Architecture, unemployment rates for people with graduate degrees range between 1.9 percent and 4.0 percent. Graduate degrees tend to outperform BA's on employment in part because advanced degrees represent higher levels of human capital development and because those degrees are more closely aligned with career pathways in particular occupations and industries.

Unemployment Rates Decline as Recent College Graduates Gain Experience and Graduate Education*

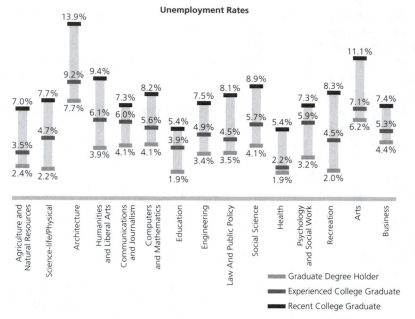

Unemployment Rates

Legend:
- Graduate Degree Holder
- Experienced College Graduate
- Recent College Graduate

Earnings Increase As Recent College Graduates Gain Experience and Graduate Education*

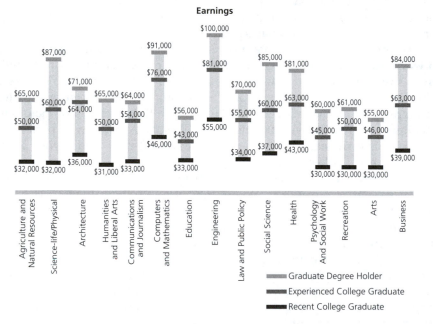

Earnings

Legend:
- Graduate Degree Holder
- Experienced College Graduate
- Recent College Graduate

*ACS 2009–2010, pooled sample. Recent college graduates are 22–26 years of age, experienced workers are 30–54 years of age. Percent unemployed are computed based on total employed and unemployed. Earnings based on full-time, full-year workers.

For example, experienced workers with BA's in healthcare have lower unemployment rates than people with graduate degrees in every other field, except the Life and Physical Sciences. Similarly, a BA in Education can make a job seeker more employable than majors in Architecture, Humanities, Journalism, Computers, Social Science, Arts and Business who go on to graduate school.

What college graduates earn also depends on what they take. Median earnings among recent college graduates vary from $55,000 among Engineering majors to $30,000 in the Arts, as well as Psychology and Social Work. In our more detailed data—which drills into the broad categories to look at results for more individual, specialized majors—the variation is even more pronounced, ranging from $60,000 for Computer Engineering graduates to $24,000 for Physiology majors.

Majors with high technical, business and healthcare content tend to earn the most among both recent and experienced college graduates. Engineering majors lead both in earnings for recent and experienced college graduates followed by Computer and Mathematics majors, and Business majors. Recent graduates in Healthcare majors start out with high earnings, but begin to lose ground to Science, Business and Engineering as college graduates gain experience and graduate degrees. Graduate school further differentiates earnings among majors.

Majors that are most closely aligned with particular industries and occupations tend to have low unemployment rates but not necessarily the highest earnings. Some majors offer both high security and high earnings, while other majors trade off earnings for job security. Healthcare, Science and Business majors have both low unemployment and the highest earnings boost from experience and graduate education. At the same time, Education, Psychology and Social Work majors have relatively low unemployment, but earnings are also low and only improve marginally with experience and graduate education.

15 Although differences remain high among majors, graduate education raises earnings across the board. The average earnings for BA's now stands at $48,000 compared with $62,000 for graduate degrees. With the exception of the Arts and Education, earnings for graduate workers range between $60,000 and $100,000.

It is easy to look at unemployment rates for new college graduates or hear stories about degree-holders forced to tend bar and question the wisdom of investing in higher education when times are bad. But those questions should last only until you compare how job seekers with college degrees are doing compared to those without college degrees.

Today's best advice, then, is that high school students who can go on to college should do so—with one caveat. They should do their homework before picking a major because, when it comes to employment prospects and compensation, not all college degrees are created equal.

Employment Projections: 2010–2020 Summary

U.S. Bureau of Labor Statistics

Industries and occupations related to health care, personal care and social assistance, and construction are projected to have the fastest job growth between 2010 and 2020, the U.S. Bureau of Labor Statistics reported [on February 1, 2012]. Total employment is projected to grow by 14.3 percent over the decade, resulting in 20.5 million new jobs. Despite rapid projected growth, construction is not expected to regain all of the jobs lost during the 2007–09 recession. The 2010–20 projections...depict education, training, and related work experience typically needed for occupations. In occupations in which a master's degree is typically needed for entry, employment is expected to grow by 21.7 percent, faster than the growth rate for any other education category. In occupations in which apprenticeship is the typical on-the-job training, employment is expected to grow by 22.5 percent, faster than for any other on-the-job training category. This news release focuses on five areas: labor force and the macroeconomy, industry employment, occupational employment, education and training, and replacement needs.

Labor force and the macroeconomy*

— Slower population growth and a decreasing overall labor force participation rate are expected to lead to slower civilian labor force growth from 2010 to 2020: 0.7 percent annually, compared with 0.8 percent for 2000–10, and 1.3 percent for 1990–2000. The projected 0.7 percent growth rate will lead to a civilian labor force increase of 10.5 million by 2020. (See table 1).[†]

— The baby-boom generation moves entirely into the 55-years-and-older age group by 2020, increasing that age group's share of the labor force from 19.5 percent in 2010 to 25.2 percent in 2020. The "prime-age" working group (ages 25 to 54) is projected to drop to 63.7 percent of the 2020 labor force. The 16- to 24-year-old age group is projected to account for 11.2 percent of the labor force in 2020. (See table 1.)

— By 2020, the number of Hispanics in the labor force is projected to grow by 7.7 million, or 34.0 percent, and their share of the labor force is expected to increase from 14.8 percent in 2010 to 18.6 percent in 2020. The labor force shares for Asians and blacks are projected to be 5.7 and 12.0 percent, respectively, up slightly from 4.7 and 11.6 percent in 2010. (See table 1.)

— Gross domestic product (GDP) is projected to grow by 3.0 percent annually, consistent with slow labor force growth, the assumption of a

---

*Macroeconomics: the study of the economy as a whole, considering such factors as unemployment, inflation, interest rates, national income, and debt.
†Directions for locating Tables 1–10 online can be found on page 188.

full-employment economy in 2020, and labor productivity growth of 2.0 percent annually.

Industry employment

— Nonagriculture wage and salary employment, which accounts for more than 9 in 10 jobs in the economy, is projected to expand to 150.2 million by 2020, up from 130.4 million in 2010. (See table 2.)
— The health care and social assistance sector is projected to gain the most jobs (5.6 million), followed by professional and business services (3.8 million), and construction (1.8 million). Despite rapid growth in the construction sector, employment in 2020 is not expected to reach its pre-recessionary annual average peak of 7.7 million in 2006. (See table 2.)
— About 5.0 million new jobs—25 percent of all new jobs—are expected in the three detailed industries projected to add the most jobs: construction, retail trade, and offices of health practitioners. Seven of the 20 industries gaining the most jobs are in the health care and social assistance sector, and five are in the professional and business services sector. (See table 3.)
— The 20 detailed industries projected to lose the largest numbers of jobs are primarily in the manufacturing sector (11 industries) and the federal government (3 industries). The largest job losses are projected for the Postal Service (–182,000), federal non-defense government (–122,000), and apparel knitting mills (–92,000). (See table 4.)

Occupational employment

— Of the 22 major occupational groups, employment in healthcare support occupations is expected to grow most rapidly (34.5 percent), followed by personal care and services occupations (26.8 percent), and healthcare practitioners and technical occupations (25.9 percent). However, the office and administrative support occupations group, with projected slower than average growth of 10.3 percent, is expected to add the largest number of new jobs (2.3 million). (See table 5.)
— The four detailed occupations expected to add the most employment are registered nurses (712,000), retail salespersons (707,000), home health aides (706,000), and personal care aides (607,000). All have large employment in 2010 and are expected to grow faster than the average of 14.3 percent. (See table 6.)
— One-third of the projected fastest growing occupations are related to health care, reflecting expected increases in demand as the population ages and the health care and social assistance industry grows. (See table 7.)
— More than one-fourth of the projected fastest growing occupations are related to construction. Employment in most of these occupations, still

at low levels in 2010 because of the 2007–09 recession, will recover along with the construction industry. But employment in most construction occupations is not expected to reach pre-recession levels. (See table 7.)
— Production occupations and office and administrative support occupations dominate the list of detailed occupations with the largest projected employment declines. However, farmers, ranchers, and other agricultural managers top the list, with a projected loss of 96,100 jobs. (See table 8.)

Education and training

— Occupations that typically need some type of postsecondary education for entry are projected to grow the fastest during the 2010–20 decade. Occupations classified as needing a master's degree are projected to grow by 21.7 percent, followed by doctoral or professional degree occupations at 19.9 percent, and associate's degree occupations at 18.0 percent. (See table 9.)
— In terms of typical on-the-job training, occupations that typically require apprenticeships are projected to grow the fastest (22.5 percent). (See table 9.)
— Of the 30 detailed occupations projected to have the fastest employment growth, 17 typically need some type of postsecondary education for entry into the occupation. (See table 7.)
— Two-thirds of the 30 occupations projected to have the largest number of new jobs typically require less than a postsecondary education, no related work experience, and short- or moderate-term on-the-job training. (See table 6.)
— Only 3 of the 30 detailed occupations projected to have the largest employment declines are classified as needing postsecondary education for entry. (See table 8.)

Replacement needs

— Over the 2010–20 decade, 54.8 million total job openings are expected. (See table 9.) While growth will lead to many openings, more than half—61.6 percent—will come from the need to replace workers who retire or otherwise permanently leave an occupation.
— In 4 out of 5 occupations, openings due to replacement needs exceed the number due to growth. Replacement needs are expected in every occupation, even in those that are declining.
— More than two-thirds of all job openings are expected to be in occupations that typically do not need postsecondary education for entry. (See table 9.)
— Eighteen of the 30 occupations with the largest number of projected total job openings are classified as typically needing less than a postsecondary education and needing short-term on-the-job training. (See table 10.)

Interpreting the projections in light of the 2007–09 recession and recovery

The BLS projections are built on the assumption of a full employment economy in 2020. The 2007–09 recession represented a sharp downturn in the economy—and the economy, especially the labor market, has been slow to recover. As a result, the 2010–20 projections reach a robust 2020 target year largely because the 2010 base year began from a relatively low point. Rapid growth rates for some measures reflect recovery from the recession and, with some important exceptions, growth beyond recovery.

A note about labor shortages and surpluses in the context of long-term economic projections

Users of these data should not assume that the difference between the projected increase in the labor force and the projected increase in employment implies a labor shortage or surplus. The BLS projections assume labor market equilibrium, that is, one in which labor supply meets labor demand except for some degree of frictional unemployment. In addition, the employment and labor force measures use different concepts. Employment is a count of jobs, and one person may hold more than one job. Labor force is a count of people, and a person is counted only once regardless of how many jobs he or she holds. For a discussion of the basic projections methodology, see "Overview of projections to 2020," Dixie Sommers and James C. Franklin, January 2012 issue of the *Monthly Labor Review*.

More information

The BLS projections are used by high school students and their teachers and parents, college students, career changers, and career development and guidance specialists. The projections are the foundation of the *BLS Occupational Outlook Handbook*, the nation's most widely used career information resource. The projections also are used by state workforce agencies to prepare state and area projections that, together with the national projections, are widely used by policymakers and education and training officials to make decisions about education and training policy, funding, and program offerings. In addition, other federal agencies, researchers, and academics use the projections to understand trends in the economy and labor market. The projections are updated every two years. More detailed information on the 2010–20 projections appears in five articles in the January 2012 issue of the Monthly Labor Review, published by the Bureau of Labor Statistics, U.S. Department of Labor. The *Monthly Labor Review* is available online at www.bls.gov/opub/mlr/mlrhome.htm. The 2012–13 edition of the *Occupational Outlook Handbook* will feature the 2010–20 projections in assessing job outlook, work activities, wages, education and training requirements, and more for detailed occupations in 341 profiles. The updated *Handbook* will be available online in late March 2012, at www.bls.gov/ooh. A graphic representation of the highlights of the projections appears in the Winter 2011–12 issue of the *Occupational Outlook Quarterly*, available online at www.bls.gov/ooq.

For ready access to Tables 1–10, listed below, go to the BLS Web site.

> **Go to: www.bls.gov**
> *Search terms: "news release February 1, 2012"*

You will find the following tables at the end of this online version of "Employment Projections: 2010–2020 Summary."

- Table 1. Civilian labor force, by age, sex, race, and ethnicity, 1990, 2000, 2010, and projected 2020
- Table 2. Employment by major industry sector, 2000, 2010, and projected 2020
- Table 3. The 20 industries with the largest projected wage and salary employment growth, 2010–20
- Table 4. The 20 industries with the largest projected wage and salary employment declines, 2010–20
- Table 5. Employment by major occupational group, 2010 and projected 2020, and median annual wage, May 2010
- Table 6. The 30 occupations with the largest projected employment growth, 2010–20
- Table 7. The 30 occupations with the fastest projected employment growth, 2010–20
- Table 8. The 30 occupations with the largest projected employment declines, 2010–20
- Table 9. Employment and total job openings by education, work experience, and on-the-job training category, 2010 and projected 2020
- Table 10. The 30 occupations with the largest projected number of total job openings due to growth and replacements, 2010–20

● Review Questions

1. When asked if college is worth the expense and time commitment, why do Carnevale et al. strongly recommend a student's getting a college degree, even in times of recession?

2. The research of Carnevale et al. shows what key relationships between the selection of an undergraduate major and employability?

3. Carnevale et al. include two summary charts presenting multiple comparative data. Review these charts. What data is being compared? What broad conclusions can you draw from these comparisons?

4. According to the Bureau of Labor Statistics *Summary*, what are the employment prospects for those with postsecondary education?

5. According to the Bureau of Labor Statistics, how much of the projected gain in employment will result from growth of the new economy, as opposed to retirement among baby-boom workers?

6. Which employment areas are projected to grow the most, according to the Bureau of Labor Statistics? Which are expected to suffer greatest declines?

7. Examine BLS Tables 6 and 7. What is the difference between the "largest employment projected growth" and the "fastest employment projected growth"?

 ## Discussion and Writing Suggestions

1. Carnevale et al. report some sobering facts about the job prospects for recent college graduates with degrees in the arts and liberal arts. Do you consider these findings an argument against pursuing degrees in these majors? Explain.

2. Carnevale et al. present two charts summarizing their research. You've likely come to college with some idea about which major(s) you expect to pursue. To what extent might you reassess your employment prospects in your intended career field, in light of the data in these charts? Do you see anything here that argues for—or against—pursuing your intended major?

3. Describe the ways in which you might use the Bureau of Labor Statistics *Summary* and Web site to investigate either broad career areas or specific jobs within a broad area.

4. The Bureau of Labor Statistics *Summary 2010–2020* is a vast resource that can provide you with credible statistical information as you complete writing assignments associated with this chapter. Take a moment to skim the synthesis assignments on pages 209–211. For any *one* assignment, locate on these Web pages a statistic that might prove useful in your writing.

5. Use information from this Bureau of Labor Statistics *Summary* to assess the accuracy of employment projections by Krugman or Kessler in this chapter or Blinder in Chapter 1. To what extent do the predictions of the writer you've selected match the projections of the BLS *Summary*?

6. Group work: Join with four classmates and study the ten tables referred to in the Bureau of Labor Statistics *Summary*. Each group member should study the content of two tables and then make an oral presentation of that content to group members.

WORK AND IDENTITY

A significant portion of your life will be spent at work. Your job will make demands of you—complex and often unanticipated demands—and you'll need to adapt in order to succeed. You may need to develop new skills and new ways of interacting with colleagues. This will change you, sometimes in subtle ways. Any activity in which you invest so much of your energy, your creativity, your intellect, and your resourcefulness will, for better or for worse, affect your life far beyond the scope of that activity. It will potentially recreate your sense of self, your sense of the kind of person you've become. If, twenty years from now, a stranger asks you who you are (beyond your name), you may well reply that you're an engineer, or a graphic designer, or a history professor—as opposed, say, to a husband or a mother. In other words, you'll define yourself in terms of your occupation; you'll think of yourself as someone who does a particular job or has a particular career.

In the third component of this chapter, sociologist Richard Sennett investigates the links between work and our sense of identity by relating the story of a man who adapted successfully to the modern workplace but paid dearly in terms of his self-worth. Sennett is best known for his writing about cities, labor, and culture. He is Centennial Professor of Sociology at the London School of Economics and Professor of the Humanities at New York University. During the 1980s, he served as president of the American Council on Work. Sennett is the author of three novels and numerous scholarly studies, including the much-cited *The Corrosion of Character: The Personal Consequences of Work in the New Capitalism* (1998), in which the following passage initially appeared.

No Long Term: New Work and the Corrosion of Character

Richard Sennett

Recently I met someone in an airport whom I hadn't seen for fifteen years. I had interviewed the father of Rico (as I shall call him) a quarter century ago when I wrote a book about blue-collar workers in America, *The Hidden Injuries of Class*. Enrico, his father, then worked as a janitor, and had high hopes for this boy, who was just entering adolescence, a bright kid good at sports. When I lost touch with his father a decade later, Rico had just finished college. In the airline lounge, Rico looked as if he had fulfilled his father's dreams. He carried a computer in a smart leather case, dressed in a suit I couldn't afford, and sported a signet ring with a crest.

Enrico had spent twenty years by the time we first met cleaning toilets and mopping floors in a downtown office building. He did so without complaining, but also without any hype about living out the American Dream. His work had one single and durable purpose, the service of his family. It had taken him fifteen years to save the money for a house, which he purchased in a suburb near Boston, cutting ties with his old Italian neighborhood because a house in the suburbs was better for the kids. Then his wife, Flavia, had gone to work, as a presser in a dry-cleaning plant; by the time I met Enrico in 1970, both parents were saving for the college education of their two sons.

What had most struck me about Enrico and his generation was how linear time was in their lives: year after year of working in jobs which seldom varied from day to day. And along that line of time, achievement was cumulative: Enrico and Flavia checked the increase in their savings every week, measured their domesticity by the various improvements and additions they had made to their ranch house. Finally, the time they lived was predictable. The upheavals of the Great Depression and World War II had faded, unions protected their jobs; though he was only forty when I first met him, Enrico knew precisely when he would retire and how much money he would have.

Time is the only resource freely available to those at the bottom of society. To make time accumulate, Enrico needed what the sociologist Max Weber called an "iron cage," a bureaucratic structure which rationalized the use of time; in Enrico's case, the seniority rules of his union about pay and the regulations organizing his government pension provided this scaffolding. When he added to these resources his own self-discipline, the result was more than economic.

5   He carved out a clear story for himself in which his experience accumulated materially and psychically; his life thus made sense to him as a linear narrative. Though a snob might dismiss Enrico as boring, he experienced the years as a dramatic story moving forward repair by repair, interest payment by interest payment. The janitor felt he became the author of his life, and though he was a man low on the social scale, this narrative provided him a sense of self-respect.

Though clear, Enrico's life story was not simple. I was particularly struck by how Enrico straddled the worlds of his old immigrant community and his new suburban-neutral life. Among his suburban neighbors he lived as a quiet, self-effacing citizen; when he returned to the old neighborhood, however, he received much more attention as a man who had made good on the outside, a worthy elder who returned each Sunday for Mass followed by lunch followed by gossipy coffees. He got recognition as a distinctive human being from those who knew him long enough to understand his story; he got a more anonymous kind of respect from his new neighbors by doing what everyone else did, keeping his home and garden neat, living without incident. The thick texture of Enrico's particular experience lay in the fact that he was acknowledged in both ways, depending in which community he moved: two identities from the same disciplined use of his time.

If the world were a happy and just place, those who enjoy respect would give back in equal measure the regard which has been accorded them. This was Fichte's idea in "The Foundations of National Law"; he spoke of the "reciprocal effect" of recognition. But real life does not proceed so generously.*

Enrico disliked blacks, although he had labored peaceably for many years with other janitors who were black; he disliked non-Italian foreigners like the Irish, although his own father could barely speak English. He could not acknowledge kindred struggles; he had no class allies. Most of all, however, Enrico disliked middle-class people. We treated him as though he were invisible, "as a zero," he said; the janitor's resentment was complicated by his fear that because of his lack of education and his menial status, we had a sneaking right to do so. To his powers of endurance in time he contrasted the whining self-pity of blacks, the unfair intrusion of foreigners, and the unearned privileges of the bourgeoisie.

Though Enrico felt he had achieved a measure of social honor, he hardly wanted his son Rico to repeat his own life. The American dream of upward mobility for the children powerfully drove my friend. "I don't understand a word he says," Enrico boasted to me several times when Rico had come home from school and was at work on math. I heard many other parents of sons and daughters like Rico say something like "I don't understand him" in harder tones, as though the kids had abandoned them. We all violate in some way the place assigned us in the family myth, but upward mobility gives that passage a peculiar twist. Rico and other youngsters headed up the social ladder sometimes betrayed shame about their parents' working-class accents and rough manners, but more often felt suffocated by the endless strategizing over pennies and the reckoning of time in tiny steps. These favored children wanted to embark on a less constrained journey.

10   Now, many years later, thanks to the encounter at the airport, I had the chance to see how it had turned out for Enrico's son. In the airport lounge, I must confess, I didn't much like what I saw. Rico's expensive suit could have been just business plumage, but the crested signet ring—a mark of elite family background—seemed both a lie and a betrayal of the father. However, circumstances threw Rico and me together on a long flight. He and I did not have one of those American journeys in which a stranger spills out his or her emotional guts to you, gathers more tangible baggage when the plane lands, and disappears forever. I took the seat next to Rico without being asked, and for the first hour of a long flight from New York to Vienna had to pry information out of him.

Rico, I learned, has fulfilled his father's desire for upward mobility, but has indeed rejected the way of his father. Rico scorns "time-servers" and others wrapped in the armor of bureaucracy; instead he believes in being open to change and in taking risks. And he has prospered; whereas Enrico had an income in the bottom quarter of the wage scale, Rico's has shot up to the top 5 percent. Yet this is not an entirely happy story for Rico.

---

*Johann Gottlieb Fichte (1762–1814): a German philosopher.

After graduating from a local university in electrical engineering, Rico went to a business school in New York. There he married a fellow student, a young Protestant woman from a better family. School prepared the young couple to move and change jobs frequently, and they've done so. Since graduation, in fourteen years at work Rico has moved four times.

Rico began as a technology adviser to a venture capital firm on the West Coast, in the early, heady days of the developing computer industry in Silicon Valley; he then moved to Chicago, where he also did well. But the next move was for the sake of his wife's career. If Rico were an ambition-driven character out of the pages of Balzac, he would never have done it, for he gained no larger salary, and he left hotbeds of high-tech activity for a more retired, if leafy, office park in Missouri. Enrico felt somewhat ashamed when Flavia went to work; Rico sees Jeannette, his wife, as an equal working partner, and has adapted to her. It was at this point, when Jeannette's career took off, that their children began arriving.

In the Missouri office park, the uncertainties of the new economy caught up with the young man. While Jeannette was promoted, Rico was downsized—his firm was absorbed by another, larger firm that had its own analysts. So the couple made a fourth move, back East to a suburb outside New York. Jeannette now manages a big team of accountants, and he has started a small consulting firm.

15　　Prosperous as they are, the very acme of an adaptable, mutually supportive couple, both husband and wife often fear they are on the edge of losing control over their lives. This fear is built into their work histories.

In Rico's case, the fear of lacking control is straightforward: it concerns managing time. When Rico told his peers he was going to start his own consulting firm, most approved; consulting seems the road to independence. But in getting started he found himself plunged into many menial tasks, like doing his own photocopying, which before he'd taken for granted. He found himself plunged into the sheer flux of networking; every call had to be answered, the slightest acquaintance pursued. To find work, he has fallen subservient to the schedules of people who are in no way obliged to respond to him. Like other consultants, he wants to work in accordance with contracts setting out just what the consultant will do. But these contracts, he says, are largely fictions. A consultant usually has to tack one way and another in response to the changing whims or thoughts of those who pay; Rico has no fixed role that allows him to say to others, "This is what I do, this is what I am responsible for."

Jeannette's lack of control is more subtle. The small group of accountants she now manages is divided among people who work at home, people usually in the office, and a phalanx of low-level back-office clerks a thousand miles away connected to her by computer cable. In her present corporation, strict rules and surveillance of phones and e-mail disciplines the conduct of the accountants who work from home; to organize the work of the back-office clerks a thousand miles away, she can't make hands-on, face-to-face judgments, but instead must work by formal written guidelines. She hasn't experienced less bureaucracy in this seemingly flexible work arrangement; indeed, her own decisions count for less than in the days when she supervised workers who were grouped together, all the time, in the same office.

As I say, at first I was not prepared to shed many tears for this American Dream couple. Yet as dinner was served to Rico and me on our flight, and he began to talk more personally, my sympathies increased. His fear of losing control, it developed, went much deeper than worry about losing power in his job. He feared that the actions he needs to take and the way he has to live in order to survive in the modern economy have set his emotional, inner life adrift.

Rico told me that he and Jeannette have made friends mostly with the people they see at work, and have lost many of these friendships during the moves of the last twelve years, "though we stay 'netted.'" Rico looks to electronic communications for the sense of community which Enrico most enjoyed when he attended meetings of the janitors' union, but the son finds communications on-line short and hurried. "It's like with your kids—when you're not there, all you get is news later."

20   In each of his four moves, Rico's new neighbors have treated his advent as an arrival which closes past chapters of his life; they ask him about Silicon Valley or the Missouri office park, but, Rico says, "they don't *see* other places"; their imaginations are not engaged. This is a very American fear. The classic American suburb was a bedroom community; in the last generation a different kind of suburb has arisen, more economically independent of the urban core, but not really town or village either; a place springs into life with the wave of a developer's wand, flourishes, and begins to decay all within a generation. Such communities are not empty of sociability or neighborliness, but no one in them becomes a long-term witness to another person's life.

The fugitive quality of friendship and local community form the background to the most important of Rico's inner worries, his family. Like Enrico, Rico views work as his service to the family; unlike Enrico, Rico finds that the demands of the job interfere with achieving the end. At first I thought he was talking about the all too familiar conflict between work time and time for family. "We get home at seven, do dinner, try to find an hour for the kids' homework, and then deal with our own paperwork." When things get tough for months at a time in his consulting firm, "it's like I don't know who my kids are." He worries about the frequent anarchy into which his family plunges, and about neglecting his children, whose needs can't be programmed to fit into the demands of his job.

Hearing this, I tried to reassure him; my wife, stepson, and I had endured and survived well a similarly high-pressure life. "You aren't being fair to yourself," I said. "The fact you care so much means you are doing the best for your family you can." Though he warmed to this, I had misunderstood.

As a boy, I already knew, Rico had chafed under Enrico's authority; he had told me then he felt smothered by the small-minded rules which governed the janitor's life. Now that he is a father himself, the fear of a lack of ethical discipline haunts him, particularly the fear that his children will become "mall rats," hanging out aimlessly in the parking lots of shopping centers in the afternoons while the parents remain out of touch at their offices.

He therefore wants to set for his son and daughters an example of resolution and purpose, "but you can't just tell kids to be like that"; he has to set an example. The objective example he could set, his upward mobility, is something they take for granted, a history that belongs to a past not their own, a story which is over. But his deepest worry is that he cannot offer the substance of his work life as an example to his children of how they should conduct themselves ethically. The qualities of good work are not the qualities of good character.

25   As I came later to understand, the gravity of this fear comes from a gap separating Enrico and Rico's generations. Business leaders and journalists emphasize the global marketplace and the use of new technologies as the hallmarks of the capitalism of our time. This is true enough, but misses another dimension of change: new ways of organizing time, particularly working time.

The most tangible sign of that change might be the motto "No long term." In work, the traditional career progressing step by step through the corridors of one or two institutions is withering; so is the deployment of a single set of skills through the course of a working life. Today, a young American with at least two years of college can expect to change jobs at least eleven times in the course of working, and change his or her skill base at least three times during those forty years of labor.

An executive for ATT points out that the motto "No long term" is altering the very meaning of work:

> In ATT we have to promote the whole concept of the work force being contingent, though most of the contingent workers are inside our walls. "Jobs" are being replaced by "projects" and "fields of work."[1]

Corporations have also farmed out many of the tasks they once did permanently in-house to small firms and to individuals employed on short-term contracts. The fastest-growing sector of the American labor force, for instance, is people who work for temporary job agencies.[2]

"People are hungry for [change]," the management guru James Champy argues, because "the market may be 'consumer-driven' as never before in history."[3] The market, in this view, is too dynamic to permit doing things the same way year after year, or doing the same thing. The economist Bennett Harrison believes the source of this hunger for change is "impatient capital," the desire for rapid return; for instance, the average length of time stocks have been held on British and American exchanges has dropped 60 percent in the last fifteen years. The market believes rapid market return is best generated by rapid institutional change.

The "long-term" order at which the new regime takes aim, it should be said, was itself short-lived—the decades spanning the mid-twentieth century. Nineteenth-century capitalism lurched from disaster to disaster in the stock markets and in irrational corporate investment; the wild swings of the business cycle provided people little security. In Enrico's generation after World War II, this disorder was brought somewhat under control in most advanced economies; strong unions, guarantees of the welfare state, and large-scale corporations combined to produce an era of relative stability. This span of thirty or so years defines the "stable past" now challenged by a new regime.

30   A change in modern institutional structure has accompanied short-term, contract, or episodic labor. Corporations have sought to remove layers of bureaucracy, to become flatter and more flexible organizations. In place of organizations as pyramids, management wants now to think of organizations as networks. "Networklike arrangements are lighter on their feet" than pyramidal hierarchies, the sociologist Walter Powell declares; "they are more readily decomposable or redefinable than the fixed assets of hierarchies."[4] This means that promotions and dismissals tend not to be based on clear, fixed rules, nor are work tasks crisply defined; the network is constantly redefining its structure.

An IBM executive once told Powell that the flexible corporation "must become an archipelago of related activities."[5] The archipelago is an apt image for communications in a network, communication occurring like travel between islands—but at the speed of light, thanks to modern technologies. The computer has been the key to replacing the slow and clogged communications which occur in traditional chains of command. The fastest-growing sector of the labor force deals in computer and data-processing services, the area in which Jeanette and Rico work; the computer is now used in virtually all jobs, in many ways, by people of all ranks....

For all these reasons, Enrico's experience of long-term, narrative time in fixed channels has become dysfunctional. What Rico sought to explain to me—and perhaps to himself—is that the material changes embodied in the motto "No long term" have become dysfunctional for him too, but as guides to personal character, particularly in relation to his family life.

Take the matter of commitment and loyalty. "No long term" is a principle which corrodes trust, loyalty, and mutual commitment. Trust can, of course, be a purely formal matter, as when people agree to a business deal or rely on another to observe the rules in a game. But usually deeper experiences of trust are more informal, as when people learn on whom they can rely when given a difficult or impossible task. Such social bonds take time to develop, slowly rooting into the cracks and crevices of institutions.

The short time frame of modern institutions limits the ripening of informal trust. A particularly egregious violation of mutual commitment often occurs when new enterprises are first sold. In firms starting up, long hours and intense effort are demanded of everyone; when the firms go public—that is, initially offer publicly traded shares—the founders are apt to sell out and cash in, leaving lower-level employees behind. If an organization whether new or old operates as a flexible, loose network structure rather than by rigid command from the top, the network can also weaken social bonds. The sociologist Mark Granovetter says that modern institutional networks are marked by "the strength of weak ties," by which he partly means that fleeting forms of association are more useful to people than long-term connections, and partly that strong social ties like loyalty have ceased to be compelling.[6] These weak ties are embodied in teamwork, in which the team moves from task to task and the personnel of the team changes in the process.

35   Strong ties depend, by contrast, on long association. And more personally they depend on a willingness to make commitments to others. Given the typically short, weak ties in institutions today, John Kotter, a Harvard Business School professor, counsels the young to work "on the outside rather than on the inside" of organizations. He advocates consulting rather than becoming "entangled" in long-term employment; institutional loyalty is a trap in an economy where "business concepts, product designs, competitor intelligence, capital equipment, and all kinds of knowledge have shorter credible life spans."[7] A consultant who managed a recent IBM job shrinkage declares that once employees "understand [they can't depend on the corporation] they're marketable."[8] Detachment and superficial cooperativeness are better armor for dealing with current realities than behavior based on values of loyalty and service.

It is the time dimension of the new capitalism, rather than high-tech data transmission, global stock markets, or free trade, which most directly affects people's emotional lives outside the workplace. Transposed to the family realm, "No long term" means keep moving, don't commit yourself, and don't sacrifice. Rico suddenly erupted on the plane, "You can't imagine how stupid I feel when I talk to my kids about commitment. It's an abstract virtue to them; they don't see it anywhere." Over dinner I simply didn't understand the outburst, which seemed apropos of nothing. But his meaning is now clearer to me as a reflection upon himself. He means the children don't see commitment practiced in the lives of their parents or their parents' generation.

Similarly, Rico hates the emphasis on teamwork and open discussion which marks an enlightened, flexible workplace once those values are transposed to the intimate realm. Practiced at home, teamwork is destructive, marking an absence of authority and of firm guidance in raising children. He and Jeannette, he says, have seen too many parents who have talked every family issue to death for fear of saying "No!," parents who listen too well, who understand beautifully rather than lay down the law; they have seen as a result too many disoriented kids.

"Things have to hold together," Rico declared to me. Again, I didn't at first quite get this, and he explained what he meant in terms of watching television. Perhaps unusually, Rico and Jeannette make it a practice to discuss with their two sons the relation between movies or sitcoms the boys watch on the tube and events in the newspapers. "Otherwise it's just a jumble of images." But mostly the connections concern the violence and sexuality the children see on television. Enrico constantly spoke in little parables to drive home questions of character; these parables he derived from his work as a janitor—such as "You can ignore dirt but it won't go away." When I first knew Rico as an adolescent, he reacted with a certain shame to these homely snippets of wisdom. So now I asked Rico if he too made parables or even just drew ethical rules from his experience at work. He first ducked answering directly—"There's not much on TV about that sort of thing"—then replied, "And well, no, I don't talk that way."

Behavior which earns success or even just survival at work thus gives Rico little to offer in the way of a parental role model. In fact, for this modern couple, the problem is just the reverse: how can they protect family relations from succumbing to the short-term behavior, the meeting mindset, and above all the weakness of loyalty and commitment which mark the modern workplace? In place of the chameleon values of the new economy, the family—as Rico sees it—should emphasize instead formal obligation, trustworthiness, commitment, and purpose. These are all long-term virtues.

40   This conflict between family and work poses some questions about adult experience itself. How can long-term purposes be pursued in a short-term society? How can durable social relations be sustained? How can a human being develop a narrative of identity and life history in a society composed of episodes and fragments? The conditions of the new economy feed instead on experience which drifts in time, from place to place, from job to job. If I could state Rico's dilemma more largely, short-term capitalism threatens to corrode his character, particularly those qualities of character which bind human beings to one another and furnishes each with a sense of sustainable self.

·   ·   ·

Rico's experiences with time, place, and work are not unique; neither is his emotional response. The conditions of time in the new capitalism have created a conflict between character and experience, the experience of disjointed time threatening the ability of people to form their characters into sustained narratives.

At the end of the fifteenth century, the poet Thomas Hoccleve declared in *The Regiment of Princes*, "Allas, wher ys this worldes stabylnesse?"—a lament that appears equally in Homer or in Jeremiah in the Old Testament.[9] Through most of human history, people have accepted the fact that their lives will shift suddenly due to wars, famines, or other disasters, and that they will have to improvise in order to survive. Our parents and grandparents were filled with anxiety in 1940, having endured the wreckage of the Great Depression and facing the looming prospect of a world war.

What's peculiar about uncertainty today is that it exists without any looming historical disaster; instead it is woven into the everyday practices of a vigorous capitalism. Instability is meant to be normal, Schumpeter's entrepreneur served up as an ideal Everyman. Perhaps the corroding of character is an inevitable consequence. "No long term" disorients action over the long term, loosens bonds of trust and commitment, and divorces will from behavior.

I think Rico knows he is both a successful and a confused man. The flexible behavior which has brought him success is weakening his own character in ways for which there exists no practical remedy. If he is an Everyman for our times, his universality may lie in that dilemma.

Notes

[1] Quoted in *New York Times*, Feb. 13, 1996, pp. D1, D6.

[2] Corporations like Manpower grew 240 percent from 1985 to 1995. As I write, the Manpower firm, with 600,000 people on its payroll, compared with the 400,000 at General Motors and 350,000 at IBM, is now the country's largest employer.

[3] James Champy, *Re-engineering Management* (New York: HarperBusiness, 1995) p. 119, pp. 39–40.

[4] Walter Powell and Laurel Smith-Doerr, "Networks and Economic Life," in Neil Smelser and Richard Swedberg, eds., *The Handbook of Economic Sociology* (Princeton: Princeton University Press, 1994), p. 381.

[5] Ibid.

[6] Mark Granovetter, "The Strength of Weak Ties, " *American Journal of Sociology* 78 (1973), 1360–80.

[7] John Kotter, *The New Rules* (New York: Dutton, 1995) pp. 81, 159.

[8] Anthony Sampson, *Company Man* (New York: Random House, 1995), pp. 226–27.

[9] Quoted in Ray Pahl, *After Success: Fin de Siècle Anxiety and Identity* (Cambridge, U.K.: Polity Press, 1995), pp. 163–64.

Review Questions

1. What does "No long term" mean—as compared to "Long term"? How does Sennett use "No long term" as a "motto" to describe changes in the new economy?

2. Sennett describes Rico and his father, Enrico, as having different life narratives. What are these narratives? How do they differ? How do they lead to Rico's distress?

3. In the new economy, according to Sennett, what changes have occurred in the structure of businesses and the ways in which workers are assigned and do work?

4. Why does Rico feel that he needs to protect his family from behavior patterns and values now commonplace in the new economy?

5. Reread ¶s 39 and 43, in which Sennett summarizes Rico's "dilemma." What is that dilemma?

● Discussion and Writing Suggestions

1. Sennett compares the old world of work and its values to modern work and its values. He suggests that workers in the new "knowledge" economy pay a psychic price for their labor. What is that price? Does the loss of those values associated with "old" work seem like a loss to you? Explain.

2. Sennett argues that a person's identity is intimately tied to the work s/he does. How so? In what ways have you (or have you not) found this connection to be true?

3. Rico's "deepest worry," according to Sennett, "is that he cannot offer the substance of his work life as an example to his children of how they should conduct themselves ethically. The qualities of good work are not the qualities of good character" (¶ 24). In your experience, is this so? If you don't feel you have the life experience to respond, pose this question to someone who you think does—someone who has worked a decade or more.

4. Is there any sense in which you find Sennett to be nostalgic—that is, longing for a world of work that is largely gone? Have you experienced in your own work any of the "old work" values discussed here? Are these values disappearing? Are they worth fighting for? Do you, as a worker, have any say in the matter? If you don't feel you have the life experience to respond, pose these questions to someone who you think does— someone who has worked a decade or more.

5. According to Sennett, "a young American with at least two years of college can expect to change jobs at least eleven times in the course of working, and change his or her skill base at least three times during those forty years of labor" (¶ 25). What is your "gut level" response to these projections concerning changes in jobs and skill base?

6. In these times, most college graduates would be happy to find a job— period. Is it too much to ask that your first job be "meaningful" in the sense Sennett describes?

7. Sennett describes Rico as a man in crisis. Do you sense a "crisis" in the modern workplace? To what extent does the work demanded of people in this economy place a burden on or confuse our identities? If you don't feel you have the life experience to respond, pose these questions to someone who you think does—someone who has worked a decade or more.

TRENDS AFFECTING WORK

The authors in this fourth and final component of readings don't use crystal balls to predict the future of working life in America. Instead, these analysts—an investigative reporter, an economist, and a former hedge-fund manager—rely on research and their own professional experience to anticipate coming changes in a dynamic job market. They are making informed guesses; and though they approach their common topic from various points of view, many of their guesses overlap. If they are right, the implications for your own working life will be substantial.

WILL YOUR JOB BE EXPORTED? [SUMMARY]

Alan S. Blinder

Alan S. Blinder is the Gordon S. Rentschler Memorial Professor of Economics at Princeton University. He has served as vice chairman of the Federal Reserve Board and was a member of President Clinton's original Council of Economic Advisers. This article first appeared in *The American Prospect* in November 2006. The following summary of "Will Your Job Be Exported?" appears in Chapter 1, in the context of a discussion on how to write summaries. See pp. 8–14 for the complete text of this important article.

In "Will Your Job Be Exported?" economist Alan S. Blinder argues that the quality and security of future jobs in America's services sector will be determined by how "offshorable" those jobs are. For the past 25 years, the greater a worker's skill or level of education, the better and more stable the job. No longer. Advances in technology have brought to the service sector the same pressures that forced so many manufacturing jobs offshore to China and India. The rate of offshoring in the service sector will accelerate, and jobs requiring both relatively little education (like call-center staffing) and extensive education (like software development) will increasingly be lost to workers overseas.

These losses will "eventually exceed" losses in manufacturing, but not all service jobs are equally at risk. While "personal services" workers (like barbers and surgeons) will be relatively safe from offshoring because their work requires close physical proximity to customers, "impersonal services" workers (like call-center operators and radiologists), regardless of their skill or education, will be at risk because their work can be completed remotely without loss of quality and then delivered via phone or computer. "[T]he relative demand for labor in the United States will [probably] shift away from impersonal services and toward personal services."

Blinder recommends three courses of action: He advises young people to plan for "a high-end personal services occupation that is not offshorable." He urges educators to prepare the future workforce by anticipating the needs of a personal services economy and redesigning classroom instruction and vocational training accordingly. Finally, he urges the government to adopt policies that will improve existing personal services jobs by increasing wages for low-wage workers; retraining workers to take on better jobs; and increasing opportunities in high-demand, well-paid areas like nursing and carpentry. Ultimately, Blinder wants America to prepare a new generation to "lead and innovate" in an economy that will continue exporting jobs that require "following and copying."

● Review Questions

1. What is "offshoring"? Why have service jobs been thought "immune to foreign competition"?

2. Explain Blinder's distinction between "personal services" and "impersonal services." Why is this distinction important?

3. In the past 25 years, what role has education played in preparing people for work? How does Blinder see that role changing in the coming decades?

4. What advice does Blinder offer to young people preparing for future work in the coming decades?

5. Why will the United States eventually lose more service-sector than manufacturing-sector jobs?

● Discussion and Writing Suggestions

1. Identify a worker (real or imagined) in a job that may be at risk for offshoring, according to Blinder. Write a letter to that person, apprising him or her of the potential danger and offering advice you think appropriate.

2. What is your reaction to Blinder's claim that educational achievement, in and of itself, will be less of a predictor of job quality and security than it once was?

3. Describe a well-paying job that would not require a college education but that should, according to Blinder, be immune to offshoring. Compare your responses to those of your classmates.

4. What work can you imagine doing in ten years? Describe that work in a concise paragraph. Now analyze your description as Blinder might. How secure is your future job likely to be?

5. Approach friends who have not read the Blinder article with his advice on preparing for future work (see Review Question 4). Report on their reactions.

6. What were your *emotional* reactions to Blinder's article? Did the piece leave you feeling hopeful, anxious, apprehensive, excited? Explain.

IS YOUR JOB AN ENDANGERED SPECIES?

Andy Kessler

Which types of jobs are most likely to go away in the new economy? This former chip designer, programmer, and hedge-fund manager presents likely candidates—in fact, a whole category of candidates. Kessler contributes frequently to the op-ed pages of the *New York Times* and the *Wall Street Journal,* in which this piece first appeared on February 17, 2011. His most recent book is *Eat People and Other Unapologetic Rules for Game-Changing Entrepreneurs* (2011). In nominating Kessler's *Eat People* for its annual award of best business books, the publisher of 800ceoread.com writes that "Kessler has made a career out of seeing the future of business, as an analyst, investment banker, venture capitalist, and hedge fund manager. Now he explains how the world's greatest entrepreneurs don't just start successful companies—they overturn entire industries."

So where the heck are all the jobs? Eight-hundred billion in stimulus and $2 trillion in dollar-printing and all we got were a lousy 36,000 jobs last month. That's not even enough to absorb population growth.

You can't blame the fact that 26 million Americans are unemployed or underemployed on lost housing jobs or globalization—those excuses are played out. To understand what's going on, you have to look behind the headlines. That 36,000 is a net number. The Bureau of Labor Statistics shows that in December some 4,184,000 workers (seasonally adjusted) were hired, and 4,162,000 were "separated" (i.e., laid off or quit). This turnover tells the story of our economy—especially if you focus on jobs lost as a clue to future job growth.

With a heavy regulatory burden, payroll taxes and health-care costs, employing people is very expensive. In January, the Golden Gate Bridge announced that it will have zero toll takers next year: They've been replaced by wireless FastTrak payments and license-plate snapshots.

Technology is eating jobs—and not just toll takers.

5   Tellers, phone operators, stock brokers, stock traders: These jobs are nearly extinct. Since 2007, the New York Stock Exchange has eliminated 1,000 jobs. And when was the last time you spoke to a travel agent? Nearly all of them have been displaced by technology and the Web. Librarians can't find 36,000 results in 0.14 seconds, as Google can. And a snappily dressed postal worker can't instantly deliver a 140-character tweet from a plane at 36,000 feet.

So which jobs will be destroyed next? Figure that out and you'll solve the puzzle of where new jobs will appear.

Forget blue-collar and white-collar. There are two types of workers in our economy: creators and servers. Creators are the ones driving productivity—writing code, designing chips, creating drugs, running search engines. Servers, on the other hand, service these creators (and other servers) by building homes, providing food, offering legal advice, and working at the Department of Motor Vehicles. Many servers will be replaced by machines, by computers and by changes in how business operates. It's no coincidence that Google announced it plans to hire 6,000 workers in 2011.

But even the label "servers" is too vague. So I've broken down the service economy further, as a guide to figure out the next set of unproductive jobs that will disappear. (Don't blame me if your job is listed here; technology spares no one, not even writers.)

- *Sloppers* are those that move things—from one side of a store or factory to another. Amazon is displacing thousands of retail workers. DMV employees and so many other government workers move information from one side of a counter to another without adding any value. Such sloppers are easy to purge with clever code.

- *Sponges* are those who earned their jobs by passing a test meant to limit supply. According to this newspaper, 23% of U.S. workers now need a state license. The Series 7 exam is required for stock brokers. Cosmetologists, real estate brokers, doctors and lawyers all need government certification. All this does is legally bar others from doing the same job, so existing workers can charge more and sponge off the rest of us.

  But eDiscovery is the hottest thing right now in corporate legal departments. The software scans documents and looks for important keywords and phrases, displacing lawyers and paralegals who charge hundreds of dollars per hour to read the often millions of litigation documents. Lawyers, understandably, hate eDiscovery.

  Doctors are under fire as well, from computer imaging that looks inside of us and from Computer Aided Diagnosis, which looks for patterns in X-rays to identify breast cancer and other diseases more cheaply and effectively than radiologists do. Other than barbers, no sponges are safe.

- *Supersloppers* mark up prices based on some marketing or branding gimmick, not true economic value. That Rolex Oyster Perpetual Submariner Two-Tone Date for $9,200 doesn't tell time as well as the free clock on my iPhone, but supersloppers will convince you to buy it. Markups don't generate wealth, except for those marking up. These products and services provide a huge price umbrella for something better to sell under.

- *Slimers* are those that work in finance and on Wall Street. They provide the grease that lubricates the gears of the economy. Financial firms provide access to capital, shielding companies from the volatility of the stock and bond and derivative markets. For that, they charge hefty fees. But electronic trading has cut into their profits, and corporations are negotiating lower fees for mergers and financings. Wall Street will always exist, but with many fewer workers.

- *Thieves* have a government mandate to make good money and a franchise that could disappear with the stroke of a pen. You know many of them: phone companies, cable operators and cellular companies are the obvious ones. But there are more annoying ones—asbestos testing and removal, plus all the regulatory inspectors who don't add value beyond making sure everyone pays them. Technologies like Skype have picked off phone companies by lowering international rates. And consumers are cutting expensive cable TV services in favor of Web-streamed video.

Like it or not, we are at the beginning of a decades-long trend. Beyond the demise of toll takers and stock traders, watch enrollment dwindle in law schools and medical schools. Watch the divergence in stock performance between companies that actually create and those that are in transition—just look at Apple, Netflix and Google over the last five years as compared to retailers and media.

10   But be warned that this economy is incredibly dynamic, and there is no quick fix for job creation when so much technology-driven job destruction is taking place. Fortunately, history shows that labor-saving machines haven't decreased overall employment even when they have made certain jobs obsolete. Ultimately the economic growth created by new jobs always overwhelms the drag from jobs destroyed—if policy makers let it happen.

● Review Questions

1. What is the main development that drives job destruction, according to Kessler? What impact does this development have on the overall economy, over time?

2. What are the two main types of workers in our economy, according to Kessler? What type of worker is in greater danger of losing his/her job today? What further subdivisions does Kessler make?

3. How is eDiscovery representative, for Kessler, of important changes underway in our economy?

● Discussion and Writing Suggestions

1. What associations do you make with the category names Kessler invents for his article? Why might Kessler have chosen these particular names in his analysis of the economy? What effect do these names have on your understanding of (and your emotional response to) the subject under discussion?

2. Conservatives generally favor a smaller, less-intrusive government with lower taxes, fewer regulations, and fewer social welfare benefits. What language does Kessler use that suggests his conservative leanings?

3. Kessler claims that an entire class of jobs is at risk. Based on what you have read in this chapter and have seen for yourself, how convincing do you find Kessler's analysis of our economy? What evidence do you see that he may be wrong or has overstated his case?

4. Describe Kessler's overall tone (see p. 38), or stance, in this article. How well matched do you find Kessler's tone for the analysis he is presenting to readers of the *Wall Street Journal*?

5. Consider the jobs you see yourself pursuing upon graduation. Where do these jobs fit into Kessler's two broadest categories; and where, if at all, into his sub-categories? Does Kessler's analysis of the economy give you confidence that the jobs that interest you will exist in ten, twenty, or thirty years?

DEGREES AND DOLLARS

Paul Krugman

Paul Krugman, Professor of Economics and International Affairs at Princeton University, won the Nobel Prize for economics in 2008 for his work on free trade and globalization. As a columnist for the *New York Times*, Krugman writes regularly on economic trends. In this piece, published in the *Times* on March 6, 2011, he sticks a pin in the conventional wisdom that to secure a good job these days, job seekers need "ever higher levels" of education. In fact, writes Krugman, jobs that require many years of schooling are vulnerable to elimination by new technologies and competition from overseas. Winner of numerous awards in addition to the Nobel, Krugman has written twenty books for both scholarly and lay audiences.

It is a truth universally acknowledged that education is the key to economic success.* Everyone knows that the jobs of the future will require ever higher levels of skill. That's why, in an appearance Friday with former Florida Gov. Jeb Bush, President Obama declared that "If we want more good news on the jobs front then we've got to make more investments in education."

But what everyone knows is wrong.

The day after the Obama-Bush event, *The Times* published an article about the growing use of software to perform legal research. Computers, it turns out, can quickly analyze millions of documents, cheaply performing

*Krugman makes a sly allusion to the opening line of Jane Austen's *Pride and Prejudice* ("It is a truth universally acknowledged, that a single man in possession of a good fortune must be in want of a wife").

a task that used to require armies of lawyers and paralegals. In this case, then, technological progress is actually reducing the demand for highly educated workers.

And legal research isn't an isolated example. As the article points out, software has also been replacing engineers in such tasks as chip design. More broadly, the idea that modern technology eliminates only menial jobs, that well-educated workers are clear winners, may dominate popular discussion, but it's actually decades out of date.

5   The fact is that since 1990 or so the U.S. job market has been characterized not by a general rise in the demand for skill, but by "hollowing out": both high-wage and low-wage employment have grown rapidly, but medium-wage jobs—the kinds of jobs we count on to support a strong middle class—have lagged behind. And the hole in the middle has been getting wider: many of the high-wage occupations that grew rapidly in the 1990s have seen much slower growth recently, even as growth in low-wage employment has accelerated.

Why is this happening? The belief that education is becoming ever more important rests on the plausible-sounding notion that advances in technology increase job opportunities for those who work with information—loosely speaking, that computers help those who work with their minds, while hurting those who work with their hands.

Some years ago, however, the economists David Autor, Frank Levy and Richard Murnane argued that this was the wrong way to think about it. Computers, they pointed out, excel at routine tasks, "cognitive and manual tasks that can be accomplished by following explicit rules." Therefore, any routine task—a category that includes many white-collar, nonmanual jobs—is in the firing line. Conversely, jobs that can't be carried out by following explicit rules—a category that includes many kinds of manual labor, from truck drivers to janitors—will tend to grow even in the face of technological progress.

And here's the thing: Most of the manual labor still being done in our economy seems to be of the kind that's hard to automate. Notably, with production workers in manufacturing down to about 6 percent of U.S. employment, there aren't many assembly-line jobs left to lose. Meanwhile, quite a lot of white-collar work currently carried out by well-educated, relatively well-paid workers may soon be computerized. Roombas are cute, but robot janitors are a long way off; computerized legal research and computer-aided medical diagnosis are already here.

And then there's globalization. Once, only manufacturing workers needed to worry about competition from overseas, but the combination of computers and telecommunications has made it possible to provide many services at long range. And research by my Princeton colleagues Alan Blinder and Alan Krueger suggests that high-wage jobs performed by highly educated workers are, if anything, more "offshorable" than jobs done by low-paid, less-educated workers. If they're right, growing international trade in services will further hollow out the U.S. job market.

10   So what does all this say about policy?

Yes, we need to fix American education. In particular, the inequalities Americans face at the starting line—bright children from poor families are less likely to finish college than much less able children of the affluent—aren't just an outrage; they represent a huge waste of the nation's human potential.

But there are things education can't do. In particular, the notion that putting more kids through college can restore the middle-class society we used to have is wishful thinking. It's no longer true that having a college degree guarantees that you'll get a good job, and it's becoming less true with each passing decade.

So if we want a society of broadly shared prosperity, education isn't the answer—we'll have to go about building that society directly. We need to restore the bargaining power that labor has lost over the last 30 years, so that ordinary workers as well as superstars have the power to bargain for good wages. We need to guarantee the essentials, above all health care, to every citizen.

What we can't do is get where we need to go just by giving workers college degrees, which may be no more than tickets to jobs that don't exist or don't pay middle-class wages.

● Review Questions

1. According to Krugman, what key attribute of a job will determine whether or not that job is likely to be replaced by technology?

2. Why does Krugman believe that those who argue that education is becoming ever more important in securing a good job are mistaken?

3. What has happened to the middle class in America in the past twenty years, according to Krugman?

● Discussion and Writing Suggestions

1. "It's no longer true that having a college degree guarantees that you'll get a good job, and it's becoming less true with each passing decade." Does this statement (in ¶ 12) alarm you? After all, you are (likely) attending college with an eye to finding a good job. Political liberals generally favor government programs that protect poor and working-class Americans, creating the conditions that they (liberals) think will lead to economic opportunities. Liberals are willing to raise taxes in order to provide these benefits. What evidence do you find in this op-ed of Krugman's liberal leanings?

2. Reread the first four paragraphs of this op-ed. What strategy does Krugman use to get the reader's attention? Do you find this strategy effective? Why?

Synthesis Activities

1. Write an explanatory synthesis that reviews the impacts of globalization and technology on the twenty-first-century workplace. What jobs are most—and least—at risk from these two forces? In developing your paper, draw on the selections by Blinder, Kessler, and Krugman.

2. Writing on trends in the twenty-first-century workplace, three authors in this chapter make distinctions that, they argue, provide the keys to future employability: Krugman writes of routine and non-routine work; Blinder, of personal services and impersonal services; and Kessler, of creators and servers. Write a comparison-contrast synthesis that explains this terminology. To what extent are these writers identifying the same trends, while using different terms? To what extent are they describing different trends?

3. Assuming that you are fortunate enough to get a job upon graduation, is it reasonable to expect this job to be personally meaningful? Draw on the selection by Sennett in developing your paper. *Note:* Relatively early in your paper, you should define (both for you and your reader) the word *meaningful*.

4. What are the attributes of workers who are likeliest to succeed in the new economy? Develop your answer into an explanation that synthesizes the attributes for success discussed by Kessler, Krugman, Rampell, Carnevale et al., and Blinder. In the second part of your paper, analyze your own prospects for workplace success based on these same attributes. Respond to two questions: To what extent do you possess these attributes now? To what extent will your intended course of study prepare you to develop these attributes?

5. Sennett concludes that the skills needed to succeed in the new economy may "corrode" one's character. He writes that the "qualities of good work [in the new economy] are not the qualities of good character." He argues that our work affects our character and, ultimately, our prospects for personal fulfillment. Do you accept this connection between work and psychic health? Use the article by Sennett along with examples from your own work experience (or the experience of someone you know well) to develop an argument.

6. In reading the article by Sennett, you may detect a tone of lament—a sense that something of value from the old world of work has been lost in the new economy. Other writers such as Kessler and Blinder look at the economy and see a dynamic transformation (or "creative destruction") taking place. Compare and contrast the degrees of optimism and pessimism among authors in this chapter, considering their

reasons (stated or not) for taking the positions they do. This paper could be an explanatory or an argument synthesis. If an argument, agree or disagree that the authors' optimism or pessimism is warranted. Include arguments supporting your own optimism or pessimism. Remember to organize your synthesis by idea, not by source.

7. Sennett writes that "a young American with at least two years of college can expect to change jobs at least eleven times in the course of working, and change his or her skill base at least three times during those forty years of labor" (¶ 26). Assuming the accuracy of this claim, how can a college student like you prepare for a life of work in which change is constant? As you develop your paper, address the following tension: On the one hand, you can major in a subject that leads you to master a specific skill (like engineering) in current demand in the workplace. (On this point, see Carnevale et al., Rampell, and Johnson.) On the other hand, assuming that the economy will require you to change skill sets, you'll need a broader training. What mix of specific and general skills will you seek in order to prepare yourself for the labor force of the twenty-first century? Develop your response into an argument synthesis that draws on the work of Sennett and Blinder.

8. Carnevale et al. and Rampell establish that students who major in the liberal arts have more trouble finding jobs postgraduation than do those who major in more skills-specific subjects, like engineering. Moreover, when liberal arts majors do find work, they earn less than their counterparts. Why, then, do students continue to major in the liberal arts? What is the value of such an education in a work environment such as the one you now face? Develop your answer in an argument synthesis. Draw on the authors in this chapter to help you make your case. (As part of your argument, you might respond to Sennett's observation about changing "skill sets," as detailed in the Synthesis Activity 7.)

9. What is the importance of your ability to adapt in the twenty-first-century workplace? First consider adaptations you can make as a student still in school—that is, *prior* to entering the workforce. Would you, for instance, consider changing what you study based on the information learned in this chapter and in related labor analyses and reports? Second, as you contemplate future employment, consider adaptations you may be called on to make *during* your working life. What adaptations are possible *as* you are working? Finally, consider both the positive and negative consequences of adaptation. Sennett, for instance, relates the story of a man whose adaptability allowed him to succeed in a corporate culture of downsizing but at the same time "corroded" his character. Develop your responses into an argument that draws on the selections in this chapter.

10. Training beyond high school can lead to a variety of degrees and certifications: the bachelor's degree from four-year institutions; a two-

year associate's degree that demonstrates competence in a particular field; a license that gains one access to a trade; apprenticeships that gain one access to a union; and more. Given the discussions of Blinder, Kessler, and Krugman concerning changes in the new economy and good jobs that are likely to remain for American workers, what are the relative values of these degrees? What can one expect, in terms of employability when pursuing one type of post–high school education over another?

11. Blinder and Krugman find public educators failing in their mission to train students for the types of jobs demanded by the twenty-first-century workplace. How do these authors think we should reform our public schools to better prepare students? Based on what you've read in this chapter, what do *you* think must be done to train students for the jobs of tomorrow? How do we fix education? Develop your answer into an argument.

12. Blinder, Kessler, and Krugman make predictions about employability in the American workplace. Choose any one of these authors. Then, using the Bureau of Labor Statistics *Summary* (with its accompanying tables), assess that author's predictions. Do you see evidence in the BLS *Summary*, for instance, of what Blinder thinks will be an accelerating loss of jobs in the impersonal services economy? Of Krugman's assessment that more education is not necessarily the ticket to stable employment? Of Kessler's categorization of the economy into creators and servers? Each of these authors makes projections that rest on assumptions about the economy. Your task is to consider these arguments in light of the BLS data. Your paper will be a critique to the extent that you are evaluating the arguments of an author; your paper will also be an argument synthesis to the extent that you are using data from one source in your evaluation of another.

13. How do the selections in this chapter illustrate the serious reality underlying "A Post-College Flow Chart of Misery and Pain" by Jenna Brager? The graphic prompts both a smile and a groan. Why? At the risk of destroying a good joke by analyzing it to death, how can the selections by Blinder, Carnevale et al., Kessler, and others help you to appreciate Brager's humor? How would you describe that humor?

RESEARCH ACTIVITIES

1. Interview several workers you know who are in their forties or, preferably, in their fifties. Ask them to describe changes they've seen in the workplace and ask how they're adapting to these changes. Frame the results of your interview in the context of several of the readings in this chapter. That is, use the readings to help make sense of the information you record in the

interviews. Your research paper could take the form of an argument or an analysis.

2. Take a thorough accounting of the "Occupational Outlook Handbook" at the Bureau of Labor Statistics Web site. Prepare a report that presents (1) the range of information available at the OOH site—and closely linked sites; (2) a strategy for mining useful information. Essentially, you will be preparing a "user's guide" to the OOH.

3. Find a copy of Studs Terkel's *Working*, select one of the interviewees reporting on his or her experiences at a particular job, and research the current status of this job or career field at the Bureau of Research Statistics Web site. Compare and contrast the experiences of the Terkel subject (mid-1970s) with those of a present-day worker.

4. Visit the career counseling office at your school; interview one or more of the staff people there, and survey the publications available at the office to determine facts about the interests and employment prospects of the student body at your school. Write a report on the success your fellow students have had in securing internships at local businesses or job placements with local employers.

5. Research the term "creative destruction" as developed by Joseph Schumpeter and report on its acceptance by present-day economists.

6. Trace the changing attitudes toward work in Western culture. Authors of interest will likely include Herbert Applebaum, Melvin Kranzberg and Joseph Gies, Richard Donkin, and Joanne Ciulla.

7. Research the origins of the Puritan work ethic and its persistence in American culture. Puritans, writes Melvin Kranzberg, "regard[ed] the accumulation of material wealth through labor as a sign of God's favor as well as of the individual's religious fervor." Be sure, in your research, to look at *The Protestant Ethic and the Spirit of Capitalism* by economist and sociologist Max Weber.

8. Research and report on one jobs-related aspect of the "Great Recession" of December 2007–June 2009, the most significant downturn in the American economy since the Great Depression of the 1930s. Here are five jobs-related topics on which you might report: "underemployment"; the fate of older, laid-off workers; the impact of the recession on American youth employment; job losses in the industries and businesses hardest hit by the recession; the emergence of "Top 10" (or 8 or 20, etc.) lists of "recession-proof" jobs.

Chapter 7

Have You Heard This?
The Latest on Rumor

Beneath the streets of New York City, countless alligators live in the sewers. Entire packs of these menacing reptiles roam the subterranean waterways, waiting to swallow unsuspecting citizens above. These are no ordinary alligators. Flushed down toilets after growing too large for their owners, fed on an endless supply of New York City rats and trash shoved from the streets into grates, they are huge, fearsome creatures. No one has actually seen these nightmarish beasts, but they are certainly lurking below, their sharp teeth just hidden from view.

The alligator rumor might be the high concept for a horror movie if it were true. But of course it isn't. This classic story is a quintessential rumor, having developed over the decades into urban legend. As it circulated and gradually took hold of public consciousness, it became, for many, as good as fact. Then, both New Yorkers and tourists began nervously watching their toes as they approached sewer grates.

How fast do rumors spread? Consider a math problem: On January 1, you tell a story to a couple of your friends. On January 2, each of your friends tells two others. On January 3, each of these tells two more. And so on, for twenty days. The spread of the rumor during the first two days can be diagrammed as follows (P = person):

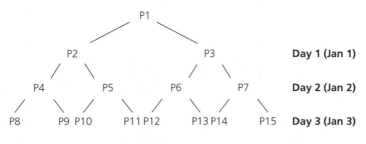

By the 20th of January, how many people will know the rumor? Answer: 2,097,151.

At some moment, a spreading rumor eventually crosses what rumor expert Cass Sunstein calls a "tipping point," the point at which so many people believe the story that it's hard to separate rumor from reality. The alligator rumor began in the 1920s but didn't reach that key moment until it hit fever pitch in the early 1980s. Of course, during the first few decades of this intervening period, there was no TV, much less cable news, and the Internet didn't become an efficient agent of rumor spreading until the '90s. Otherwise, the tipping point for the Big Apple's subterranean alligators would likely have been reached much earlier.

Reconsider the math problem above, which assumes one-day-at-a-time distribution via word of mouth. How would the same problem work in the digital age? In 2012, we can e-mail an entire address book with a simple touch of the "Send" button or "share" with all of our Facebook friends with a quick tap of "Enter." Within seconds, minutes, or hours, a rumor can "go viral," moving from a whispered piece of gossip to an e-mail chain, a Twitter feed, or a recurring story on cable news. As the transition from rumor to perceived reality becomes near-instantaneous, rumors become virtually uncontrollable, both by those who originate them and those who are targeted.

What do rumors tell us about those who start and spread them? Or, as psychologist Nicholas DiFonzo asks, "What is it about being human that sets the stage for rumor activity?" As you will discover in this chapter, rumors can be understood as expressions of our collective fears, hopes, and attitudes about the community and the world we live in. They are outward signs of the way we view one another, individually and in groups. They help us make sense of a sometimes confusing or threatening world by confirming the truth of our world views or our beliefs about how particular groups of people behave. Some rumors encapsulate what Robert H. Knapp calls our "pipe dreams"—our fervent, if unrealistic, hopes. Others offer thinly veiled covers for our anxieties, our concerns about the bad things that might happen. They often confirm what we already believe to be true (even if it isn't). They also drive further apart individuals and groups who are already suspicious of one another. In examining rumors, we discern the psychological, emotional, and intellectual life of our personal and business relationships, our popular culture, our politics, and our society.

Consider political rumors, which often arise out of fears about what a president or political party might do unless stopped. During the health care debate of 2009, so many rumors were competing for public attention (among them, the government's "death panels") that the White House eventually created a Web site to attempt to set the record straight. Two years later, President Obama felt compelled to release his long-form birth certificate to put to rest the stubbornly persistent rumor that he was not born in the

United States. But as *Los Angeles Times* columnist Gregory Rodriguez explains, once we accept as true a rumor that is supported by our own belief system, even hard evidence is unlikely to sway us. The release of the president's birth certificate counted for nothing to some of his opponents, who went to great lengths to explain why the released document was not real or was of suspect origin.

The falsehoods about Barack Obama's citizenship are the most prominent recent manifestations of rumor in American presidential politics. As former John McCain presidential campaign manager Richard H. Davis explains, political rumors have long been a feature of American history. During the 1828 presidential campaign, supporters of Andrew Jackson spread a rumor that his opponent, incumbent President John Quincy Adams, had procured an American woman to provide sexual services for the czar of Russia. Later that century, rumors circulated that Abraham Lincoln was actually the illegitimate son of a Smoky Mountain man named Abram Elroe. Other presidential rumors are rooted in religious bigotry: that Lincoln was a Catholic, that Franklin Roosevelt was a Jew, that Barack Obama is a Muslim. Among the more bizarre recent political rumors was the Clinton "body count," a list of more than fifty suspicious deaths of colleagues, friends, advisors, and other citizens who were allegedly preparing to testify against the Clintons in the wake of the Monica Lewinsky scandal.

Rumors driven by anxiety, fear, and prejudice also proliferate in the immediate wake of national disasters. After the Japanese attack on Pearl Harbor in December 1941, rumors spread that Roosevelt and Churchill had actually plotted the raids as a pretext for U.S. entry into World War II, and even that some of the attacking airplanes were piloted by British and American flyers. After 9/11, rumors spread that the American and Israeli governments were involved in planning the attacks on the World Trade Center and the Pentagon, and that 4,000 Jews stayed home from work that day because they had been told in advance of the targeting of the twin towers. (In fact, such beliefs are almost conventional wisdom among many in the Middle East.)

Many other rumors are focused on the personal—on what is happening, or what could happen, to ordinary people: Dave and his next door neighbor are having a fling; the company where we work is closing down next month (or, if actually scheduled to close down, will stay in business, after all); school jobs in the community are being given to illegal aliens from Jamaica; vaccinations cause autism (or cancer); or—to look back at our model analysis in Chapter 4—travelers abroad who are rash enough pick up sexual companions in lounges risk having their kidneys surgically removed.

In the following pages, then, we explore this problematic but ubiquitous phenomenon of rumor. Among our chief concerns:

- How and why do rumors start?
- How do rumors spread? What are their mechanisms, and what can we do to stop them—or at least, to neutralize them?

- Why do rumors spread? Why are people apt to believe them, even when the evidence suggests they are false? How may rumors confirm what people already believe or suspect to be true?
- In what ways do people use rumors for political, professional, or personal gain?
- What do our rumors suggest about *us*?

The chapter consists of three types of selections: works of art or literature, case studies of particular rumors, and theoretical or reflective pieces that attempt to explain how rumors work. The works of art serve as bookends to the chapter. We begin with the famous *Saturday Evening Post* cover "The Gossips" by the beloved American painter Norman Rockwell, which vividly—and humorously—illustrates the communal spread of rumor. We end by directing readers online to a short story by John Updike, famed chronicler of twentieth-century middle-class suburban angst. In "The Rumor," Updike creates a tale of a long-married couple dealing in unexpected ways with an amusing but potentially damaging rumor.

The case studies offer extended examples of particular rumors. "Frankenchicken" discusses one of the first Internet-fueled rumors, the supposedly genetically modified chicken offered by a popular fast food chain. In "That Old Devil Moon," Sandra Salmans explores the supposed satanic company logo of a major American company. Alan Glenn's "Paul is Dead (said Fred)" traces the life of a Beatles rumor. And focusing on presidential politics, the selections by Richard H. Davis and Samuel G. Freedman dissect the longstanding nature of political rumor mongering, that rare aspect of political discourse that's truly bipartisan.

The theoretical selections attempt to explain how and why rumors work and how they can be fought. In "Truth Is in the Ear of the Beholder," Gregory Rodriguez examines how we accept rumors that confirm our worldview (and reject facts that don't). The classic "A Psychology of Rumor" by Robert H. Knapp explores three particular types of rumor and their causes and responds to the question "What are the qualities that make for a good rumor?" In "It's Clear That It's Unclear," Nicholas DiFonzo explores the ways in which rumors help us to make sense of a complex and sometimes threatening world. Next, in a chapter from his recent book *On Rumors*, Cass Sunstein discusses the manner in which rumors expand through "cascades" and how they are reinforced by "group polarization." Finally, in "Managing Rumors," public relations experts John Doorley and Helio Fred Garcia offer businesspeople a systematic approach to counteracting false stories and reports.

Together, these selections should help you understand rumors in many of their forms and venues: why they're created, how they work, and how we all contribute to their enduring power.

THE GOSSIPS

Norman Rockwell

As children, most of us have played the "telephone game." One person shares a piece of information with a friend, who tells it to another, who tells it to another, and so on. By the time the last person hears the news, the original story has changed into something else entirely. "The sky is blue" can turn somewhere along the line into "the sky is going to fall on you." In the painting below, which originally appeared as the cover of the March 6, 1948, edition of the *Saturday Evening Post*, Norman Rockwell (1894–1978) humorously traces this kind of error-compounding pattern.

One of America's most beloved artists, Rockwell created quintessential, wholesome, and often whimsical images of American life, many of them originally appearing

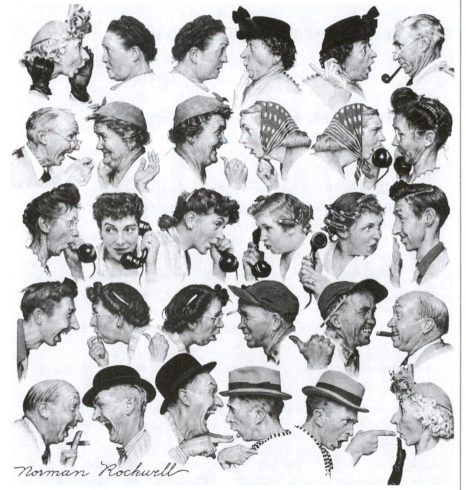

Printed by permission of the Norman Rockwell Family Agency, Copyright © 1948
The Norman Rockwell Family Entities

in the *Saturday Evening Post* (322 of his paintings were published as *Post* covers over a period of 47 years). As his career progressed, Rockwell began to explore the complex issues of his time: civil rights, poverty, and even space travel. His critics sometimes accused him of idealizing and sentimentalizing American life; but Rockwell's reputation has grown in recent years, culminating with exhibitions in art museums in New York, Washington, Raleigh, Chicago, Phoenix, Tacoma, and San Diego, as well as in the White House. Whether depicting an archetypal Thanksgiving meal, a father seeing his son off to military service, or a young African-American girl accompanied by federal marshals as she enrolls in a previously all-white school, Rockwell's work indelibly memorialized mainstream American life. In "The Gossips," he shows the sometimes amusing, sometimes insidious play of that most mainstream of American, indeed human, activities—rumor.

● Discussion and Writing Suggestions

1. Rockwell's painting is called "The Gossips." In your own mind and experience, what are the main similarities and differences between gossip and rumor?

2. Most of us have found ourselves in a situation similar to the one Rockwell portrays here, at least once in our lives. Where was your placement in the line? How did the initial message change during the course of the communication?

3. When a piece of information is transmitted on a wave of gossip, the content of that information—its meaning and implications—often changes drastically. Think about an event from your own life affected by a rumor. In what ways did changes in the informational content of the rumor affect your life? Can you think of a current (or historical) event that has been affected by the mutating nature of gossip?

4. Several figures in this painting are clearly pleased by the gossip. Why do you think some people enjoy getting and passing along salacious information (of sometimes dubious reliability) about their friends and neighbors?

5. Aside from pleasure, what other responses are represented by the figures in the painting?

6. The last two figures in the painting suggest that the end result of gossip is negative. Can you think of any *positive* aspects of sharing information in this manner?

7. Rockwell was known for painting "American" scenes and images. What does this particular piece suggest about American culture—at least in the era (the late 1940s) when this painting was created?

FRANKENCHICKEN

One of life's guilty pleasures is occasionally digging into a plate of crispy fried chicken. But suppose someone told you that what you were eagerly ingesting wasn't really chicken, but a "frankenfood" bird, genetically engineered to have shrunken bones, no beak, and no feet and to be technologically optimized for preparing and cooking? According to the rumor described in the following selection, frankenbirds are exactly what the popular fast food chain KFC uses for its chicken. This rumor has the distinction of being one of the first to spread worldwide via e-mail. In the following selection, the popular site Snopes.com tackles this rampant early Internet rumor and explains why it was just that—a rumor, not the truth. A vast cornucopia of fascinating rumor lore, Snopes.com was formed in 1995 to help Web surfers get to the bottom of online rumors.

Go to: Snopes.com

Search terms: "tastes like chicken"

● Review Questions

1. As it worked its way across the Internet, many people accepted this apparently absurd rumor without question. Why did they find it so plausible? What "facts" were offered in support?

2. What elements of the story (e.g., about corporate practices and corporate deception) seemed reasonable to readers and to those spreading the rumor?

3. While this rumor implies a distrust of corporate practices, how does it also reflect a lack of faith in government?

4. In what ways did contemporary scientific developments contribute this particular rumor?

● Discussion and Writing Suggestions

1. Reading about this rumor in hindsight can make it seem absurd. But plenty of people believed it when it worked its way across the Internet. Why do you think that people found it so plausible?

2. The piece alludes to other popular fast food restaurant rumors, including worms at McDonald's and roaches at Taco Bell. What other restaurant-focused rumors have you heard about? Did you believe them? Why or why not?

3. Snopes.com offers some reasons for the spread of this rumor. Which reason seems most persuasive—and why? What might motivate someone to help spread a rumor like this?

4. Considering how quickly Internet stories can spread, a company can find itself on the wrong side of a rumor in the blink of an eye. If you were running a business, how would you respond to this sort of rumor? (For instance, would you respond at all?)

5. Clearly, the KFC rumor may have affected the public's eating patterns—or at least those of a segment of the population. Have you ever altered your behavior based on a rumor? Tell the story—in a paragraph.

6. What does the wide reach of this particular rumor suggest about rumor transmission in general?

TRUTH IS IN THE EAR OF THE BEHOLDER

Gregory Rodriguez

In this op-ed, published on September 28, 2009, in the *Los Angeles Times*, columnist Gregory Rodriguez argues that rumors thrive because those who hear them are "predisposed to believe them." Drawing upon rumor theorists such as Robert H. Knapp and Cass Sunstein, represented later in this chapter, he explores the ways in which rumors emerge from our anxieties and belief systems. Rumors that support and validate our prior convictions are hard to disprove, even when countered with cold hard facts and solid reasoning. A founding director of Arizona State University's Center for Social Cohesion, Rodriguez writes about civic engagement and political and cultural trends.

Rumors and conspiracy theories can only thrive in the minds of people who are predisposed to believe them. Successful propagators of fringe theories don't just send random balloons into the atmosphere. Rather, they tap into the preexisting beliefs and biases of their target audiences.

Plenty of studies have shown that people don't process information in a neutral way—"biased assimilation" they call it. In other words, rather than our opinions being forged by whatever information we have available, they tend to be constructed by our wants and needs. With all their might, our minds try to reduce cognitive dissonance—that queasy feeling you get when you are confronted by contradictory ideas simultaneously. Therefore, we tend to reject theories and rumors—and facts and truths—that challenge our worldview and embrace those that affirm it.

It's easy to assume that lack of education is the culprit when it comes to people believing rumors against logic and evidence—for instance, that Barack Obama, whose mother was an American citizen and whose state of birth has repeatedly said his birth records are in good order, isn't a legitimate American citizen. But one 1994 survey on conspiracy theories found that educational level or occupational category were not factors in whether you believed in them or not.

What was significant? Insecurity about employment. That finding ties into psychologist Robert H. Knapp's 1944 thesis that rumors "express and gratify the emotional needs" of communities during periods of social duress. They arise, in his view, to "express in simple and rationalized terms the uncertainties and hostilities which so many feel."

5   If, on the one hand, you think you should blame rumormongers and rumor believers for not doing their homework, you can, on the other hand, give them credit for striving pretty hard to explain phenomena they find threatening. Rumors and conspiracy theories often supply simplified, easily digestible explanations (and enemies) to sum up complex situations. However crass, they're both fueled by a desire to make sense of the world.

Can false rumors and off-the-wall theories be corrected by broadcasting the truth? Sometimes, but not always. Access to information, evidently, is not a silver bullet. In his just-published book, *On Rumors*, legal scholar (and new head of the White House Office of Information and Regulatory Affairs) Cass R. Sunstein argues that efforts at correcting rumors can sometimes even hurt the cause of truth.

He cites a 2004 experiment in which liberals and conservatives were asked to examine their views on the existence of weapons of mass destruction in Iraq After reading a statement that declared that Iraq had WMD, the subjects were asked to reveal their views on a five-point scale, from "strongly agree" to "strongly disagree."

Then they were handed a mock news article in which President George W. Bush defended the war, in part by suggesting that Saddam Hussein had weapons of mass destruction. After reading that article, participants were also asked to read about the CIA's Duelfer report, which showed that the Bush administration was wrong to think Iraq had such weapons. Finally, they were again asked their opinion of the original statement on the same five-point scale.

What the researchers found is that the outcome depended on the participants' political point of view. The liberals shifted in the direction of greater disagreement, while the conservatives showed a significant shift in agreeing with the original statement. As the researchers put it, "The correction backfired—conservatives who received the correction telling them that Iraq did not have WMD were more likely to believe that Iraq had WMD."

10   Are you scared yet? I am.

Sunstein's book goes on to explore ways that society can hold rumormongers accountable without eliciting a chilling effect on the freedom of speech. He's concerned that crazy rumors in the Internet Age can gum up the machinery of democracy itself.

I applaud the effort, but I'd prefer to do away with the insecurity and uncertainty that feed wacko theories and rumors in the first place. A modicum of stability, a fair and functioning economy and polity—those have to be what we strive for.

But in the meantime, don't forget psychologist Knapp. "To decry the ravages of rumor-mongering is one thing," he wrote, "to control it is yet another." Pass it on.

● Review Questions

1. Define "biased assimilation."

2. Which factors concerning rumors were found *not* to be of importance, according to a 1994 study? Which *were* found significant?

3. In what ways are the views of psychologist Robert H. Knapp supported by the 1994 findings discussed here?

4. How did researchers draw a connection between the political stance of participants and their beliefs about the justification for the Iraq War?

● Discussion and Writing Suggestions

1. Rodriguez suggests that when confronted with information that flies in the face of our personal ideologies, we often ignore the new information and stick with what we already believe. Discuss an occasion when you changed your mind on a subject based on new information or— conversely—a time when you ignored or rationalized away new data in order to justify sticking with your existing belief or set of values.

2. Rodriguez describes a 2004 study concerning participants' changing views about the justification of the U.S. war in Iraq—both before and after participants were presented with the "facts" about Iraq's weapons of mass destruction. What other recent events or controversies have sparked broad, vocal opinions about "facts" that have since been discredited? Consider stories such as the controversies over the president's birth certificate and religious beliefs. In these or other like cases, to what extent do you find that facts, when eventually revealed, make a difference to people's convictions?

3. Rodriguez summarizes Cass Sunstein's view that trying to correct false rumors is often counterproductive. Cite examples of situations in which attempts to clarify a rumor only reinforces it.

4. How does the Internet affect both the spread and the attempted refutation of rumors? What seem to you the differences between reading a correction online, reading a correction in a traditional print source, and being given the correction face-to-face by another person?

5. Discussing those who don't change their opinions after being confronted with the facts, Rodriguez says that we can at least "give them credit for striving pretty hard to explain phenomena they find threatening." What does he mean? To what extent do you agree?

FIGHTING THAT OLD DEVIL RUMOR

Sandra Salmans

Might buying a can of coffee be a way of supporting "black magic?" Could baking a cake be a form of devil worship? If we are to believe a long-standing rumor about Procter & Gamble, the company behind products such as Folger's coffee and Duncan Hines baking mixes, the answer is yes. Rumors suggesting that the company's distinctive moon and stars logo was a sign of some satanic affiliation became so widespread that the company had to go to court to clear its name. Over the years, P&G sued a number of individuals and other companies it claimed were spreading this devil-worship rumor, including the Amway Corporation. After a court process that dragged on for seventeen years, P&G was awarded over $19 million in damages. By that time, the company had already modified its logo in an attempt to put the rumors to rest. That attempt—a major concession to the rumormongers—helped to quiet the story; it also illustrated that once a rumor takes hold, its grip remains tenacious. In this October 1982 *Saturday Evening Post* article, Sandra Salmans traces the ongoing reverberations of a rumor that grew out of reactions to a simple line drawing. *Note:* To view the logo in question, Google or Bing "procter and gamble logo controversy."

Cathy Gebing's telephone rings every few minutes, and the question is always the same: Is the moon-and-stars design on Procter & Gamble's 70-odd products the mark of the devil?

"No, sir, that's a false rumor," Mrs. Gebing answers patiently. "That's our trademark, we've had it about 100 years."

Normally the consumer services department, this is now the rumor control center for Procter, the consumer goods giant that has lately become the focus of a nationwide rumor campaign.

The rumors, first appearing about two years ago, essentially contend that Procter's 132 year-old trademark, which shows the man in the moon and 13 stars representing the original colonies, is a symbol of Satanism and devil worship. The rumor-mongering also urges a Christian boycott of Procter's products, which include Pampers, Duncan Hines and Folgers, plus dozens of other well-known names.

5   After a great deal of indecision about how to combat the rumors, Procter took formal action in July, filing libel suits against seven individuals for spreading "false and malicious" rumors. The company has said that it may file more suits. "What we have to do is make people realize that we mean business," said Robert Norrish, Procter's public relations director.

It is, in fact, a public relations problem and a difficult one.

"Legal recourse isn't a happy way to go," said Robert Schwartz, president of Manning, Selvage & Lee, a leading New York public relations firm, "but they probably had very few alternatives. The company was diverting resources to deal with this, and at some point, you have to call a halt." However, Mr. Schwartz added, if Procter loses the suits, its image will certainly suffer.

Procter has firmly rejected suggestions that it simply remove the offending symbol from its packages. That, however, increases the suspicions of some consumers.

"If it causes controversy, I don't see why they have to have it." said Faye Dease, a clinic supervisor at Womack Army Hospital in Fort Bragg, North Carolina. Mrs. Dease said that, when a mirror is held up to the logo, the curlicues in the man's beard become 666—the sign of the Antichrist.

10   Procter is not the only company to have fallen siege to rumors. McDonald's has found itself subject to whisper campaigns contending alternately that the restaurant chain was giving to Satan or that it was putting worms in its hamburgers. Entenmann's, the bakery owned by the Warner-Lambert Company, was rumored to be owned by the Rev. Sun Myung Moon's Unification Church.

But the rumors have been more enduring at Procter, and the company's course—to go not only to news organizations and clergy for help, but also the courts—has been more aggressive.

Procter is going after the rumor with all the diligence that it devotes to a new product introduction. A three-inch-thick file documents the company's strategy: a map of the United States, showing the geographical sweep of the rumors; tallies, state by state, of the queries to the consumer services department; tallies, day by day, of the nature of the complaint ("Satanic"; "Mentions lawsuits"; "Has heard/seen media reports"; "Check more than one if appropriate").

At the consumer services department, whose toll-free telephone number is printed on every Procter package, the calls first began trickling in two years ago, the company said.

Individuals in a handful of Middle Western states said they had heard that Procter was owned by the Rev. Sun Myung Moon's followers. In November 1980 Procter felt compelled to answer the charges by writing to news organizations in those states.

15   But in December 1981, there were suddenly 1,152 queries, by the company's tally, mainly from the West Coast, and the focus shifted from the Moon church to the devil. "In the beginning, God made the tree," a 75-year-old woman wrote the company. "Where did Satan get Charmin?"

Many callers reported hearing that Procter's "owner" had appeared on a television talk show where he admitted selling his soul to the devil in order to gain the company's success.

Anonymous fliers, usually misspelling the company's name, began to appear at supermarkets. "Proctor & Gamble," one said, "announced on

The Phil Donahue Show Friday that they contribute 10 percent of their earnings to the Satanic religion (which is devil worship)."

"Do you realize," another anonymous flier said, "that if all the Christians in the world would stop buying Proctor and Gamble Products this Company would soon be out of business?"

Procter did a second mailing, to news organizations on the West Coast. But this time there was no letup. By last spring, Procter was getting 12,000 queries monthly about its relationship with the devil. There were reports of ministers, mainly in small Fundamentalist churches, attacking Procter from the pulpit and urging their congregations to boycott its products.

20 Given the dubious results of the news media campaign, John Smale, Procter's president, decided on a less public line of attack. The company wrote to local clergy and enclosed testaments of faith from very prominent clerics, including preachers who led an earlier attack on Procter for sponsoring television shows of what they regarded as questionable morality. The Rev. Jerry Falwell, leader of Moral Majority, a church-based conservative political-action group, wrote that he had talked with Procter's chairman, "and I am certain neither he nor his company is associated in any way with Satanism or devil worship."

By June, however, the center was receiving more than 15,000 queries monthly, including a few from Alaska and Hawaii.

Mr. Smale told Procter's public relations department to forget his earlier cautions. On June 10, "We presented our recommendations to Mr. Smale." William Dobson, of the public relations department, recalled. "It was essentially to go on the offensive."

On July 1, Procter announced its first lawsuits. The litigation was "a very hard-nosed way to generate publicity." Mr. Dobson said. "We were working on the traditional Procter concepts: reach and frequency."

The subjects of those lawsuits and a second wave later in the month— Mike Campbell of Atlanta, William and Linda Moore of Pensacola, Florida, Guy Sharpe of Atlanta, Elma and Ed Pruitt of Clovis, New Mexico, and Sherman and Margaret McCord of Tullahoma, Tennessee—were chosen simply because "they just happened to be the first people where we felt we had enough evidence to go to court," Mr. Dobson said.

25 Most of the leads to ministers had evaporated, and in any case, a suit against a member of the clergy, "frankly, wasn't our optimum choice," Mr. Dobson said.

All but one of the defendants sell products of competing consumer-goods companies, according to Procter. The Moores and Mr. Pruitt are distributors for the Amway Corporation, which sells soap and other consumer products door-to-door. The McCords are distributors for Shaklee, which sells vitamins, household cleaners and personal care products. Mr. Campbell works for a grocery brokerage firm that represents manufacturers of household cleaning products.

However, "there is no evidence that companies are pushing this rumor," Mr. Norrish said. Nor is it clear that they were economically inspired. "We didn't try to figure out motives," he added. "We just want to stop them."

Most of the defendants denied the charges or said that they were convinced the rumors were false.

Mrs. McCord said that she had printed the rumor in her newsletter to other Shaklee distributors, but had realized her mistake and apologized in both the newsletter and a letter to Procter. Mrs. Pruitt said she and her husband stopped distributing anti-Procter leaflets after learning that the rumor was false.

30   William Hurst, the lawyer for Mr. Campbell, said that his client did hand an anti-Procter circular to a supermarket clerk when he was stocking the shelves with Clorox, but it was his only copy, and "he did not believe it."

Mr. Sharpe, a well-known weatherman for WXIA-TV in Atlanta and a Methodist lay preacher, issued a denial that he had made defamatory remarks against Procter & Gamble.

The lawsuits provoked the hoped for flurry of publicity, including network television coverage, and the number of queries to the consumer services department has fallen by half, Procter says. But few of the remaining 250 or so callers each day have heard of the lawsuits. "How do you reach them?" Mr. Norrish wonders.

● Review Questions

1. What do the images in the Procter & Gamble logo actually represent?

2. Which component of the logo occasioned the "devil worship" rumor?

3. Aside from exercising its legal recourse, what did P&G hope to accomplish with its first lawsuits?

4. Why did Procter president John Smale reach beyond the usual media outlets in an effort to deflate the rumor?

● Discussion and Writing Suggestions

1. The logo rumor led many people to boycott Procter & Gamble. Have you ever been asked to boycott a company? Why? In hindsight, to what extent was the boycott based on rumor?

2. Why do you think that the Procter & Gamble rumor was so persuasive and so resistant over the years to the company's attempts at refuting it? In formulating your response, speculate on some of the possible motivations of those who began the rumor and those who spread it; speculate also on the worldviews of those who were so receptive to its content.

3. P&G took a variety of approaches over the years to handling the charges of Satanism, ultimately filing lawsuits that took years to resolve. In the meantime, the company changed its logo. Assume you worked at Procter & Gamble during the years that the devil-worship rumor took hold. How might you have advised the company to adopt a different rumor-fighting strategy? In developing your answer, draw upon both your business sense and what you understand about human nature. In the final analysis, how well (or badly) do you think the company dealt with this persistent rumor?

4. The Procter & Gamble rumor is intertwined with religious beliefs and fears. History is filled with rumors of this nature—for example, the Salem witch trials of 1692. What other rumors have you personally encountered, or do you know of, that you can attribute to religious belief, fear, or just simple misunderstanding? How did these rumors spread, and what were their outcomes?

5. This particular rumor spread in the early 1980s, before the widespread availability of the Internet. At that time, rumors were not spread with the same instantaneous pace as they are now; similarly, companies could not simply respond within seconds by "tweeting" a response in an effort to deflate the rumor. How might the slower exchange of information during the 1980s have affected both the life of this rumor and the company's attempts at refutation? Had the rumor started today, do you think its life span would have been as long as it turned out to be?

A PSYCHOLOGY OF RUMOR

Robert H. Knapp

During World War II, psychologist Robert H. Knapp attempted to classify and identify the numerous rumors circulating at the time (rumors being everywhere in time of war). In his classic article "A Psychology of Rumor," Knapp examined some of the rumors currently or recently in circulation and attempted to create a framework for further study. In this selection, he classifies three main types of rumor, each based on the human emotion that drives it: wish, fear, or hostility. At the time he wrote this paper, Knapp headed rumor control for the Massachusetts Committee on Public Safety. Though the paper (excerpted here) was published nearly seventy years ago, Knapp's classification system continues to be influential in the academic study of rumor and remains useful in accounting for the features of the countless rumors we encounter daily.

[W]e shall define rumor as a *proposition for belief of topical reference disseminated without official verification.* So formidably defined, rumor is but

Knapp, Robert H., "A Psychology of Rumor" from *The Public Opinion Quarterly* 8:1 (Spring 1944): pages 22–31, by permission of Oxford University Press.

a special case of informal social communications, including myth, legend, and current humor. From myth and legend it is distinguished by its emphasis on the topical. Where humor is designed to provoke laughter, rumor begs for belief.

So defined, rumors have three basic characteristics. They have, first, a distinct and characteristic mode of transmission—mostly by word of mouth. Being spread by means of this primitive medium, rumors are more subject than the formal modes of transmission to inaccuracy and capricious distortion.

A second characteristic of rumors is that they provide "information." A rumor is always about some particular person, happening, or condition.

Finally, rumor satisfies. Mythology, folklore, and humor gather impetus from the emotional gratifications which they afford. The same may be said of rumor. Rumors *express* and *gratify* the emotional needs of the community in much the same way as day dreams and fantasy fulfill the needs of the individual. For convenience of notation, this importance aspect of rumors will be called the "expressive" characteristic.

● ● ●

The Classification of Rumors

5 We present here a three-fold classification, based upon the already observed fact that rumors almost invariably gratify some emotional need. In practice it has been found that the emotional needs most frequently served by rumors are wish, fear, and hostility. Accordingly, three basic types of rumors can be delineated.

The *Pipe-dream or Wish Rumor*. Such rumors express the wishes and hopes of those among they circulate. They can be popularly identified with "wishful thinking." The following, found in circulation in Boston during the winter of 1942, are typical examples:

> The Japanese do not have enough oil to last six months.
> There will be a revolution in Germany before summer.
> Lloyd's of London Wall Street are betting 10 to 1 that the war will be over by autumn.

The *Bogie Rumor*. The precise opposite of the pipe-dream rumor is the bogie rumor. Just as the former mirrors the wishes and hopes of the group, so the bogie is essentially derived from fears and anxieties. Bogies range all the way from rumors with a dour and pessimistic quality to the panic rumors so familiar to social psychologists. Typical examples of this type are these:

> The entire Pacific Fleet was destroyed at Pearl Harbor.
> Several thousand bodies of soldiers have washed up off the town of X.
> Crab meat packed by the Japanese contains ground glass.

The *Wedge-driving Aggression Rumor*. The wedge-driving rumor is so termed because of its effect in dividing groups and destroying loyalties its essential motivation is aggression or hatred. In practice almost all aggression rumors turn out to be directed against elements of our own population or our allies. The following are typical examples:

> Churchill blackmailed Roosevelt into provoking war with Japan.
> The British are sabotaging their own ships in American ports so that they will not have to put out to sea.
> The Catholics in America are trying to evade the draft.

• • •

What Makes a Good Rumor

10   1. No successful rumor may exceed a length or complexity greater than the memory span of the group through which it passes Rumor by its very nature must depend upon the memory of its successive tellers. Typically the successful rumor is short, simple and salient. . . .
2. As perception and memory simplify the things we see, so do they simplify the rumors we hear and read. In time, a successful rumor becomes a "good story." This process of heightening some elements, of leveling or deleting others, is accomplished by the following typical distortions:

> addition of a humorous twist
> addition of striking and aesthetic detail
> deletion of qualifications and syntactic complexities
> simplification of plot and circumstances
> assumption of a more familiar form
> exaggeration

> Through the operation of these several processes, the successful rumor emerges with the same vigor that characterizes the folk ballad, the popular witticism, and other products of extensive oral transmission.

3. There are conditions which make it easier for rumors to become distorted. The farther a rumor is removed from known or confirmed fact, the more easily does it seem to get twisted when passed on. Distortion appears to take its greatest toll when a rumor is kept entirely on the person-to-person level and does not appear in the press or on the air. Finally, when there is either great unrest (as in panic) or an acute need for information, rumor tends to undergo its most drastic changes.
4. Names, numbers, and places are typically the most unstable components of any rumor. There are abundant examples of rumors circulating in different totalitarian nations, all of identical plot, yet each employing the names and places familiar to the local populations. Similarly with respect to numbers, rumors are notoriously capricious.
5. From whatever humble beginning a rumor may spring, it is soon attributed to a high authoritative source. This gives the rumor both prestige and the appearance of veracity.

6. Rumors become harmonized with the cultural traditions of the group in which they circulate. The rumors of the secret weapon, rife in France during the early days of the present war, were cast in terms of the Big Bertha* of the last war....

7. The successful rumor, to thrive, must always adapt *itself* to the *immediate* as well as to the traditional circumstances of the group; it must ride the tide of current swings in public opinion and interest. Typically, rumors come in clusters dealing with a single subject. Thus in Boston, rumors of anti-semitic character would dominate the grapevine for one month, only to subside and be replaced with anti-British rumors. The primitive grapevine mentality seems almost incapable of sustaining more than three or four basic ideas at a time. Similarly, in respect to expressive character, rumors at a given time tend to follow a single expressive pattern. This was very clearly demonstrated in England during the last war when waves of "bogie" rumors of defeat or of military disaster were dispelled almost over night by waves of "pipe-dream" rumors telling of the arrival of Russian troops in England.

● Review Questions

1. Identify the three basic characteristics of rumor as established by Knapp.

2. Describe Knapp's classification system for rumor.

3. How do successful rumors become heightened into "good stories" as time goes on?

4. Which aspects of a rumor tend to be the most unstable?

● Discussion and Writing Suggestions

1. Use each of Knapp's categories to classify a rumor you've read about in this chapter.

2. Based on your own experience, and using Knapp's categories, classify at least one rumor that you have heard or helped spread. How does this rumor meet the criteria of the particular category?

3. Knapp's examples of rumor are a product of the public anxieties associated with wartime. What recent rumors can you think of that spring from uneasiness about contemporary events?

---

*Big Bertha was a howitzer—a heavy artillery piece with a 16.5-inch diameter barrel—developed by the German armament manufacturer Krupp just before World War I.

4. The World War II examples used here are specific to Knapp's time. Since then, the United States has been involved in a number of wars and other conflicts. What role do you think rumor plays in this country's current military engagements? Consider both rumors that develop on the home front and rumors that develop among soldiers, sailors, and airmen.

5. Knapp states that rumor is transmitted "mostly by word of mouth." To what extent have you found this still to be the case? How is information that is spread by various methods of transmission interpreted in different ways?

6. Knapp suggests that all rumors grow out of basic human emotions such as hope or anxiety. In what ways have you found his observation to be true (or false) in your own experience or the experiences of people you know?

"PAUL IS DEAD!" (SAID FRED)

Alan Glenn

In the late 1960s, The Beatles were the most commercially successful rock band in the world, and Paul McCartney perhaps its most well-known and beloved singer. So when a rumor started in 1969 that Paul might have died three years earlier, music fans were jolted. According to the rumor, Paul's death had been hushed up, but (in the spirit of imaginative fun) the band had left "clues" about the truth throughout its albums for their fans to decipher. Of course, this morbid scheme would have been outrageous if true. But was it? Originating at a college radio station, the rumor, initially intended as a lark for local audiences, spread across the country. In the pre-Internet age, the rumor moved at record speed, inviting audiences to research the "clues" and find their own. Here, in an article from the November 11, 2009, edition of the University of Michigan's *Michigan Today*, Alan Glenn, a columnist for the *Ann Arbor Chronicle*, explores the relatively innocent beginnings of the rock world's most enduring rumor: "Paul is dead." What happened subsequently is a textbook case of how rumor can spread across the pop-culture landscape. Note: additional illustrations to accompany this selection can be found online. Google or Bing "paul is dead said fred."

In the fall of 1969 a strange and mysterious rumor was circulating on the fringes of college campuses in the Midwest: Paul McCartney of the Beatles was dead.

According to the rumor, McCartney had died three years previously in a horrific car crash. His death—so the story went—was covered up, the surviving Beatles found a double to replace him, and ever since had been hiding clues in their songs and album covers that revealed the truth about their ex-bandmate's grisly fate.

No one knows for certain how the rumor started, or where. But in mid-October it exploded on to the national scene, sweeping the ranks of youth from coast to coast in a matter of days. Suddenly it seemed as if everyone under the age of 30 was either debating the possibility of McCartney's demise or poring over their Beatles records, searching for clues.

The power of the rumor was such that, four decades later, plenty of Baby Boomers still vividly recall the tingling sensation they felt when they first heard an eerie backwards voice emanating from their turntables, and began to consider that Paul might actually be dead.

5   What many do not know is that the rumor might not have come to their attention at all except for a mischievous young U-M natural resources student named Fred LaBour. Indeed, if the McCartney death rumor can be called a modern myth, then Beatles expert Devin McKinney may be correct to identify LaBour as its Homer.

Today, Fred LaBour is best known as "Too Slim," bassist-cum-jokester for the country and western act Riders in the Sky. Forty years ago he was an equally jocular staff writer for the *Michigan Daily* who had been assigned to review *Abbey Road*, the Beatles' latest album.

On October 12, 1969, LaBour was tuned in to radio station WKNR from Detroit when disc jockey Russ Gibb took a call from a listener who wanted to talk about a rumor going around that Paul McCartney was dead. Gibb was skeptical at first, but became intrigued when the caller explained that there were clues pointing to McCartney's death hidden in the Beatles' music.

For the next hour thousands of listeners, including LaBour, stayed glued to their radios as Gibb and his callers discussed the supposed evidence and what could be behind it. The following day LaBour got out his Beatles records, lined them up on his desk, and sat down to write one of the oddest and most influential record reviews ever printed.

On the morning of October 14, the university community awoke to the shocking and incredible report that one of the world's most popular and beloved entertainers was no more. The headline blazoned across the second page of the Michigan Daily proclaimed the awful news:

"McCartney dead; new evidence brought to light."

"Paul McCartney was killed in an automobile accident in early November, 1966," began Fred LaBour's accompanying full-page article, "after leaving EMI recording studios tired, sad, and dejected." McCartney was found four hours later, "pinned under his car in a culvert with the top of his head sheared off. He was deader than a doornail."

10 What LaBour had written was less record review than conspiracy-age fable. He related in detail how the accident had been covered up and a look-alike found to replace the dead musician—not as a rumor, but as if it were fact The mysterious clues were held to be part of a strange and disturbing plot orchestrated by John Lennon, who had it in mind to found a new religion with himself as god and the "reborn" McCartney a Christ-like figure at his side.

According to rumors, the Beatles left clues to Paul's death. Abbey Road's album cover (above) was supposedly flush with such clues, such as Paul's bare feet, and a cigarette in his right hand.

LaBour's story electrified the campus. The *Daily* sold out its entire run by mid-morning, and a second printing was ordered to meet demand. "I remember walking down Ann Arbor streets hearing Beatles music from every single apartment and house," LaBour says. He also recalls occasionally hearing someone trying to play a record backwards—listening for clues.

Indeed, the enigmatic clues seemed to draw most people into the rumor's web—and LaBour's article contained an abundance of evidence for clue-hungry readers to digest.

For instance, the inside cover of *Sgt. Pepper's Lonely Hearts Club Band* features a photo in which McCartney is wearing an arm patch that seems to read O.P.D.—according to LaBour, an abbreviation for "Officially Pronounced Dead," the British equivalent of DOA. On the album's back cover is a photo in which McCartney is the only one of the Beatles facing away from the camera.

15   LaBour also pointed out that on the front cover of *Abbey Road* McCartney is barefoot, signifying death because that is how corpses are buried. Furthermore, in the photo Paul holds a cigarette in his right hand, whereas the "real" McCartney is left-handed.

Then there were the now-famous clues to be found by playing certain songs backwards. When reversed, "Revolution 9" reveals something that sounds eerily like "Turn me on, dead man," while from the outro of "I Am the Walrus" seems to emerge a creepy chorus of "Ha ha! Paul is dead."

"I cannot tell you how many times I listened to those records backwards," says actress Christine Lahti (*Chicago Hope*), who in the fall of 1969 was a nineteen-year-old U-M theater student. Dubious at first, after many repetitions—and the encouragement of friends—she found herself more willing to believe. "After a point you started to hear it," she explains, "just by the power of suggestion."

Lahti suspects that this Rorschach-like nature of the clues accounts for much of the rumor's appeal. "It might also have had something to do with the mind-altering drugs that many people were involved with," she adds with a laugh.

Filmmaker Ric Burns (*New York: A Documentary Film*), then a teenaged Beatlemaniac attending Ann Arbor's Pioneer High School, remembers spending hours hunting for clues and debating the rumor with friends. Like Lahti, he believes that a major part of the attraction was the ambiguity of the purported evidence.

20   "It was not some 'x-marks-the-spot' clue," Burns explains. "You could sort of hear it, but you couldn't. It was like you were seeing the tip of the iceberg of a larger reality."

But most people did not realize that many of the clues were nothing more than a college prank.

Fred LaBour's article in the *Daily* presented more than two-dozen clues, most of which he originated himself. Of those, many went on to become an integral part of the rumor.

But LaBour admits—and has always admitted—that he made up his clues on the spot, as a joke. A prime example is his assertion that "walrus"—as in the lyric "the walrus was Paul"—is Greek for "corpse." (It isn't.) LaBour also brazenly fabricated many other "facts": identifying, for instance, McCartney's replacement as a Scottish orphan named William Campbell. (He had considered calling the impostor "Glen" Campbell, after the country singer, but decided it would be too obvious.)

LaBour never expected his article to be taken at face value, and was astonished when the national press picked it up as a serious piece of news. "The story was quoted extensively everywhere," he recalls. "First the Detroit papers, then Chicago, then, by the weekend, both coasts."

25   After this the rumor truly seemed to catch fire. Suddenly LaBour's playful inventions were being soberly, discussed on the evening news of all three major television networks, and in prestigious national magazines such as *Time* and *Life*.

Exactly why LaBour's story was so influential is unclear. It was not the only article on the rumor, nor was it the first. The rumor was also being heavily promoted on alternative radio. But many agree with Beatleologist Andru J. Reeve, who opines that LaBour's story was "the single most significant factor in the breadth of the rumor's spread."

LaBour recalls being worried about his unintentional role in sending the rumor spiraling out of control. "But after a few days," he says, "the theatrical aspect became clearer to me, and, shy as I was in the face of all the attention, I began to enjoy the ride."

The culmination of that ride was being invited to Hollywood in early November to participate in an RKO television special that featured celebrity attorney F. Lee Bailey conducting a mock trial in which he examined various expert "witnesses" on the subject of McCartney's alleged death.

30   "I was a nervous college kid, way out of my league," LaBour recalls. "I told Bailey during our pre-show meeting that I'd made the whole thing up. He sighed, and said, 'Well, we have an hour of television to do. You're going to have to go along with this.' I said okay."

By the time the program was scheduled for broadcast, however, public interest in the rumor had cooled. It received only a single airing, on a local television station in New York City on November 30, 1969.

The popular mania surrounding the "Paul is dead" rumor was short-lived—but even today, despite the thorough debunking of nearly all the so-called evidence, it continues to circulate, mainly among conspiracy buffs and inquisitive Beatles fans.

Fred LaBour doesn't think his adoptive brainchild will ever completely disappear. "Like it or not," he says, "the rumor will be with us as long as the Beatles are with us."

Which will be a very long time indeed.

Review Questions

1. After LaBour published his article, the campus was "electrified" by the story. Given that the McCartney rumor was already in verbal circulation before his piece was published, why did it have such a galvanizing force?

2. What quality of LaBour's "clues" appeared to draw in the most readers, and ultimately spread the rumor further?

3. The speed and popularity of this particular rumor taught LaBour a lesson about being the "source" of a rumor. What did he learn?

4. What did LaBour discover, through his experience on television, about the popular media's attitude toward rumor?

Discussion and Writing Suggestions

1. This rumor highlights two aspects of human nature: a fascination with celebrity and a morbid curiosity with death. What does this intersection of rumor, fame, and mortality suggest about human nature?

2. How do you account for the remarkable success of the "Paul is dead" rumor in spreading so quickly and persuading so many people of its truth? To what distinctive elements do you attribute its appeal and its power? Compare this rumor—and the evidence offered for its support—to one or more other rumors you have heard or read about concerning particular celebrities today.

3. To what extent is a rumor more or less believable when its details are ambiguous, as compared, say, to the very particular details associated with the missing-kidney rumor discussed in Chapter 4 (pp. 128–135)? Based on your own experience, compare and contrast examples of ambiguous rumors and rumors in which details are precise.

4. On its surface, the "Paul is dead" rumor seems worlds away from the political and military nature of Knapp's examples and his theoretical framework for classifying rumors. Still, can you detect ways in which this case falls within Knapp's framework of rumor? Consider his three types of rumor, along with his analyses of what happens to a rumor as it spreads. Consider, too, Knapp's discussion of the factors that create successful rumors.

POLITICAL SMEAR RUMORS: TWO CASE STUDIES

During a particularly tense town hall meeting in 2008, a prospective voter declared to Republican presidential candidate John McCain that his Democratic opponent, Barack Obama, was "an Arab." This kind of charge had been floating for months across segments of the political landscape: Obama was a Muslim, a socialist, even a terrorist conspirator. While some Obama opponents tried to capitalize on such sentiments shared by certain segments of the electorate, the Republican candidate himself demurred, and to the disapproval of many of his listeners, gently corrected the audience member. Through personal experience, McCain knew both how unfair and how damaging to a presidential campaign such a rumor could be. In 2000 he himself had been the victim of malicious rumor when anonymous political opponents falsely charged that McCain had fathered a child outside of marriage.

We may think that this kind of strategic rumor mongering is a relatively recent development of a hyper-partisan era; unfortunately, such smears have a long history in American politics. During their presidential campaigns, both Thomas Jefferson and Grover Cleveland were accused of fathering out of wedlock offspring. (Both men were elected, despite the rumors, which in Jefferson's case were probably true.)

The selections in this cluster focus on the specific cases of Obama and McCain, but they also look back to rumors of a previous era. *New York Times* columnist Samuel Freedman, author of six acclaimed books about journalism and American history, explores the 2008 rumors about Obama. His piece, "In Untruths About Obama," sets those untruths in the context of a campaign run 80 years earlier. In "Anatomy of a Smear Campaign" (available online), Richard H. Davis, who served twice as John McCain's national campaign manager, shares his inside knowledge of the smears that derailed McCain's 2000 presidential bid.

In Untruths About Obama, Echoes of a Distant Time

Samuel G. Freedman

During the presidential campaign of 1928, a photograph began circulating in rural areas of the Southwest showing Alfred E. Smith shaking hands with a fellow politician on the roadway of a tunnel. The image depicted Smith as he was officially opening the Holland Tunnel, which had been built during his tenure as governor of New York.

The people thousands of miles away who received copies of the picture were given a decidedly different explanation: Smith planned to extend the tunnel under the Atlantic Ocean all the way to the Vatican, so he could take secret orders from the pope. As just about any informed voter that year already knew, Smith was the first Roman Catholic ever to win a major party's presidential nomination.

At the remove of 80 years, it is tempting to laugh off such a crude attempt at fearmongering and character assassination. With Catholics unquestionably part of the American mainstream—one of the most coveted swing groups of voters in the current race [2008] for the White House—the misrepresentation of the photo might seem the artifact of a benighted past.

Except for two things.

5   The first is that the climate of anti-Catholic bigotry, which ran from the refined arena of the *Atlantic* magazine to the cross burnings of the Ku Klux Klan, not only contributed to Smith's crushing defeat by Herbert Hoover but also helped keep any other Catholic from mounting a serious run for the presidency until John F. Kennedy in 1960. The hate campaign, in other words, worked.

As for the second point, scholars of Smith's career and of American Catholicism say nothing in presidential history since 1928 more closely resembles the smearing of Al Smith than the aura of anti-Muslim agitation that has swirled around Barack Obama these past two years.

The insinuations of disloyalty to America, the caricature of the candidate as less than genuinely American—these tactics could have come from the playbook of Smith's basest opponents, the scholars say.

The biggest single difference may be the postmodern aspect of the attacks against Mr. Obama. He is vilified not for the religion he follows but for the one he doesn't, and much of his campaign's energy has gone into reiterating that he is a Christian. Either way, the underlying premise of the rumors remains that a Muslim is unfit to be president.

"What is similar in Smith's time is that there was a widespread belief there was something dangerous about electing a Catholic as president," said Allan J. Lichtman, an American University historian who is the author of *Prejudice and the Old Politics: The Presidential Election of 1928.* "You couldn't be a good American and serve American interests if you were a Catholic, because you were beholden to a foreign potentate called the pope and Catholicism held autocratic tenets.

10   "Likewise today, there is a widespread belief that somehow you cannot be a good American and be a Muslim at the same time, that being a Muslim means you have loyalties outside the United States—and, like Catholics in the 1920s, they are dangerous loyalties to militant groups seeking to do harm. There's no truth to the allegations, then or now, but they are tenaciously held."

In Smith's case, foes from the highbrow end of society, as well as K.K.K. bottom feeders, disparaged Catholic faith as incompatible with democracy. Admittedly, the smears against Mr. Obama have not achieved the comparable legitimacy in elite circles.

In the blogosphere and through mass e-mail, however, and even on Fox News and in *Insight* magazine, the disinformation has proliferated that Mr. Obama was raised as a Muslim, educated in a madrassa, influenced by an Islamist stepfather and sworn into the Senate holding a Koran.

These calumnies, no matter how often contradicted, have nourished virulent behavior at Republican campaign rallies. At an event for John McCain and Sarah Palin in Bethlehem, Pa., National Public Radio captured the voice of one participant shouting: "Obama's a Muslim! He's a terrorist himself!"

Robert A. Slayton, author of the Smith biography *Empire Statesman,* suggested in a recent interview that the religious bias against Smith and Mr. Obama served in part as a proxy for nativist resistance to an increasingly diverse nation. The United States in both the 1920s and the 2000s has been bitterly divided over mass immigration—by Jews and Catholics then, Hispanics and Muslims now.

15   Smith's opponents conflated his Catholic faith with his Irish heritage, urban roots and even New York accent to cast him outside the Anglo-Saxon, Protestant, small-town norms of America. Mr. Obama, of course, is of mixed race and has a Muslim middle name, Hussein, which has been flourished by some Republicans as proof of his foreignness.

"The most remarkable parallel to 1928 has to do with the idea that Smith was one of 'those people,' that the people he represented weren't real Americans," said Mr. Slayton, a professor of American history at Chapman University in Orange, Calif. "And when Sarah Palin talks about the 'real America' now, I hear an echo of that."

If there is a lesson from Al Smith about all this, then it came during a speech he delivered on Sept. 20, 1928, in Oklahoma City.

"This country, to my way of thinking, cannot be successful if it ever divides on sectarian lines," he declared. "If there are any considerable number of our people that are going to listen to appeals to their passion and to their prejudice, if bigotry and intolerance and their sister vices are going to succeed, it is dangerous for the future life of the Republic. And the best way to kill anything un-American is to drag it out into the open, because anything un-American cannot live in the sunlight."

THE ANATOMY OF A SMEAR CAMPAIGN: THE CASE OF JOHN MCCAIN

Richard H. Davis

Go to: Google or Bing

Search terms: "mccain campaign smear spurstalk"

 ## Review Questions

1. What method did political operatives use to spread the rumor about McCain in 2000?

2. Why did the McCain campaign choose not to directly refute the rumor?

3. Aside from the fact that the Obama rumor was untrue, what thinly veiled underlying fear does it represent for some members of the public?

4. Despite the similarities between the rumors concerning Al Smith and Barack Obama, in what key way did they differ, according to Freedman?

Discussion and Writing Suggestions

1. Davis asserts that "if you're responding, you're losing." What do you think of this approach—that is, doing nothing to handle "tawdry attacks"? In what ways is doing nothing effective from a political and/or personal perspective? In what ways is doing nothing ineffective?

2. Contorting facts into a rumor for political use clearly worked against McCain in 2000. Is "all fair" in politics? To what extent should candidates be prepared to handle such situations? What do these methods, and responses, indicate about the participants?

3. Freedman asserts that a deeper anxiety lay beneath the Smith and Obama rumors. Can you think of other cases, whether in politics or in your personal life, where rumors about an individual are rooted in a deeper anxiety? How did these rumors operate?

4. Considering the cases of both McCain and Obama, do you think the responses of their campaigns were appropriate? Is it possible for a response to be appropriate, but not effective? Explain.

5. Put yourself in the shoes of a campaign manager, whether for McCain or Obama. Create a plan of action for responding to the rumors faced by their respective campaigns.

6. How do the rumors discussed in these two selections fit within Knapp's framework? How would you classify them, according to his scheme? To what extent do they exhibit the qualities that make for "good" or successful rumors?

How Rumors Help Us Make Sense of an Uncertain World

Nicholas DiFonzo

On general principle we may disapprove of rumors, but their pervasiveness throughout history and across cultures suggests that they serve important personal and social purposes. In the following selection, Nicholas DiFonzo, Professor of Psychology at Rochester Institute of Technology and the author of numerous books and articles on rumor, discusses why both individuals and groups find it necessary and even desirable to create and spread rumors. "How Rumors Help Us Make Sense of an Uncertain World" forms Chapter 3 of DiFonzo's best-known book *The Watercooler Effect* (2008). Offering examples from his own experience, together with other cultural and historical examples, DiFonzo shows how rumors develop on both personal and social levels.

I was proofreading a manuscript about the history of rumor research on the morning of September 11, 2001, when my wife called and told me to turn on the television. As I sat in spellbound silence, I saw jetliners crash into the World Trade Center, erupt into fireballs, and each of the Twin Towers collapse. The TV announcers were silent at that moment— too stunned to even comment. That morning in Sarasota, Florida, the president called for a moment of silence to honor those killed in the attacks. And in the week that followed, the sky was also eerily silent—no planes were permitted to fly.

These spaces of silence punctuated the long expanses of conversation—and conjecture—in the aftermath of that memorable day. America had been attacked; she felt physically and psychologically threatened and a heightened sense of unity and patriotism. We spontaneously gathered in houses of worship to pray. We monitored the Internet, radio, and television news for information. We talked to one another and wondered aloud: Why? What's next? During these very unusual days rumors flourished: "The Justice Department has advised all employees to avoid using the [Washington, D.C.] Metro to get home because of a subway attack." "Arabs employed at Dunkin' Donuts and International House of Pancakes celebrated in reaction to news of the attacks." "A hijacked plane is headed for the Sears Tower in Chicago." None of these rumors were true, but they were part of how we tried to make sense of the new (to us) threat of terrorism.

These 9/11 rumors dramatically illustrate some of the key elements of rumors that I will explore in this chapter. Up to this point I've tried to show that rumors are prevalent, that various types of rumors exist, and that rumors cause or contribute to a variety of outcomes. But exactly what do we mean by the term "rumor"? In the introduction, I described rumor as shared human sensemaking par excellence, but *how* do rumor help people make sense of their worlds? . . .

Let's begin by defining our term. Rumors are unverified information statements that circulate about topics that people perceive as important; arise in situations of ambiguity, threat, or potential threat; and are used by people attempting to make sense or to manage risk. There are three questions that this definition addresses: What do rumor statements consist of? What types of situations do they tend to arise from? And what are people trying to do with them?

5   First, rumors consist of information statements—noun and verb statements that purport to inform us. "Harry Potter is dead" proposes that J. K. Rowling, the author of the famed children's book series, "killed off" the hero in its last installment. (This rumor—uncertain at the time—lured Potter fans into clicking Web links that contained a computer worm.) "Tropical Fantasy Fruit Punch is owned by the KKK" alleges that the Brooklyn Bottling Company is controlled by the Ku Klux Klan. (False—it is owned by Eric Miller.) "As part of a grisly initiation rite, gang members in Illinois—driving with their headlights off—have killed unsuspecting motorists who blink their headlights at them." (False—the Illinois State Police call this the "headlights hoax.") These rumors are all declarative—they tell us something.

Second, rumors consist of statements that circulate among people; they are never merely a private thought held by an individual. Rumor is a group phenomenon, something that happens between at least two people (usually more). I may know that my boss is unhappy in his job, that he was recently scolded unfairly by his superiors, and that he has taken a few days off. I may speculate to myself that he has flown to another city for a job interview, but this thought is not yet a rumor until I share it with another person. Rumors are therefore not synonymous with another person. Rumors are therefore not synonymous with prejudices, stereotypes, beliefs, or attitudes, although each of these may be conveyed in a rumor. Rather, rumors are fundamentally acts of communication.

Third, rumors consist of statements in circulation that people generally consider significant or of interest to tellers and hearers. They tend to be about topics that we regard as relatively more urgent, vital, consequential, or imperative. The classic rumor is often embedded in the anxiety-filled utterance "I heard that our department is being downsized; did you hear anything?" Obviously, a department layoff would be of great importance to employees because unemployment is a threat to well-being. Or, rumors about stocks that I own are important to me because they're relevant to my financial bottom line. This sense of importance can stem from our interest in anything we hold dear or cherish. For example, sports rumors reflect the intense interest of fans. Soccer player Michael Owen was beset by many rumors of his supposed intention to leave his Newcastle team, perhaps originating from his absence from play due to many injuries over two seasons. In the realm of political games, if I'm a solid Democrat or Republican, rumors about politicians from either group greatly interest me. Ralph Rosnow called these sorts of concerns "outcome relevant"—the outcome of a particular situation or issue is relevant to me, my welfare, my well-being, or my sense of self.

Fourth, and most important, these information statements in circulation are not verified—they are not supported, buttressed, checked, or authenticated. A verified statement has a stamp of approval on it: an imprimatur if you will; a person or source that will vouch for the validity of the information. A verified statement is not necessarily the same as a true statement: True means that the information corresponds with objective reality, while verified means that someone vouches for its correspondence with objective reality. News is typically—though not always—verified; rumor is not.

Some examples will help clarify what "unverified" means. Let's consider the two possibilities: statements that a person thinks are unverified, and those he or she classifies as verified. Perhaps most readily identified as unverified are statements that the sender himself classifies as unverified— that is, those he is openly unsure of: "I'm not sure that this is true, but I heard that management is now requiring that nurses in our department be 'on call' nights and weekends." The cautionary prefix "I'm not sure that this is true..." is a dead giveaway that the statement is unverified. It doesn't matter whether the information following the prefix is true or false; at the moment of transmission it's imparted as a rumor. Of course, this unverified rumor could be true or false.

10   Next, consider statements that a person classifies as verified. These could also be true or false. Verified statements that are true are certainly not rumors. What about "verified" statements that are false? That is, statements that are false, but which people—the transmitter, the receivers, or both—vouch for as true. False statements might be vouched for as true by con men and propagandists, or by the misinformed and mistaken. Verification in all such cases is necessarily weak—because the statement is false—even if it has been vouched for by the most impeccable source. The impeccable source is either lying or mistaken. Misinformation spread by propagandists is rumor. Saddam Hussein regularly spread rumors about his ability to spy on and punish ordinary Iraqi citizens to discourage potential rebels. A less intentional example are the exaggerated reports of raping, killing, and pillaging by the citizens of New Orleans following Hurricane Katrina that were reported by credible news agencies—it seemed a reasonable course of action to believe them at the time—yet they turned out to be objectively false. They were therefore rumors—the evidence that buttressed these statements crumbled. Statements that are *apparently* verified also fall into this category. Flyers and e-mails circulating in the 1980s and 1990s proclaimed that the head of Procter & Gamble (P&G) announced on the *Phil Donahue Show* that the corporation donates to the Church of Satan. The flyers urged recipients to contact the show for a transcript as proof. Anyone who took the time to do so found out, of course, that P&G's CEO has never been on this show (indeed—on any talk show). The "evidence" upon which the statement rested failed on closer examination. False statements that people believe to be verified are ultimately unverifiable—and are therefore always properly considered rumors.

So, rumors consist of unverified information statements in circulation that are perceived to be important or of interest. What types of situations give rise to these kinds of statements?

Recall the GM automotive factory workers in Ypsilanti, Michigan. These workers were told that by the end of the summer of 1993, the plant would close. Not much else was revealed, leaving employees with a lot of questions: When will it happen? How will the shutdown proceed? Who will be laid off? How will these decisions be made? Information was also missing in a large consumer loan corporation where I interviewed managers several years ago. This corporation faced an extensive restructuring involving the relocation of one large division to another city. Motivated to give only solid information to employees, managers were quite secretive about the reorganization plans. They actually gave the reorganization effort a secret code name and were instructed not to discuss it with workers. Rumors abounded.

Rumors tend to arise in situations that are ambiguous and/or pose a threat or potential threat—situations in which meanings are uncertain, questions are unsettled, information is missing, and/or lines of communication are absent.

Similarly, during natural disasters lines of communication are sometimes knocked out, often resulting in an information blackout. One wintry day in the early 1990s, I had difficulty returning home on my daily commute because a severe ice storm had disrupted transportation—including my train—throughout all of southeastern Pennsylvania and New Jersey. My fellow passengers and I were unable to gather information that would have helped us answer some key questions: How long will the storm last? Are there any other trains running in my direction? Are the roads safe enough to drive on?

15   Even the prevalence of cell phones doesn't necessarily disambiguate such weather-related snafus. Traveling through O'Hare airport on a recent summer day, I—along with thousands of other passengers—looked at the departing flights roster and read "FLIGHT CANCELED." No other information was given. Clearly, it was an unclear situation. I started talking with perfect strangers and, through rumor, I learned that the reason for cancellations was high winds, that the proper response was to "get in line" at the United Airlines desk, and that in these situations it was best to make hotel reservations immediately for that night. (I made it home after a couple of days in Chicago.)

Ambiguous situations also occur when one bit of information contradicts another—a common occurrence in life. Not long ago, I happened to be in Memphis, Tennessee, and I took the opportunity to visit the National Civil Rights Museum. The museum is housed in the Lorraine Motel, where Dr. Martin Luther King Jr. was assassinated on April 4, 1968. Across the street is another part of the museum: the Main Street rooming house where James Earl Ray allegedly fired the fatal shot resulting in King's death. In March 1969, Ray confessed to shooting Dr. King and was sentenced to ninety-nine years in prison. However, he recanted three days after he confessed and hinted that he had been an unwilling patsy as part of a conspiracy. He spent the rest of his life seeking a retrial and denying his alleged part in Dr. King's murder.

Lloyd Jowers, a restaurant owner in Memphis, claimed in 1993 that King's death was the result of a conspiracy involving the Mafia and the U.S. government. In 1999, a civil suit against Jowers found that a conspiracy to kill Dr. King did exist. Dr. King's family also became convinced of Ray's innocence and issued a statement to that effect that same year. Despite this, a U.S. Justice Department investigation completed in 2000 disagreed. It didn't find any of these allegations to be credible. Confused? So are many people, and as a result, rumors about what happened to Dr. King on that April day in 1968 are alive and well.

Rumors also tend to arise in situations that pose a threat or potential threat—possibly to one's welfare or even survival. This explains why rumor statements are generally considered important by rumor discussants.

At the beginning of this chapter I recounted some of the rumors that arose out of the widespread feelings of vulnerability in the weeks following September 11, 2001. Continued terrorist activity and ubiquitous security checking have refreshed this unease and fueled more rumors. In July 2007, police arrested a suspected terrorist in the port city of Santander, northern Spain, who had been found with a gun and a timer. Unsubstantiated reports then circulated that plans had been found on him to bomb a ferry line to the United Kingdom. Rumors then flourished that the *Pont-Aven*, a vessel connecting Santander and Plymouth, was the target of a terrorist bombing plot. The potential threat posed in this situation was obviously to human life

20   But anything that challenges one's welfare or well-being is a potential threat. A computer consultant company owner I once interviewed, recounted how his organization was the target of a negative rumor campaign. The campaign was orchestrated by employees who preyed upon fears that the new computer system would make job duties more difficult and even lead to layoffs. Rumors were spread purposely that the consultant was "incompetent."

Similar, rumors circulated among staff in an organization I helped change toward a measurement culture. Some employees feared that the proposed changes would make it much more difficult to do their jobs, and even that they might not be able to perform the new tasks at all. Negative rumors about the change surfaced: "Management will not adequately support the change." The rumors were an attempt to identify and cope with potential threats. Change of any stripe can be scary—it may lead us into situations that we can't handle.

The threat posed can be psychological in nature. A situation may challenge a belief, attitude, mind-set, or sense of identity. Strong feelings of defensiveness can be called forth when we—or groups that we identify with—are criticized or derogated; we can *feel* very threatened indeed. Rumors can neutralize such threats, for example, by denigrating the source of the challenge or by bolstering our own position, cause, or group.

In 2007, WorldPublicOpinion.org conducted an in-depth survey of citizens from four predominately Muslim countries—Egypt, Morocco, Pakistan, and Indonesia; the sample was representative of the population of each of these countries. The survey explored sentiments toward the United States and Al Qaeda, and attitudes about the use of violence on civilian populations. Very large majorities of participants opposed violence against civilians, as exemplified in the acts of September 11, 2001, perpetrated by Al Qaeda. However, because American intentions are widely believed to be hostile to Islam, respondents were motivated not to criticize any group—including Al Qaeda—antagonistic to the United States.

Among a number of interesting findings were the perceptions of who was responsible for the attacks of September 11. A very small minority— 2 percent of Pakistanis, for example—thought that Al Qaeda orchestrated the attacks. When pressed in focus groups that Osama bin Laden had taken responsibility for the attacks on videotape, many participants became visibly uncomfortable and defensive, expressed disbelief, and suggested that the video was fake. A common response was that "Hollywood can create anything."

25   Instead, many thought that unknown persons, Israel, or even the United States was behind the events. To wit, rumors persist that four thousand Jews were told by the Israeli Secret Service on September 10, 2001, not to report to work at the World Trade Center the next day—the implication being that Israel bombed the buildings to incite anti-Arab sentiment. Rumors portraying Israel or the United States as masterminding September 11 are likely to spring up in situations where participants feel defensive about Al Qaeda's role in the attacks. Arab nations, of course, do not have a monopoly on such rumors—they circulate among all people whenever defensive sentiments arise.

So, rumors arise in situations that are ambiguous, or pose some threat or potential threat. But how do they help people deal with ambiguity and threat?

In the early summer of 2007, five happy and carefree young women died in a horrible head-on collision with a tractor-trailer on a two-lane highway near Rochester, New York. One week earlier, they had graduated from high school. They were in an SUV headed to a summer house at 10:00 p.m. along a two-lane rural road, when they passed a sedan, then inexplicably swerved into the path of the oncoming eighteen-wheeler. Fuel lines were broken and their vehicle erupted in a terrible conflagration. The force of the impact was so great that the young women were killed instantly. Why had their SUV swerved into the path of the oncoming truck?

The answer to that question will probably never be definitively known, but a grieving community tried to answer it as part of an effort to make sense of the tragedy. Out of this sensemaking, two false rumors were fashioned. One was that the driver of the sedan had sped up as he was being passed, forcing the SUV into the truck's path. This was in fact the opposite of what happened: The sedan slowed down to allow the SUV to safely pass. Another was that the oncoming eighteen-wheeler didn't reduce its speed before the collision. False again: The truck driver jammed on the brakes as soon as he saw the SUV enter his lane—he left more than 120 feet of skid marks before the impact. These rumors were put to rest weeks later at a news conference during which it was revealed that the SUV driver's cell phone had sent and received text messages just seconds before the crash. It appears likely that distraction due to cell phone usage was at the heart of this sad event. The rumors that arose served as hypotheses to people trying to make sense of what happened.

It's clear that rumors help people make some sort of sense out of unclear situations. The GM workers in Ypsilanti circulated rumors in an attempt to achieve clarity about the impending plant closing. Employees in the lending institution I interviewed passed rumors as a way of ferreting out the facts of the restructuring situation. My fellow stranded train and plane travelers and I used rumors to sift a picture of the weather, transportation routes, and appropriate courses of action. People set forth rumors about the death of Dr. King in order to resolve the contradictory statements associated with this national tragedy. Human nature abhors an explanation vacuum. People in groups use rumors to construct, evaluate, and refine explanations for the ambiguous situation.

30   In situations that pose a threat or potential threat, rumors also help people manage that threat by encouraging them to deal with it through positive action, or by simply making them feel better about it. Rumors about the bombing of the *Pont-Aven* alerted patrons not to travel via that ferry; passengers could avoid the possibility of a sudden death by delaying their trip or choosing another route. Rumors that a computer consultant is incompetent warned clients not to use that consultant; company officials could avoid years of computer-related troubles by simply choosing a different consultant or by not installing a computer system at all. A rumor that "the Port Jervis dam is breaking!" instructs Port Jervis residents to flee the scene immediately if they know what's good for them; they could preserve their lives by acting quickly.

A rumor in 2001 warned: "Avoid Boston on September 22 because drunken Arabs at a bar let it slip that there would be a second wave of attacks that day." By staying out of town on the twenty-second, Bostonians and others could evade the dangers encountered by people living and working in New York City on September 11. Rumors among college students about professors—"Milgram is a hard but fair grader"; "Rogers is an easy A"; "Allport is a phenomenal lecturer"—help students avoid unfavorable experiences such as unfair grades, low marks, and boring lectures. In all of these examples, the rumor implies a course of action that—if available—will supposedly aid the hearer in avoiding a negative or achieving a positive out come.

Many negative outcomes in life are, of course, unavoidable. For these, rumors assist people by helping them emotionally cope with the dreaded event or state of affairs. Rumors can help do this by, again, simply helping people make sense of an unclear situation. Merely understanding why a bad thing is happening is a good emotional coping strategy.

Understanding that the GM plant will be closing down this summer because foreign labor is cheaper won't alter the negative outcome for employees—losing employment—but is will remove a sense of arbitrariness from the situation. The plant closing can be understood as the result of larger economic forces, globalization, or corporate greed. Understanding how the SUV with five young women crossed into the opposing lane will not bring them back to life or lessen the feelings of loss felt by family and community—but it will set the event into a larger context. The crash could have come about, for example, as part of larger patterns of cell phone distraction, aggressive driving, or time pressures faced by truck drivers. We search for explanations in part because the very presence of an explanation is comforting. Rumors often often help people by providing a ready-made explanation.

Rumors can also help people cope emotionally by neutralizing a psychological threat—especially a challenge to our positive view of ourselves. In conflict situations, this is particularly so. In the study investigating sentiments toward Al Qaeda, focus group respondents presumably latched on to rumors that the United States or Israel organized the events of September 11 because they deflect the threatening idea that Al Qaeda was responsible for killing nearly three thousand civilians. Similarly, negative racial attitudes are distasteful—we don't like to think of ourselves as judgmental toward a person based solely on the color of his skin, her gender, or country of origin. We consider ourselves fair-minded people. How is it that we sometimes exhibit racial prejudice, then?

35   Wedge-driving rumors—negative stories about members of the rival or targeted group—can justify distasteful attitudes. In the aftermath of Hurricane Katrina, false rumors about black individuals in New Orleans engaged in looting, raping, and shooting at rescuers were widespread. False rumors that groups of unruly black persons vandalized rest stop facilities while being bussed from New Orleans at taxpayer expense were also common. Such rumors can make prejudiced individuals feel better about their negative racial attitudes toward African-Americans. Conversely, false rumors that New Jersey State troopers and their dogs chased a black child, causing the boy to fall into the Raritan Canal near Princeton and drown, spread quickly in the African-American community one hot summer in the late 1980s. Such rumors can make prejudiced persons feel better about having negative racial attitudes toward European Americans.

In a similar vein, we don't like to think of ourselves as prejudiced against even a rival group. But prejudice against any rival group can be legitimated by negative rumors about that group. Politics has always been a hot topic, but what can explain the current acrimony between Democrats and Republicans? Negative rumors about politicians from the opposing party help people justify their intense biases. I receive negative political e-rumors from both sides of the aisle. These rumors are always of "the other side is bad" variety. They are never checked for veracity, but simply forwarded to friends believed to be like-minded. These rumors serve a purpose—to justify negative prejudice toward the rival group—in this case, the opposing political party. We would normally consider such bias for what it is—unfair and distasteful; rumors, however, can make it palatable.

Central to our discussion of rumors is their role in human sense-making. So, to better understand what rumor is, we need to understand how we make sense generally and the role of rumors in that process. More specifically, how do individuals make sense and how do rumors affect this individual sense-making? And how do groups make sense together and how do rumors affect this group sense-making?

Not long ago, my wife and I were exiting a movie theater just past midnight. The theater was located near a large Barnes and Noble bookstore, around which stood a huge crowd alternately cheering and clapping as they awaited their turn to purchase *Harry Potter and the Deathly Hallows*, the seventh and last installment of J. K. Rowling's amazingly popular children's book series. I slowly drove by the fringe of the crowd; it was New Year's Eve in the middle of July. People of all ages had waited in line the entire day in order to be among the first to receive the coveted volume. Three news stations were also present, adding to the circus-like fanfare. It was a happy event. My wife and I couldn't recall such excitement over the release of a book. Many would stay up all night to read the 784-page tome and then attend a brunch to discuss it with other bleary-eyed enthusiasts. Some would go straight from the bookstore to parties where the main social activity was sitting and reading. What could *explain* the Harry Potter phenomenon?

40   What was it about this children's book, our culture, or media that led to this unprecedented interest and fanfare at this moment in time? Any satisfactory explanation would convey the desires, beliefs, and aims of the many people involved in Pottermania, and clarify the underlying psychological, sociological, and literary underpinnings of this muggle (ordinary human) event. Good candidate explanations might appeal to the literary quality of Rowling's epic, an increasing desire for a sense of wonder in our modern age, contagion phenomena, global interconnectedness resulting from the growth of the Internet, or the increasing media savvy of marketers.

To ask how individuals make sense of things is really to ask how they go about the task of explanation. Explanation is aimed at increasing comprehension and understanding. It can involve offering details of a situation that enable us to understand it, or the reasons—i.e., the desires, beliefs, or aims—of the actors involved. Good explanations clarify meanings, ideas, or thoughts.

Psychologists have outlined the process an individual undergoes when seeking to explain an event, situation, or feature of their experience that is unclear. The process has a common-sense flavor to it; explanation is a universal human activity. A person first becomes aware of an event—it is noticed. It is then interpreted—an initial explanation is set forth. If so motivated and able, the person can then iteratively test and revise this interpretation, or generate alternatives for testing and revision. This iterative testing may involve searching for additional information. At some point, the individual settles on a final explanation. Noticing and interpreting happen automatically; that is, they occur in an almost reflex fashion, without effort or thought. Testing, revising, generating alternatives, and selecting a final explanation, however, take effort.

Whether automatic or effortful, each of the tasks in the explanation process is guided by cognitive structures. I introduced this term in Chapter 2; it refers to associations of ideas, such as stereotypes or frameworks. Cognitive structures are activated by bringing ideas to mind. For example, if I say the word "Italian," several ideas are brought to mind or become more accessible in our awareness: pasta, large close-knit families, Roman noses, expressive gestures, espresso coffee, medieval art, Mediterranean climate, and Mafia. These elements are associated with one another around the concept "Italian"; they form a stereotype.

Cognitive structures guide the explanation process at each step. For example, they help us notice events. Upon learning that our new neighbor's name is DiFonzo, their facial features, expressive gestures, and many children become more salient to us—we notice them. When we encounter an event that puzzles us, cognitive structures help us interpret the event automatically—without thinking. We learn that Mr. Difonzo's uncle in Sicily was found dead from a gunshot wound; we privately wonder if it was a Mafia-related killing. Cognitive structures guide us in the effortful generation of alternate explanations as well. We know that the Sicilian uncle collected guns for a hobby and—guided by the cognitive structure "gun collecting"—we inquire as to whether he accidentally shot himself while cleaning his guns.

45   Rumors affect this process of explanation at several points along the way, often by simply delivering the relevant cognitive structure. First of all, they help us to notice events. Many times this is a simple matter of the rumor calling attention to a particular incident, theme, characteristic, or situation. False rumors that Snapple is owned by the Ku Klux Klan brought attention to the kosher symbol—signified on the Snapple label by the letter *K* with a circle around it. In addition, rumors often also convey an initial interpretation of an event. To continue our Snapple example, the presence of the *K* symbol on the Snapple label, according to the rumor, indicated that the company was owned by the KKK.

The false rumors of Paul McCartney's death both called attention to and interpreted why he was barefoot on the cover of the *Abbey Road* album: according to the rumor, the deceased are customarily interred without shoes in Britain. (Actually, this isn't true.) Rumors activated the cognitive structures that guided the noticing and interpreting in each of these examples. This "rumor guidance" often happens automatically—without effort, intention, or thought.

Rumors may also activate the cognitive structures that motivate and guide the effortful search for new information to help us evaluate an explanation. A rumor that American Home Mortgage Investment Corporation had shut down part of its lending operation inspired information-seeking about the company's lending practices. The company had indeed engaged in risky practices; it had issued many loans to borrowers without requiring extensive documentation. The rumor resulted in a 23 percent reduction in the company's stock value in one day, despite protests by company officials that the rumor was untrue.

One particular type of cognitive structure that rumors frequently deliver to individuals is the stable cause—a cause that lasts over time. In the previous chapter, I discussed how a rumor that "Goodyear profits are up because of good management practices" activated the stable cause idea that good management will continue, thereby leading to the prediction that Goodyear stock would continue to rise. In experiments, these rumors did indeed lead to predictions that Goodyear stock would continue to rise and in this way systematically affected buying behavior—but, as it turns out, unprofitably.

In another study I discussed in Chapter 2, rumors that Sophie (a fictional character) has some form of mental illness conveyed the idea that Sophie was mentally ill, activated the stable cause idea that mental illness lasts over time, and thereby led to the conclusion that her mental illness was likely to continue. Mental illness would presumably impair her judgments and adversely affect her desirability as a friend. Students (not educated about mental illness) were then less likely to vote for Sophie as class president and to desire to be socially close with her.

50   The point is that rumors often affect individual sensemaking by activating a stable, lasting cause to explain events; this frequently leads to predicting that the recent events, behaviors, or conditions will continue. Put another way, rumors often lead to this kind of sensemaking simply because they often supply a lasting cause for the current state of affairs or trend of events: The way things are going now will continue into the future.

For individuals, then, rumors make us think about some events, affect how we frame these events, and affect what we continue to learn about these events. But what about collections of connected individuals? That is, what about groups? How do groups make sense together and how do rumors affect group sensemaking?

In the mid-1990s, Internet discussion groups were a new phenomenon. A small percentage of people at that time participated in email Listservs. My colleague, Prashant Bordia, was one of them. He noticed that discussions of rumors on these groups were sensemaking activities and he carefully recorded and analyzed these electronic posts.

One discussion in particular intrigued him and became the subject of his master's thesis: people on one particular Usenet site were concerned that Prodigy—a large Internet service provider at the time—was spying on customers' personal files. The false rumor asserted that this profit-driven corporation was uploading private information from subscribers' hard drives without their knowledge or consent. Prodigy then allegedly sifted through this information for marketing purposes—that is, to develop a clearer demographic and psychological picture of their customers so that they might be more successful at selling them additional products and services. Demographic and psychological profiling was not new at this time, but the idea that a large company would, without permission, upload private customer files was a key part of the rumor that sparked concern and discussion.

Broadly speaking, group sensemaking resembles individual sensemaking in that particular tasks are performed by many different people rather than just one. There is a division of labor. That noticing, interpreting, revising, and settling on a final explanation are performed by members of the group rather than by a Single person. One task, for example, is to first bring a rumor to the group. The sociologist Tamotsu Shibutani called this the messenger role. After analysis of the types of statements that people actually include in their posts, Prashant and I categorized such roles as "communicative postures." For example, the messenger role is best represented in an explanation delivering posture. In the Prodigy rumor discussion, a discussant might post "I don't know if this is true, but I heard that Prodigy is uploading our private files for use by their marketing departments"—the person delivers an explanation to the group along with a cautionary statement that it might be false.

55   We dubbed such tasks "postures" because they represent the temporary role that a person may play while "taking their turn" at any given point in the discussion. That is, "posture" conveys that the role that one plays in a discussion may change over time. A person might cautiously deliver an explanation at one stage of a discussion, but then later perform a different role in that same discussion. She might, for example, later express disbelief in that explanation and present an argument supporting her contention that Prodigy was not surreptitiously uploading customer data (we dubbed this an explanation falsifying posture): "I don't believe that Prodigy is uploading information because to do so would take up too much bandwidth."

Prashant's analysis detected other communicative postures displayed in these discussions. A post that was explanation evaluating would analyze and interpret the rumor explanation. For example: "Perhaps the Prodigy cache file grows over time because they are first compressing the user's personal files, then adding it into the cache file before uploading!" Explanation accepting posts would express belief in the rumor: "I believe they are doing this." Explanation verifying postures would go further and express belief in the rumor along with a supporting argument: "I believe Prodigy is doing this because they are solely interested in making a profit and would not hesitate to violate our privacy rights." Of course, when people are collectively analyzing a rumor explanation, they need to search for, find, deliver, and analyze additional information.

A directing posture would provide information and suggest a strategy for further information gathering: "Whenever I dial in to Prodigy, my modem light turns on intermittently, even if I'm not sending or receiving information; someone should find out if this is the way modems ordinarily operate." Information-seeking postures would simply state the gaps in knowledge needed in order to generate or evaluate a rumor and would often be in the form of a question: "What do we know about the Prodigy cache file?" Information reporting postures would share information and personal experience: "Ever since I subscribed to Prodigy, my computer has been operating more slowly." Other postures performed the functions of motivating participants to continue sensemaking by either considering negative outcomes ("I'm scared about what this could mean about my privacy") or positive ones ("I wish our private files would remain private")....

The point in pondering these postures is that people, when they "take their turn" in an electronic discussion by posting a message, perform a particular function in service of the group's goal of making sense of the situation. Clearly, rumor discussions are not simply telephone game transmissions, otherwise known as "whispers down the lane"—A tells B a rumor, who then tells C, who then tells D...and so on down the line. This common conception of rumor is simplistic and individualistic—it frames rumor as something that primarily happens with an individual rather than a group. Instead, a group sensemaking discussion around a rumor consists of a sometimes confusing interchange of news, information statements, opinions, explanations, commands, questions, motivators, and digressions.

But even though the discussion seems unwieldy, there are clear trends as it moves forward. At first, people display explanation delivering and directing postures: they cautiously bring the rumor to the group, and strategies are proposed to find out more information. Supported by information seeking and reporting, and motivated to continue by considering negative or positive outcomes, they engage in explanation evaluating postures—they are actively sifting, sorting, and making sense of the rumor. Finally, people participate more casually as a consensus in reached or interest dies down. They move on to other topics or simply stop participating. Despite the apparent chaos and confusion, these discussions are colorful and purposeful interchanges that—collectively—proceed in a fairly predictable fashion around the central task of sensemaking.

● Review Questions

1. Summarize the four major characteristics of rumor, according to DiFonzo.

2. Explain the difference between unverified and verified rumor.

3. DiFonzo explains that rumors sometimes help us cope with the fact that "negative outcomes in life are...unavoidable." How does he support this assertion?

4. Define wedge-driving rumors. Cite two examples of such rumors, according to DiFonzo.

5. What is the "messenger role?" Define what DiFonzo calls "postures."

Discussion and Writing Suggestions

1. How does DiFonzo's analysis of rumor square with your own understanding of rumor? Recall a particular rumor that concerned you, someone you know, or some group of which you are (or were) a member. In your response, address some of the following questions: (1) What event(s) or concern(s) sparked this rumor? (2) To what extent did this rumor fulfill the terms of DiFonzo's definition of rumor? (3) Who took on the "messenger role"? (4) How did the rumor affect "group sensemaking"? (5) What "postures" were involved? (6) How did these postures operate to spread and transform the rumor? Drawing on DiFonzo's insights, explain how this rumor helped you or others "make sense of an uncertain world."

2. DiFonzo explains that "in situations that pose a threat...rumors also help people manage that threat by encouraging them to deal with it through positive action, or by simply making them feel better about it." In what ways can rumors make us "feel better?" Alternately, how might threat-managing rumors have a negative impact? Provide examples from your own experience.

3. DiFonzo's account of the accident in which five young women in an SUV died demonstrates how people use rumor to help make sense of tragedy. The initial stories concerning the accident misrepresented key facts but may have helped the grief-stricken community of the victims better come to terms with the accident. The actual cause of the accident was more difficult for the community to accept. Can you think of other examples from your own experience, or the experiences of people you know, demonstrating the ways in which rumors sometimes provide comfort in the face of realities we prefer to avoid?

4. Through his example of the airport mishap, DiFonzo demonstrates how rumor can lead to useful "positive action." What other occasions come to mind, whether from your own life or from social situations in your experience, suggesting that rumors sometimes serve a useful purpose?

5. DiFonzo explains that group rumor making is more complex than a game of "telephone." Based on your own experiences and observations, recount an example of how a rumor develops through group discussion.

6. This selection begins by referencing the events of 9/11 and continues throughout discussing the rumors involving the events of that day. To what extent, positively and/or negatively, did these rumors help "people deal with ambiguity and threat"?

7. Recall once again a rumor from your own experience. Reconstruct a stretch of dialogue between you and a group of friends that illustrates how the rumor was created, transformed, and spread. Incorporate into the dialogue some of the phenomena DiFonzo discusses: threat neutralization, communicative postures, group sensemaking, and so on.

RUMOR CASCADES AND GROUP POLARIZATION

Cass R. Sunstein

Picture a snowball rolling down a steep hill. As it gathers momentum, collecting more snow, its diameter rapidly swells. By the time it hits bottom, its mass is considerably larger than it was at the top. According to legal scholar Cass Sunstein, rumors operate in a like manner. Sunstein asserts that rumors move and grow in various types of "cascades," pulling in new believers in the process. Before long, rumors have reached the point at which a majority of listeners or readers believes them. This dynamic can have positive effects: As Sunstein points out, informational cascades helped spur the worldwide movement for sexual equality into near-universal acceptance. But the dynamic can just as easily spread misinformation as rumors cascade into believability and take on an aura of "fact" to large groups of people. These cascaded "truths" might be relatively innocuous urban myths (such as alligators living in city sewers); they might just as easily be political smears that damage or destroy campaigns. Cass Sunstein is the author of numerous books, including *Risk and Reason* (2002), *Why Societies Need Dissent* (2003), and *Infotopia: How Many Minds Produce Knowledge* (2006). Much of his recent work has focused on the impact of rumor cascades involving government conspiracy theories and how to best counteract them. The following selection first appeared as a chapter in Sunstein's book *On Rumors* (2009), published shortly after he was chosen to head the Obama White House Office of Information and Regulatory Affairs.

Learning from Others 1: Informational Cascades

Rumors frequently spread through informational cascades. The basic dynamic behind such cascades in simple: once a certain number of people appear to believe a rumor, others will believe it too, unless they have good reason to believe that it is false. Most rumors involve topics on which people lack direct or personal knowledge, and so most of us defer to the crowd. As more people defer, thus making the crowd grow, there is a real risk that large groups of people will believe rumors even though they are entirely false.

Imagine a group of people who are deciding whether Senator Jones has done something scandalous.[1] Each member of the group is announcing his view in sequence. Andrew is the first to speak; perhaps he is the propagator of the rumor. Andrew states that Senator Jones has indeed done something scandalous. Barbara now knows Andrew's judgment. Exercising her own independent judgment on the basis of what she knows of the senator, she might agree with Andrew. If she has no knowledge at all about Senator Jones, she might also agree with Andrew; perhaps she accepts Andrew's claim that he knows what he is talking about. Or suppose that her independent judgment is that Senator Jones probably did not engage in the scandalous conduct. Even if so, she still might end up believing the rumor, just because of what Andrew has said. If she trusts Andrew no more and no less than she trusts herself, she might not know what to think or do; she might simply flip a coin.

Now consider a third person, Carl. Suppose that both Andrew and Barbara suggest that they believe the rumor, but that Carl's own information, though far from conclusive, indicates that their belief is wrong. Even in that event, Carl might well ignore what he knows and follow Andrew and Barbara. It is likely, after all, that both Andrew and Barbara had reasons for reaching their conclusion, and unless Carl thinks that his own information is better than theirs, he may follow their lead. If he does, Carl is in a cascade.

Now suppose that Carl is agreeing with Andrew and Barbara; lacking any personal information about Senator Jones, he thinks they are probably right. Suppose too that other group members—Dennis, Ellen, and Frances—know what Andrew, Barbara, and Carl think and said, and believe that their judgments are probably reasonable. In that event, they will do exactly what Carl did: accept the rumor about Senator Jones even if they have no relevant knowledge. Our little group might accept the rumor even if Andrew initially said something that he knew to be false or spoke honestly but erroneously. Andrew's initial statement, in short, can start a cascade in which a number of people accept and spread serious misinformation.

5   All this might seem unrealistic, but cascades often do occur in the real world. In fact, this little account helps to explain the transmission of many rumors. Even among specialists, cascades are common. Thus an article in *The New England Journal of Medicine* explores "bandwagon diseases," in which doctors act like "lemmings, episodically and with a blind infectious enthusiasm pushing certain diseases and treatments primarily because everyone else is doing the same."[2] There can be serious consequences in the real world. "Most doctors are not at the cutting edge of research; their inevitable reliance upon what colleagues have done and are doing leads to numerous surgical fads and treatment-caused illnesses."[3] Some medical practices, including tonsillectomy, "seem to have been adopted initially based on weak information," and extreme differences in tonsillectomy frequencies (and other procedures, including vaccinations) provide good evidence that cascades are at work.[4]

On the Internet, informational cascades happen every day, and even when they involve baseless rumors, they greatly affect our beliefs and our behavior. Consider the fact that YouTube videos are far more likely to attract many more viewers if they have already attracted many viewers—a clear example of a cascade.

It is also true that many cascades spread truth, and they can do a lot of good. Cascades help account for the beliefs that the earth is round, that racial segregation is wrong, that people should be allowed to engage in free speech, and that democracy is the best form of government. A bank might really be failing, and a politician might really be corrupt, and if a cascade spreads these facts, so much the better. The belief that the earth is round, the attack on apartheid in South Africa, and the global movement for sexual equality were all fueled by informational cascades. But false rumors often also set off cascades, and when they do, two major social problems occur. First and most important, people can come to believe a falsehood, possibly a damaging one. Such cascades can ruin relationships, businesses, and even careers. Second, those who are in the cascade generally do not disclose their private doubts. People may know that Senator Jones is unlikely to have done what he is accused of doing, but they follow the lead of those who came before them. Recall the self-interested or malicious motivations of many propagators; we can now have a better sense of why it is important to chill the falsehoods they circulate.

With respect to rumors, of course, people start with different levels of information. Many of us lack any relevant information at all. Once we hear something that seems plausible but alarming, those of us who lack information may believe what we hear if we do not know anything to the contrary. Other people are not ignorant; they do know something that is relevant, but not enough to overcome the shared beliefs of many others, at least when those others are trusted. Still other people have a significant amount of relevant information, but are nonetheless motivated to accept the false rumor. Recall the importance of tipping points: rumors often spread through a process in which they are accepted by people with low thresholds first, and, as the number of believers swells, eventually by others with higher thresholds who conclude, not unreasonably, that so many people cannot be wrong.[5] The ultimate result is that large numbers of people end up accepting a false rumor even though it is quite baseless. Return to the Internet. A propagator makes a statement on a blog; other blogs pick up the statement; and eventually the accumulation of statements makes a real impression, certainly among people within specific social networks, and perhaps far more generally. Both truths and falsehoods spread in this fashion.

A study not of rumors but of music downloads is revealing about this process. The Princeton sociologist Matthew Salganik and his coauthors[6] created an artificial music market among 14,341 participants who were visitors to a website that was popular among young people. The participants were given a list of previously unknown songs from unknown bands. They were asked to listen to selections of any of the songs that interested them, to decide which songs (if any) to download, and to assign a rating to the songs they chose. About half the participants made their decisions based on their own independent judgments about the quality of the music. This was the control group. The participants outside that group were randomly assigned to one of eight possible "worlds." Within these worlds, participants could see how many times each song had been downloaded. Each of these worlds evolved on its own; participants in any particular world could see only the downloads in their own world. The key question was whether people would be affected by the visible choices of others—and whether different music would become popular in different worlds. What do you expect would happen? Would people be affected by the judgments of others?

10   It turned out that people were dramatically influenced by the choices of their predecessors. In every one of the eight worlds, people were far more likely to download songs that had been previously downloaded in significant numbers—and far less likely to download songs that had not been so popular. Most strikingly, the success of songs was highly unpredictable. The songs that did well or poorly in the control group, where people did not see other people's judgments, could perform very differently in the "social influence" worlds. In those worlds, a song could become very popular or very unpopular, with everything depending on the choices of the first participants to decide whether to download it. The identical song could be a hit or a failure, simply because other people, at the start, chose to download it or not. As Salganik and his coauthors put it: "In general, the 'best' songs never do very badly, and the 'worst' songs never do extremely well," but—and this is the remarkable point—"almost any other result is possible."[7]

In a related study, Salganik and his coauthors, acting not unlike propagators, attempted to influence the process. They told people, falsely, that certain songs had been downloaded in large numbers, even though they had actually proved unpopular.[8] More particularly, the researchers actually inverted true popularity, so that people would see the least popular songs as having the most downloads and the most popular songs as having the fewest. Their key finding was that they were able to produce self-fulfilling prophecies, in which false perceptions of popularity produced actual popularity over time. When people think songs are popular, songs actually become popular, at least in the short run. True, the most popular songs did in fact recover their popularity, but it took a while, and songs that had previously been among the least popular—before the inversion—continued to be at or toward the top of the list. This is a striking demonstration of how people's behavior can be affected by an understanding, even a false one, what other people think and do.

The music download experiments help to explain how rumors spread. Alleged facts about a politician or a country or a company do move far more in some "worlds" than in others—and in different worlds, people will believe different "facts." The variable success of rumors provides a real-world analogue to the concept, so popular in science fiction novels, of "parallel worlds. "Even without self-conscious efforts at manipulation, certain rumors will become entrenched in some places and have no success at all in others. If propagators are clever, they will attempt to convince people that others have come to believe the rumor that they are creating or spreading. One propagator will have terrific success in some worlds but none at all in others; another propagator will show a radically different pattern of success and failure. Quality, assessed in terms of correspondence to the truth, might not matter a great deal or even at all. Recall that on YouTube, cascades are common, as popular videos attract increasing attention not necessarily because they are good but because they are popular.

In light of this, we can see why some social groups hold quite tenaciously to false rumors while other groups treat them as implausible or even ridiculous. An example is the existence of widely divergent judgments among differing groups about the origins and causes of AIDS—with some groups believing, falsely, that the first cases were observed in Africa as a result of sexual relations between human beings and monkeys, and other groups believing, also falsely, that the virus was produced in government laboratories.[9] Another example is the existence of widely divergent views about the causes of the 9/11 attacks—views that attribute the attacks to many sources, including Israel and the United States.

The multiple views about AIDS and the attacks of 9/11 are products of social interactions and in particular of informational cascades. The same process occurs when groups come to believe some alleged fact about the secret beliefs, foolishness, or terrible misdeeds of a public or private figure. In each instance, an informational cascade is often at work. And when cascade-propelled rumors turn into firm beliefs, the combination can be devastating. Recall that people holding similar beliefs are especially likely to accept some rumors and to discount others. Suppose that one group (in, say, Utah or Iran) has been subject to a rumor-driven cascade, while another group (in, say, New York or Canada) has not. If so, those in the different "worlds" will develop strong prior beliefs with which they will approach whatever they hear later—beliefs that may make corrections hard to accept. . . .

Learning from Others 2: Conformity Cascades

15 Sometimes people believe rumors because other people believe them. But sometimes people just act as if they do.

They censor themselves so that they can appear to agree with the crowd. Conformity pressures offer another account of how rumors spread.

To see how conformity works, let us consider some classic experiments by Solomon Asch, who explored whether people would be willing to overlook the unambiguous evidence of their own senses.[10] In these experiments, the subject was placed into a group of seven to nine people who seemed to be other subjects in the experiment but who were actually Asch's confederates. Their ridiculously simple task was to match a particular line, shown on a large white card, to the one of three "comparison lines" that was identical to it in length. The two nonmatching lines were substantially different, with the differential varying from an inch and three quarters to three quarters of an inch.

In the first two rounds of the Asch experiments, everyone agreed about the right answer. "The discriminations are simple; each individual monotonously calls out the same judgment."[11] But "suddenly this harmony is disturbed at the third round."[12] All other group members made what is obviously, to the subject and to any reasonable person, a glaring error, matching the line at issue to one that is conspicuously longer or shorter. In these circumstances, the subject had a choice: she could maintain her independent judgment or instead accept the view of the unanimous majority.

What happened? Remarkably, most people ended up yielding to the group at least once in a series of trials. When asked to decide on their own, without seeing judgments from others, people erred less than 1 percent of the time. But in rounds in which group pressure supported the incorrect answer, people erred 36.8 percent of the time.[13] Indeed, in a series of twelve questions, no less than 70 percent of people went along with the group, and defied the evidence of their own senses, at least once.[14]

20   Why did this happen? Several conformists stated, in private interviews, that their own opinions must have been wrong—an answer suggesting that they were moved not by peer pressure but instead by a belief that the shared belief of others is probably correct. On the other hand, experimenters using the same basic circumstances of Asch's experiments have generally found significantly reduced error when the subject is asked to give a private answer.[15] In short, when people know that conformity or deviation will be easily identified, they are more likely to conform.[16] These findings suggest that peer pressure matter—and that it induces what the economist Timur Kuran has called *knowledge falsification*, that is, public statements in which people misrepresent their actual knowledge.[17] Here, then, is a clue to the relationship between successful rumors and conformity pressures. People will falsify their own knowledge, or at least squelch their own doubts, in the face of the apparent views of a crowd.

Rumors often spread as a result of conformity cascades, which are especially important in social networks made up of tightly knit groups or in which there is a strong stake in a certain set of beliefs. In a conformity cascade, people go along with the group in order to maintain the good opinion of others—no matter their private views or doubts. Suppose that Albert suggests that a certain political figure is corrupt and that Blanche concurs with Albert, not because she actually thinks that Albert is right, but because she does not wish to seem, to Albert, to be ignorant or indifferent to official corruption. If Albert and Blanche say that the official is corrupt, Cynthia might not contradict them publicly and might even appear to share their judgment. She does so not because she believes that judgment to be correct, but because she does not want to face their hostility or lose their good opinion.

It should be easy to see how this process might generate a special kind of cascade. Once Albert, Blanche, and Cynthia offer a united front on the issue, their friend David might be reluctant to contradict them even if he thinks that they are wrong. The apparently shared view of Albert, Blanche, and Cynthia imparts its own information: their view might be right. But even if David is skeptical or has reason to believe that they are wrong, he might not want to break with them publicly.

Conformity cascades can certainly produce convergence on truth. Maybe unduly skeptical people are silencing themselves—not the worst thing if their skepticism is baseless. But conformity cascades often help to account for the spread of false rumors. Especially when people operate within a tightly knit group or live in some kind of enclave, they may silence themselves in the face of an emerging judgment or opinion even if they are not sure whether it is right. Often people will be suspicious of a rumor, or believe that it is not true, but they will not contradict the judgment of the relevant group, largely in order to avoid social sanctions. Consider far-left and far-right groups, in which well-organized social networks often spread damaging falsehoods, frequently about their political opponents, with the indispensable aid of conformity pressures.

In the actual world of group decisions, people are of course uncertain whether publicly expressed statements are a product of independent knowledge, participation in an informational cascade, or the pressure of conformity. Much of the time, we overestimate the extent to which the actions of others are based on independent information rather than on social pressures. False rumors become entrenched as a result. And here too, of course, diverse thresholds matter a great deal. Blanche may silence herself and agree with the group only when the pressure to conform is intense; David might be more easily led to go along with the crowd. But if most of the world consists of people like David, then the Blanches are more likely eventually to yield. There are tipping points for conformity no less than for information.

Learning from Others 3: Group Polarization

Deliberation among like-minded people often entrenches false rumors.[18] The explanations here overlap with those that account for social cascades, but the dynamics are distinctive. Here again, we can understand why some groups will end up firmly believing rumors that seem ludicrously implausible to others.

The Basic Finding

In the summer of 2005, a small experiment in democracy was held in Colorado.[19] Sixty American citizens were brought together and assembled into ten groups, each consisting of six people. Members of each group were asked to deliberate on several issues, including one of the most controversial of the day: Should the United States sign an international treaty to combat global warming? To answer that question, people had to come to terms with what were, in a loose sense, rumors. They had to ask whether climate change was real or a hoax, whether the American economy would be badly harmed by participation in an international agreement, and whether such an agreement was necessary to prevent an imminent or long-term disaster for the United States.

As the experiment was designed, the groups consisted of "liberal" and "conservative" members—the former from Boulder, the latter from Colorado Springs. In the parlance of election years, there were five "blue state" groups and five "red state" groups—five groups whose members initially tended toward liberal positions on climate change and five whose members tended toward conservative positions on that issue. People were asked to state their opinions anonymously both before and after fifteen minutes of group discussion. What was the effect of discussion?

The results were simple. In almost every group, members ended up holding more extreme positions after they spoke with one another. Most of the liberals in Boulder favored an international treaty to control global warming before discussion; they favored it more strongly after discussion. Many of the conservatives in Colorado Springs were somewhat skeptical about that treaty before discussion; they strongly opposed it after discussion. Aside from increasing extremism, the experiment had an independent effect: it made both liberal groups and conservative groups significantly more homogeneous—and thus squelched diversity. Before their members started to talk, both the red and the blue groups displayed a fair bit of internal disagreement. The disagreements were reduced as a result of a mere fifteen-minute discussion. Even in their anonymous statements, group members showed far more consensus after discussion than before.

30   Moreover, the rift between liberals and conservatives widened as a result of discussing. And after discussion, opinions among like-minded group members narrowed to the point where everyone mostly agreed with everyone else.

The Colorado experiment is a case study in group polarization: when like-minded people deliberate, they typically end up adopting a more extreme position in line with their pre-deliberation inclinations.[20] Group polarization is pervasive in human life. If a group of people tends to believe that the nation's leader is a criminal, or that some corporate executive is a scoundrel, or that one of their own members has betrayed them, their belief to this effect will be strengthened after they speak among themselves. In the context of rumor transmission, the implication is simple: when group members begin with an antecedent commitment to a rumor, internal deliberations will strengthen their belief in its truth. The antecedent commitment might involve a specific claim, including a bit of gossip about an apparently powerful person. Or it might involve a more general belief with which the rumor easily fits. The key point is that internal deliberations further entrench the rumor.

Notes

[1] I draw here on David Hirshleifer, "The Blind Leading the Blind: Social Influence, Fads, and Information Cascades," in *The New Economics of Human Behavior*, edited by Mariano Tommasi and Kathryn Ierulli (Cambridge, Mass.: Cambridge University Press, 1995), 188, 193–95, and on the discussion in Cass R. Sunstein, *Why Societies Need Dissent* (Cambridge, Mass.: Harvard University Press, 2003), 55–73.

[2] John F. Burnham, "Medical Practice á la Mode: How Medical Fashions Determine Medical Care," *The New England Journal of Medicine* 317 (1987): 1220, 1201.

[3]Hirshleifer, "Blind Leading the Blind," 204.

[4]Sushil Bikhchandani et al., "Learning from the Behavior of Other: Conformity, Fads, and Informational Caseades." *The Journal of Economic Perspectives* 12 (1998): 151, 167. On YouTube cascades, see Clarice Sim and W. Wayne Fu, "Riding the 'Hits' Wave: Informational Cascades in Viewership of Online Videos" (unpublished manuscript, 2008), available at www.isu.uzh.ch/enterpreneurship/workshop/fu.pdf.

[5]For many illustrations, see Terry Ann Knof, *Rumors, Race, and Riots* (New York: Transaction, 2006).

[6]Matthew J. Salganik et al., "Experimental Study of Inequality and Unpredictability in an Artificial Cultural Market," *Science* 311 (2006): 854–56.

[7]Ibid.

[8]Matthew J. Salganik et al., "Leading the Herd Astray: An Experimental Study of Self-Fulfilling Prophecies in an Artificial Cultural Market," *Social Psychology Quarterly* (forthcoming).

[9]Fabio Lorenzi-Cioldi and Alain Clèmence, "Group Processes and the Construction of Social Representations," in *Blackwell Handbook of Group Psychology: Group Processes,* edited by Michael A. Hogg and R. Scott Tindale (Oxford: Blackwell Publishing, 2011), 311, 315–17.

[10]See the overview in Solomon Asch, "Opinions and Social Pressure," in *Readings About the Social Animal,* edited by Elliott Aronson (New York: W. H. Freeman, 1995), 13.

[11]Solomon Asch, *Social Psychology* (Oxford: Oxford University Press, 1952), 453.

[12]Asch, "Opinions and Social Pressure," 13.

[13]Ibid., 16.

[14]Ibid.

[15]Aronson, *Readings About the Social Animal,* 23–24.

[16]Robert Baron and Norbert Kerr, *Group Process, Group Decision, Group Action* (Pacific Grove, Calif.: Brooks/Cole, 1992), 66.

[17]Kuran, *Private Truths, Public Lies.*

[18]Allport and Postman, *Psychology of Rumor,* 35.

[19]Reid Hastie, David Schkade, and Cass R. Sunstein, "What Really Happened in Deliberation Day", *California Law Review* 95 (2007): 915–40.

[20]Roger Brown, *Social Psychology,* 2nd ed. (New York: Free Press, 1986).

Review Questions

1. What are the various types of cascades?

2. What is "the basic dynamic behind" rumor cascades, according to Sunstein?

3. How does Sunstein draw from an article in the *New England Journal of Medicine* to reinforce the concept of rumor cascades?

4. In what way does YouTube act as an ideal example of cascade movement?

5. Cite some examples offered by Sunstein to explain how cascades can also spread and reinforce truth, thereby having a positive impact on the world.

6. What kind of problems can occur, according to Sunstein, when false rumors spark cascades?

7. What paradox arises during the group polarization process?

● Discussion and Writing Suggestions

1. Patients may suffer harm when physicians allow medical cascades to influence their diagnoses and prescriptions. Drawing on your own experiences and observations, as well as on your reading, discuss other ways in which cascades can cause personal damage.

2. Cascades don't spread false rumors only; they may also spread beliefs about important social and scientific developments. In recent years, we have seen social media help spread news of democracy and help mobilize social movements. In what ways have you witnessed or read about positive information spread through a cascade?

3. Sunstein identifies three specific cascades in this selection. Consider each type—the root cause, the methods of delivery, the audience, and the impact. Which type of cascade do you believe has the greatest impact on the public at large? Explain, using specific examples and drawing upon Sunstein's text.

4. Sunstein describes an experiment conducted by Princeton sociologist Matthew Salganik, who used music sharing as a way of illustrating cascade thinking. The experiment showed the workings of a self-fulfilling prophecy through which "false perceptions of popularity produced actual popularity over time." Were you surprised by the results of this experiment? To what extent do you think that cascade thinking might have affected your own musical tastes or your assessment of particular songs—or the artists who created these songs?

5. Referencing Solomon Asch's famous experiments (pp. 259–261), Sunstein suggests that people conform to the views of a crowd even when they doubt the crowd's collective judgment. Why do you think the pressure to conform is so strong? On a personal level, discuss an occasion when you have been faced with a conformity cascade. What were the circumstances? Write a narrative describing how you gave into the group thinking, or stood up to it. Did you express your reservations?

6. In "Truth Is in the Ear of the Beholder," Rodriguez refers to and expands upon Sunstein's discussion of group polarization, particularly the latter's point that during the process of speaking with each other, individuals in political groups become ever more entrenched in their beliefs. Using one or more examples from your own experience, discuss how this phenomenon works, both in terms of the impact upon individuals in the group and upon the progress of the rumor itself.

MANAGING RUMORS

John Doorley and Helio Fred Garcia

We see the pattern repeatedly in the media: A rumor breaks into the news, and the embarrassed or outraged subject hires a public relations firm, releases a statement (or appears at a press conference, his pained but supportive spouse by his side), appears on a talk show, and attempts in various—and often fruitless—ways to stop the rumor in its tracks. The subject may be a business (such as a Procter & Gamble representative appearing on *Donahue*), a personality (Paul McCartney performing a concert to prove that he is, in fact, alive), a public official, or a candidate for office. Battling rumor has reached all the way to the White House. As a candidate, Barack Obama featured a "Fighting Rumors" link on his Web site, tasked with tackling rumors about his religion or his birthplace as they appeared. More recently, as the President worked toward his health care reform, White House staff launched a Web site specifically designed to address rumors about the plan.

These developments are emblematic of the concepts John Doorley and Helio Fred Garcia, authors of *Reputation Management* (2006), explore in "Understanding and Managing Rumors." Using a formula devised by rumor experts Gordon Allport and Leo Postman in the 1940s, these experts create a schedule for responding to rumor, for minimizing negative impact. The next time you see a company spokesperson clarifying a rumor on CNN, chances are he or she is following the kind of guidelines suggested by Doorley and Garcia.

The Morphing of Rumors

One of the defining elements of rumors is that they are not static. As a rumor passes from person to person, it tends to change through processes that social psychologists call leveling, sharpening and assimilation.

In the 1940s, two Harvard University psychologists, Gordon W. Allport and Leo Postman, conducted experiments on how the content of rumors changes as the rumor passes from person to person. They concluded that as a rumor travels, it tends to grow shorter, more concise and more easily told: In subsequent versions [of the rumor] more and more original details are leveled out, fewer words are used and fewer items are mentioned…As the leveling of details proceeds, the remaining details are necessarily sharpened. Sharpening refers to the selective perception, retention and reporting of a few details from the originally larger context. Although sharpening, like leveling, occurs in every series of reproductions, the same items are not always emphasized. Much depends on the constitution of the group in which the tale is transmitted. Those items will be selected for sharpening which are of particular interest to the reporter. Assimilation has to do with the powerful attractive force exerted upon the rumor by habits, interests and sentiments existing in the reader's mind. Items become sharpened or leveled to fit the leading motif of the story, and they become consistent with this motif in such a way as to make the resultant story more coherent.

Allport and Postman emphasize that while leveling, sharpening and assimilation are independent mechanisms, they function simultaneously. The result is that a story becomes more coherent and interesting, and therefore, more believable with each retelling.

• • •

Controlling Rumors Mathematically

Fortunately, rumors tend to follow predictable patterns, and intervention in specific ways can help an organization overcome, or even kill, a rumor.

5   Breakthrough research on rumors was conducted during World War II by Allport and Postman. Much of their work was classified, but after the war it was published, first in *Public Opinion Quarterly* in 1946 and then in their 1947 book, *The Psychology of Rumor*. One of their most significant contributions to the study of rumors was a mathematical formula that described the way a rumor works. The formula further suggests ways to control or eliminate a rumor.

The two factors that influence a rumor are its importance to the listener and its ambiguity. To control a rumor, one must either diminish the importance assigned to the rumor if true, or eliminate the ambiguity around the factual basis of the rumor, or both. Eliminating ambiguity is particularly important if the rumor is completely false. But even when the rumor has a mixture of truth and fiction, eliminating ambiguity about the fiction can control the rumor and ground it in reality. Once an unambiguous reality is established, it may be possible to reduce the importance of the information in the rumor, thereby decelerating its transmission.

The Basic Law of Rumor

Allport and Postman elaborate below on how the two factors of importance and ambiguity work together and note that there is a mathematical relationship:

> The two essential conditions of importance and ambiguity seem to be related to rumor transmission in a roughly quantitative manner. A formula for the intensity of rumor might be written as follows: $R \sim i \times a$

In words, this formula means that the amount of rumor in circulation will vary with the importance of the subject to the individuals concerned (*i*) times the ambiguity of the evidence pertaining to the topic at issue (*a*). The relation between importance and ambiguity is not additive but multiplicative, for if either importance or ambiguity is zero, there is no rumor. Ambiguity alone does not sustain rumor. Nor does importance.

Because the relationship between importance and ambiguity is multiplicative, an incremental decline in either can result in a greater-than-incremental decline in the scope of the rumor.

Here's how the math works: Assume a scale of zero to 10, zero being nonexistent and 10 being certain. If both importance and ambiguity are high, say 10, the scope of the rumor will be quite strong:

$$R \sim i \times a \qquad R \sim 10 \times 10 \qquad R \sim 100$$

10　In other words, when both importance and ambiguity are at their highest, the scope of the rumor will be at its highest. But reduce just one of the factors, and the scope of the rumor declines considerably. Assume that importance remains at 10 but that ambiguity can be reduced to 3.

The scope of the rumor has declined from 100 to 30, or by more than two-thirds. And because anything multiplied by zero equals zero, if either ambiguity or importance is reduced to zero, the rumor disappears.

In practical terms, this formula lets a professional communicator and a management team do several powerful things. Knowing that importance and ambiguity drive a rumor, a company can more efficiently identify what it needs to do and say. Second, knowing the formula gives clients and bosses confidence that they can influence the interpretation of events. The formula empowers management to focus communications in ways that can impact how the company is perceived. Best of all, the formula can disarm negative information, killing a rumor and preventing further damage.

Dynamics of Controlling a Rumor in the News Cycle

When applying the $R \sim i \times a$ formula, one critical element of success is how early one can influence importance and ambiguity. Corporate management often has little appreciation for the need to pre-empt rumors or for the seemingly arbitrary and somewhat confusing deadlines under which journalists work. The Allport and Postman model empowers crisis communicators and companies to disclose more information sooner, controlling the rumor and decreasing the likelihood of a negative story.

The Rule of 45 Minutes, Six Hours, Three Days and Two Weeks

At specific points in a news cycle it is possible to kill a negative story or control a partially accurate story. Miss one of these points and you will suffer reputational damage. Worse, the distance between the points, the intensity of the crisis and the potential for reputational harm grow in an almost exponential fashion as bad news spreads.

15   And while these points result from careful observation of how the news cycles and the rumor formula interact, the same orders of magnitude apply beyond the media, when progressively larger groups of people, overtime, become invested in a rumor.

The first 45 minutes: You have maximum influence on the outcome of a story in the first moments after the rumor arises. During this time, only a small number of people, and possibly only one reporter, know about a rumor or are working on a story. If you follow the $R \sim i \times a$ formula to persuade a reporter not to pursue a story in those first 45 minutes, chances are high that the story will disappear. On the other hand, if you are unable to respond within that 45-minute time frame, a number of negative things happen. First, the original reporter is likely to be on the phone trying to confirm the rumor, retelling it to sources who can pass it along to other reporters. Second, given the proliferation of all-news media, chances are good that the story will break quickly. Third, in the retelling of the rumor from the first reporter to other sources, the substance of the rumor will change. As the rumor becomes known in slightly different forms by many different people, it will become harder to find a definitive demonstration to put the rumor to rest.

Controlling the rumor now becomes less a function of persuasion—a private intervention with a single reporter—than of a public statement to influence your constituencies.

Six hours: Once a story crosses a wire service, is broadcast on television or radio, or appears on the Internet, it may still be possible to eventually control the rumor, but now it will be much more difficult. As a general rule, once a story is broadcast you can expect to have at least six hours of negative coverage.

During these six hours, more reporters come to the story and more people become aware of the rumor. Your customers, employees, suppliers, competitors, regulators and local community hear about it and begin to react.

20   If, during this part of the cycle, you consider the $R \sim i \times a$ formula as you plan your public statements, chances are high that the rumor can be controlled and the story will fade, though reputational damage may have been done.

If you are unable to control the story during this phase of the cycle, expect several days of negative news—all the while, the processes of leveling, sharpening, assimilating and snowballing are morphing the rumor into something far less manageable.

Three days: Once a story hits the daily newspapers, you can expect it to be alive for several days. The day the story appears, there is likely to be television and radio commentary about the story, as well as gossip among your customers, employees and competitors, with all the attendant distortion.

During this period it is still possible to use the $R \sim i \times a$ formula to your advantage. You will have suffered several days of reputational damage and will have seen a wide range of people exposed to the negative rumor. If you cannot control the story during these three days, expect at least two weeks of negative coverage.

Two weeks: After the daily newspapers have had their run, there is still a further news cycle that includes weekly and bimonthly magazines, industry trade publications, and the Sunday-morning talk shows. During this period you can still use the $R \sim i \times a$ formula to kill the rumor. You will have suffered several weeks of negative coverage and reputational harm. If you are unable to control the story in this time frame, expect continuous coverage. A company is unlikely to recover quickly from this kind of scrutiny.

25   All of this suggests that it is a fundamental mistake for corporations to make decisions about crisis communications on their own timelines. They need to recognize that however arbitrary and at times irrational media deadlines may seem, companies can control their destinies better if they can kill rumors as early as possible in a news cycle.

Failure to recognize the power of both the $R \sim i \times a$ formula and the rule of 45 minutes, six hours, three days and two weeks puts the company at the mercy of the rumor mill, gossipmongers and the irrational-seeming dynamics of the news media. Successfully employing them can help prevent reputational damage and keep the company focused on its own agenda.

Review Questions

1. According to Allport and Postman, what three processes occur as a rumor develops? Describe what is involved in these processes.

2. What two factors most influence a rumor? Express the relationship between these factors as a formula.

3. Indicate the time frames Doorley and Garcia establish as the benchmarks in rumor management.

Discussion and Writing Suggestions

1. Doorley and Garcia establish clear time-frame benchmarks for dealing with rumor. Consider some of the previous readings in this chapter about particular rumors. To what extent did the subjects attempt to meet these time frames? How did their success—or failure—in meeting these deadlines affect the spread and effectiveness of the rumors?

2. The writers indicate that the longer we wait to address a rumor, the more difficult it becomes to control. Can you think of any public cases (either recent or historical) where swift response failed to help? What about cases where delayed responses did, in fact, settle the matter? How were those situations handled?

3. Consider a recent rumor from any realm of public interest (politics, entertainment, business, etc.). How did the target address the rumor? To what extent was the chosen strategy effective? How closely did the subject use Doorley and Garcia's rumor-control framework?

4. Put yourself in the shoes of a public figure (business executive, celebrity, public official, etc.) at the heart of a rumor. Identify yourself and describe the rumor. Using the four time frames established in this selection, create a plan of action for each level.

5. Doorley and Garcia discuss Allport and Postman's concepts of leveling, sharpening, and assimilation. Select any of the rumors discussed in this chapter—or another rumor with which you are familiar—and explain how any or all of these processes may apply.

THE RUMOR

John Updike

We've become familiar with the public face of rumor: the instantaneous surge of an allegation across the Internet and onto YouTube, the press releases on company letterhead, the politician's talk show appearances. But what happens behind closed doors—when, for example, a rumor ricochets inside the home, affecting both a couple and their circle of friends and colleagues? In the following story, John Updike traces the effects of gossip on a marriage. Updike (1932–2009) was a "Renaissance man" among American writers of the second half of the twentieth century: novelist, short-story writer, poet, essayist, literary critic, art critic. A two-time Pulitzer Prize winner, he is best known for his "Rabbit" novels—*Rabbit, Run* (1960), *Rabbit Redux* (1971), *Rabbit is Rich* (1981), and *Rabbit at Rest* (1990)—which trace the life of Harry C. ("Rabbit") Angstrom, former high school basketball star, car salesman, and indifferent husband and father, as he struggles to make sense of—and break free from—his middle class, suburban life. Like Norman Rockwell earlier in this chapter, Updike is best known for his portrayal of "average" Americans and mainstream life. In this story, originally published by *Esquire* in June 1991, he presents a vivid portrait of a marriage. While initially dismissing as falsehood a rumor that comes to engulf their life, the couple is nonetheless quietly enthralled by it.

Go to: Google or Bing
Search terms: "updike rumor"

Discussion and Writing Suggestions

1. Even as she dismisses the rumors, Sharon is surprised by her friends' certainty about its truth. Do you think she has doubts? Why? Is she bothered—or excited—by the rumor?

2. The rumor in this story is "factually untrue." During the course of the story, however, Frank begins to wonder whether it might be at least partially true. He even wonders whether it would be a good thing for the rumor to be *perceived* as true by his wife and his colleagues. Can you think of other rumors, whether from your own life or from the public stage, that may have been false but have been accepted or even embraced by the subjects?

3. How do Frank's feelings toward his mother and father, as well as his feelings about the kind of men he admires, lend support to his feelings about the rumor?

4. Most of the previous selections in this chapter have focused on rumor functioning on a societal scale. This story, however, deals with the personal life of the Whittiers. How do some of the theories explored in the chapter (by Knapp, Sunstein, and DiFonzo) apply here? Consider specific moments in the story: How do the phone calls link up with Sunstein's "cascades"? Which of Knapp's categories does the rumor fit (from the perspective of the friends, as well as Frank himself)?

5. Frank entertains the notion that there may be value, or at least allure, in the rumor's spread. Create a rumor about yourself that you would like to see circulate among your friends and community. What is it? Why would you want people to believe this rumor?

6. Do you like Frank and Sharon Whittier? Why or why not? Do their thoughts and actions seem plausible? Explain.

7. This story is centered on married life, not on a larger societal context like most of the other readings in this chapter. That said, the implications of "The Rumor" might also be applied to larger arenas. What other situations come to mind, whether from other chapter selections or from your own experience, where a company, a politician, or a celebrity indulges in or even encourages a rumor instead of correcting it?

SYNTHESIS ACTIVITIES

1. Write a synthesis that explains *why* and *how* rumors spread. In your discussion, refer to the theories of Knapp, Sunstein, and DiFonzo. Use any of the example rumors treated in this chapter (as well as the stolen-kidney case in Chapter 4, "Analysis," pp. 128–135) to support your discussion.

2. Select one of the rumors treated at length in this chapter. Briefly analyze this rumor from the perspective of the theoretical approaches of Knapp (three categories of rumor; qualities of good rumors), Rodriguez ("biased assimilation"), Sunstein (cascades and group polarization), and DiFonzo (dealing with ambiguity and threat). Then, in an argument synthesis, explain which theoretical approach most compellingly reveals the whys and wherefores of the rumor you have selected.

3. Some rumors are created in the spirit of fun and are relatively harmless in their effects—for example, those New York alligators that led off our introduction or the "Paul is dead" rumor described by Alan Glenn. Other rumors arise from malicious intent and often devastate their targets. In an argument synthesis, rank several types of rumors on a scale of benevolence/malevolence, according to the motives of those who create and spread them. Draw upon some of the case studies treated in this chapter, as well as the "missing kidney" rumor. Don't hesitate to bring into the discussion rumors based on your own personal knowledge and experience. Also use some of the theoretical pieces such as those of Rodriguez, Knapp, Sunstein, and DiFonzo to help account for and justify your rankings.

4. Select any three of the cases of rumor from this chapter or from Chapter 4, "Analysis" (the missing kidney). Compare and contrast these rumors, taking account of their origins (and the rationales behind their creation), their spread, and their impact. Try to select cases that appear similar on the surface but may have subtle or even major differences below the surface. Alternately, choose cases that appear quite different but that, according to your analysis, are essentially similar in nature. A key part of your comparison-contrast synthesis will be answering the *So what?* question. Having worked the comparison, what observations can you make about the three rumors you have discussed—and, provisionally (based on your small sample size), about rumor itself?

5. In his article on McCain's presidential bid of 2000, Davis writes of the campaign manager's feeling that to respond to a rumor would only give it weight. Considering everything you have read in this chapter—not just that particular piece—to what extent do you agree with this cautious approach? Should a rumor be addressed at its first sign, or should it be allowed to run its course, however long that takes? What factors should bear most on how best to counteract damaging rumors? Use examples from the readings, as well as the ideas of theorists such as Sunstein and DiFonzo to support your argument.

6. In 2011, President Obama and his aides attempted to quell the long-standing rumor that he was not born in the United States. Attempting to put the claim to rest, he eventually released the full-length version of his birth certificate. Even in the face of this hard evidence, the rumor

persisted, and public figures such as Donald Trump and Rick Perry suggested that the evidence presented by the new document was insufficient or questionable. What does the refusal to accept concrete evidence suggest about human nature and political affiliation? In drafting your response, an argument synthesis, consider the points made by at least two of the following: Rodriguez, Knapp, Sunstein.

7. Conventional wisdom suggests that our digital lifestyle (think e-mail, Facebook, Twitter, computers, smartphones, and so on) has accelerated the spread of rumor. To what extent do you find this belief true? In the digital age, can attempts to quell rumors move at the same speed as the rumors themselves? Use examples from the selections in this chapter, along with cases of rumor known to you personally, to develop an argument in response to this question. It might be helpful to consider a rumor from the pre-Internet era, as well as one from the present day.

8. Knapp and DiFonzo explain that rumors are often symptoms of our hopes and fears. What hopes and fears are reflected by one of the following rumors: (1) the genetically modified chicken, (2) the "satanic logo," or (3) "Paul is dead"? Model your response on the analysis paper in Chapter 4, which applied Knapp's categories to the "missing kidney" rumor.

9. Imagine that you work for a public relations firm, hired by someone targeted by a rumor. This might be a rumor similar to one covered in this chapter or another you have come across outside of class. Create an argument synthesis that takes the form of an action plan for your client. (A model for such an action plan might be the one offered by Doorley and Garcia.)

10. You work for a book publisher that is preparing a new edition of Sunstein's *On Rumors*. For this latest edition, the author wants to update the examples offered, to demonstrate various types of "cascades." Considering the readings from this chapter (and elsewhere), write a memo to Sunstein offering current examples for his discussions of "informational cascades," "conformity cascades," and "group polarization." In your memo, be sure to explain how each example fulfills Sunstein's criteria.

11. After the "Paul is dead" rumor spread, as documented by Glenn, the Beatles seemed to have fun playing along with the story. In John Updike's "The Rumor," we see an untrue rumor spark a sense of excitement in its subject and a surprising determination to keep the rumor alive. What is it about a rumor that, occasionally, might be alluring to its subject? Drawing upon some of the particular cases covered in this chapter, or cases known to you personally, develop your response into an argument synthesis.

RESEARCH ACTIVITIES

1. Throughout his discussion, DiFonzo refers to the numerous rumors that grew out of the terrorist attacks of September 11, 2001. As he explains, some of these rumors were developed as a coping mechanism, and some grew out of newly discovered anxieties and fears about the identity and the nature of our enemies. Research another catastrophic event in American history, and identify some of the rumors that were created in its wake. Knapp offers a glimpse into the rumors circulating around World War II. What about the Vietnam War? The Kennedy assassination? The Martin Luther King assassination? Explore some of the rumors associated with these events (or another such national calamity) and the ways in which theories by Knapp, DiFonzo, or Sunstein help account for them.

2. While some rumors eventually go national and even global, others affect a more limited group of people: employees of a particular company, customers of local establishments, soldiers in a particular military unit, students at a particular school. In the fall of 2011, Smith College was overrun with an explosive culinary news item: All campus dining services were going vegan. This announcement sparked Twitter feeds, campus protests, and even coverage from the leading vegan lifestyle magazine. But the news was a hoax, fueled by the power of rumor. Research two or three other hoaxes of limited impact, and discuss their spread and their impact (try searching for "local rumors" on Snopes.com or the archives of local newspapers). How and why did these rumors spread so fast and alarm so many? Draw upon Sunstein's concept of "cascades" to support your discussion, as well as DiFonzo's ideas about how rumors help us make sense of an uncertain world. What does public willingness to accept these hoaxes as true say about human nature?

3. Some rumors, such as "the missing kidney" (see Chapter 4), have entered popular culture as "urban legends." Urban legends (which often have nothing to do with cities) are defined by DiFonzo as "narratives about strange, funny, or horrible events that could have happened, the details of which change to fit particular locales or time periods, and which frequently contain a moral lesson." There's even a horror film named *Urban Legend*. Picture yourself as a film executive or screenwriter looking for an idea to develop into a movie. Research other urban legends (start with Snopes.com), and write a pitch for a movie based on one that appeals to you. Why do you think audiences will connect to this story? What features about it will engage viewers? What does it have in common with other rumors?

4. In an op-ed for the *Washington Post* (November 17, 2011), Paul Farhi asserts that "the e-mail rumor mill is run by conservatives." While he discusses political rumors associated with both Republicans and

Democrats, Farhi claims that "when it comes to generating and sustaining specious and shocking stories, there's no contest. The majority of the junk comes from the right, aimed at the left." Research some of the more notorious rumors that have been a feature of recent politics. Describe and characterize them. To what extent are their agendas and political purposes clear? Based on your research, do you agree with Farhi? Develop your argument using Knapp's scheme. What do your findings suggest about political discourse in both parties?

5. Samuel Freedman draws parallels between the anti-Muslim sentiment in the 2008 election and anti-Catholicism in the 1930s, showing us that political rumormongering has a long, dishonorable history. The targets may change, but for centuries the rumor mill has operated the same way. Research two or three politically connected rumors from earlier historical periods. (Again, a good starting point is Snopes.com, along with works by the authors in this chapter, such as DiFonzo and Sunstein, and the bibliographies or endnotes in their articles and books.) Discuss the rumors themselves and explain how they affected the political landscape at the time. Consider the causes, agendas, and hopes and fears expressed by the rumors.

6. If you were to receive an e-mail sharing a story about a "missing kidney," you might assume that the alleged events in the story represented a new phenomenon. As Robert Dingwall explains, however (see the model analysis in Chapter 4), the kidney rumor stretches back many years, undergoing transformations in different countries and at different periods of its development. During this transformative process, particularly potent rumors go through what rumor scholars Gordon Allport and Leo Postman describe as "leveling, sharpening, and assimilation" (as discussed by Doorley and Garcia in "Managing Rumor").

Research and discuss another fear-driven rumor. (Once again, a good starting point is Snopes.com. Then learn more about your selected rumor from additional sources). How far back does the rumor go in the public consciousness? How has it changed over the years? How has it—to use Allport and Postman's terms—leveled, sharpened, and assimilated?

7. The Chris Dussold case involved charges of sexual harassment. Research the sexual harassment guidelines in place at various colleges and universities. Based on these guidelines, what do you conclude is the appropriate way to handle allegations based on rumors of sexual harassment? Locate other cases similar to Dussold's, taking account of both their similarities and differences.

8. Robert H. Knapp's theory of rumor, included in this chapter, was written over half a century ago, a fact that accounts for his choice of examples relating to World War II. Imagine that you work for a publisher looking

to release an updated version of his article, with content footnotes providing examples more likely to be familiar to contemporary readers. Locate new examples of rumor (not treated in this chapter) that illustrate each of Knapp's three categories. In your memo to the publisher, identify each rumor, categorize it, and explain how it fulfills the criteria for that type of rumor.

9. Research the new crop of "reputation defender" services available to those who find their online identities under siege. (Start by googling terms like "managing rumor.") Based on your findings, discuss these services and explain how they work and why they may or may not be effective. To what extent do these services follow an approach similar to the one recommended by Doorley and Garcia?

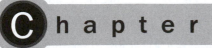

Green Power

Our wealth, our society, our being is driven by oil and carbon. And when we say that we have to make a shift, that is extremely difficult. It is intellectually dishonest to say that we can get some lightbulbs, or we can get a Prius, and we're all done. No—this is going to take massive technological innovation. It's going to take changes in the way we live and work. It's going to take cooperation of unprecedented degree among businesses and government and among countries. That's where we are. There's no other word except "daunting."

—Jerry Brown, Governor of California

In 2006, climber and filmmaker David Braeshears made his way up to a Himalayan outcrop on a steep ridge 19,000 feet high. From that familiar vantage point he had a clear view of the Rongbuk Glacier in Tibet, a frozen river of ice that flows from the north slope of Mount Everest. Comparing what he was seeing to a photograph taken in 1921 from the same vantage point by British explorer George Mallory, he was appalled by how much the ice had melted. "The glacier's just gone," he remarked to *Frontline* producer Martin Smith. It had, in fact, lost some 40% of its mass in the past eighty-five years.

The shrunken Himalayan glacier is but one more indication—along with collapsing ice shelves in Antarctica and polar bears stranded on ice floes—of the extent of climate change since the middle of the twentieth century. Climate experts warn of nothing short of an apocalypse unless current global warming trends are reversed. The earth's population faces the prospect of more frequent and severe hurricanes, fires, declining agricultural yields, the extinction of species, and rising ocean levels that threaten to flood coastal cities. Author and *New York Times* columnist Thomas Friedman quotes environmental consultant Rob Watson on the nature of the challenge we confront: "People don't seem to realize...that it is not like we're on the *Titanic* and we have to avoid the iceberg. *We've already hit the iceberg.* The water is rushing in below. But some people just don't want to leave the dance floor; others don't want to give up on the buffet."

What's causing climate change? Experts point to increasing levels of greenhouse gases—chiefly carbon dioxide, or CO_2. (Other greenhouse gases include methane, ozone, and water vapor.) These gases trap the sun's heat in the atmosphere by preventing infrared rays from escaping into space—and, therefore, they keep living things from freezing to death. (Like cholesterol, a certain quantity of greenhouse gases is essential to survival.) For most of human history, greenhouse gases have remained at a life-supporting equilibrium. But accelerating levels of industrialization during the twentieth century, and particularly during the latter half of that century, have changed the equilibrium by measurably increasing atmospheric levels of CO_2, a by-product of the burning of fossil fuels such as coal and oil, energy sources that are integral to the existence of modern civilization. More than half of the nation's electricity is generated by the burning of coal. It takes 9½ tons of coal to produce the quantity of electricity used by the average American each year. And, of course, the overwhelming majority of the world's vehicles are fueled by gasoline, or refined petroleum.

The internal combustion, CO_2-spewing engine that has powered vehicles of every type since the dawn of the automobile era in the early twentieth century has long been viewed as one of the greatest culprits in creating air pollution—and, more recently, in contributing to climate change. And bad as the situation is now, it is expected to get far worse. The number of cars in the world, about 625 million, is anticipated to double by 2020. China and India—whose populations account for a third of humanity—will soon overtake the United States as the world's biggest oil importers.

In recent years, interest in and development of alternative energy sources that do not release CO_2 (or, at least, not *as much* CO_2) into the atmosphere—and thus that serve to slow, if not reverse, the pace of global climate change—has intensified. Automakers are now taking the first serious steps away from gasoline-powered vehicles in an effort to "green" the transportation industry—as evidenced by the popularity of the Toyota Prius and other hybrids, the advent of plug-in hybrid vehicles such as the Chevrolet Volt, and all-electric cars such as the Nissan Leaf. Increasingly, natural gas and biofuels are being used to power cars and buses; and on the horizon are cars powered by hydrogen fuel cells.

Wind and solar power continue to gain ground as sources of electricity for home and industry. In 2008, Texas oilman T. Boone Pickens launched a highly visible public relations campaign explaining his plan to build the world's largest wind farm in Texas, which would generate and transmit enough electricity to power one million homes. As the recession that began later that year deepened, however, the scarcity of credit and the falloff in natural gas prices (making wind power economically less attractive) forced Pickens to scale back his ambitious project in favor of a series of smaller wind farms in the Midwest.

More controversial is nuclear power, owing chiefly to questions of safety and cost. The safety issues surrounding nuclear energy were thrown into sharp relief in 2011 when three nuclear reactors at the Fukushima Daiichi facility in northeastern Japan experienced a meltdown in the wake of a major earthquake and tsunami. Building a nuclear power plant costs between $5 and $10 billion, and no application for a new nuclear power plant has been approved since 1979 (the year of the Three Mile Island reactor accident). Other renewable sources of electrical power include hydroelectric (generated by the force of flowing water); geothermal (generated by heat from the earth's core, transmitted to the surface); and biomass (generated by the burning of organic matter such as wood, leaves, manure, and crops). As of 2011, however, only about 12% of the nation's energy consumption was being generated from renewable sources—as opposed to 40% from fossil fuels such as petroleum and 22% from coal.

The development of green power, of renewable energy sources, is not only a global imperative, but it is also a matter of public policy. That is, it involves questions of what government does or does not do to encourage or discourage particular activities by businesses, nonprofit organizations, educational institutions, and individuals. Governments issue regulations, pass laws, tax and spend, subsidize, make grants, reward those who comply with their rules, and penalize those who do not. In the 1970s, the U.S. government attempted to impose CAFE (Corporate Average Fuel Efficiency Standards) regulations mandating minimum fuel efficiency standards for vehicles. But automakers have long resisted such controls and have pressured their elected representatives to ease or abandon them.

Other government efforts to curb greenhouse gas emissions have not survived industry opposition. Environmentalists were encouraged by the election of Barack Obama, who favored the development of renewable energy sources and of a "smart" national energy grid. Obama also proposed reducing the nation's reliance on fossil fuels by increasing fuel efficiency standards through such programs as cap and trade. Between 2009 and 2011, the Obama Interior Department approved 27 renewable energy projects, both wind and solar, capable of generating 6,500 megawatts (compared with about 1,800 megawatts in all prior years). But the new president, faced with staunch congressional opposition (even among some fellow Democrats) to his green energy programs, found it difficult to get many of his proposals passed into law. And green energy development suffered a major public relations setback after the Solyndra Corporation, a government-subsidized company that manufactured improved solar panels, went bankrupt—a debacle costing the taxpayers more than $500 million. In terms of public policy on green power, the states may end up having more of an impact than the federal government. In April 2011, for example, California governor Jerry Brown signed a law requiring that by 2020, 33% of the state's energy (an increase over the previous mandate of 20%) be generated by renewable energy sources.

The selections in this chapter offer multiple perspectives on how we can reduce (if not entirely eliminate) our dependence on fossil fuels and support the development of alternative, renewable energy sources. As you might expect, experts disagree not only about the nature of the problem and its causes, but also about needed solutions. Therefore, we present represent some of these disagreements, which will give you ample opportunity to evaluate, respond, and form your own informed opinions.

The chapter is organized into two sections. The first lays out the more general challenges we face in addressing a carbon emission–related climate crisis and in working to reduce our dependence on fossil fuels. The second section considers particular alternative, renewable energy sources such as nuclear, solar, and wind.

We begin with "Going Green: A Wedge Issue." In his recent book *Hot, Flat, and Crowded* (2008), Thomas Friedman argues that there are no easy ways to save the earth. You'll view part of his dynamic presentation on the topic in a lecture at M.I.T., in which he asserts that we must "change or die." Then you'll go online to read about the very difficult things we, as citizens of the planet earth, must do to ensure that our world remains capable of sustaining life. Closing this first section, in "The Dangerous Delusions of Energy Independence," Robert Bryce throws cold water on those who believe that we can free ourselves of reliance upon oil produced in other countries. "Energy independence is hogwash," he declares. "Worse yet, the inane obsession with the idea of energy independence is preventing the U.S. from having an honest and effective discussion about the energy challenges it now faces."

The second half of the chapter, organized into three clusters, focuses on several types of alternative energy. In the nuclear power cluster, columnists Holman Jenkins, Jr., Eugene Robinson, William Tucker, and Anne Applebaum offer four contrasting viewpoints in the debate over the safety and viability of nuclear power in the wake of the Fukushima accident of 2011. In the solar power cluster, *Los Angeles Times* reporter Marla Dickerson discusses what the state of California has done to convert a significant part of its power generation from coal to solar; Nobel Prize–winning economist Paul Krugman discusses the politics of solar energy; and *Washington Post* blogger Brad Plumer argues that solar power is about to reach the breakout stage. In the wind power cluster, *New Yorker* writer Elizabeth Kolbert reports on the fascinating case of the Danish island of Samsø ("island in the wind"), whose citizens decided to convert to electrical power generated entirely by wind turbines. In "Wind Power Puffery," however, H. Sterling Burnett dismisses the prospect of wind power as a significant response to our energy problems.

And so the debate continues, not only between businesspeople and environmentalists, but also among environmentalists themselves. To return to Thomas Friedman: "there is no 'Easy' button we can press to make the world green."

GOING GREEN: A WEDGE ISSUE

We begin our exploration of Green Power by inviting you to virtually attend a lively presentation at M.I.T. by *New York* Times columnist Thomas Friedman. Then go online to read a provocative discussion, by scientists Robert H. Socolow and Stephen W. Pacala, about the kind of massively scaled energy projects that will be required to reduce planet-wide CO_2 emissions in meaningful ways.

Thomas Friedman, foreign affairs columnist for the *Times,* has won three Pulitzer Prizes for his books, which include *From Beirut to Jerusalem* (1989), *The Lexus and the Olive Tree* (1999), and *The World is Flat* (2005). (We offer an excerpt from *The World is Flat* in Chapter 9, "The Changing Landscape of Work in the Twenty-First Century.") In his M.I.T., talk Friedman discusses issues covered in his more recent book *Hot, Flat, and Crowded: Why We Need a Green Revolution—And How It Can Renew America* (2008).

Go to: YouTube.com

Search terms: "thomas friedman mit green energy"

Using less restrictive search terms (e.g., "thomas friedman green energy"), you can find clips of Friedman in many other academic venues and in TV interviews. Look, especially, for an interview with Friedman by Fareed Zakaria. In *Hot, Flat, and Crowded,* Friedman discusses the startling findings of Socolow and Pacala concerning just how much hard work will be required to truly accomplish a "green revolution"—and not just a "green party." In their September 2006 *Scientific American* article, Socolow and Pacala introduce the concept of "wedges"—each wedge of the circle representing an activity that reduces the world's carbon levels by 25 billion tons over the next 50 years. A workable carbon strategy, according to Socolow and Pacala, requires the implementation of seven such wedges. Socolow and Pacala head the Carbon Migration Initiative at Princeton University. Socolow is a professor of mechanical engineering. Pacala is a professor of ecology.

Go to: Google *or* Bing

Search terms: "a plan to keep carbon in check"

Discussion and Writing Suggestions

1. Friedman pokes fun at what passes for a "green revolution"—and what he calls a "green party." Why? Do you agree with him? To what extent have you bought into the kind of "eco-chic" for which Friedman has such scorn? Do you think he is not sufficiently appreciative of well-intentioned (if ineffectual) efforts on the part of individuals?

2. Both in his talks and his writing, Friedman uses a breezy, punchy manner of delivery. "Washington today," he claims, is "brain dead." We cannot keep being "as dumb as we want to be." He sneers at people who strive to be "green" by buying Priuses or low energy light

bulbs. To what extent is this style effective for you? Did you find it, for instance, refreshing? irreverent? offensive?

3. Friedman lays partial blame on the government for not effectively responding to the threat of climate change. "If we had a government that was as alive as the country," he charges, "no one would touch us." Friedman also suggests that a smarter set of regulations—and in particular, raising taxes on fossil fuel energy—would increase the real cost of oil to the planet so that green energy sources would become competitive. Do you believe that government policy could help to bring about a genuine green revolution? If so, how? Alternatively, should government "get out of the way," as conservatives recommend, and let private industry take the lead? To what extent do you think that government policy since the time Friedman gave his presentation (during the last months of the George W. Bush administration) has begun to effectively address the problems posed by climate change?

4. Friedman asks, "Have you ever seen a revolution where no one got hurt?" The underlying principle here is that in real revolutions people *do* get hurt—not necessarily physically, but perhaps economically, or in such a way as to significantly change their preferred lifestyle. "Change or die!" he admonishes. Write an analysis in which you apply this or another of Friedman's principles or definitions to a particular situation of which you have personal knowledge or about which you have read. See the guidelines and model analyses in Chapter 4 for ideas on how to proceed.

5. Examine Socolow and Pacala's chart "15 Ways to Make a Wedge." Which of these wedges—or sets of wedges—do you believe are the most realizable, the most likely to be accomplished in the next 50 years? Why? The least likely? Why? What are the potential roadblocks? For those wedges that you view as most practical, discuss the combination of government policies and private/commercial initiatives that you think are most necessary.

6. For each of the wedge groups in Socolow and Pacala's chart—e.g., alternative energy sources, carbon capture and storage (CCS), or power generation—which industrial or political interests do you think would be most opposed to progress? What do you imagine their arguments would be? What are some counter-arguments? What is your position?

7. Socolow and Pacala describe nuclear power as "probably the most controversial of all the wedge strategies." Among the drawbacks of nuclear power: the potential for catastrophic accidents, the problem of nuclear waste disposal, and the possibility that some governments would convert civilian application of nuclear energy to weapons development. What is your view, at this point, of the potential for nuclear power to alleviate the world's energy problems and avoid catastrophic climate change? Note: the "Debate on Nuclear Power, Post-Fukushima," later in this chapter, may give you additional food for thought on this subject.

THE DANGEROUS DELUSIONS OF ENERGY INDEPENDENCE

Robert Bryce

In the following selection, Robert Bryce argues that it is neither possible nor desirable for the United States to become independent of foreign energy supplies. Those who advocate such independence, he claims, are "woefully ignorant about the fundamentals of energy and the energy business." Bryce's provocative conclusion flies in the face of often unexamined assumptions held by many politicians, as well as environmentalists.

Robert Bryce, a fellow at the Institute for Energy Research and a managing editor of the *Energy Tribune*, has written about energy for more than two decades. His articles have appeared in such publications as the *Atlantic Monthly*, the *Guardian*, and the *Nation*. His books include *Cronies: Oil, the Bushes, and the Rise of Texas, America's Superstate* (2004) and *Power Hungry: The Myths of Green Energy and the Real Fuels of the Future* (2010). This selection is excerpted from the introduction ("The Persistent Delusion") to his book *Gusher of Lies: The Dangerous Delusions of "Energy Independence"* (2008).

Americans love independence.

Whether it's financial independence, political independence, the Declaration of Independence, or grilling hotdogs on Independence Day, America's self-image is inextricably bound to the concepts of freedom and autonomy. The promises laid out by the Declaration—life, liberty, and the pursuit of happiness—are the shared faith and birthright of all Americans.

Alas, the Founding Fathers didn't write much about gasoline.

Nevertheless, over the past 30 years or so—and particularly over the past 3 or 4 years—American politicians have been talking as though Thomas Jefferson himself warned about the dangers of imported crude oil. Every U.S. president since Richard Nixon has extolled the need for energy independence. In 1974, Nixon promised it could be achieved within 6 years.[1] In 1975, Gerald Ford promised it in 10.[2] In 1977, Jimmy Carter warned Americans that the world's supply of oil would begin running out within a decade or so and that the energy crisis that was then facing America was "the moral equivalent of war."[3]

5   The phrase "energy independence" has become a prized bit of meaningful-sounding rhetoric that can be tossed out by candidates and political operatives eager to appeal to the broadest cross section of voters. When the U.S. achieves energy independence, goes the reasoning, America will be a self-sufficient Valhalla, with lots of good-paying manufacturing jobs that will come from producing new energy technologies. Farmers will grow fat, rich, and happy by growing acre upon acre of corn and other plants that can be turned into billions of gallons of oil-replacing ethanol. When America arrives at the promised land of milk, honey, and supercheap motor fuel, then U.S. soldiers will never

again need visit the Persian Gulf, except, perhaps, on vacation. With energy independence, America can finally dictate terms to those rascally Arab sheikhs from troublesome countries. Energy independence will mean a thriving economy, a positive balance of trade, and a stronger, better America.

The appeal of this vision of energy autarky has grown dramatically since the terrorist attacks of September 11. That can be seen through an analysis of news stories that contain the phrase "energy independence." In 2000, the Factiva news database had just 449 stories containing that phrase. In 2001, there were 1,118 stories. By 2006, that number had soared to 8,069.

The surging interest in energy independence can be explained, at least in part, by the fact that in the post–September 11 world, many Americans have been hypnotized by the conflation of two issues: oil and terrorism. America was attacked, goes this line of reasoning, because it has too high a profile in the parts of the world where oil and Islamic extremism are abundant. And buying oil from the countries of the Persian Gulf stuffs petrodollars straight into the pockets of terrorists like Mohammad Atta and the 18 other hijackers who committed mass murder on September 11.

Americans have, it appears, swallowed the notion that all foreign oil—and thus, presumably, all foreign energy—is bad. Foreign energy is a danger to the economy, a danger to America's national security, a major source of funding for terrorism, and, well, just not very patriotic. Given these many assumptions, the common wisdom is to seek the balm of energy independence. And that balm is being peddled by the Right, the Left, the Greens, Big Agriculture, Big Labor, Republicans, Democrats, senators, members of the House, [former president] George W. Bush, the opinion page of the *New York Times*, and the neoconservatives. About the only faction that dismisses the concept is Big Oil. But then few people are listening to Big Oil these days.

Environmental groups like Greenpeace and Worldwatch Institute continually tout energy independence.[4] The idea has long been a main talking point of Amory Lovins, the high priest of the energy-efficiency movement and the CEO of the Rocky Mountain Institute.[5] One group, the Apollo Alliance, which represents labor unions, environmentalists, and other left-leaning groups, says that one of its primary goals is "to achieve sustainable American energy independence within a decade."[6]

10   Al Gore's 2006 documentary about global warming, *An Inconvenient Truth*, implies that America's dependence on foreign oil is a factor in global warming.[7] The film, which won two Academy Awards (for best documentary feature and best original song), contends that foreign oil should be replaced with domestically produced ethanol and that this replacement will reduce greenhouse gases.[8] (In October 2007, Gore was awarded the Nobel Peace Prize.)

The leading Democratic candidates for the White House in 2008 have made energy independence a prominent element of their stump speeches. [Former] Illinois senator Barack Obama has declared that "now is the time for serious leadership to get us started down the path of energy independence."[9] In January 2007, in the video that she posted on her Website that kicked off her presidential campaign, New York senator Hillary Clinton said she wants to make America "energy independent and free of foreign oil."[10]

The Republicans are on board, too. In January 2007, shortly before Bush's State of the Union speech, one White House adviser declared that the president would soon deliver "headlines above the fold that will knock your socks off in terms of our commitment to energy independence."[11] In February 2007, Arizona senator and presidential candidate John McCain told voters in Iowa, "We need energy independence. We need it for a whole variety of reasons."[12] In March 2007, former New York mayor Rudolph Giuliani insisted that the federal government "must treat energy independence as a matter of national security." He went on, saying that "we've been talking about energy independence for over 30 years and it's been, well, really, too much talk and virtually no action.... I'm impatient and I'm single-minded about my goals, and we will achieve energy independence."[13]

• • •

Polls show that an overwhelming majority of Americans are worried about foreign oil. A March 2007 survey by Yale University's Center for Environmental Law and Policy found that 93 percent of respondents said imported oil is a serious problem and 70 percent said it was "very" serious.[14] That finding was confirmed by an April 2007 poll by Zogby International, which found that 74 percent of Americans believe that cutting oil imports should be a high priority for the federal government. And a majority of those surveyed said that they support expanding the domestic production of alternative fuels.[15]

The energy independence rhetoric has become so extreme that some politicians are even claiming that lightbulbs will help achieve the goal. In early 2007, U.S. Representative Jane Harman, a California Democrat, introduced a bill that would essentially outlaw incandescent bulbs by requiring all bulbs in the U.S. to be as efficient as compact fluorescent bulbs. Writing about her proposal in the *Huffington Post*, Harman declared that such bulbs could "help transform America into an energy efficient and energy independent nation."[16]

15   While Harman may not be the brightest bulb in the chandelier, there's no question that the concept of energy independence resonates with American voters and explains why a large percentage of the American populace believes that energy independence is not only doable but desirable.

But here's the problem: It's not and it isn't.

Energy independence is hogwash. From nearly any standpoint—economic, military, political, or environmental—energy independence makes no sense. Worse yet, the inane obsession with the idea of energy independence is preventing the U.S. from having an honest and effective discussion about the energy challenges it now faces.

[Let's] acknowledge, and deal with, the difference between rhetoric and reality. The reality is that the world—and the energy business in particular—is becoming ever more interdependent. And this interdependence will likely only accelerate in the years to come as new supplies of fossil fuel become more difficult to find and more expensive to produce. While alternative and renewable forms of energy will make minor contributions to America's overall energy mix, they cannot provide enough new supplies to supplant the new global energy paradigm, one in which every type of fossil fuel—crude oil, natural gas, diesel fuel, gasoline, coal, and uranium—gets traded and shipped in an ever more sophisticated global market.

Regardless of the ongoing fears about oil shortages, global warming, conflict in the Persian Gulf, and terrorism, the plain, unavoidable truth is that the U.S., along with nearly every other country on the planet, is married to fossil fuels. And that fact will not change in the foreseeable future, meaning the next 30 to 50 years. That means that the U.S. and the other countries of the world will continue to need oil and gas from the Persian Gulf and other regions. Given those facts, the U.S. needs to accept the reality of *energy interdependence*.

20   The integration and interdependence of the $5-trillion-per-year global energy business can be seen by looking at Saudi Arabia, the biggest oil producer on the planet.[17] In 2005, the Saudis *imported* 83,000 barrels of gasoline and other refined oil products per day.[18] It can also be seen by looking at Iran, which imports 40 percent of its gasoline needs. Iran also imports large quantities of natural gas from Turkmenistan.[19] If the Saudis, with their 260 billion barrels of oil reserves, and the Iranians, with their 132 billion barrels of oil and 970 trillion cubic feet of natural gas reserves, can't be energy independent, why should the U.S. even try?[20]

An October 2006 report by the Council on Foreign Relations put it succinctly: "The voices that espouse 'energy independence' are doing the nation a disservice by focusing on a goal that is unachievable over the foreseeable future and that encourages the adoption of inefficient and counterproductive policies."[21]

America's future when it comes to energy—as well as its future in politics, trade, and the environment—lies in accepting the reality of an increasingly interdependent world. Obtaining the energy that the U.S. will need in future decades requires American politicians, diplomats, and business people to be actively engaged with the energy-producing countries of the world, particularly the Arab and Islamic producers. Obtaining the country's future energy supplies means that the U.S. must embrace the global market while acknowledging the practical limits on the ability of wind power and solar power to displace large amounts of the electricity that's now generated by fossil fuels and nuclear reactors.

The rhetoric about the need for energy independence continues largely because the American public is woefully ignorant about the fundamentals of energy and the energy business.[22] It appears that voters respond to the phrase, in part, because it has become a type of code that stands for foreign policy isolationism—the idea being that if only the U.S. didn't buy oil from the Arab and Islamic countries, then all would be better. The rhetoric of energy independence provides political cover for protectionist trade policies, which have inevitably led to ever larger subsidies for politically connected domestic energy producers, the corn ethanol industry being the most obvious example.

But going it alone with regard to energy will not provide energy security or any other type of security. Energy independence, at its root, means protectionism and isolationism, both of which are in direct opposition to America's long-term interests in the Persian Gulf and globally.

25   Once you move past the hype and the overblown rhetoric, there's little or no justification for the push to make America energy independent. And that's the purpose of this book: to debunk the concept of energy independence and show that none of the alternative or renewable energy sources now being hyped—corn ethanol, cellulosic ethanol, wind power, solar power, coal-to-liquids, and so on—will free America from imported fuels. America's appetite is simply too large and the global market is too sophisticated and too integrated for the U.S. to secede.

Indeed, America is getting much of the energy it needs because it can rely on the strength of an ever-more-resilient global energy market. In 2005, the U.S. bought crude oil from 41 different countries, jet fuel from 26 countries, and gasoline from 46.[23] In 2006, it imported coal from 11 different countries and natural gas from 6 others.[24] American consumers in some border states rely on electricity imported from Mexico and Canada.[25] Tens of millions of Americans get electricity from nuclear power reactors that are fueled by foreign uranium. In 2006, the U.S. imported the radioactive element from 8 different countries.[26]

Yes, America does import a lot of energy. But here's an undeniable truth: It's going to continue doing so for decades to come. Iowa farmers can turn all of their corn into ethanol, Texas and the Dakotas can cover themselves in windmills, and Montana can try to convert all of its coal into motor fuel, but none of those efforts will be enough. America needs energy, and lots of it. And the only way to get that energy is by relying on the vibrant global trade in energy commodities so that each player in that market can provide the goods and services that it is best capable of producing.

Notes

[1]Richard Nixon, State of the Union address, January 30, 1974. Available: http://www.thisnation.com/library/sotu/1974rn.html.

[2]Gerald Ford, State of the Union address, January 15, 1975. Available: http://www.ford.utexas.edu/LIBRARY/SPEECHES/750028.htm.

[3]Jimmy Carter, televised speech on energy policy, April 18, 1977. Available: http://www.pbs.org/wgbh/amex/carter/filmmore/ps_energy.html.

[4]Greenpeace is perhaps the most insistent of the environmental groups regarding energy independence. This 2004 statement is fairly representative: http://www.greenpeace.org/international/campaigns/no-war/war-on-iraq/it-s-about-oil. For Worldwatch, see its press release after George W. Bush's 2007 State of the Union speech, which talks about "increased energy independence." Available: http://www.worldwatch.org/node/4873.

[5]See any number of presentations by Lovins on energy independence. One sample: his presentation before the U.S. Senate Committee on Energy and Natural Resources on March 7, 2006. Available: http://energy.senate.gov/public/index.cfm?FuseAction=Hearings.Testimony&Hearing_ID=1534&Witness_ID=4345. Or see *Winning the Energy Endgame*, by Lovins et al., 228, discussing the final push toward "total energy independence" and the move to the hydrogen economy.

[6]National Apollo Alliance Steering Committee statement. Available: http://www.apolloalliance.org/about_the_alliance/who_we_are/steeringcommittee.cfm.

[7]At approximately 1:32 into the movie, in a section that discusses what individuals can do to counter global warming, a text message comes onto the screen: "Reduce our dependence on foreign oil, help farmers grow alcohol fuels."

[8]AMPAS data. Available: http://www.oscars.org/79academyawards/nomswins.html.

[9]Barack Obama, "Energy Security Is National Security," Remarks of Senator Barack Obama to the Governor's Ethanol Coalition, February 28, 2006. Available: http://obama.senate.gov/speech/060228-energy_security_is_national_security/index.html.

[10]Original video at www.votehillary.org. See also, http://www.washingtonpost.com/wp-dyn/content/article/2007/01/20/AR2007012000426.html.

[11]*New York Times*, "Energy Time: It's Not about Something for Everyone," January 16, 2007.

[12]Shailagh Murray, "Ethanol Undergoes Evolution as Political Issue," *Washington Post*, March 13, 2007, A06. Available: http://www.washingtonpost.com/wp-dyn/content/article/2007/03/12/AR2007031201722_pf.html.

[13]Richard Perez-Pena, "Giuliani Focuses on Energy," *The Caucus: Political Blogging from the New York Times*, March 14, 2007. Available: http://thecaucus.blogs.nytimes.com/2007/03/14/giuliani-focuses-on-energy.

[14]Yale Center for Environmental Law and Policy, 2007 Environment survey. Available: http://www.yale.edu/envirocenter/YaleEnvironmentalPoll2007Keyfindings.pdf.

[15]UPI, "Americans Want Energy Action, Poll Says," April 17, 2007. Available: http://www.upi.com/Energy/Briefing/2007/04/17/americans_want_energy_action_poll_says.

[16]Jane Harman, "A Bright Idea for America's Energy Future," *Huffington Post*, March 15, 2007. Available: http://www.huffingtonpost.com/rep-jane-harman/a-bright-idea-for-america_b_43519.html.

[17]http://www.infoplease.com/ipa/A0922041.html.

[18]Organization of Arab Petroleum Exporting Countries (OPEC), *Annual Statistical Report 2006*, 75. Available: http://www.oapecorg.org/images/A%20S%20R%20 2006.pdf.

[19] Nazila Fathi and Jad Mouawad, "Unrest Grows amid Gas Rationing in Iran," *New York Times*, June 29, 2007. According to this story, Iran imports gasoline from 16 countries. Iran has been importing natural gas from Turkmenistan since the late 1990s. In 2008, those imports will likely be about 1.3 billion cubic feet of natural gas per day. The fuel will be used to meet demand in northern Iran. For more, see, David Wood, Saeid Mokhatab, and Michael J. Economides, "Iran Stuck in Neutral," *Energy Tribune*, December 2006, 19.

[20] EIA oil reserve data for Saudi Arabia available: http://www.eia.doe.gov/emeu/cabs/saudi.html. EIA oil reserve data for Iran available: http://www.eia.doe.gov/emeu/cabs/Iran/Oil.html. EIA natural gas data for Iran available: http://www.eia.goe.gov/emeu/cabs/Iran/NaturalGas.html.

[21] Council on Foreign Relations, "National Security Consequences of U.S. Oil Dependency," October 2006, 4. Available: http://www.cfr.org/content/publications/attachments/EnergyTFR.pdf.

[22] A June 2007 survey done by Harris Interactive for the American Petroleum Institute found that only 9 percent of the respondents named Canada as America's biggest supplier of oil for the year 2006. For more on this, see Robert Rapier, "America's Energy IQ," R-Squared Energy Blog, June 29, 2007. Available: http://i-r-squared.blogspot.com/2007/06/americas-energy-iq.html#links. For the results of the entire survey, see: http://www.energytomorrow.org/energy_issues/energy_iq/energy_iq_survey.html.

[23] EIA crude import data available: http://tonto.eia.doe.gov/dnav/pet/pet_move_impcus_a2_nus_epc0_im0_mbbl_a.htm. EIA data for jet fuel available: http://tonto.eia.doe.gov/dnav/pet/pet_move_impcus_a2_nus_EPJK_im0_mbbl_a.htm. EIA data for finished motor gasoline available: http://tonto.eia.doe.gov/dnav/pet/pet_move_impcus_a2_nus_epm0f_im0_mbbl_a.htm.

[24] EIA coal data available: http://www.eia.doe.gov/cneaf/coal/quarterly/html/t18p01p1.html. For gas imports, EIA data available: http://tonto.eia.doe.gov/dnav/ng/ng_move_impc_s1_a.htm.

[25] EIA data available: http://www.eia.doe.gov/cneaf/electricity/epa/epat6p3.html.

[26] Information from 2006, EIA data available: http://www.eia.doe.gov/cneaf/nuclear/umar/table3.html.

Review Questions

1. Why are Americans so obsessed with independence, according to Bryce?

2. Why does Bryce believe that renewable energy sources such as wind power and solar power cannot supplant fossil fuels in the foreseeable future?

3. How does Bryce explain the American public's (and their leaders') rhetoric about independence?

● Discussion and Writing Suggestions

1. What is Bryce's chief objection to the premise that the United States should strive to become energy independent? To what extent do you agree with his objection?

2. To what extent do you believe that Bryce is overly pessimistic about the prospects for renewable energy sources supplanting fossil fuels in the near term? Explain.

3. Bryce employs sarcasm plentifully throughout this piece. Cite examples. Do you think that he uses this rhetorical device effectively? Explain.

4. Bryce argues that "the U.S. needs to accept the reality of *energy interde-pendence*." What implications does such an acceptance have for (1) domestic suppliers of fossil fuels (coal, oil, natural gas); (2) domestic consumption of energy from both fossil and renewable sources; (3) our relations with oil-supplying nations of the Middle East?

5. Critique Bryce's argument. Use as guidelines the principles discussed in Chapter 2. Consider first the main questions: (1) To what extent does Bryce succeed in his purpose? (2) To what extent do you agree with him? Then move to the specifics: Do you find Bryce's arguments com-pelling? Has he argued logically? What are his assumptions, and how do you assess their validity? You may want to draw upon other authors in this chapter—for example, Friedman or Gore—to provide support in your critique of Bryce. Keep in mind that this selection by Bryce is part of the introduction to a book-length treatment of the subject, during which he goes into much greater detail and a more extended argument than you will find in this relatively brief excerpt. Nevertheless, the heart of Bryce's argument is contained in this passage.

6. Locate a specific principle or definition that Bryce uses in this selection. For example, in ¶1 he asserts that "Americans love independence" and in ¶17 he contends that "the world—and the energy business in particular—is becoming ever more interdependent. And this interde-pendence will likely only accelerate in the years to come . . ." Write an analysis in which you apply this or another principle or definition by Bryce to a particular situation of which you have personal knowledge or about which you have read. See the guidelines and model analyses in Chapter 4 for ideas on how to proceed.

A DEBATE ON THE FUTURE OF NUCLEAR POWER, POST-FUKUSHIMA

On March 11, 2011, a magnitude 9.0 earthquake off the northeastern coast of Japan, followed by a massive tsunami that flooded the Tohoku region, caused extensive damage to the Fukushima Daiichi power plant, a complex of six nuclear reactors operated by the Tokyo Electric Power Company. In the days that followed, three of the reactors experienced a nuclear meltdown when power failures caused the cooling-water levels in the nuclear core to drop, exposing and overheating the uranium fuel rods (see diagram below). A series of hydrogen explosions and the release of radioactive cesium into the atmosphere hampered plant workers from shutting down the reactors and controlling the damage. Residents within a 20 km. (12 mile) radius were evacuated, and the government subsequently banned the sale

HOW A NUCLEAR REACTOR WORKS

All power plants convert a source of energy or fuel into electricity. Most large plants do that by heating water to create steam, which turns a turbine that drives an electric generator. Inside the generator, a large electromagnet spins within a coil of wire, producing electricity.

A fossil plant burns coal or oil to make the heat that creates the steam. Nuclear power plants…make the steam from heat that is created when atoms split apart—called fission.

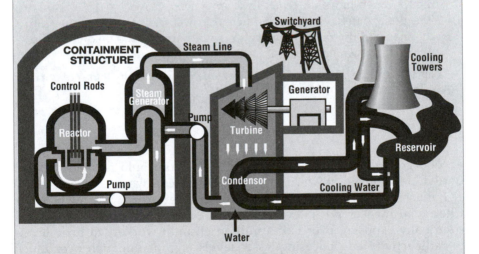

The fuel for nuclear power plants is uranium, which is made into pellets and sealed inside long metal tubes, called fuel rods. The rods are located in the reactor vessel.

The fission process takes place when the nucleus of a uranium atom is split when struck by a neutron. The "fissioning" of the nucleus releases two or three new neutrons and energy in the form of heat. The

(continued)

released neutrons then repeat the process, releasing more neutrons and producing more nuclear energy. The repeating of the process is called a chain reaction and creates the heat needed to turn water into steam.

In a pressurized water reactor...water is pumped through the reactor core and heated by the fission process. The water is kept under high pressure inside the reactor so it does not boil.

The heated water from the reactor passes through tubes inside four steam generators, where the heat is transferred to water flowing around the tubes. The water boils and turns to steam.

The steam is piped to the turbines. The force of the expanding steam drives the turbines, which spin a magnet in coil of wire—the generator—to produce electricity.

After passing through the turbines, the steam is converted back to water by circulating it around tubes carrying cooling water in the condenser. The condensed steam—now water—is returned to the steam generators to repeat the cycle.

The cooling water from the condenser is sprayed into the air inside the cooling tower and falls about 60 feet, which cools it before it is continuously recycled to condense more steam. Water in the vapor rising from the cooling tower is replenished to the condenser cooling system using [pumped-in water, generally from a nearby river].

The three water systems at [a nuclear power plant] are separate from each other, and the radioactive water is not permitted to mix with other nonradioactive water systems.

Adapted from "How Sequoyah Works," Tennessee Valley Authority, http://www.tva. gov/power/nuclear/sequoyah_howworks.htm.

of food grown in the region. The plant's reactors would not be stabilized until mid-December, at which time 160,000 residents were still displaced.

Fukushima was the worst nuclear disaster since 1986, when the Chernobyl nuclear power reactor in the Ukraine suffered a meltdown, eventually exposing over half a million cleanup workers to toxic levels of radioactivity and releasing lesser levels of contamination over much of the western USSR and Europe. Hundreds of miles around Chernobyl remain uninhabitable today. The Fukushima accident renewed the long-dormant debate over the safety of nuclear power, just at the time when this technology was increasingly being viewed as a financially viable and relatively green alternative to the burning of coal as a source of electricity.

That debate is represented in the following four brief selections, originally published as op-eds in American newspapers soon after the disaster occurred. In "The Future of Nukes, and Japan," published on 16 March,

2011, *Wall Street Journal* columnist Holman W. Jenkins asserts that the impact of the nuclear accident at Fukushima was ultimately minimal but fears that "antinuclear panic" will forestall the further development of nuclear power in this country. Eugene Robinson, writing on 15 March 2011 for the *Washington Post*, argues in "Japan's Nuclear Crisis Might Not Be Its Last" that the kind of disaster that struck Japan could also strike the United States. In his 23 April 2011 op-ed for the *Wall Street Journal*, William Tucker reminds us that all fuel sources (even ones considered "green") have their costs and drawbacks. Finally, in an op-ed published on 15 March 2011, *Washington Post* commentator Anne Applebaum wonders: "If the Japanese Can't Build a Safe Reactor, Who Can?"

THE FUTURE OF NUKES, AND OF JAPAN

Holman W. Jenkins, Jr.

You can't beat for drama the struggle of Japanese operators to manage the emergency cool-down of nuclear reactors in the tsunami zone. For the things that matter most, though—life and safety—the nuclear battle has been a sideshow. Hundreds were feared dead when entire trains went missing. Whole villages were wiped out with the loss of thousands of inhabitants. So far one worker at one nuclear plant is known to have died in a hydrogen explosion and several others have exhibited symptoms of radiation poisoning.

As for environmental degradation, video testifies to the brown murk that the tsunami waters became when they crossed into land. An infinity of contaminants—sewage, fuels, lubricants, cleaning solvents—have been scattered across the Earth and into aquifers. Radiation releases, meanwhile, haven't been a serious threat to anyone but the plant's brave workers.

Just under a decade ago, when Americans were worried about the vulnerability of nuclear plants to deliberate terrorist destruction, Nuclear Regulatory Commission Chairman Nils Diaz gave a notable speech: "In general, I do not believe nuclear power is being portrayed in a balanced manner.... This is probably the fault of all of us who know better since there have been strong currents for not mentioning consequences [of nuclear accidents] out loud."

He proceeded to lay out the consequences of Chernobyl, a uniquely bad nuclear accident, in which a graphite core reactor burned in the open air for more than a week. Along with 59 firemen and workers who lost their lives, the failure to evacuate or take other precautionary steps led to 1,800 thyroid cancer cases among children, though fewer than a dozen deaths. "Leukemia has been expected to be among the early primary latent health effects seen among those exposed to significant amounts of radiation," Mr. Diaz continued, "yet excess cases of leukemia that can be attributed to Chernobyl have not been detected."

5   Do not pretty up what Mr. Diaz was saying. He was not offering risk-free energy. Now think about Japan. It suffered its worst earthquake in perhaps 1,100 years, followed by a direct-hit tsunami on two nuclear plants. Plenty of other industrial systems on which the Japanese rely—transportation, energy, water, food, medical, public safety—were overwhelmed and failed. A mostly contained meltdown of one or more reactors would not be the worst event of the month.

Note, as a matter of realism, we say "mostly contained." In a full or partial meltdown, you don't really know what you will get unless you know the condition of the containment structure and, even more, what's going on inside it, especially in terms of fluids and gases that might have to be vented. Complicating matters in Japan's case is also the failed cooling of spent fuel, yesterday contributing to a burst of emissions that alarmed but didn't threaten the wider public. Tokyo Electric has an almighty mess to clean up, but even in circumstances compounded by a region-wide natural disaster a Chernobyl-scale release seems likely to be avoided—in which case this year's deaths from nuclear power will be less than those from coal-mining accidents.

So here's a question: The world has gas and coal with which to produce electricity. Nuclear is a hot-house plant, requiring lots of government support. Environmental groups, with their perhaps unmerited moral authority, have insisted for years that curbing carbon is the greatest human challenge, and those groups that haven't opted for escapism, insisting wind and solar somehow can make up the difference, have quietly recognized that the only alternative to fossil energy is nuclear.

Where will these groups be in the morning? China and India, two fast-growing producers of greenhouse gases, have dozens of nuclear plants planned or under construction. India being a democracy, that country is particularly ripe to be turned off course by political reaction to Japan. If they believe their climate rhetoric, will environmentalists speak up in favor of nuclear realism or will they succumb to the fund-raising and media lure of antinuclear panic?

We suspect we already know the answer. In the unlikely event the world was ever going to make a concerted dent in CO2 output, nuclear was the key. Let's just guess this possibility is now gone, for better or worse.

NO FAIL-SAFE OPTION

Eugene Robinson

Nuclear power was beginning to look like a panacea—a way to lessen our dependence on oil, make our energy supply more self-sufficient and significantly mitigate global warming, all at the same time. Now it looks more like a bargain with the devil.

I wish this were not so. In recent years, some of the nation's most respected environmentalists—including Stewart Brand, founder of the Whole Earth Catalog—have come to champion nuclear power. But as Japanese engineers struggle frantically to keep calamity from escalating into catastrophe, we cannot ignore the fact that nuclear fission is an inherently and uniquely toxic technology.

The cascading sequence of system failures, partial meltdowns and hydrogen explosions at the Fukushima Daiichi nuclear power plant was touched off by a once-in-a-lifetime event: the most powerful earthquake in Japan's recorded history, which triggered a tsunami of unimaginable destructive force. It is also true that the Fukushima reactors are of an older design, and that it is possible to engineer nuclear plants that would never suffer similar breakdowns.

But it is also true that there is no such thing as a fail-safe system. Stuff happens.

5   The Earth is alive with tectonic movement, volcanism, violent weather. We try to predict these phenomena, but our best calculations are probabilistic and thus imprecise. We have computers that are as close to infallible as we can imagine, but the data they produce must ultimately be interpreted by human intelligence. When a crisis does occur, experts must make quick decisions under enormous pressure; usually they're right, sometimes they're wrong.

The problem with nuclear fission is that the stakes are unimaginably high. We can engineer nuclear power plants so that the chance of a Chernobyl-style disaster is almost nil. But we can't eliminate it completely—nor can we envision every other kind of potential disaster. And where fission reactors are concerned, the worst-case scenario is so dreadful as to be unthinkable.

Engineers at the Fukushima plant are struggling to avert a wholesale release of deadly radiation, which is the inherent risk of any fission reactor. In the Chernobyl incident, a cloud of radioactive smoke and steam spread contamination across hundreds of square miles; even after 25 years, a 20-mile radius around the ruined plant remains off-limits and uninhabitable. Studies have estimated that the release of radioactivity from Chernobyl has caused at least 6,000 excess cases of thyroid cancer, and scientists expect more cancers to develop in the years to come.

It seems unlikely that the Fukushima crisis will turn into another Chernobyl, if only because there is a good chance that prevailing winds would blow any radioactive cloud out to sea. Japanese authorities seem to be making all the right decisions. Yet even in a nation with safety standards and technological acumen that are second to none, look at what they're up against—and how little margin for error they have to work with.

At first, the focus was on the Unit 1 reactor and the struggle to keep the nuclear fuel rods immersed in water—which is necessary, at all times, to avoid a full meltdown and a catastrophic release of radiation. Pumping sea water into the reactor vessel seemed to stabilize the situation, despite a hydrogen explosion—indicating a partial meltdown—that blew the roof off the reactor's outer containment building.

10   But then, attention shifted to Unit 3, which may have had a worse partial meltdown; it, too, experienced a hydrogen explosion. Officials said they believed they were stabilizing that reactor but acknowledged that it was hard to be sure. Meanwhile, what could be the most crucial failure of all was happening in Unit 2, which suffered an explosion Tuesday after its fuel rods were twice fully exposed. Scientists had no immediate way of knowing how much of that reactor's fuel had melted—or what the consequences might be.

The best-case scenario is that Japanese engineers will eventually get the plant under control. Then, I suppose, it will be possible to conclude that the system worked. As President Obama and Congress move forward with a new generation of nuclear plants, designs will be vetted and perhaps altered. We will be confident that we have taken the lessons of Fukushima into account.

And we will be fooling ourselves, because the one inescapable lesson of Fukushima is that improbable does not mean impossible. Unlikely failures can combine to bring any nuclear fission reactor to the brink of disaster. It can happen here.

WHY I STILL SUPPORT NUCLEAR POWER, EVEN AFTER FUKUSHIMA

By William Tucker

It's not easy being a supporter of nuclear energy these days. The events in Japan have confirmed many of the critics' worst predictions. We are way past Three Mile Island. It is not quite Chernobyl, but the possibilities of widespread radioactive contamination remain real.

Still, other energy technologies are not without risk. In 1944 a natural gas explosion in Cleveland leveled an entire neighborhood and killed 130 people. Yet we still pipe gas right into our homes. Coal mining killed 100,000 workers in the 20th century, and still kills an average of six a day in China, but we haven't given up coal. A hydroelectric dam collapsed in Japan during the earthquake, wiping away 1,800 homes and killing an undetermined number of people, yet nobody has paid much attention.

But talk about the risks of other energy sources really doesn't cut to the issue. The obvious question people are asking is, "Why do we have to mess with this nuclear stuff in the first place? Why do we have to risk these horrible accidents when other better technologies are available?" The answer is that there are no better alternatives available. If we are going to maintain our standard of living—or anything approximating it—without overwhelming the earth with pollution, we are going to have to master nuclear technology.

Consider: Uranium fuel rods sit in a reactor core for five years. During that time six ounces of their weight—six ounces!—will be completely transformed into energy. But the energy produced by that transformation will be enough to power a city the size of San Francisco for five years.

5   A coal plant must be fed by a 100-car freight train arriving every 30 hours. A nuclear reactor is refueled by a fleet of six trucks arriving once every two years. There are 283 coal mines in West Virginia and 449 in Kentucky. There are only 45 uranium mines in the entire world. Russia is offering to supply uranium to most of the developing world with the output from one mine. That is why the environmental impact of nuclear is infinitely smaller.

What about natural gas? Huge reservoirs of shale gas have been unlocked by hydrofracking. But "fracking" has been able to proceed so rapidly only because it has been exempted from federal regulations governing air and water pollution. Now that concern has arisen about damaged aquifers, natural gas production may slow as well.

So what about hydro, wind and solar? These energy sources will not bring about utopia. The only reason we don't object to the environmental effects of these renewables is because we haven't yet encountered them.

The amount of energy that can be derived from harnessing wind or water is about 15 orders of magnitude less than what can be derived from uranium. Thus a hydroelectric dam such as Hoover must back up a 250-square-mile reservoir (Lake Mead) in order to generate the same electricity produced by a reactor on one square mile.

Windmills require even more space, since air is less dense than water. Replacing just one of the two 1,000-megawatt reactors at Indian Point in Westchester County, N.Y., would require lining the Hudson River from New York to Albany with 45-story windmills one-quarter mile apart—and then they would generate electricity only about one-third of the time, when the wind is blowing.

10   Solar collectors must be built to the same scale. It would take 20 square miles of highly polished mirrors or photovoltaic cells to equal

the output of one nuclear reactor—and then only when the sun shines. Such facilities may one day provide supplementary power or peaking output during hot summer afternoons, but they will never be able to supply the uninterrupted flow of electricity required by an industrial society.

It will be impossible to meet the consumer demands of a contemporary society without a reliable source of energy like nuclear. Other countries have already acknowledged this. There are 65 reactors under construction around the world (far safer and more advanced than the 30-year-old technology at Fukushima Daiichi), but none in the U.S.

The Russians' sale of uranium to the world comes with an offer to take back the "nuclear waste" and reprocess it into more fuel, at a profit. The Chinese have commercialized their first Integral Fast Breeder, a reactor that can burn any kind of "waste" and promises unlimited quantities of cheap energy.

We have become the world's predominant industrial power because our forebears were willing to take the risks and make the sacrifices necessary to develop new technologies—the steam engine, coal mining, electricity, automobiles, airplanes, electronics, space travel. If we are not willing to take this next set of risks, others will. Then the torch will be passed to another generation that is not our own and our children and grandchildren will live with the consequences.

IF THE JAPANESE CAN'T BUILD A SAFE NUCLEAR REACTOR, WHO CAN?

Anne Applebaum

In the aftermath of a disaster, the strengths of any society become immediately visible. The cohesiveness, resilience, technological brilliance and extraordinary competence of the Japanese are on full display. One report from Rikuzentakata—a town of 25,000, annihilated by the tsunami that followed Friday's massive earthquake—describes volunteer firefighters working to clear rubble and search for survivors; troops and police efficiently directing traffic and supplies; survivors are not only "calm and pragmatic" but also coping "with politeness and sometimes amazingly good cheer."

Thanks to these strengths, Japan will eventually recover. But at least one Japanese nuclear power complex will not. As I write, three reactors at the Fukushima Daiichi nuclear power station appear to have lost their cooling capacity. Engineers are flooding the plant with seawater—effectively destroying it—and then letting off radioactive steam. There have been two explosions. The situation may worsen in the coming hours.

Yet Japan's nuclear power stations were designed with the same care and precision as everything else in the country. More to the point, as the only country in the world to have experienced true nuclear catastrophe, Japan had an incentive to build well, as well as the capability, laws and regulations to do so. Which leads to an unavoidable question: If the competent and technologically brilliant Japanese can't build a completely safe reactor, who can?

It can—and will—be argued that the Japanese situation is extraordinary. Few countries are as vulnerable to natural catastrophe as Japan, and the scale of this earthquake is unprecedented. But there are other kinds of extraordinary situations and unprecedented circumstances. In an attempt to counter the latest worst-possible scenarios, a Franco-German company began constructing a super-safe, "next-generation" nuclear reactor in Finland several years ago. The plant was designed to withstand the impact of an airplane—a post-Sept. 11 concern—and includes a chamber allegedly able to contain a core meltdown. But it was also meant to cost $4 billion and to be completed in 2009. Instead, after numerous setbacks, it is still unfinished—and may now cost $6 billion or more.

5   Ironically, the Finnish plant was meant to launch the renaissance of the nuclear power industry in Europe—an industry that has, of late, enjoyed a renaissance around the world, thanks almost entirely to fears of climate change. Nuclear plants emit no carbon. As a result, nuclear plants, after a long, post-Chernobyl lull, have became fashionable again. Some 62 nuclear reactors are under construction at the moment, according to the World Nuclear Association; a further 158 are being planned and 324 others have been proposed.

Increasingly, nuclear power is also promoted because it safe. Which it is—except, of course, when it is not. Chances of a major disaster are tiny, one in a hundred million. But in the event of a statistically improbable major disaster, the damage could include, say, the destruction of a city or the poisoning of a country. The cost of such a potential catastrophe is partly reflected in the price of plant construction, and it partly explains the cost overruns in Finland: Nobody can risk the tiniest flaw in the concrete or the most minimal reduction in the quality of the steel.

But as we are about to learn in Japan, the true costs of nuclear power are never reflected even in the very high price of plant construction. Inevitably, the enormous costs of nuclear waste disposal fall to taxpayers, not the nuclear industry. The costs of cleanup, even in the wake of a relatively small accident, are eventually borne by government, too. Health-care costs will also be paid by society at large, one way or another. If there is true nuclear catastrophe in Japan, the entire world will pay the price.

I hope that this will never, ever happen. I feel nothing but admiration for the Japanese nuclear engineers who have been battling catastrophe for several days. If anyone can prevent a disaster, the Japanese can do it. But I also hope that a near-miss prompts people around the world to think twice about the true "price" of nuclear energy, and that it stops the nuclear renaissance dead in its tracks.

 ## Review Questions

1. Why does Jenkins believe that the nuclear accident at Fukushima does not constitute a convincing case against the continued use of nuclear power?

2. Eugene Robinson warns that though we can plan to the best of our ability, designing and building the most modern and effective nuclear plants, we cannot create a "risk-free system." Why not?

3. In what specific ways are even "green" energy sources bad for the environment, according to Tucker?

4. How does Applebaum refute the claims of pronuclear activists that nuclear power is more cost-effective than other forms of energy?

Discussion and Writing Suggestions

1. Jenkins concludes by observing that the possibility of the world turning to nuclear power "to make a concerted dent in CO_2 output...is now gone, for better or worse." If true, is the world "better" or "worse" off in your view? Why?

2. Robinson thinks that turning to nuclear energy to deal with global warming looks like "a bargain with the devil." Do you agree? Why or why not? While all energy production carries some degree of risk and danger (for example, since 1949, about 250,000 people in China have been killed in coal-mining accidents), at what point should we conclude that the degree of risk posed by one particular technology is simply too much to bear? How can we best weigh risks against benefits?

3. Tucker examines the major alternatives to nuclear power—coal, natural gas, hydroelectric, wind, and solar power—and concludes that for all its drawbacks, nuclear power remains the best choice. Has he convinced you? Explain. What flaws, if any, do you find in his arguments?

4. Applebaum asks a provocative question in her title and later in the body of her op-ed: "If the Japanese can't build a safe reactor, who can?" Her implied answer, of course: "no one." To what extent do you think she has posed a fair question? To what extent do you agree with her implied answer? In your response, consider the positions of such other authors in this section as Jenkins and Tucker.

5. In the wake of the Japanese earthquake, some countries were quick to shut down their own nuclear plants or put on hold their further development. To what extent do you think such decisions were prudent? To what extent rash or premature?

6. Write a letter to the editor, responding to one of these op-eds on nuclear power. In your response, draw upon and expand with your own arguments and examples the ideas of some of the authors in this section. Keep in mind that energy policy has become highly politicized. The op-eds supportive of nuclear power come from an editorially conservative newspaper (*Wall Street Journal*), and those against it from one (*Washington Post*) generally viewed as liberal. In taking a side of the issue, keep these editorial biases in mind, and aim to win over those who may disagree.

SOLAR POWER

To many environmentalists, solar power is about as near-perfect an energy source as you can get. Energy from the sun is clean, free, abundant, and infinitely renewable. It emits no noxious fumes. It is not dangerous to produce. It does not need to be extracted at great human, financial, and environmental cost from below the ground.

Yet at the present time, owing to a number of major drawbacks, solar energy in the United States remains a marginal power source. Electricity derived from solar power is expensive to produce and transmit and cannot, unless subsidized by the government, compete economically with power derived from fossil fuels. Solar power is intermittent (no power is gathered when the sun doesn't shine) and is difficult to store. And solar arrays large enough to provide significant quantities of energy—enough, say, to supply medium-sized cities—require huge amounts of acreage. Even environmentalists have turned against solar power when construction of solar arrays has threatened millions of acres of fragile desert land.

In addition to these long-term problems, solar power suffered a major public relations setback in a 2011 scandal that will almost certainly jeopardize crucial government support of the industry in the near future[1]—this at a time when U.S. solar's most potent competitor, China, is heavily subsidizing its solar industry.[2]

---

[1] In 2009, the Obama administration authorized loan guarantees of more than $500 million to the Solyndra Corporation, which built innovative (and cylindrical) solar panels, with the promise that such government support would help create 4,000 new jobs. When Solyndra filed for bankruptcy two years later, the government was left holding the financial bag.

[2] The irony was that Solyndra's solar panels were technologically superior to conventional flat panels for generating large quantities of electrical energy. But the company was unable to compete with Chinese solar power producers, subsidized even more heavily by *their* government. [China is one of the world's largest producers of solar energy, accounting for about half of the world's annual production (in 2007) of 3,800 megawatts.]

The selections that follow offer some current perspectives on solar power. In "State Solar Power Plans Are Big as the Great Outdoors," *Los Angeles Times* writer Marla Dickerson explains how California has used incentives and goal posts to promote solar power. She also acknowledges some of the adverse environmental effects of this push. In "Here Comes the Sun," Paul Krugman, a *New York Times* columnist and Nobel Prize winner in economics, explores the real possibility that the cost of solar power may soon drop substantially enough to make the technology economically viable. In "Solar Power Is Getting Cheaper, But How Far Can It Go?" *Washington Post* writer Brad Plumer claims that with the right choices, solar power can move "squarely out of 'cute' territory" and become a legitimate alternative to fossil fuels. Considered together, these selections provide an overview of an industry poised for expansion.

State Solar Plans Are as Big as All Outdoors

Marla Dickerson

Just up the road, past pump jacks bobbing in California's storied oil patch, look sharp and you'll catch a glimpse of the state's energy future.

Rows of gigantic mirrors covering an area bigger than two football fields have sprouted alongside almond groves near California 99. This is a power plant that uses the sun's heat to produce electricity for thousands of homes.

Owned by Palo Alto-based Ausra Inc., it's the first so-called solar thermal facility to open in California in nearly two decades. It's part of a drive to build clean electricity generation using the sun, wind and other renewable sources with an urgency not seen since the days of environmentalist Gov. Jerry Brown.* Add President-elect Barack Obama's stated intention to push for more renewable power, and you've got the equivalent of a green land rush.

At least 80 large solar projects are on the drawing board in California, more than in any other place in the country. The scale of some is unrivaled on the planet. One facility planned for the Mojave Desert is projected to take up a land mass the size of Inglewood.†

5   "The expectation is that renewables will transform California's electricity system," said Terry O'Brien, who helps vet sites for new facilities for the California Energy Commission.

---

*Jerry Brown served as governor of California from 1975 to 1983 and was again elected to the governorship in 2011. His father Pat Brown also served as California governor from 1959 to 1967.
†Inglewood: a city in southwestern Los Angeles County; area: 9.1 square miles

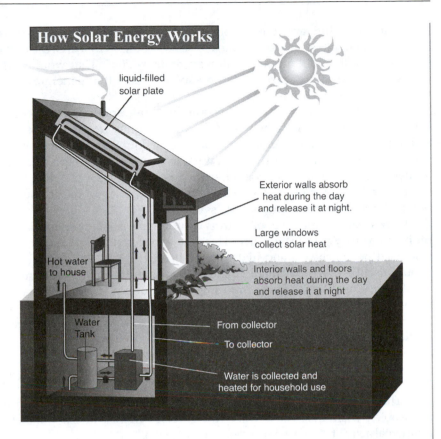

How Solar Energy Works

liquid-filled
solar plate

Exterior walls absorb
heat during the day
and release it at night.

Large windows
collect solar heat

Hot water
to house

Interior walls and floors
absorb heat during the day
and release it at night

Water
Tank

From collector

To collector

Water is collected and
heated for household use

It's a daunting challenge for the world's eighth-largest economy. Despite the nation's toughest mandates for boosting green energy and reducing greenhouse gases, California remains addicted to burning fossil fuels to keep the lights on.

Excluding large hydroelectric operations, less than 12% of the state's electricity came from renewable sources in 2007, according to the commission. Solar ranked last, supplying just 0.2% of California's needs. Rooftop photovoltaic panels are unaffordable or impractical for most Californians even with generous state incentives.

Enter Big Solar.

Proponents say utility-scale solar is a way to get lots of clean megawatts online quickly, efficiently and at lower costs. Solar thermal plants such as Ausra's are essentially giant boilers made of glass and steel. They use the sun's heat to create steam to power turbines that generate electricity.

10   Costing about 18 cents a kilowatt-hour at present, solar thermal power is roughly 40% cheaper than that generated by the silicon-based panels that sit on the roofs of homes and businesses, according to a June report

by Clean Edge Inc. and the Co-op American Foundation. Analysts say improved technology and economies of scale should help lower the cost of solar thermal to about 5 cents a kilowatt-hour by 2025. That would put it on par with coal, the cheap but carbon-spewing fuel that generates about half the nation's electricity.

Size matters, said Sun Microsystems Inc. co-founder-turned-venture-capitalist Vinod Khosla, whose Khosla Ventures has invested more than $30 million in Ausra. A square patch of desert about 92 miles long on each side blanketed with Ausra's technology could generate enough electricity to meet the entire nation's demand, company executives say. "Utility-scale solar is probably the only way to achieve real scale…and reduce our carbon emissions" significantly, Khosla said.

Critics fear that massive solar farms would create as many environmental problems as they purport to solve. This new-age electricity still requires old-fashioned power towers and high-voltage lines to get it to people's homes. A proposed 150-mile transmission line known as the Sunrise Powerlink that would carry renewable power from Imperial County to San Diego has run into stiff resistance from grass-roots groups and environmentalists.

Solar plants require staggering amounts of land, which could threaten fragile ecosystems and mar the stark beauty of America's deserts. And in contrast to rooftop panels, which enable homeowners to pursue energy independence, these centralized facilities keep consumers tethered to utility companies.

"They are trying to perpetuate the old Big Energy paradigm into the renewable-energy era," said Sheila Bowers, a Santa Monica attorney and environmental activist. "They have a monopoly agenda."

15   California already has the largest operating collection of solar thermal facilities in the world: nine plants totaling just over 350 megawatts in San Bernardino County. Built in the 1980s, they were part of a drive toward energy self-sufficiency stemming from the '70s oil shocks. The boom ended when California dropped requirements forcing utilities to buy renewable power.

The push is back. The 2000–01 energy crisis exposed California's continued dependence on outsiders—more than 30% of its electricity still comes from out of state. Renewable forms of energy are once again central to efforts to shore up supply and fight global warming.

State lawmakers have told investor-owned utilities that they must procure 20% of their electricity from renewable sources by 2010; Gov. Arnold Schwarzenegger is pushing for a minimum of 33% by 2020. A landmark 2006 state law forcing California to reduce its greenhouse gas emissions to 1990 levels within 12 years also is boosting green generation. Most of the proposed utility-scale solar plants are slated for San Bernardino and Riverside counties, whose vast deserts offer abundant sunshine and plenty of open space for the behemoths. The U.S. Bureau of Land Management is juggling so many requests from companies looking to build on federal land—79 at last count, covering more than 690,000 acres—that it had to stop accepting applications for a few weeks last summer. Many of these facilities may never get built. Environmentalists are mobilizing. U.S. credit markets are in a deep freeze. Oil and natural gas prices are falling, reducing some of the urgency to go green.

Still, the obstacles haven't clouded the ambitions of solar start-ups such as Ausra.

"Our investors perceive there is a huge opportunity here," said Bob Fishman, Ausra's president and chief executive. A group of dignitaries that included Schwarzenegger gathered near here in October to get a close-up look at the 5-megawatt operation Ausra opened.

20   The company uses a technology known as a compact linear Fresnel reflector. Acres of mirrors are anchored to metal frames and held roughly 6 feet off the ground in parallel rows. Controlled by computers, these panels make hundreds of barely perceptible movements throughout the day, tracking the sun's path across the sky.

The mirrors catch the sun's rays and reflect them onto a cluster of water pipes overhead. The intense heat—it can reach 750 degrees—generates pressurized steam inside the pipes. That steam is then fed into a turbine whose spinning generates electricity.

"It's like when you were a kid and you used a magnifying glass to fry a bug" on a sunny day, said Dave DeGraaf, vice president of product development. "We're focusing all that energy."

Despite its mammoth size, this pilot plant generates a modest amount of electricity, enough to power just 3,500 homes when the sun is shining. Ausra is thinking much bigger.

It has set up a manufacturing facility in Nevada that will supply a 177-megawatt solar plant planned for a site near Carrizo Plain National Monument in eastern San Luis Obispo County.

25   The facility's mirrors will occupy a full square mile of terrain. The project is still in the permitting process. Ausra has never tried something on this scale. But Pacific Gas & Electric is confident enough that is has agreed to buy the power from Carrizo to help it meet its green energy needs.

Other companies looking to shine in California with utility-scale plants include Solel Inc., whose proposed 553-megawatt project in the Mojave Desert would span nine square miles; BrightSource Energy Inc. of Oakland; SunPower Corp. of San Jose; OptiSolar Inc. of Hayward, Calif.; Stirling Energy Systems Inc. of Phoenix; and FPL Energy of Juno Beach, Fla.

"Climate change is the greatest challenge that mankind has ever faced," said Peter Darbee, president and chief executive of Pacific Gas & Electric and head of its parent, San Francisco-based PG&E Corp. "It's imperative to seek out the most cost-effective solutions."

Here Comes the Sun

Paul Krugman

For decades the story of technology has been dominated, in the popular mind and to a large extent in reality, by computing and the things you can do with it. Moore's Law—in which the price of computing power falls roughly 50 percent every 18 months—has powered an ever-expanding range of applications, from faxes to Facebook.

Our mastery of the material world, on the other hand, has advanced much more slowly. The sources of energy, the way we move stuff around, are much the same as they were a generation ago.

But that may be about to change. We are, or at least we should be, on the cusp of an energy transformation, driven by the rapidly falling cost of solar power. That's right, solar power.

If that surprises you, if you still think of solar power as some kind of hippie fantasy, blame our fossilized political system, in which fossil fuel producers have both powerful political allies and a powerful propaganda machine that denigrates alternatives.

5   Speaking of propaganda: Before I get to solar, let's talk briefly about hydraulic fracturing, aka fracking.

Fracking—injecting high-pressure fluid into rocks deep underground, inducing the release of fossil fuels—is an impressive technology. But it's also a technology that imposes large costs on the public. We know that it produces toxic (and radioactive) wastewater that contaminates drinking water; there is reason to suspect, despite industry denials, that it also contaminates groundwater; and the heavy trucking required for fracking inflicts major damage on roads.

Economics 101 tells us that an industry imposing large costs on third parties should be required to "internalize" those costs—that is, to pay for the damage it inflicts, treating that damage as a cost of production. Fracking might still be worth doing given those costs. But no industry should be held harmless from its impacts on the environment and the nation's infrastructure.

Yet what the industry and its defenders demand is, of course, precisely that it be let off the hook for the damage it causes. Why? Because we need that energy! For example, the industry-backed organization *energyfromshale. org* declares that "there are only two sides in the debate: those who want our oil and natural resources developed in a safe and responsible way; and those who don't want our oil and natural gas resources developed at all."

So it's worth pointing out that special treatment for fracking makes a mockery of free-market principles. Pro-fracking politicians claim to be against subsidies, yet letting an industry impose costs without paying compensation is in effect a huge subsidy. They say they oppose having the government "pick winners," yet they demand special treatment for this industry precisely because they claim it will be a winner.

10   And now for something completely different: the success story you haven't heard about.

These days, mention solar power and you'll probably hear cries of "Solyndra!" Republicans have tried to make the failed solar panel company both a symbol of government waste—although claims of a major scandal are nonsense—and a stick with which to beat renewable energy.

But Solyndra's failure was actually caused by technological success: the price of solar panels is dropping fast, and Solyndra couldn't keep up with the competition. In fact, progress in solar panels has been so dramatic and sustained that, as a blog post at *Scientific American* put it, "there's now frequent talk of a 'Moore's law' in solar energy," with prices adjusted for inflation falling around 7 percent a year.

This has already led to rapid growth in solar installations, but even more change may be just around the corner. If the downward trend continues—and if anything it seems to be accelerating—we're just a few years from the point at which electricity from solar panels becomes cheaper than electricity generated by burning coal.

And if we priced coal-fired power right, taking into account the huge health and other costs it imposes, it's likely that we would already have passed that tipping point.

15   But will our political system delay the energy transformation now within reach?

Let's face it: a large part of our political class, including essentially the entire G.O.P., is deeply invested in an energy sector dominated by fossil fuels, and actively hostile to alternatives. This political class will do everything it can to ensure subsidies for the extraction and use of fossil fuels, directly with taxpayers' money and indirectly by letting the industry off the hook for environmental costs, while ridiculing technologies like solar.

So what you need to know is that nothing you hear from these people is true. Fracking is not a dream come true; solar is now cost-effective. Here comes the sun, if we're willing to let it in.

SOLAR IS GETTING CHEAPER, BUT HOW FAR CAN IT GO?

Brad Plumer

The usual take on solar power is that it's a niche energy source, too pricey and erratic to meet more than a sliver of our electricity needs. Bill Gates has mocked solar as "cute." But, as Paul Krugman reminds us today, that's changing far more quickly than people realize. "In fact," Krugman writes, "progress in solar panels has been so dramatic and sustained that, as a blog post at *Scientific American* put it, 'there's now frequent talk of a Moore's law in solar energy,' with prices adjusted for inflation falling around 7 percent a year."

A couple of things are driving the drop in costs. Solar-panel technology is getting more efficient, true, but that's just part of the tale. China is also heavily subsidizing its domestic industry, driving a 40 percent plunge in prices over the past year (and bulldozing a few U.S. companies into bankruptcy). But it's not all about over-production from China, either. Solar companies are figuring out how to set up systems cheaply: installation and other non-module costs in the United States dropped 17 percent in 2010.

One big point to add to Krugman's column is that solar is *already* being deployed on a large scale. Tom Dinwoodie, chief technical officer at SunPower, notes that the industry has been growing at a 65 percent annual rate in the past five years. In 2010, some 17 gigawatts of solar power were manufactured, shipped and installed—the equivalent of 17 large nuclear power plants. So just how far can solar go?

One key question is whether solar can reach "grid parity"—the point at which it can compete with fossil fuels without subsidies. As Shayle Kann explains at Greentech Media, this could happen in two ways. One, solar would become attractive to utilities even after accounting for the fact that the sun doesn't always shine. At some point, for example, power companies may decide to rely on solar for hot, electricity-gobbling afternoons instead of relying on dirty natural-gas peaking plants. Alternatively, solar could reach the point at which huge numbers of retail consumers see big savings on their energy bills from installing rooftop solar.

5   It's hard to know when, exactly, grid parity will arrive. Kees van der Leun, of the energy consulting firm Ecofys, predicts that solar could be competitive with fossil fuels by 2018 or so. On the other hand, as Tyler Cowen notes, energy markets don't appear to be betting on this development. If it does happen at some point, though, a steep plunge in solar costs could be incredibly transformative. The International Energy Agency projects that solar could provide more than half of the world's energy needs by 2060 if costs fell to $100 per megawatt hour—around 50 cents per watt installed. (At the moment, solar panels are gunning for the $1-per-watt threshold.)

A lot depends on government policy. The progress being made by the U.S. solar industry will likely slow at the end of this year if a federal grant program that makes a production tax credit more accessible is allowed to expire. A price on carbon would also make a big difference in giving solar a leg up against fossil fuels, which currently offload some of their total cost into the atmosphere. And the Energy Department is pushing research into energy storage and other technologies—check out the Optical Cavity Furnace—to bring prices down. So there are a lot of variables here. But at this point, it's safe to say that solar has moved squarely out of "cute" territory.

Review Questions

1. "Size matters," says Sun Microsystems cofounder Vinod Khosla, referring to solar power systems. What does he mean?

2. What are the disadvantages of the solar thermal power systems of the kind described by Dickerson?

3. Summarize Krugman's objections to hydraulic fracking.

4. Why does Krugman reject the charge that the Solyndra case is an example of government waste and of the failure of solar technology?

5. What is the role of government in encouraging the development of solar power, according to Plumer?

Discussion and Writing Suggestions

1. All three writers acknowledge the public skepticism about solar power. To what extent has this skepticism persuaded you that solar power is not a practical way of generating sufficiently large quantities of power to replace the use of fossil fuels—and therefore is not a significant way of addressing the global warming problem?

2. How do you think Thomas Friedman would feel about the kind of solar projects described by Dickerson? Might such projects fall into the category of "an energy party"? Why or why not?

3. Large scale solar power projects are often faced with the NIMBY issue: "not in my back yard." Would you be prepared to live in an area near one of the large-scale solar facilities described in this article, knowing that the generation of solar power in large quantities could significantly reduce the volume of carbon dioxide released into the atmosphere from the burning of coal? Explain.

4. Discussing the debate over the environmental consequences of "fracking," or hydraulic fracturing, Krugman quotes an assertion from an energy-backed organization Web site: "there are only two sides in this debate: those who want our oil and natural resources developed in a safe and responsible way; and those who don't want our oil and natural gas resources developed at all." On which side would you place Krugman, based on his arguments? To what extent do you agree that that statement actually represents the choices we face? Do you see other alternatives in this particular area of energy development? Explain.

5. Both Krugman and Plumer cite "Moore's Law" to illustrate how solar technology is on its way to becoming more widespread and

commercially viable. Look up and summarize "Moore's Law." What are some other technologies to which Moore's Law applies?

6. Imagine that you work for a public relations firm. You have been hired by the solar power industry to create a campaign that will win over those who view solar energy as a "fantasy." What points will you highlight? Consider the viability of government support as discussed by Dickerson, the implications of other energy techniques explored by Krugman, and the path to reality specified by Plumer. How will you use those authors to convince opponents that solar power is worth pursuing?

7. Each writer here mentions, to varying degrees, governmental involvement in energy industries. To what extent do you think it is helpful, and/or appropriate for the government to participate in this arena? To what extent does government support represent an unwarranted use of taxpayer money and unwarranted interference in the private sector? Explain, referring to the selections.

WIND POWER

As one heads southwest toward San Francisco on Route 580 in northern California, approaching the barren hills of the Altamont Pass between Livermore and Tracy, an eerie sight gradually reveals itself. Lining the hillsides and hilltops on both sides of the highway, numerous columns of wind turbines stand sentry as if waiting to attack the vehicles passing below. The Livermore wind farm was one of the first in the world and is still one of the largest, consisting of over 4,900 medium-size wind turbines that generate 576 megawatts (thousand watts) of electricity per year. There are hundreds of wind farms around the world. China's turbines annually generate more than 44 gigawatts (thousand megawatts) of the world's total estimated consumption of more than 1,700 gigawatts—1.7 terawatts—of electricity. The United States' wind farms generate 40 gigawatts, followed by Germany (27 gigawatts), Spain (20), and India (13). Collectively, the world's wind farms create 194 gigawatts. Denmark (treated in Kolbert, below), at 3.7 gigawatts, generates almost 20% of its energy from wind power.

Many of the advantages and disadvantages of solar power also apply to wind power. Both are clean, renewable sources of energy. Neither needs to be laboriously and dangerously extracted from the earth. The raw materials are free. But so far, neither solar nor wind power can generate electricity on anything approaching the scale of fossil fuels or nuclear power. Both solar and wind are intermittent energy sources: Just as the sun doesn't always shine, the wind doesn't always blow. When the sun and the wind stop, backup power must be provided by fossil fuels, unless the energy has been stored. So far, however, large-scale energy storage from these sources is not viable. Additionally, wind farms, even more than industrial solar arrays, require vast amounts of acreage. Besides being unsightly (to some), wind turbines kill bats and birds (including eagles). Environmentalists worry about them damaging fragile ecosystems. Others oppose them on both aesthetic and economic grounds. In the acerbic opinion of British broadcaster Eric Robson, "It's surely self-evident that wind farms are an economic and technological nonsense, sustainable only if the government stuffs their owners' mouths with money, but slack-brained environmentalists hail them as the answer to all our prayers."*

Two perspectives on wind power are presented in the following selections. In "The Island in the Wind," excerpted from a longer article in the *New Yorker*, Elizabeth Kolbert describes in vivid imagery "an unlikely social movement": how the people of the Danish island of Samsø got all their homes and farms to run on electricity generated entirely by wind power. Kolbert is a journalist who specializes in environmental issues. She wrote for the *New York Times* from 1984 to 1999 and has been a staff reporter for *The New Yorker* since 1999. She is the author of *Field Notes from a Catastrophe: Man and Nature and Climate Change* (2006). In "Wind Power Puffery," H. Sterling Burnett discusses the limitations and drawbacks of wind power. Burnett is a senior fellow with the National Center for Policy Analysis. In 2000 he served as a member of the Environment and Natural Resources Task Force in the Texas Comptroller's e-Texas commission. His articles and opinion pieces have been published in *Environmental Ethics*, *International Studies in Philosophy*, *USA Today*, the *Los Angeles Daily News*, *Rocky Mountain News*, and the *Seattle Times*. This piece appeared in the *Washington Times* on 4 February 2004.

---

*Eric Robson, *Outside Broadcaster*, Frances Lincoln Ltd, 2007: p. 177.

THE ISLAND IN THE WIND

Elizabeth Kolbert

Jørgen Tranberg is a farmer who lives on the Danish island of Samsø. He is a beefy man with a mop of brown hair and an unpredictable sense of humor. When I arrived at his house, one gray morning this spring, he was sitting in his kitchen, smoking a cigarette and watching grainy images on a black-and-white TV. The images turned out to be closed-circuit shots from his barn. One of his cows, he told me, was about to give birth, and he was keeping an eye on her. We talked for a few minutes, and then, laughing, he asked me if I wanted to climb his wind turbine. I was pretty sure I didn't, but I said yes anyway.

We got into Tranberg's car and bounced along a rutted dirt road. The turbine loomed up in front of us. When we reached it, Tranberg stubbed out his cigarette and opened a small door in the base of the tower. Inside were eight ladders, each about twenty feet tall, attached one above the other. We started up, and were soon huffing. Above the last ladder, there

Catching the wind

Alternative energy sources are getting a new look as demand for fossil fuels increases worldwide, and as technical innovations help reduce the costs of alternatives. California produces more wind-generated electricity than any state except Texas and Iowa. A look at wind farms:

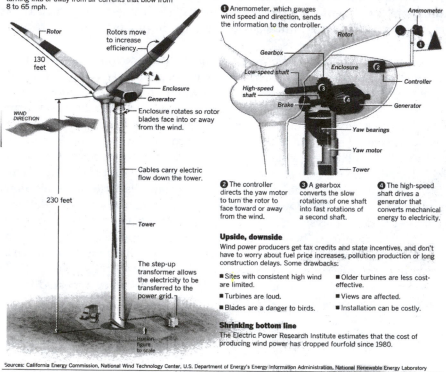

Wind turbine
These modern windmills catch the wind by either turning into or away from air currents that blow from 8 to 65 mph.

Rotor
130 feet
Rotors move to increase efficiency.
Enclosure
Generator
WIND DIRECTION
Enclosure rotates so rotor blades face into or away from the wind.
Cables carry electric flow down the tower.
230 feet
Tower
The step-up transformer allows the electricity to be transferred to the power grid.
Human figure to scale

How it works
Wind moves a propeller, which turns shafts to work a generator.

❶ Anemometer, which gauges wind speed and direction, sends the information to the controller.

Anemometer
Rotor
Gearbox
Low-speed shaft
High-speed shaft
Enclosure ❷
Controller
❸
❹
Brake
Generator
Yaw bearings
Yaw motor
Tower

❷ The controller directs the yaw motor to turn the rotor to face toward or away from the wind.

❸ A gearbox converts the slow rotations of one shaft into fast rotations of a second shaft.

❹ The high-speed shaft drives a generator that converts mechanical energy to electricity.

Upside, downside
Wind power producers get tax credits and state incentives, and don't have to worry about fuel price increases, pollution production or long construction delays. Some drawbacks:

■ Sites with consistent high wind are limited.
■ Turbines are loud.
■ Blades are a danger to birds.

■ Older turbines are less cost-effective.
■ Views are affected.
■ Installation can be costly.

Shrinking bottom line
The Electric Power Research Institute estimates that the cost of producing wind power has dropped fourfold since 1980.

Sources: California Energy Commission, National Wind Technology Center, U.S. Department of Energy's Energy Information Administration, National Renewable Energy Laboratory

DOUG STEVENS Los Angeles Times

was a trapdoor, which led to a sort of engine room. We scrambled into it, at which point we were standing on top of the generator. Tranberg pressed a button, and the roof slid open to reveal the gray sky and a patchwork of green and brown fields stretching toward the sea. He pressed another button. The rotors, which he had switched off during our climb, started to turn, at first sluggishly and then much more rapidly. It felt as if we were about to take off. I'd like to say the feeling was exhilarating; in fact, I found it sickening. Tranberg looked at me and started to laugh.

Samsø, which is roughly the size of Nantucket, sits in what's known as the Kattegat, an arm of the North Sea. The island is bulgy in the south and narrows to a bladelike point in the north, so that on a map it looks a bit like a woman's torso and a bit like a meat cleaver. It has twenty-two villages that hug the narrow streets; out back are fields where farmers grow potatoes and wheat and strawberries. Thanks to Denmark's peculiar geography, Samsø is smack in the center of the country and, at the same time, in the middle of nowhere.

For the past decade or so, Samsø has been the site of an unlikely social movement. When it began, in the late nineteen-nineties, the island's forty-three hundred inhabitants had what might be described as a conventional attitude toward energy: as long as it continued to arrive, they weren't much interested in it. Most Samsingers heated their houses with oil, which was brought in on tankers. They used electricity imported from the mainland via cable, much of which was generated by burning coal. As a result, each Samsinger put into the atmosphere, on average, nearly eleven tons of carbon dioxide annually.

5   Then, quite deliberately, the residents of the island set about changing this. They formed energy coöperatives and organized seminars on wind power. They removed their furnaces and replaced them with heat pumps. By 2001, fossil-fuel use on Samsø had been cut in half. By 2003, instead of importing electricity, the island was exporting it, and by 2005 it was producing from renewable sources more energy than it was using.

The residents of Samsø that I spoke to were clearly proud of their accomplishment. All the same, they insisted on their ordinariness. They were, they noted, not wealthy, nor were they especially well educated or idealistic. They weren't even terribly adventuresome. "We are a conservative farming community" is how one Samsinger put it. "We are only normal people," Tranberg told me. "We are not some special people."

This year, the world is expected to burn through some thirty-one billion barrels of oil, six billion tons of coal, and a hundred trillion cubic feet of natural gas. The combustion of these fossil fuels will produce, in aggregate, some four hundred quadrillion B.T.U.s of energy. It will also yield around thirty billion tons of carbon dioxide. Next year, global consumption of fossil fuels is expected to grow by about two per cent, meaning that emissions will rise by more than half a billion tons, and the following year consumption is expected to grow by yet another two per cent.

When carbon dioxide is released into the air, about a third ends up, in relatively short order, in the oceans. (CO_2 dissolves in water to form a weak acid; this is the cause of the phenomenon known as "ocean acidification.") A quarter is absorbed by terrestrial ecosystems—no one is quite sure exactly how or where—and the rest remains in the atmosphere. If current trends in emissions continue, then sometime within the next four of five decades the chemistry of the oceans will have been altered to such a degree that many marine organisms—including reef-building corals—will be pushed toward extinction. Meanwhile, atmospheric CO_2 levels are projected to reach five hundred and fifty parts per million—twice pre-industrial levels—virtually guaranteeing an eventual global temperature increase of three or more degrees. The consequences of this warming are difficult to predict in detail, but even broad, conservative estimates are terrifying: at least fifteen and possibly as many as thirty per cent of the planet's plant and animal species will be threatened; sea levels will rise by several feet; yields of crops like wheat and corn will decline significantly in a number of areas where they are now grown as staples; regions that depend on glacial runoff or seasonal snowmelt—currently home to more than a billion people—will face severe water shortages; and what now counts as a hundred-year drought will occur in some parts of the world as frequently as once a decade.

Today, with CO_2 levels at three hundred and eighty-five parts per million, the disruptive impacts of climate change are already apparent. The Arctic ice cap, which has shrunk by half since the nineteen-fifties, is melting at an annual rate of twenty-four thousand square miles, meaning that an expanse of ice the size of West Virginia is disappearing each year. Over the past ten years, forests covering a hundred and fifty million acres in the United States and Canada have died from warming-related beetle infestations. It is believed that rising temperatures are contributing to the growing number of international refugees—"Climate change is today one of the main drivers of forced displacement," the United Nations' high commissioner for refugees, António Guterres, said recently—and to armed conflict: some experts see a link between the fighting in Darfur, which has claimed as many as three hundred thousand lives, and changes in rainfall patterns in equatorial Africa.

10   "If we keep going down this path, the Darfur crisis will be only one crisis among dozens of other," President Nicolas Sarkozy, of France, told a meeting of world leaders in April. The Secretary-General of the United Nations, Ban Ki-moon, has called climate change "the defining challenge of our age."

In the context of this challenge, Samsø's accomplishments could be seen as trivial. Certainly, in numerical terms they don't amount to much: all the island's avoided emissions of the past ten years are overwhelmed by the CO_2 that a single coal-fired power plant will emit in the next three weeks, and China is building new coal-fired plants at the rate of roughly four a month. But it is also in this context that the island's efforts are most significant. Samsø transformed its energy systems in a single decade. Its experience suggests how the carbon problem, as huge as it is, could be dealt with, if we were willing to try.

Samsø set out to reinvent itself thanks to a series of decisions that it had relatively little to do with. The first was made by the Danish Ministry of Environment and Energy in 1997. The ministry, looking for ways to promote innovation, decided to sponsor a renewable-energy contest. In order to enter, a community had to submit a plan showing how it could wean itself off fossil fuels. An engineer who didn't actually live on Samsø thought the island would make a good candidate. In consultation with Samsø's mayor, he drew up a plan and submitted it. When it was announced that Samsø had won, the general reaction among residents was puzzlement. "I had to listen twice before I believed it," one farmer told me.

The brief surge of interest that followed the announcement soon dissipated. Besides its designation as Denmark's "renewable-energy island," Samsø received basically nothing—no prize money or special tax breaks, or even government assistance. One of the few people on the island to think the project was worth pursuing was Søren Hermansen.

Hermansen, who is now forty-nine, is a trim man with close-cropped hair, ruddy cheeks, and dark-blue eyes. He was born on Samsø and, save for a few stints away, to travel and go to university, has lived there his entire life. His father was a farmer who grew, among other things, beets and parsley. Hermansen, too, tried his hand at farming—he took over the family's hundred acres when his father retired—but he discovered he wasn't suited to it. "I like to talk, and vegetables don't respond," he told me. He leased his fields to a neighbor and got a job teaching environmental studies at a local boarding school. Hermansen found the renewable-energy-island concept intriguing. When some federal money was found to fund a single staff position, he became the project's first employee.

15   For months, which stretched into years, not much happened. "There was this conservative hesitating, waiting for the neighbor to do the move," Hermansen recalled. "I know the community and I know this is what usually happens." Rather than working against the islanders' tendency to look to one another, Hermansen tried to work with it.

"One reason to live here can be social relations," he said. "This renewable-energy project could be a new kind of social relation, and we used that." Whenever there was a meeting to discuss a local issue—any local issue—Hermansen attended and made his pitch. He asked Samsingers to think about what it would be like to work together on something they could all be proud of. Occasionally, he brought free beer along to the discussions. Meanwhile, he began trying to enlist the support of the island's opinion leaders. "This is where the hard work starts, convincing the first movers to be active," he said. Eventually, much as Hermansen had hoped, the social dynamic that had stalled the project began to work in its favor. As more people got involved, that prompted others to do so. After a while, enough Samsingers were participating that participation became the norm.

"People on Samsø started thinking about energy," Ingvar Jørgensen, a farmer who heats his house with solar hot water and a straw-burning furnace, told me. "It became a kind of sport."

"It's exciting to be a part of this," Brian Kjæ, an electrician who installed a small-scale turbine in his back yard, said. Kjæ's turbine, which is seventy-two feet tall generates more current than his family of three can use, and also more than the power lines leading away from his house can handle, so he uses the excess to heat water, which he stores in a tank that he rigged up in his garage. He told me that one day he would like to use the leftover electricity to produce hydrogen, which could potentially run a fuel-cell car.

"Søren, he has talked again and again, and slowly it's spread to a lot of people," he said.

20   Since becoming the "renewable energy island," Samsø has increasingly found itself an object of study. Researchers often travel great distances to get there, a fact that is not without its own irony. The day after I arrived, from New York via Copenhagen, a group of professors from the University of Toyama, in Japan, came to look around. They had arranged a tour with

Hermansen, and he invited me to tag along. We headed off to meet the group in his electric Citroën, which is painted blue with white puffy clouds on the doors. It was a drizzly day, and when we got to the dock the water was choppy. Hermansen commiserated with the Japanese, who had just disembarked from the swaying ferry; then we all boarded a bus.

Our first stop was a hillside with a panoramic view of the island. Several wind turbines exactly like the one I had climbed with Tranberg were whooshing nearby. In the wet and the gray, they were the only things stirring. Off in the distance, the silent fields gave way to the Kattegat, where another group of turbines could be seen, arranged in a soldierly line in the water.

All told, Samsø has eleven large land-based turbines. (It has about a dozen additional micro-turbines.) This is a lot of turbines for a relatively small number of people, and the ratio is critical to Samsø's success, as is the fact that the wind off the Kattegat blows pretty much continuously; flags on Samsø, I noticed, do not wave—they stick straight out, as in children's drawings. Hermansen told us that the land-based turbines are a hundred and fifty feet tall, with rotors that are eighty feet long. Together, they produce some twenty-six million kilowatt-hours a year, which is just about enough to meet all the island's demands for electricity. (This is true in an arithmetic sense; as a practical matter, Samsø's production of electricity and its needs fluctuate, so that sometimes it is feeding power into the grid and sometimes it is drawing power from it.) The offshore turbines, meanwhile, are even taller—a hundred and ninety-five feet high, with rotors that extend a hundred and twenty feet. A single offshore turbine generates roughly eight million kilowatt-hours of electricity a year, which, at Danish rates of energy use, is enough to satisfy the needs of some two thousand homes. The offshore turbines—there are ten of them—were erected to compensate for Samsø's continuing use of fossil fuels in its cars, trucks, and ferries. Their combined output, of around eighty million kilowatt-hours a year, provides the energy equivalent of all the gasoline and diesel oil consumed on the island, and then some; in aggregate, Samsø generates about ten per cent more power than it consumes.

"When we started, in 1997, nobody expected this to happen," Hermansen told the group. "When we talked to local people, they said, Yes, come on, maybe in your dreams." Each land-based turbine cost the equivalent of eight hundred and fifty thousand dollars. Each offshore turbine cost around three million dollars. Some of Samsø's turbines were erected by a single investor, like Tranberg; others were purchased collectively. At least four hundred and fifty island residents own shares in the onshore turbines, and a roughly equal number own shares in those offshore. Shareholders, who also include many nonresidents, receive annual dividend checks based on the prevailing price of electricity and how much their turbine has generated.

"If I'm reduced to being a customer, then if I like something I buy it, and if I don't like it I don't buy it," Hermansen said. "But I don't care about the production. We care about the production, because we own the wind turbines. Every time they turn around, it means money in the bank. And, being part of it, we also feel responsible." Thanks to a policy put in place by Denmark's government in the late nineteen-nineties, utilities are required to offer ten-year fixed-rate contracts for wind power that they can sell to customers elsewhere. Under the terms of these contracts, a turbine should—barring mishap—repay a shareholder's initial investment in about eight years.

25   From the hillside, we headed to the town of Ballen. There we stopped at a red shed-shaped building made out of corrugated metal. Inside, enormous bales of straw were stacked against the walls. Hermansen explained that the building was a district heating plant that had been designed to run on biomass. The bales, each representing the equivalent of fifty gallons of oil, would be fed into a furnace, where water would be heated to a hundred and fifty-eight degrees. This hot water would then be piped underground to two hundred and sixty houses in Ballen and in the neighboring town of Brundby. In this way, the energy of the straw burned at the plant would be transferred to the homes, where it could be used to provide heat and hot water.

Samsø has two other district heating plants that burn straw—one in Tranebjerg, the other in Onsbjerg—and also a district plant, in Nordby, that burns wood chips. When we visited the Nordby plant, later that afternoon, it was filled with what looked like mulch. (The place smelled like a potting shed.) Out back was a field covered in rows of solar panels, which provide additional hot water when the sun is shining. Between the rows, sheep with long black faces were munching on the grass. The Japanese researchers pulled out their cameras as the sheep snuffled toward them, expectantly.

Of course, burning straw or wood, like burning fossil fuels, produces CO_2. The key distinction is that while fossil fuels release carbon that otherwise would have remained sequestered, biomass releases carbon that would have entered the atmosphere anyway, through decomposition. As long as biomass regrows, the CO_2 released in its combustion should be reabsorbed, meaning that the cycle is—or at least can be—carbon neutral. The wood chips used in the Nordby plant come from fallen trees that previously would have been left to rot. The straw for the Ballen-Brundby plant comes mainly from wheat stalks that would previously have been burned in the fields. Together, the biomass heating plants prevent the release of some twenty-seven hundred tons of carbon dioxide a year.

In addition to biomass, Samsø is experimenting on a modest scale with biofuels: a handful of farmers have converted their cars and tractors to run on canola oil. We stopped to visit one such farmer, who grows his own seeds, presses his own oil, and feeds the leftover mash to his cows. The farmer couldn't be located, so Hermansen started up the press himself. He stuck a finger under the spout, then popped it into his mouth. "The oil is very good," he announced. "You can use it in your car, and you can use it on your salad."

After the tour, I went back with Hermansen to his office, in a building known as the Energiakademi. The academy, which looks like a Bauhaus interpretation of a barn, is covered with photovoltaic cells and insulated with shredded newspapers. It is supposed to serve as a sort of interpretive center, though when I visited, the place was so new that the rooms were mostly empty. Some high-school students were kneeling on the floor, trying to put together a miniature turbine.

30   I asked Hermansen whether there were any projects that hadn't worked out. He listed several, including a plan to use natural gas produced from cow manure and an experiment with electric cars that failed when one of the demonstration vehicles spent most of the year in the shop. The biggest disappointment, though, had to do with consumption.

"We made several programs for energy savings," he told me. "But people are acting—what do you call it?—irresponsibly. They behave like monkeys." For example, families that insulated their homes better also tended to heat more rooms, "so we ended up with zero." Essentially, he said, energy use on the island has remained constant for the past decade.

I asked why he thought the renewable-energy-island effort had got as far as it did. He said he wasn't sure, because different people had had different motives for participating. "From the very egoistic to the more over-all perspective, I think we had all kinds of reasons."

Finally, I asked what he thought other communities might take from Samsø's experience.

"We always hear that we should think globally and act locally," he said. "I understand what that means—I think we as a nation should be part of the global consciousness. But each individual cannot be part of that. So 'Think locally, act locally' is the key message for us."

35   "There's this wish for showcases," he added. "When we are selected to be the showcase for Denmark, I feel ashamed that Denmark doesn't produce anything bigger than that. But I feel proud because we are the showcase. So I did my job, and my colleagues did their job, and so did the people of Samsø."

WIND POWER PUFFERY

H. Sterling Burnett

Whenever there is a discussion of energy policy, many environmentalists and their political allies tout wind power as an alternative to burning fossil fuels. Even if electricity from wind power is more expensive than conventional fuel sources, and it is, wind advocates argue its environmental benefits are worth it. In particular, proponents claim increased reliance on wind power would reduce air pollution and greenhouse gas emissions.

But is this assertion correct? No, the truth is wind power's environmental benefits are usually overstated, while its significant environmental harms are often ignored.

Close inspection of wind power finds the promised air pollution improvements do not materialize. There are several reasons, the principal one being that wind farms generate power only when the wind blows within a certain range of speed. When there is too little wind, wind towers don't generate power. Conversely, when the wind is too strong, they must be shut off for fear of being blown down.

Due to this fundamental limitation, wind farms need conventional power plants to supplement the power they supply and to replace a wind farm's expected supply to the grid when the towers are not turning. After all, the power grid requires a regulated constant flow of energy to function properly.

5   Yet bringing a conventional power plant on line to supply power is not as simple as turning on a switch. Most "redundant" fossil fuel power stations must run, even if at reduced levels, continuously. When these factors are combined with the emissions of pollutants and CO_2 caused by the manufacture and maintenance of wind towers and their associated infrastructure, very little of the air quality improvements actually result from expansion of wind power.

There are other problems. A recent report from Great Britain—where wind power is growing even faster than in the U.S.—says that as wind farms grow, wind power is increasingly unpopular. Why? Wind farms are noisy, land-intensive and unsightly. The industry has tricked its way into unspoiled countryside in "green" disguise by portraying wind farms as "parks." In reality, wind farms are more similar to highways, industrial buildings, railways and industrial farms. This wouldn't be a major consideration if it weren't that, because of the prevailing wind currents, the most favorable locations for wind farms usually are areas with particularly spectacular views in relatively wild places.

Worse, wind farms produce only a fraction of the energy of a conventional power plant but require hundreds of times the acreage. For instance, two of the biggest wind "farms" in Europe have 159 turbines and cover thousands of acres between them. But together they take a year to produce less than four days' output from a single 2,000-megawatt conventional power station—which takes up 100 times fewer acres. And in the U.S., a proposed wind farm off the coast of Massachusetts would produce only 450 megawatts of power but require 130 towers and more than 24 square miles of ocean.

Perhaps the most well-publicized harmful environmental impact of wind power relates to its effect on birds and bats. For efficiency, wind farms must be located where the wind blows fairly constantly. Unfortunately, such locations are prime travel routes for migratory birds, including protected species like Bald and Golden Eagles. This motivated the Sierra Club to label wind towers "the Cuisinarts of the air."

Indeed, scientists estimate as many as 44,000 birds have been killed over the past 20 years by wind turbines in the Altamont Pass, east of San Francisco. The victims include kestrels, red-tailed hawks and golden eagles—an average of 50 golden eagles are killed each year.

10   These problems are exacerbated, explains one study, as "Wind farms have been documented to act as both bait and executioner—rodents taking shelter at the base of turbines multiply with the protection from raptors, while in turn their greater numbers attract more raptors to the farm."

Deaths are not limited to the United States or to birds. For example, at Tarif, Spain, thousands of birds from more than 13 species protected under European Union law have been killed by the site's 269 wind turbines. During last fall's migration, at least 400 bats, including red bats, eastern pipistrelles, hoary bats and possible endangered Indiana bats, were killed at a 44-turbine wind farm in West Virginia.

As a result of these problems and others, lawsuits are either pending or being considered to prevent expansion of wind farms in West Virginia and California and to prevent the construction of offshore wind farms in a number of New England states.

Indeed, the Audubon society has called for a moratorium on new wind development in bird-sensitive areas—which, because of the climatic conditions needed for wind farms, includes the vast majority of the suitable sites for proposed construction.

Wind power is expensive, doesn't deliver the environmental benefits it promises and has substantial environmental costs. In short, wind power is no bargain. Accordingly, it doesn't merit continued government promotion or funding.

Review Questions

1. Locate the one or two sentences in Kolbert's article that make the connection between Samsø's experience with wind power and the reduction of global CO_2 emissions.

2. How did Samsø's geographical circumstances play a role in the success of its conversion to renewable energy?

3. Why is the process of burning biomass substances, such as bales of straw or wood chips, more carbon-neutral than the burning of coal, according to Kolbert?

Discussion and Writing Suggestions

1. Why do you think Kolbert begins this article as she does, with a verbal picture of Jørgen Tranberg, rather than with, say, the data on CO_2 emissions in ¶ 7 or the consequences of heightened levels of CO_2 in the atmosphere in ¶s 8 and 9?

2. Kolbert describes a "social dynamic" through which one committed citizen convinced a number of his fellow citizens to participate in a community project; and they in turn convinced others, some with particular skills, until the committed few became a community-wide movement dedicated to productive change. Have you witnessed or been a part of such a movement in your own or another community? Describe what happened and the conclusions you draw from this experience. What obstacles did you face? How were they overcome? Which factors or events were most helpful? Most surprising? Most frustrating? Most rewarding? What advice do you have for others considering such community projects?

3. To what extent do you think the experience of Samsø concerning renewable energy sources such as wind is repeatable elsewhere, particularly in the United States? In what ways might the different geographical, cultural, and political circumstances in the United States make it difficult to repeat Samsø's experience here? In what respects might the circumstances be similar?

4. What conclusions, if any, can you draw from the Samsø experience with wind power about the role of government in encouraging the use of renewable energy? About the role of entrepreneurship? The role of individual initiative? The role of civic duty?

5. To what extent do you view the problems with wind power cited by Burnett as serious enough to rule out this energy source as viable? To what extent do you think we should proceed with large-scale construction of wind farms, considering the realities of (1) intermittent power that must be periodically supplemented by conventional power plants; (2) the poor ratio of power generated to acreage of land consumed by wind turbines; (3) the danger to birds?

6. Conduct a brief Google (or other Internet) search, and then respond to some of Burnett's concerns about wind power with the information you find. To what extent are Burnett's objections well-founded? To what extent might it be possible to deal effectively with the problems he discusses?

7. The danger to birds posed by spinning wind turbines is analogous to the danger to whales posed by sonar tests conducted by Navy submarines. In one case, the benefit is renewable energy; in the other case, the benefit is (according to the military and civilian Department of Defense

officials) enhanced national security. How should we weigh such conflicting interests and decide between them?

8. Critique Burnett's argument. Use as guidelines the principles discussed
in Chapter 2. Consider first the main questions: (1) To what extent does
Burnett succeed in his purpose? (2) To what extent do you agree with
him? Then move to the specifics: e.g., to what extent do you agree with
his contention that wind turbines pose too great a risk to birds? Before
writing your critique, you may want to reread what Elizabeth Kolbert and
other authors in this chapter have written about wind power.

SYNTHESIS ACTIVITIES

1. Write an explanatory synthesis, as if it were a cover story for a weekly
newsmagazine, in which you (1) lay out the essential drawbacks of this
county's continuing dependence upon oil and (2) discuss the range of
alternative, renewable energy sources available now or in the near future.
Your synthesis will therefore roughly follow the organization of the "Green
Power" chapter itself.

   Begin by drawing on sources like Socolow and Pacala to indicate the
nature and scope of the problem posed by this country's over-reliance on
the burning of fossil fuels. Describe some of the proposals for dealing with
the problem. In the second half of your synthesis, summarize some of the
particular forms of renewable energy—nuclear, wind, and solar power, drawing upon the authors represented in the second half of this chapter.

   Conclude by indicating which of these forms of green energy, and which
policies, appear to the authors of your sources as the most promising or practical.

2. Write an argument synthesis in which you advocate a policy or a set of
policies that you believe should govern the nation's use of energy over
the next fifty years. Socolow and Pacala offer some policies for consideration. Some of the articles in the latter half of the chapter cover policies
already in place: for example, California's mandate to derive 33% of the
state's energy sources from renewable energy by 2020.

   Based upon your reading in this chapter and elsewhere, as well as on your
own sense of what must be done, make the case for your policies. Remember
that it is not sufficient to simply advocate broad goals (we must steadily convert to renewable energy sources): you must also indicate what government,
industry, smaller business, and individuals must *do* to achieve significant re-
ductions in greenhouse gas emissions.

3. How, in the years ahead, are green technologies likely to change our
daily lives? Write an article for a magazine dated December 2025
(or 2050) on the subject of how the national quest to address the

climate crisis and to develop alternative energy sources has, since 2000, changed the way Americans live and work. Draw upon as many sources in this chapter as are helpful; but use your imagination (and a reasonable degree of probability) to analyze how the world of the near future developed from policy decisions and technological innovations being made today and over the next few years.

4. Given what you have read about the need for renewable energy, what do you believe are an *individual's* responsibilities, if any, in reducing energy use? Thomas Friedman appears to believe that the climate crisis cannot effectively be addressed by individuals, arguing that unless solutions are scaled to a massive degree, they are token gestures that will be inconsequential in resolving the larger problem. What, amid all this incoming data, is your position? Is it necessary or useful for an individual to have an energy policy? What would your policy be? How effective would this policy be in reducing carbon emissions? If it is symbolic only (or mostly), is symbolism still important and necessary? Draw upon Socolow and Pacala and any other authors in this chapter as you develop your response.

5. Imagine that you work for an advertising agency that is competing for a contract with a large company that generates either nuclear, wind, or solar power for a particular state or a particular region. Your job is to try to win the contract by preparing a brief plan that lays out to the power company executives a potential advertising campaign. Draw upon some of the authors in this chapter to prepare your written prospectus. (List the Works Cited on a separate page at the end of the document.) Indicate the key idea of your proposed campaign that will sell nuclear/wind/solar power. Explain why the type of energy the company is offering is superior to other types of energy. Do not misrepresent or distort the information presented by the authors in this chapter. Rather, use their information and arguments to best advantage. Organize your plan so that it has an introductory section, a body section containing specifics and a persuasive argument, and a conclusion.

6. Explain how some of the selections in this chapter may have changed your perception of the way you and those around you use energy, and how your life may be affected by the necessity of developing alternative sources of energy. Which authors' analyses have done the most to impress upon you the seriousness of the challenge? Which have most concerned you? For example, when Thomas Friedman asks, "Have you ever seen a revolution where no one got hurt?" he implies that saving the earth will require considerable sacrifice. To what extent are you prepared to make sacrifices: to pay increased taxes to help ensure a cleaner, safer environment and a more stable climate; to give up a degree of ease of movement; to take different jobs; to buy different cars,

homes, and appliances; to live in places located near power generation stations, whether wind, solar, or nuclear? Draw upon whichever
authors in the chapter seem best suited to help you grapple with such
questions.

7. Discuss the prospects of achieving the goals in some of Socolow and
    Pacala's wedges by drawing upon information in the latter half of this
    chapter. In developing your answer, consider electricity generation
    using nuclear, wind, and solar power as discussed by authors like
    Kolbert.

8. Robert Bryce forcefully argues that we should not succumb to the
    "delusions of energy independence." Much as we would prefer it, he
    asserts, there is no prospect of achieving independence from Middle
    Eastern oil during the next few decades. Which other authors in this
    chapter might support that position? Write an argument supporting or
    refuting Bryce's conclusion, based upon arguments made and informa-
    tion presented by other authors in the second part of this chapter.

9. Thomas Friedman and others have argued that the most effective way to
    spur the development of energy-efficient vehicles and alternative fuels
    for transportation is to make gasoline so expensive that it becomes
    financially painful to drive vehicles powered by internal-combustion
    engines. "As long as gas is cheap," he writes, "people will go out and
    buy used S.U.V.'s and Hummers." Imposing a steep gas tax will force
    people to change their habits and their preferred modes of transpor-
    tation. In an editorial, argue for or against the federal government's
    imposing a gas tax sufficient to make gasoline in the United States as
    expensive as it is in Europe—between $5 and $7 a gallon. Draw upon
    some of the authors in this chapter to help you make the case for or
    against such a tax.

10. You have read about the conflicts between those who would pursue
    renewable energy projects (such as solar power in California) and locals
    who scream NIMBY (not in my backyard). Many people live in remote
    areas, away from cities and suburbs because they like the view, and
    they don't want to see wind turbines or solar power arrays cluttering
    the landscape. It comes as no surprise, then, that the construction of
    a power grid needed to send electricity from a wind farm in Texas to
    office buildings in Los Angeles may be delayed, according to a recent
    Los Angeles Times article, because "municipalities and landowners
    have protested plans to string transmission networks through their
    backyards."

    What can we do to get beyond the NIMBY syndrome? Draw on the
    readings in this chapter, particularly those in the latter part, in develop-
    ing your answer.

RESEARCH ACTIVITIES

1. After the presidential election of 2008, many people were hopeful that the policies of the incoming Obama administration would be far more responsive to environmental concerns than the policies of the previous administration. The new president campaigned partially on the promise to take climate change seriously, to transform the automobile industry to make more energy-efficient vehicles, and to build a high-tech energy infrastructure to transmit electricity from wind and solar power plants in rural areas to the cities. The president also promised to push for higher federal fuel-economy standards and to support a cap-and-trade program with the goal of reducing carbon emissions by 80% by mid-century.

   Investigate the success of the Obama administration in achieving these goals. What policies and programs have been proposed, what regulations have been issued, what laws have been passed? What kind of hurdles has the federal government encountered as it attempts to achieve its green energy goals?

2. Robert Bryce is one of many who dismiss as impractical the goal of energy independence. Research how energy independent the United States in fact is—or could be reasonably soon. To what degree are we more independent of Middle Eastern oil than we were five or ten years ago? To what degree are plug-in hybrids more of a reality than they were at the turn of the present century? To what extent has the amount of power generated by wind and solar sources significantly supplanted coal-fired electricity during the past few years? Write a report summarizing your findings.

3. In the report "American's Energy 'Independence'" published on the Web <http://www.abc.net.au/unleashed/stories/s2274315.htm>, Dennis Phillips, a professor of foreign policy at the University of Sydney in Australia, notes that the environmental agenda often clashes with the economic and employment agenda, particularly in Third World countries. He argues:

   > All the world's poor are entitled to a much higher standard of living, but in order to progress, the world's poorest three billion will need to access and consume vastly increased quantities of energy. "Renewables" like wind and solar power are not going to do the job in the short term.

   > Do we tell the world's poor to be patient and wait? In the "ethanol fiasco" we have done worse than that. We have processed staple crops like corn and soybeans to pour into our fuel tanks, forcing up food prices that ignited riots around the world.

   Research the energy situation in one or two non-European countries, to determine (1) energy requirements for sustainability and economic development; (2) chief energy sources; (3) carbon footprints; and (4) prospects for

developing and using clean, renewable energy. How, if at all, have governments and businesses in these countries attempted to reconcile the environmental costs of increased energy use on the one hand and the need for
increased energy to spur economic development on the other?

4. To what extent are other countries, particularly in Europe, further along
    in developing and using clean energy than the United States? Select one
    European country and research its government's energy policy, its patterns
    of energy use, and its development of renewable energy plants and infra-
    structure. Determine the extent to which the experiences of this country,
    particularly its successes, may be transferable to the United States.

5. In 2008, Texas oilman T. Boone Pickens, declaring that "the United
    States is the Saudi Arabia of wind power," attempted to counteract our
    dependence upon foreign oil by launching an ambitious plan to build
    the world's largest wind farm in Texas. Investing millions of dollars of his
    own money, Pickens founded Mesa Power to oversee the project, which
    involved over 2,500 wind turbines—sufficient, he anticipated, to even-
    tually produce electricity to power 1.3 million homes. Launching a na-
    tionwide publicity campaign on television, newspapers, and magazines
    to promote his plan, Pickens also proposed that natural gas—which is
    abundant in this country and which does not produce CO_2—should
    replace gasoline as the fuel for all automobiles. Pickens's plan ran into
    a snag with the credit crunch of late 2008 (it was difficult for him to
    get the necessary financing), but he remained hopeful that the setback
    would be temporary.

    Research the Pickens plan and its current status and prospects. How
    many wind turbines have been built? How much power is being supplied?
    What kind of progress has been made in converting automobiles to use nat-
    ural gas? To what extent do energy experts and environmentalists view the
    Pickens plan as offering a viable solution to the environmental crisis?

6. Opponents of nuclear power argue that nuclear accidents such as oc-
    curred at Fukushima, Japan (2011), the Three Mile Island reactor in
    Pennsylvania (1979), and at the Chernobyl reactor in the former Soviet
    Union (1986) risk a cataclysm that makes nuclear power generation too
    dangerous. Others point to the perfect safety record of nuclear reactors
    in France, where, after a 25-year conversion process, 80% of the coun-
    try's energy comes from nuclear reactors. Investigate the safety factor of
    nuclear reactors used for power generation. What steps have been taken
    since Three Mile Island and Chernobyl to decrease the risks of radioac-
    tive particles being released into the atmosphere following a nuclear ac-
    cident? Have experts arrived at a consensus about the safety concerns, or
    is there still significant controversy over this issue?

7. Investigate the proposals to discourage use of fossil fuels and to encour-
    age renewable power generation by *one* of the following methods: (1)

cap and trade; (2) carbon taxes; (3) increased gasoline taxes. Consider not only proposed U.S. government programs, but also state programs, such as California's mandate to generate at least 33% of its power from renewable sources by 2010. Consider also policies proposed at international environmental conferences such as occurred at the UN Conference on Environment and Development (the "Earth Summit," Rio de Janeiro, 1992), in Kyoto (the Kyoto Protocol, 1997), and at the United Nations Climate Change Conferences (Bali, 2007; Copenhagen, 2009; Cancun, 2010; Durban, South Africa, 2011). Which proposals and programs to discourage carbon greenhouse gas pollution and to encourage green energy generation have met with most success? Which have been the most controversial?

8. In recent years, natural gas (the source of about one quarter of domestic electricity needs) has shown dramatic new promise for reducing American energy dependence. New methods of drilling have opened up vast new deposits of a form of previously inaccessible natural gas known as shale gas. As a recent *Time* report indicated, shale gas appears to be "a relatively clean, relatively cheap fuel that can help fill the world's needs during the transition to a truly green economy." The process used to extract shale gas from deep within the earth—hydraulic fracturing, or "fracking,"—involves injecting highly pressurized fluids into rock, then setting off explosive charges, to create channels for the extraction of fossil fuels. As critics such as Paul Krugman have noted, fracking may have potentially severe environmental costs, with the potential for major spills that contaminate groundwater and create air pollution. Research the current status of fracking, perhaps in a particular geographic area of the United States, and assess the costs and benefits of this new technology.

9. Research the latest developments in either (1) plug-in hybrid technology or (2) hydrogen fuel-cell technology. If you choose to study plug-in hybrid technology, pay particular attention to the quest to develop relatively low-cost, long-range batteries. If you choose hydrogen fuel-cell technology, pay particular attention to the quest to separate pure hydrogen from its other bound elements, as well as to store and distribute hydrogen through a national infrastructure.

10. Investigate the latest developments in either wind or solar power. For the energy source you select, investigate the actual growth of this technology over the past decade or so and the projected growth over the next ten years. How much of the nation's power requirements are currently being supplied by this particular technology? How much is projected to be supplied 10, 20, or 50 years down the road? What government incentives are available for the construction and operation of wind power or solar power? If you research solar power, to what extent are large-scale ground arrays overtaking rooftop solar panels in popularity? To what extent are

environmental concerns, political wrangling, and bureaucratic roadblocks hindering the development of wind or solar power?

11. For many years there was great excitement about ethanol, an alcohol-based fuel that is blended with gasoline. The most popular formulation, known as E85, consists of 85% corn ethanol and 15% gasoline. In the past, presidential candidates campaigning in Iowa often felt compelled to express their undying support for ethanol, because Iowan and other Midwestern farmers grew and sold the corn necessary for its manufacture. More recently, ethanol's stock has fallen. Research the history of ethanol as an alternative fuel, focusing on the economic and political aspects of its role in the search for alternatives to straight gasoline.

12. Research another form of alternative energy not significantly covered in this chapter—for instance, biomass, diesel, biodiesel, geothermal, natural gas, ethanol, or algae. To what extent does this form of energy promise to help us achieve a greater degree of energy independence? To what degree is it likely to supplant fossil fuels, such as oil and coal? What are its advantages and disadvantages? What are the implications for the environment of large-scale use of this form of energy? What major players currently control or are likely to control the supply of this energy? Which parties stand most to gain by such large-scale use? Which stand most to lose?

New and Improved: Six Decades of Advertising

Possibly the most memorable ad campaign of the twentieth century (dating from the late 1920s) took the form of a comic strip. A bully kicks sand into the face of a skinny man relaxing on the beach with his girlfriend. Humiliated, the skinny man vows to get even. "Don't bother, little boy!" huffs the scornful girlfriend, who promptly dumps him. At home, the skinny man kicks a chair in frustration, declares that he's sick of being a scarecrow, and says that if Charles Atlas (once a "97-lb. weakling" himself) can give him a "real body," he'll send for his FREE book. In the next frame, the once-skinny man, now transformed into a hunk thanks to Atlas's "Dynamic Tension" fitness program, admires himself in front of the mirror: "Boy, it didn't take Atlas long to do this for me. Look, how those muscles bulge!... That big stiff won't dare insult me now!" Back on the beach, the bully is decked by the once-skinny man, as his adoring girlfriend looks on: "Oh Mac! You are a real man after all!"

Crude? Undoubtedly. But variations of this ad, which made Atlas a multimillionaire, ran for decades (his company is still in business). Like other successful ads, it draws its power from skillful appeals to almost-primitive urges—in this particular case, the urge to gain dominance over a rival for the attention of the opposite sex. Of course, effective ads don't always work on such a primal level. Another famous ad of the 1920s appeals to our need to gain respect from others for accomplishments higher than punching out opponents. Headlined "They Laughed When I Sat Down at the Piano—But When I Started to Play...!" the text offers a first-person account of a man who sits down to play the piano at a party. As he does so, the guests make good-natured fun of him; but once he began to play, "a tense silence fell on the guests. The laughter died on their lips as if by magic. I played through the first bars of Liszt's immortal 'Liebenstraum.' I heard gasps of amazement. My friends sat breathless—spellbound." For sixteen additional paragraphs, the writer goes on to detail the effect of his playing upon the guests and to explain how "You, too, can now *teach yourself* to be an accomplished musician—right at home," by purchasing the program of the U.S. School of Music. Again, the reader is encouraged to send for the free booklet. And by the way, "Forget the old-fashioned idea that you need 'special talent'" to play an instrument.

The ubiquity of advertising is a fact of modern life. In fact, advertising can be traced as far back as ancient Roman times, when pictures were inscribed on walls to promote gladiatorial contests. In those days, however, the illiteracy of most of the population and the fact that goods were made by hand and could not be mass produced limited the need for more-widespread advertising. One of the first American advertisers was Benjamin Franklin, who pioneered the use of large headlines and made strategic use of white space. But advertising as the mass phenomenon we know is a product of the twentieth century, when the United States became an industrial nation—and particularly of the post–World War II period, when a prosperous economy created our modern consumer society, marked by the middle-class acquisition of goods, the symbols of status, success, style, and social acceptance. Today, we are surrounded not only by a familiar array of billboards, print ads, and broadcast ads, but also by the Internet, which has given us "spam," the generic name for an entire category of digital pitches for debt reduction, low mortgage rates, and enhanced body parts—compared to which the average Buick ad in a glossy magazine reads like great literature.

Advertisements are more than just appeals to buy; they are windows into our psyches and our culture. They reveal our values, our (not-so-hidden) desires, our yearnings for a different lifestyle. For example, the Marlboro man, that quintessence of taciturn cowboy masculinity, at home only in the wide-open spaces of Marlboro Country, is a mid-twentieth-century American tribute to (what is perceived as) nineteenth-century American values, popularized in hundreds of Westerns. According to James Twitchell, a professor of English and advertising at the University of Florida, "He is what we have for royalty, distilled manhood. . . . The Marlboro Man needs to tell you nothing. He carries no scepter, no gun. He never even speaks. Doesn't need to." He is also the product of a bolt of advertising inspiration: Previously, Marlboro had been marketed—unsuccessfully—as a woman's cigarette.

Another example of how ads reveal culture is the memorable campaign for the Volkswagen Beetle in the 1960s. That campaign spoke to the counterculture mentality of the day: Instead of appealing to the traditional automobile customer's desire for luxury, beauty, size, power, and comfort, Volkswagen emphasized how small, funny looking, bare bones—but economical and sensible—their cars were. On the other hand, snob appeal—at an affordable price, of course—has generally been a winning strategy. In the 1980s and 1990s, Grey Poupon mustard ran a successful campaign of TV commercials featuring one Rolls-Royce pulling up alongside another. A voice from one vehicle asks, "Pardon me. Do you have any Grey Poupon?" "But of course!" replies a voice in the other car, and a hand with a jar of mustard reaches out from the window of the second car, to pass the jar to the unseen occupant of the first car. This campaign is a perfect illustration of what University of California at Davis history professor Roland Marchand calls the appeal of the democracy of goods: "the wonders of modern mass production and distribution enable…everyone to enjoy society's most desirable pleasures, conveniences, or benefits."

So pervasive and influential has advertising become that it has created a significant backlash among social critics. Among the most familiar charges against advertising: It fosters materialism, it psychologically manipulates people to buy things they don't need, it perpetuates gender and racial stereotypes (particularly in its illustrations), it is deceptive, it is offensive, it debases the language, and it is omnipresent—we cannot escape it. Although arguing the truth or falsity of these assertions makes for lively debate, our focus in this chapter is not on the ethics of advertising, but rather on how it works. What makes for successful advertising? How do advertisers—and by advertisers we mean not only manufacturers but also the agencies they hire to produce their advertisements—pull our psychological levers to influence us to buy (or think favorably of) their products? What are the textual and graphic components of an effective advertisement—of an effective advertising campaign? How—if at all—has advertising evolved over the past several decades? (You may be interested in seeking out the documentary film *Art and Copy* (2009), about some of the great ad campaigns created during this period.)

Advertising has seen significant changes in the six decades since the end of World War II. It is unlikely that the comic-strip Charles Atlas ad or the verbose "They Laughed When I Sat Down at the Piano" ad would succeed today. Both seem extremely dated. More representative of today's advertising style is the successful milk campaign; each ad featured a celebrity such as Bernie Mac or Lauren Bacall with a milk mustache, a headline that says simply "Got milk?" and a few short words of text supposedly spoken by the pictured celebrity. But the changes in advertising during the six decades covered in this chapter are more of style than of substance. On the whole, the similarities between an ad produced in the 1950s and one produced today are more significant than the differences. Of course, hair and clothing styles change with the times, message length recedes, and both text and graphics assume a lesser degree of apple-pie social consensus on values. But on the whole, the same psychological appeals, the same principles of headline and graphic design that worked 60 years ago, continue to work today. We choose one automobile over another, for instance, less because our vehicle of choice gets us from point A to point B, than because we invest it—or the advertiser does—with rich psychological and cultural values. In 1957, the French anthropologist and philosopher Roland Barthes wrote (in a review of a French automobile, the Citroën DS), "I think that cars today are almost the exact equivalent of the great Gothic cathedrals: I mean the supreme creation of an era, conceived with passion by unknown artists, and consumed in image if not in usage by a whole population which appropriates them as a purely magical object." Barthes might have had a good career as an advertising copywriter.

How advertising works, then, is the subject of the present chapter. By applying a variety of theoretical and practical perspectives to a gallery of six decades of advertisements (and on other ads of your own choosing), you'll be able to practice your analytical skills on one of the more fascinating areas of American mass culture. You will find the main objects of your analyses later in this chapter: (1) a portfolio of *print advertisements* that originally appeared in such magazines as *Time, Newsweek, U.S. News and World Report*, and *Sunset*; and (2) a portfolio of memorable *TV commercials*, available for viewing on the YouTube Web site. For ease of comparison and contrast, most of the print ads can be classified into a relatively few categories: cigarettes, alcohol, automobiles, food, and "miscellaneous." We have selected both the print ads and the TV commercials for their inherent interest, as well as for the variety of tools employed to communicate their message about what sets their product or service apart from the competition—what some advertisers call their *USP*, or unique selling proposition.

The first two selections in the chapter provide analytical tools, particular perspectives from which to view individual advertisements. In "Advertising's Fifteen Basic Appeals," Jib Fowles offers a psychological perspective. Fowles identifies and discusses the most common needs to which advertisers attempt to appeal—among these the need for sex, affiliation with other people, dominance, and autonomy. In "Making the Pitch in Print Advertising," Courtland Bovée and his colleagues outline the key elements of the textual component of effective advertising—including headlines, subheadlines, and body text. Next, in "Selling Happiness: Two Pitches from *Mad Men*," we see how a great advertising man (in a great TV series) can transform the operation of a mechanical device into a powerful emotional experience or can reassure users of a deadly product that they can consume it safely.

Charles O'Neill, an independent marketing consultant, has written, "Perhaps, by learning how advertising works, we can become better equipped to sort out content from hype, product values from emotions, and salesmanship from propaganda." We hope that the selections in this chapter will equip you to do just that, as well as to develop a greater understanding of one of the most pervasive components of American mass culture.

ADVERTISING'S FIFTEEN BASIC APPEALS

Jib Fowles

Our first selection provides what you will likely find the single most useful analytical tool for studying advertisements. Drawing upon studies of numerous ads and upon interviews with subjects conducted by Harvard psychologist Henry A. Murray, Fowles developed a set of fifteen basic appeals he believes to be at the heart of American advertising. These appeals, according to Fowles and to Murray, are directed primarily to the "lower brain," to those "unfulfilled urges and motives swirling in the bottom half of [our] minds," rather than to the part of the brain that processes our more rational thoughts and impulses. As you read Fowles's article and his descriptions of the individual appeals, other examples from contemporary print and broadcast ads may occur to you. You may find it useful to jot down these examples for later incorporation into your responses to the discussion and synthesis questions that follow.

Fowles has written numerous articles and books on the popular media, including *Mass Advertising as Social Forecast: A Method for Futures Research* (1976), *Why Viewers Watch: A Reappraisal of Television's Effects* (1992), *Advertising and Popular Culture* (1996), and *The Case for Television Violence* (1999). This selection first appeared in *ETC.* 39:3 (1982) and was reprinted in *Advertising and Popular Culture*.

Emotional Appeals

The nature of effective advertisements was recognized full well by the late media philosopher Marshall McLuhan. In his *Understanding Media,* the first sentence of the section on advertising reads, "The continuous pressure is to create ads more and more in the image of audience motives and desires."

By giving form to people's deep-lying desires, and picturing states of being that individuals privately yearn for, advertisers have the best chance of arresting attention and affecting communication. And that is the immediate goal of advertising: to tug at our psychological shirtsleeves and slow us down long enough for a word or two about whatever is being sold. We glance at a picture of a solitary rancher at work, and "Marlboro" slips into our minds.

Advertisers (I'm using the term as a shorthand for both the products' manufacturers, who bring the ambition and money to the process, and the advertising agencies, who supply the know-how) are ever more compelled to invoke consumers' drives and longings; this is the "continuous pressure" McLuhan refers to. Over the past century, the American marketplace has grown increasingly congested as more and more products have entered into the frenzied competition after the public's dollars. The economies of other nations are quieter than ours since the volume of goods being hawked does not so greatly exceed demand. In some economies, consumer wares are scarce enough that no advertising at all is necessary. But in the United States, we go to the other extreme. In order to stay in business, an advertiser must strive to cut through the considerable commercial hub-bub by any means available—including the emotional appeals that some observers have held to be abhorrent and underhanded.

The use of subconscious appeals is a comment not only on conditions among sellers. As time has gone by, buyers have become stoutly resistant to advertisements. We live in a blizzard of these messages and have learned to turn up our collars and ward off most of them. A study done a few years ago at Harvard University's Graduate School of Business Administration ventured that the average American is exposed to some 500 ads daily from television, newspapers, magazines, radio, billboards, direct mail, and so on. If for no other reason than to preserve one's sanity, a filter must be developed in every mind to lower the number of ads a person is actually aware of—a number this particular study estimated at about seventy-five ads per day. (Of these, only twelve typically produced a reaction—nine positive and three negative, on the average.) To be among the few messages that do manage to gain access to minds, advertisers must be strategic, perhaps even a little underhanded at times.

5   There are assumptions about personality underlying advertisers' efforts to communicate via emotional appeals, and while these assumptions have stood the test of time, they still deserve to be aired. Human beings, it is presumed, walk around with a variety of unfulfilled urges and motives swirling in the bottom half of their minds. Lusts, ambitions, tendernesses, vulnerabilities—they are constantly bubbling up, seeking resolution. These mental forces energize people, but they are too crude and irregular to be given excessive play in the real world. They must be capped with the competent, sensible behavior that permits individuals to get along well in society. However, this upper layer of mental activity, shot through with caution and rationality, is not receptive to advertising's pitches. Advertisers want to circumvent this shell of consciousness if they can, and latch on to one of the lurching, subconscious drives.

In effect, advertisers over the years have blindly felt their way around the underside of the American psyche, and by trial and error have discovered the softest points of entree, the places where their messages have the greatest likelihood of getting by consumers' defenses. As McLuhan says elsewhere, "Gouging away at the surface of public sales resistance, the ad men are constantly breaking through into the *Alice in Wonderland* territory behind the looking glass, which is the world of subrational impulses and appetites."

An advertisement communicates by making use of a specially selected image (of a supine female, say, or a curly-haired child, or a celebrity) which is designed to stimulate "subrational impulses and desires" even when they are at ebb, even if they are unacknowledged by their possessor. Some few ads have their emotional appeal in the text, but for the greater number by far the appeal is contained in the artwork. This makes sense, since visual communication better suits more primal levels of the brain. If the viewer of an advertisement actually has the importuned motive, and if the appeal is sufficiently well fashioned to call it up, then the person can be hooked. The product in the ad may then appear to take on the semblance of gratification for the summoned motive. Many ads seem to be saying, "If you have this need, then this product will help satisfy it." It is a primitive equation, but not an ineffective one for selling.

Thus, most advertisements appearing in national media can be understood as having two orders of content. The first is the appeal to deep-running drives in the minds of consumers. The second is information regarding the good[s] or service being sold: its name, its manufacturer, its picture, its packaging, its objective attributes, its functions. For example, the reader of a brassiere advertisement sees a partially undraped but blandly unperturbed woman standing in an otherwise commonplace public setting, and may experience certain sensations; the reader also sees the name "Maidenform," a particular brassiere style, and, in tiny print, words about the material, colors, price. Or, the viewer of a television commercial sees a demonstration with four small boxes labeled 650, 650, 650, and 800; something in the viewer's mind catches hold of this, as trivial as thoughtful consideration might reveal it to be. The viewer is also exposed to the name "Anacin," its bottle, and its purpose.

Sometimes there is an apparently logical link between an ad's emotional appeal and its product information. It does not violate common sense that Cadillac automobiles be photographed at country clubs, or that Japan Air Lines be associated with [all things Asian] Orientalia. But there is no real need for the linkage to have a bit of reason behind it. Is there anything inherent to the connection between Salem cigarettes and mountains, Coke and a smile, Miller Beer and comradeship? The link being forged in minds between product and appeal is a pre-logical one.

10   People involved in the advertising industry do not necessarily talk in the terms being used here. They are stationed at the sending end of this communications channel, and may think they are up to any number of things—Unique Selling Propositions, explosive copywriting, the optimal use of demographics or psychographics, ideal media buys, high recall ratings, or whatever. But when attention shifts to the receiving end of the channel, and focuses on the instant of reception, then commentary becomes much more elemental: an advertising message contains something primary and primitive, an emotional appeal, that in effect is the thin end of the wedge, trying to find its way into a mind. Should this occur, the product information comes along behind.

When enough advertisements are examined in this light, it becomes clear that the emotional appeals fall into several distinguishable categories, and that every ad is a variation on one of a limited number of basic appeals. While there may be several ways of classifying these appeals, one particular list of fifteen has proven to be especially valuable.

Advertisements can appeal to:

1. The need for sex
2. The need for affiliation

3. The need to nurture

4. The need for guidance

5. The need to aggress

6. The need to achieve

7. The need to dominate

8. The need for prominence

9. The need for attention

10. The need for autonomy

11. The need to escape

12. The need to feel safe

13. The need for aesthetic sensations

14. The need to satisfy curiosity

15. Physiological needs: food, drink, sleep, etc.

Murray's List

Where does this list of advertising's fifteen basic appeals come from? Several years ago, I was involved in a research project which was to have as one segment an objective analysis of the changing appeals made in post–World War II American advertising. A sample of magazine ads would have their appeals coded into the categories of psychological needs they seemed aimed at. For this content analysis to happen, a complete roster of human motives would have to be found.

The first thing that came to mind was Abraham Maslow's famous four-part hierarchy of needs. But the briefest look at the range of appeals made in advertising was enough to reveal that they are more varied, and more profane, than Maslow had cared to account for. The search led on to the work of psychologist Henry A. Murray, who together with his colleagues at the Harvard Psychological Clinic has constructed a full taxonomy of needs. As described in *Explorations in Personality*, Murray's team had conducted a lengthy series of in-depth interviews with a number of subjects in order to derive from scratch what they felt to be the essential variables of personality. Forty-four variables were distinguished by the Harvard group, of which twenty were motives. The need for achievement ("to overcome obstacles and obtain a high standard") was one, for instance; the need to defer was another; the need to aggress was a third; and so forth.

Murray's list had served as the groundwork for a number of subsequent projects. Perhaps the best-known of these was David C. McClelland's extensive study of the need for achievement, reported in his *The Achieving Society*. In the process of demonstrating that a people's high need for achievement is predictive of later economic growth, McClelland coded achievement imagery and references out of a nation's folklore, songs, legends, and children's tales.

15   Following McClelland, I too wanted to cull the motivational appeals from a culture's imaginative product—in this case, advertising. To develop categories expressly for this purpose, I took Murray's twenty motives and added to them others he had mentioned in passing in *Explorations in Personality* but not included on the final list. The extended list was tried out on a sample of advertisements, and motives which never seemed to be invoked were dropped. I ended up with eighteen of Murrays' motives, into which 770 print ads were coded. The resulting distribution is included in the 1976 book *Mass Advertising as Social Forecast.*

Since that time, the list of appeals has undergone refinements as a result of using it to analyze television commercials. A few more adjustments stemmed from the efforts of students in my advertising classes to decode appeals; tens of term papers surveying thousands of advertisements have caused some inconsistencies in the list to be hammered out. Fundamentally, though, the list remains the creation of Henry Murray. In developing a comprehensive, parsimonious inventory of human motives, he pinpointed the subsurface mental forces that are the least quiescent and most susceptible to advertising's entreaties.

Fifteen Appeals

1. Need for Sex. Let's start with sex, because this is the appeal which seems to pop up first whenever the topic of advertising is raised. Whole books have been written about this one alone, to find a large audience of mildly titillated readers. Lately, due to campaigns to sell blue jeans, concern with sex in ads has redoubled.

The fascinating thing is not how much sex there is in advertising, but how little. Contrary to impressions, unambiguous sex is rare in these messages. Some of this surprising observation may be a matter of definition: the Jordache ads with the lithe, blouse-less female astride a similarly clad male is clearly an appeal to the audience's sexual drives, but the same cannot be said about Brooke Shields* in the Calvin Klein commercials. Directed at young women and their credit-card carrying mothers, the image of Miss Shields instead invokes the need to be looked at. Buy Calvins and you'll be the center of much attention, just as Brooke is, the ads imply; they do not primarily inveigle their target audience's need for sexual intercourse.

In the content analysis reported in *Mass Advertising as Social Forecast* only two percent of ads were found to pander to this motive. Even *Playboy*

---

*Brooke Shields (b. 1965) is a model (at age 3 she was the Ivory Snow baby), as well as a stage (*Grease*), TV, and film actress; her most well-known films are *Pretty Baby* (1978) and *Blue Lagoon* (1980).

ads shy away from sexual appeals: a recent issue contained eighty-three full-page ads, and just four of them (or less than five percent) could be said to have sex on their minds.

20   The reason this appeal is so little used is that it is too blaring and tends to obliterate the product information. Nudity in advertising has the effect of reducing brand recall. The people who do remember the product may do so because they have been made indignant by the ad; this is not the response most advertisers seek.

To the extent that sexual imagery is used, it conventionally works better on men than women; typically a female figure is offered up to the male reader. A Black Velvet liquor advertisement displays an attractive woman wearing a tight black outfit, recumbent under the legend, "Feel the Velvet." The figure does not have to be horizontal, however, for the appeal to be present as National Airlines revealed in its "Fly me" campaign. Indeed, there does not even have to be a female in the ad; "Flick my Bic"* was sufficient to convey the idea to many.

As a rule, though, advertisers have found sex to be a tricky appeal, to be used sparingly. Less controversial and equally fetching are the appeals to our need for affectionate human contact.

2. Need for Affiliation.   American mythology upholds autonomous individuals, and social statistics suggest that people are ever more going it alone in their lives, yet the high frequency of affiliative appeals in ads belies this. Or maybe it does not: maybe all the images of companionship are compensation for what Americans privately lack. In any case, the need to associate with others is widely invoked in advertising and is probably the most prevalent appeal. All sorts of goods and services are sold by linking them to our unfulfilled desires to be in good company.

According to Henry Murray, the need for affiliation consists of desires "to draw near and enjoyably cooperate or reciprocate with another; to please and win affection of another; to adhere and remain loyal to a friend." The manifestations of this motive can be segmented into several different types of affiliation, beginning with romance.

25   Courtship may be swifter nowadays, but the desire for pair-bonding is far from satiated. Ads reaching for this need commonly depict a youngish male and female engrossed in each other. The head of the male is usually higher than the female's, even at this late date; she may be sitting or leaning while he is standing. They are not touching in the Smirnoff vodka ads, but obviously there is an intimacy, sometimes frolicsome, between them. The couple does touch for Martell Cognac when "The moment was Martell." For Wind Song perfume they have touched, and "Your Wind Song stays on his mind."

---

*"Flick my Bic" became a famous and successful slogan in advertisements for Bic cigarette lighters during the late 1970s and 1980s. Fowles hints at the not-too-subtle sexual implications of the line.

Depending on the audience, the pair does not absolutely have to be young—just together. He gives her a DeBeers diamond, and there is a tear in her laugh lines. She takes Geritol* and preserves herself for him. And numbers of consumers, wanting affection too, follow suit.

Warm family feelings are fanned in ads when another generation is added to the pair. Hallmark Cards brings grandparents into the picture, and Johnson and Johnson Baby Powder has Dad, Mom, and baby, all fresh from the bath, encircled in arms and emblazoned with "Share the Feeling." A talc has been fused to familial love.

Friendship is yet another form of affiliation pursued by advertisers. Two women confide and drink Maxwell House coffee together; two men walk through the woods smoking Salem cigarettes. Miller Beer promises that afternoon "Miller Time" will be staffed with three or four good buddies. Drink Dr. Pepper, as Mickey Rooney is coaxed to do, and join in with all the other Peppers. Coca-Cola does not even need to portray the friendliness; it has reduced this appeal to "a Coke and a smile."

The warmth can be toned down and disguised, but it is the same affiliative need that is being fished for. The blonde has a direct gaze and her friends are firm businessmen in appearance, but with a glass of Old Bushmill you can sit down and fit right in. Or, for something more upbeat, sing along with the Pontiac choirboys.

30   As well as presenting positive images, advertisers can play to the need for affiliation in negative ways, by invoking the fear of rejection. If we don't use Scope, we'll have the "Ugh! Morning Breath" that causes the male and female models to avert their faces. Unless we apply Ultra Brite or Close-Up to our teeth, it's good-bye romance. Our family will be cursed with "House-a-tosis" if we don't take care. Without Dr. Scholl's antiperspirant foot spray, the bowling team will keel over. There go all the guests when the supply of Dorito's nacho cheese chips is exhausted. Still more rejection if our shirts have ring-around-the-collar, if our car needs to be Midasized. But make a few purchases, and we are back in the bosom of human contact.

As self-directed as Americans pretend to be, in the last analysis we remain social animals, hungering for the positive, endorsing feelings that only those around us can supply. Advertisers respond, urging us to "Reach out and touch someone," in the hopes our monthly [phone] bills will rise.

3. Need to Nurture.   Akin to affiliative needs is the need to take care of small, defenseless creatures—children and pets, largely. Reciprocity is of less consequence here, though; it is the giving that counts. Murray uses synonyms like "to feed, help, support, console, protect, comfort, nurse, heal." A strong

---

*The original Geritol (a combination of the words "geriatric" and "tolerance") was an iron tonic and vitamin supplement marketed to people over 40 between 1950 and 1979 with the slogan, "Do you have iron poor, tired blood?" Though today Geritol is the label on a group of health-related products, the name became famous—and, to some extent, funny—as a means of restoring energy and youthful vigor to middle-age and elderly people.

need it is, woven deep into our genetic fabric, for if it did not exist we could not successfully raise up our replacements. When advertisers put forth the image of something diminutive and furry, something that elicits the word "cute" or "precious," then they are trying to trigger this motive. We listen to the childish voice singing the Oscar Mayer wiener song, and our next hot-dog purchase is prescribed. Aren't those darling kittens something, and how did this Meow Mix get into our shopping cart?

This pitch is often directed at women, as Mother Nature's chief nurturers. "Make me some Kraft macaroni and cheese, please," says the elfin preschooler just in from the snowstorm, and mothers' hearts go out, and Kraft's sales go up. "We're cold, wet, and hungry," whine the husband and kids, and the little woman gets the Manwiches ready. A facsimile of this need can be hit without children or pets: the husband is ill and sleepless in the television commercial, and the wife grudgingly fetches the NyQuil.

But it is not women alone who can be touched by this appeal. The father nurses his son Eddie through adolescence while the John Deere lawn tractor survives the years. Another father counts pennies with his young son as the subject of New York Life Insurance comes up. And all over America are businessmen who don't know why they dial Qantas Airlines* when they have to take a trans-Pacific trip; the koala bear knows.

35   **4. Need for Guidance.**   The opposite of the need to nurture is the need to be nurtured: to be protected, shielded, guided. We may be loath to admit it, but the child lingers on inside every adult—and a good thing it does, or we would not be instructable in our advancing years. Who wants a nation of nothing but flinty personalities?

Parent-like figures can successfully call up this need. Robert Young[†] recommends Sanka coffee, and since we have experienced him for twenty-five years as television father and doctor, we take his word for it. Florence Henderson[‡] as the expert mom knows a lot about the advantages of Wesson oil.

The parent-ness of the spokesperson need not be so salient; sometimes pure authoritativeness is better. When Orson Welles[§] scowls and intones, "Paul Masson will sell no wine before its time," we may not

---

*Qantas Airlines is an Australian airline whose ads during the 1980s and 1990s featured a cuddly koala bear standing in for both the airline and the exotic delights of Australia.

[†]Robert Young (1907–1988) acted in movies (including Alfred Hitchcock's *Secret Agent* (1936) and *Crossfire* (1947) and TV (starring in the long-running 1950s series *Father Knows Best* and the 1960s series *Marcus Welby, M.D.*). A classic father figure, in his later career he appeared in ads for Sanka coffee.

[‡]Florence Henderson (b. 1934), acted on Broadway and TV (primarily in musical and comedy roles). Her most famous TV show was *The Brady Bunch* (1968–74), where she played a mother of three daughters who married a man with three sons.

[§]Orson Welles (1915–1985) was a major American filmmaker and actor whose films include *Citizen Kane* (1941—generally considered the greatest American film of all time), *The Magnificent Ambersons* (1942), *The Lady from Shanghai* (1947), *Macbeth* (1948), and *Touch of Evil* (1958). Toward the end of his life—to the dismay of many who revered him—the magisterial but financially depleted Welles became a spokesman for Paul Masson wines.

know exactly what he means, but we still take direction from him. There is little maternal about Brenda Vaccaro* when she speaks up for Tampax, but there is a certainty to her that many accept.

A celebrity is not a necessity in making a pitch to the need for guidance, since a fantasy figure can serve just as well. People accede to the Green Giant, or Betty Crocker, or Mr. Goodwrench.† Some advertisers can get by with no figure at all: "When E. F. Hutton‡ talks, people listen."

Often it is tradition or custom that advertisers point to and consumers take guidance from. Bits and pieces of American history are used to sell whiskeys like Old Crow, Southern Comfort, Jack Daniel's. We conform to traditional male/female roles and age-old social norms when we purchase Barclay cigarettes, which informs us "The pleasure is back."

40   The product itself, if it has been around for a long time, can constitute a tradition. All those old labels in the ad for Morton salt convince us that we should continue to buy it. Kool-Aid says "You loved it as a kid. You trust it as a mother," hoping to get yet more consumers to go along.

Even when the product has no history at all, our need to conform to tradition and to be guided are strong enough that they can be invoked through bogus nostalgia and older actors. Country-Time lemonade sells because consumers want to believe it has a past they can defer to.

So far the needs and the ways they can be invoked which have been looked at are largely warm and affiliative; they stand in contrast to the next set of needs, which are much more egoistic and assertive.

5. Need to Aggress.   The pressures of the real world create strong retaliatory feelings in every functioning human being. Since these impulses can come forth as bursts of anger and violence, their display is normally tabooed. Existing as harbored energy, aggressive drives present a large, tempting target for advertisers. It is not a target to be aimed at thoughtlessly, though, for few manufacturers want their products associated with destructive motives. There is always the danger that, as in the case of sex, if the appeal is too blatant, public opinion will turn against what is being sold.

Jack-in-the-Box sought to abruptly alter its marketing by going after older customers and forgetting the younger ones. Their television commercials had a seventy-ish lady command, "Waste him," and the Jack-in-the-Box clown exploded before our eyes. So did public reaction until the commercials

---

*Brenda Vaccaro (b. 1939) is a stage, TV, and film actress; her films include *Midnight Cowboy* (1969), *Airport '77* (1977), *Supergirl* (1984), and *The Mirror Has Two Faces* (1996).
†Mr. Goodwrench (and the slogan "Looking for Mr. Goodwrench"), personified as an engaging and highly capable auto mechanic, is a product of the General Motors marketing department.
‡E. F. Hutton (named after its founder, Edward Francis Hutton) was a major brokerage firm that was brought down in the 1980s by corporate misconduct. Its most famous TV ad portrayed, typically, two well-dressed businesspeople in conversation in a crowded dining room or club room. The first man says to the other, "My broker says..." The second man listens politely and responds, "Well, my broker is E. F. Hutton, and *he* says...," and everyone else in the room strains to overhear the conversation. The tag line: "When E. F. Hutton talks, people listen."

were toned down. Print ads for Club cocktails carried the faces of octogenarians under the headline, "Hit me with a Club"; response was contrary enough to bring the campaign to a stop.

45   Better disguised aggressive appeals are less likely to backfire: Triumph cigarettes has models making a lewd gesture with their uplifted cigarettes, but the individuals are often laughing and usually in close company of others. When Exxon said, "There's a Tiger in your tank," the implausibility of it concealed the invocation of aggressive feelings.

Depicted arguments are a common way for advertisers to tap the audience's needs to aggress. Don Rickles* and Lynda Carter[†] trade gibes, and consumers take sides as the name of Seven-Up is stitched on minds. The Parkay [margarine] tub has a difference of opinion with the user; who can forget it, or who (or what) got the last word in?

6. Need to Achieve.   This is the drive that energizes people, causing them to strive in their lives and careers. According to Murray, the need for achievement is signalled by the desires "to accomplish something difficult. To overcome obstacles and attain a high standard. To excel one's self. To rival and surpass others." A prominent American trait, it is one that advertisers like to hook on to because it identifies their product with winning and success.

The Cutty Sark ad does not disclose that Ted Turner failed at his latest attempt at yachting's America Cup; here he is represented as a champion on the water as well as off in his television enterprises. If we drink this whiskey, we will be victorious alongside Turner. We can also succeed with O. J. Simpson[‡] by renting Hertz cars, or with Reggie Jackson[§] by bringing home some Panasonic equipment. Cathy Rigby** and Stayfree maxipads will put people out front.

---

*Don Rickles (b. 1926) is a nightclub comedian (who has also appeared in TV and films) famous for his caustic wit and for humorously insulting people in the audience.

[†]Lynda Carter (b. 1951) is an actress whose most famous role was as the heroine of the 1976 TV series *Wonder Woman*.

[‡]O. J. Simpson (b. 1957) is a famous football player turned film actor (*The Naked Gun*) and defendant in a notorious murder trial in the 1990s. In a highly controversial decision, Simpson was acquitted of killing his ex-wife Nicole Simpson and her friend Ron Goldman; but in a subsequent civil trial, he was found liable for the two deaths. Before the trial, Simpson was well known for his TV commercials for Hertz rental cars, featuring him sprinting through airports to get to the gate, to demonstrate what you *wouldn't* have to do if you rented a car through Hertz.

[§]Reggie Jackson (b. 1946), a member of the Baseball Hall of Fame, played as an outfielder between 1967 and 1987. Known as "Mr. October" for his dramatic game-winning at-bats during post-season play, he had more strikeouts (2,597) than any other player. He was the first baseball player to have a candy bar (the "Reggie Bar") named after him, and toward the end of his career was a pitchman for Panasonic televisions.

**Cathy Rigby, an Olympian, was the first American gymnast to win a medal (in 1970) at the World Championships. She went on to star in a Broadway revival of the musical *Peter Pan* (surpassing Mary Martin for the greatest number of performances). Subsequently, she became a sportscaster for ABC Sports.

Sports heroes are the most convenient means to snare consumers' needs to achieve, but they are not the only one. Role models can be established, ones which invite emulation, as with the profiles put forth by Dewar's scotch. Successful, tweedy individuals relate they have "graduated to the flavor of Myer's rum." Or the advertiser can establish a prize: two neighbors play one-on-one basketball for a Michelob beer in a television commercial, while in a print ad a bottle of Johnnie Walker Black Label has been gilded like a trophy.

50   Any product that advertises itself in superlatives—the best, the first, the finest—is trying to make contact with our needs to succeed. For many consumers, sales and bargains belong in this category of appeals, too; the person who manages to buy something at fifty percent off is seizing an opportunity and coming out ahead of others.

7. Need to Dominate.   This fundamental need is the craving to be powerful—perhaps omnipotent, as in the Xerox ad where Brother Dominic exhibits heavenly powers and creates miraculous copies. Most of us will settle for being just a regular potentate, though. We drink Budweiser because it is the King of Beers, and here comes the powerful Clydesdales to prove it. A taste of Wolfschmidt vodka and "The spirit of the Czar lives on."

The need to dominate and control one's environment is often thought of as being masculine, but as close students of human nature, advertisers know it is not so circumscribed. Women's aspirations for control are suggested in the campaign theme, "I like my men in English Leather, or nothing at all." The females in the Chanel No. 19 ads are "outspoken" and wrestle their men around.

Male and female, what we long for is clout; what we get in its place is Mastercard.

8. Need for Prominence.   Here comes the need to be admired and respected, to enjoy prestige and high social status. These times, it appears, are not so egalitarian after all. Many ads picture the trappings of high position; the Oldsmobile stands before a manorial doorway, the Volvo is parked beside a steeplechase. A book-lined study is the setting for Dewar's 12, and Lenox China is displayed in a dining room chock full of antiques.

55   Beefeater gin represents itself as "The Crown Jewel of England" and uses no illustrations of jewels or things British, for the words are sufficient indicators of distinction. Buy that gin and you will rise up the prestige hierarchy, or achieve the same effect on yourself with Seagram's 7 Crown, which ambiguously describes itself as "classy."

Being respected does not have to entail the usual accoutrements of wealth: "Do you know who I am?" the commercials ask, and we learn that the prominent person is not so prominent without his American Express card.

9. Need for Attention.   The previous need involved being *looked up to*, while this is the need to be *looked at*. The desire to exhibit ourselves in such a way as to make others look at us is a primitive, insuppressible instinct. The clothing and cosmetic industries exist just to serve this need, and this is the way they pitch their wares. Some of this effort is aimed at males, as the ads for Hathaway shirts and Jockey underclothes. But the greater bulk of such appeals is targeted singlemindedly at women.

To come back to Brooke Shields: this is where she fits into American marketing. If I buy Calvin Klein jeans, consumers infer, I'll be the object of fascination. The desire for exhibition has been most strikingly played to in a print campaign of many years' duration, that of Maidenform lingerie. The woman exposes herself, and sales surge. "Gentlemen prefer Hanes" the ads dissemble, and women who want eyes upon them know what they should do. Peggy Fleming* flutters her legs for L'eggs, encouraging females who want to be the star in their own lives to purchase this product.

The same appeal works for cosmetics and lotions. For years, the little girl with the exposed backside sold gobs of Coppertone, but now the company has picked up the pace a little: as a female, you are supposed to "Flash 'em a Coppertone tan." Food can be sold the same way, especially to the diet-conscious; Angie Dickinson poses for California avocados and says, "Would this body lie to you?" Our eyes are too fixed on her for us to think to ask if she got that way by eating mounds of guacamole.†

60   **10. Need for Autonomy.**   There are several ways to sell credit card services, as has been noted: Mastercard appeals to the need to dominate, and American Express to the need for prominence. When Visa claims, "You can have it the way you want it," yet another primary motive is being beckoned forward—the need to endorse the self. The focus here is upon the independence and integrity of the individual; this need is the antithesis of the need for guidance and is unlike any of the social needs. "If running with the herd isn't your style, try ours," says Rotan-Mosle, and many Americans feel they have finally found the right brokerage firm.

The photo is of a red-coated Mountie on his horse, posed on a snow-covered ledge; the copy reads, "Windsor—One Canadian stands alone." This epitome of the solitary and proud individual may work best with male customers, as may Winston's man in the red cap. But one-figure advertisements also strike the strong need for autonomy among American women. As Shelly Hack‡ strides for Charlie perfume, females respond to her obvious pride and flair; she is her own person. The Virginia Slims tale is of people who have come a long way from subservience to independence. Cachet perfume feels it does not need a solo figure to work this appeal, and uses three different faces in its ads; it insists, though, "It's different on every woman who wears it."

Like many psychological needs, this one can also be appealed to in a negative fashion, by invoking the loss of independence or self-regard.

---

*Peggy Fleming (b. 1948), an Olympic figure skater and Gold Medal winner (1968), later became a TV sports commentator and a representative for UNICEF (the United Nations Children's Emergency Fund).
†Angie Dickinson (b. 1931) is an American film and TV actress. She appeared in *Rio Bravo* (1959), *Ocean's 11* (1960 and 2001), *Point Blank* (1967), and *Dressed to Kill* (1980); she also starred in the 1970s TV series *Police Woman*.
‡Shelly Hack (b. 1952) portrayed Tiffany Welles in the 1970s TV show *Charlie's Angels*.

Guilt and regrets can be stimulated: "Gee, I could have had a V-8." Next time, get one and be good to yourself.

11. Need to Escape.   An appeal to the need for autonomy often co-occurs with one for the need to escape, since the desire to duck out of our social obligations, to seek rest or adventure, frequently takes the form of one-person flight. The dashing image of a pilot, in fact, is a standard way of quickening this need to get away from it all.

Freedom is the pitch here, the freedom that every individual yearns for whenever life becomes too oppressive. Many advertisers like appealing to the need for escape because the sensation of pleasure often accompanies escape, and what nicer emotional nimbus could there be for a product? "You deserve a break today," says McDonald's, and Stouffer's frozen foods chime in, "Set yourself free."

65   For decades men have imaginatively bonded themselves to the Marlboro cowboy who dwells untarnished and unencumbered in Marlboro Country some distance from modern life; smokers' aching needs for auton-omy and escape are personified by that cowpoke. Many women can iden-tify with the lady ambling through the woods behind the words, "Benson and Hedges and mornings and me."

But escape does not have to be solitary. Other Benson and Hedges ads, part of the same campaign, contain two strolling figures. In Salem ciga-rette advertisements, it can be several people who escape together into the mountaintops. A commercial for Levi's pictured a cloudbank above a city through which ran a whole chain of young people.

There are varieties of escape, some wistful like the Boeing "Someday" campaign of dream vacations, some kinetic like the play and parties in soft drink ads. But in every instance, the consumer exposed to the advertise-ment is invited to momentarily depart his everyday life for a more carefree experience, preferably with the product in hand.

12. Need to Feel Safe.   Nobody in their right mind wants to be in-timidated, menaced, battered, poisoned. We naturally want to do what-ever it takes to stave off threats to our well-being, and to our families'. It is the instinct of self-preservation that makes us responsive to the ad of the St. Bernard with the keg of Chivas Regal. We pay attention to the stern talk of Karl Malden* and the plight of the vacationing couples who have lost all their funds in the American Express travelers cheques commercials. We want the omnipresent stag from Hartford Insurance to watch over us too.

In the interest of keeping failure and calamity from our lives, we like to see the durability of products demonstrated. Can we ever forget that Timex

---

*Karl Malden (1912–2009), with his familiar craggy face and outsized nose, was a stage and later a film actor. He was the original Mitch in the Broadway production of Tennessee Williams's *Streetcar Named Desire*, a role he reprised in the 1951 movie version. His films include *On the Waterfront* (1954), *Cheyenne Autumn* (1964), and *Patton* (1970), and he starred in the 1972 TV series *Streets of San Francisco*. Malden became famous to a later generation of viewers as a pitchman for the American Express card, with the slogan "Don't leave home without it!"

takes a licking and keeps on ticking? When the American Tourister suitcase bounces all over the highway and the egg inside doesn't break, the need to feel safe has been adroitly plucked.

70   We take precautions to diminish future threats. We buy Volkswagen Rabbits for the extraordinary mileage, and MONY insurance policies to avoid the tragedies depicted in their black-and-white ads of widows and orphans.

We are careful about our health. We consume Mazola margarine because it has "corn goodness" backed by the natural food traditions of the American Indians. In the medicine cabinet is Alka-Seltzer, the "home remedy"; having it, we are snug in our little cottage.

We want to be safe and secure; buy these products, advertisers are saying, and you'll be safer than you are without them.

13. Need for Aesthetic Sensations.   There is an undeniable aesthetic component to virtually every ad run in the national media: the photography or filming or drawing is near-perfect, the type style is well chosen, the layout could scarcely be improved upon. Advertisers know there is little chance of good communication occurring if an ad is not visually pleasing. Consumers may not be aware of the extent of their own sensitivity to artwork, but it is undeniably large.

Sometimes the aesthetic element is expanded and made into an ad's primary appeal. Charles Jordan shoes may or may not appear in the accompanying avant-grade photographs; Kohler plumbing fixtures catch attention through the high style of their desert settings. Beneath the slightly out of focus photograph, languid and sensuous in tone, General Electric feels called upon to explain, "This is an ad for the hair dryer."

75   This appeal is not limited to female consumers: J&B scotch says "It whispers" and shows a bucolic scene of lake and castle.

14. Need to Satisfy Curiosity.   It may seem odd to list a need for information among basic motives, but this need can be as primal and compelling as any of the others. Human beings are curious by nature, interested in the world around them, and intrigued by tidbits of knowledge and new developments. Trivia, percentages, observations counter to conventional wisdom—these items all help sell products. Any advertisement in a question-and-answer format is strumming this need.

A dog groomer has a question about long distance rates, and Bell Telephone has a chart with all the figures. An ad for Porsche 911 is replete with diagrams and schematics, numbers and arrows. Lo and behold, Anacin pills have 150 more milligrams than its competitors; should we wonder if this is better or worse for us?

15. Physiological Needs.   To the extent that sex is solely a biological need, we are now coming around full circle, back toward the start of the list. In this final category are clustered appeals to sleeping, eating, drinking. The art of photographing food and drink is so advanced, sometimes these temptations are wondrously caught in the camera's lens: the crab meat in the Red Lobster restaurant ads can start us salivating, the

Quarterpounder can almost be smelled, the liquor in the glass glows invitingly. Imbibe, these ads scream.

Styles

Some common ingredients of advertisements were not singled out for separate mention in the list of fifteen because they are not appeals in and of themselves. They are stylistic features, influencing the way a basic appeal is presented. The use of humor is one, and the use of celebrities is another. A third is time imagery, past and future, which goes to several purposes.

80   For all of its employment in advertising, humor can be treacherous, because it can get out of hand and smother the product information. Supposedly, this is what Alka-Seltzer discovered with its comic commercials of the late sixties; "I can't believe I ate the whole thing," the sad-faced husband lamented, and the audience cackled so much it forgot the antacid. Or, did not take it seriously.

But used carefully, humor can punctuate some of the softer appeals and soften some of the harsher ones. When Emma says to the Fruit-of-the-Loom fruits, "Hi, cuties. Whatcha doing in my laundry basket?" we smile as our curiosity is assuaged along with hers. Bill Cosby gets consumers tickled about the children in his Jell-O commercials, and strokes the need to nurture.

An insurance company wants to invoke the need to feel safe, but does not want to leave readers with an unpleasant aftertaste; cartoonist Rowland Wilson creates an avalanche about to crush a gentleman who is saying to another, "My insurance company? New England Life, of course. Why?" The same tactic of humor undercutting threat is used in the cartoon commercials for Safeco when the Pink Panther wanders from one disaster to another. Often humor masks aggression: comedian Bob Hope in the outfit of a boxer promises to knock out the knock-knocks with Texaco; Rodney Dangerfield, who "can't get no respect," invites aggression as the comic relief in Miller Lite commercials.

Roughly fifteen percent of all advertisements incorporate a celebrity, almost always from the fields of entertainment or sports. The approach can also prove troublesome for advertisers, for celebrities are human beings too, and fully capable of the most remarkable behavior. If anything distasteful about them emerges, it is likely to reflect on the product. The advertisers making use of Anita Bryant* and Billy Jean King† suffered

---

*Anita Bryant (b. 1940), a singer and entertainer (and as Miss Oklahoma, runner-up in the 1958 Miss America competition) became controversial during the late 1970s with her campaigns against homosexuality and AIDS. At the time, she was making ads and TV commercials for Florida orange juice, but was dropped by the sponsor after boycotts by activists.

†Billy Jean King (b. 1943) was a championship tennis player in the late 1960s and 1970s. In 1973, she was named *Sports Illustrated*'s "Sportsperson of the Year," the first woman to win this honor. She won four U.S. championships and six Wimbledon's single championships. In 1973, in a much publicized "Battle of the Sexes" match, King won all three sets against the 55-year-old Bobby Riggs (once ranked as the best tennis player in the world), who had claimed that "any half-decent male player could defeat even the best female players."

several anxious moments. An untimely death can also react poorly on a product. But advertisers are willing to take risks because celebrities can be such a good link between producers and consumers, performing the social role of introducer.

There are several psychological needs these middlemen can play upon. Let's take the product class of cameras and see how different celebrities can hit different needs. The need for guidance can be invoked by Michael Landon, who plays such a wonderful dad on "Little House on the Prairie"; when he says to buy Kodak equipment, many people listen. James Garner* for Polaroid cameras is put in a similar authoritative role, so defined by a mocking spouse. The need to achieve is summoned up by Tracy Austin and other tennis stars for Canon AE-1; the advertiser first makes sure we see these athletes playing to win. When Cheryl Tiegs[†] speaks up for Olympus cameras, it is the need for attention that is being targeted.

85   The past and future, being outside our grasp, are exploited by advertisers as locales for the projection of needs. History can offer up heroes (and call up the need to achieve) or traditions (need for guidance) as well as art objects (need for aesthetic sensations). Nostalgia is a kindly version of personal history and is deployed by advertisers to rouse needs for affiliation and for guidance; the need to escape can come in here, too. The same need to escape is sometimes the point of futuristic appeals but picturing the avant-garde can also be a way to get at the need to achieve.

Analyzing Advertisements

When analyzing ads yourself for their emotional appeals, it takes a bit of practice to learn to ignore the product information (as well as one's own experience and feelings about the product). But that skill comes soon enough, as does the ability to quickly sort out from all the non-product aspects of an ad the chief element which is the most striking, the most likely to snag attention first and penetrate brains farthest. The key to the appeal, this element usually presents itself centrally and forwardly to the reader or viewer.

Another clue: the viewing angle which the audience has on the ad's subjects is informative. If the subjects are photographed or filmed from below and thus are looking down at you much as the Green Giant does, then the need to be guided is a good candidate for the ad's emotional

---

*James Garner (b. 1928) is an American actor in movies and TV shows. His most famous TV roles were as the title character in the 1950s western-comedy series *Maverick* and as the hero of the 1970s detective series *The Rockford Files*. Garner also appeared in the movies *Sayonara* (1957), *The Great Escape* (1963), and *The Americanization of Emily* (1964).

[†]Cheryl Tiegs (b. 1947) is a supermodel perhaps best known for her affiliation with the *Sports Illustrated Swimsuit Edition*. A 1978 poster of Tiegs in a pink swimsuit became a cultural icon. Recently, she has entered the business world with an accessory and wig line for Revlon.

appeal. If, on the other hand, the subjects are shot from above and appear deferential, as is often the case with children or female models, then other needs are being appealed to.

To figure out an ad's emotional appeal, it is wise to know (or have a good hunch about) who the targeted consumers are; this can often be inferred from the magazine or television show it appears in. This piece of information is a great help in determining the appeal and in deciding between two different interpretations. For example, if an ad features a partially undressed female, this would typically signal one appeal for readers of *Penthouse* (need for sex) and another for readers of *Cosmopolitan* (need for attention).

It would be convenient if every ad made just one appeal, were aimed at just one need. Unfortunately, things are often not that simple. A cigarette ad with a couple at the edge of a polo field is trying to hit both the need for affiliation and the need for prominence; depending on the attitude of the male, dominance could also be an ingredient in this. An ad for Chimere perfume incorporates two photos: in the top one the lady is being commanding at a business luncheon (need to dominate), but in the lower one she is being bussed (need for affiliation). Better ads, however, seem to avoid being too diffused; in the study of post–World War II advertising described earlier, appeals grew more focused as the decades passed. As a rule of thumb [only twenty percent of ads have one primary appeal], about sixty percent have two conspicuous appeals; the last twenty percent have three or more. Rather than looking for the greatest number of appeals, decoding ads is most productive when the loudest one or two appeals are discerned, since those are the appeals with the best chance of grabbing people's attention.

90   Finally, analyzing ads does not have to be a solo activity and probably should not be. The greater number of people there are involved, the better chance there is of transcending individual biases and discerning the essential emotional lure built into an advertisement.

Do They or Don't They?

Do the emotional appeals made in advertisements add up to the sinister manipulation of consumers?

It is clear that these ads work. Attention is caught, communication occurs between producers and consumers, and sales result. It turns out to be difficult to detail the exact relationship between a specific ad and a specific purchase, or even between a campaign and subsequent sales figures, because advertising is only one of a host of influences upon consumption. Yet no one is fooled by this lack of perfect proof; everyone knows that advertising sells. If this were not the case, then tight-fisted American businesses would not spend a total of fifty billion dollars annually on these messages.

But before anyone despairs that advertisers have our number to the extent that they can marshal us at will and march us like automatons to the check-out counters, we should recall the resiliency and obduracy of the American consumer. Advertisers may have uncovered the softest spots in minds, but that does not mean they have found truly gaping apertures. There is no evidence that advertising can get people to do things contrary to their self-interests. Despite all the finesse of advertisements, and all the subtle emotional tugs, the public resists the vast majority of the petitions. According to the marketing division of the A. C. Nielsen Company, a whopping seventy-five percent of all new products die within a year in the marketplace, the victims of consumer disinterest which no amount of advertising could overcome. The appeals in advertising may be the most captivating there are to be had, but they are not enough to entrap the wily consumer.

The key to understanding the discrepancy between, on the one hand, the fact that advertising truly works, and, on the other, the fact that it hardly works, is to take into account the enormous numbers of people exposed to an ad. Modern-day communications permit an ad to be displayed to millions upon millions of individuals; if the smallest fraction of that audience can be moved to buy the product, then the ad has been successful. When one percent of the people exposed to a television advertising campaign reach for their wallets, that could be one million sales, which may be enough to keep the product in production and the advertisements coming.

95   In arriving at an evenhanded judgment about advertisements and their emotional appeals, it is good to keep in mind that many of the purchases which might be credited to these ads are experienced as genuinely gratifying to the consumer. We sincerely like the goods or service we have bought, and we may even like some of the emotional drapery that an ad suggests comes with it. It has sometimes been noted that the most avid students of advertisements are the people who have just bought the product; they want to steep themselves in the associated imagery. This may be the reason that Americans, when polled, are not negative about advertising and do not disclose any sense of being misused. The volume of advertising may be an irritant, but the product information as well as the imaginative material in ads are partial compensation.

A productive understanding is that advertising messages involve costs and benefits at both ends of the communications channel. For those few ads which do make contact, the consumer surrenders a moment of time, has the lower brain curried, and receives notice of a product; the advertiser has given up money and has increased the chance of sales. In this sort of communications activity, neither party can be said to be the loser.

Review Questions

1. Why is advertising more common in highly industrialized countries such as the United States than in countries with "quieter" economies?

2. How are advertisers' attempts to communicate their messages, and to break through customer resistance, keyed to their conception of human psychology, according to Fowles?

3. What are the "two orders of content" of most advertisements, according to Fowles?

4. How is Fowles indebted to Henry Murray?

5. Why must appeals to our need for sex and our need to aggress be handled carefully, according to Fowles?

6. How does the use of humor or the use of celebrities fit into Fowles's scheme?

Discussion and Writing Suggestions

1. In ¶ 4, Fowles cites a study indicating that only a fraction of the advertisements bombarding consumers every day are even noticed, much less acted upon. How do the results of this study square with your own experience? About how many of the commercial messages that you view and hear every day do you actually pay attention to? What kinds of messages draw your attention? What elicits positive reactions? Negative reactions? What kinds of appeals are most successful in making you want to actually purchase the advertised product?

2. What do you think of Fowles's analysis of "advertising's fifteen basic appeals"? Does this classification seem an accurate and useful way of accounting for how most advertising works upon us? Would you drop any of his categories, or perhaps incorporate one set into another set? Has Fowles neglected to consider other appeals that you believe to be equally important? If so, can you think of one or more advertisements that employ such appeals omitted by Fowles?

3. Categorize several of the print ads in the ad portfolio later in the chapter (pp. 362–377), using Fowles's schema. Explain how the headlines, body text, and graphics support your categorization choices.

4. Fowles asserts that "[c]ontrary to impressions, unambiguous sex is rare in [advertising] messages." This article first appeared in 1982. Does Fowles's statement still seem true today? To what extent do you believe

that advertisers in recent years have increased their reliance on overt sexual appeals? Cite examples.

5. Fowles believes that "the need to associate with others [affiliation]...is probably the most prevalent appeal" in advertising. To what extent do you agree with this statement? Locate or cite print or broadcast ads that rely on the need for affiliation. How do the graphics and text of these ads work on what Fowles calls "the deep running drives" of our psyches or "the lower brain"?

6. Locate ads that rely upon the converse appeals to nurture and to guidance. Explain how the graphics and text in these ads work upon our human motivations. If possible, further categorize the appeal: For example, are we provided with guidance from a parent figure, some other authority figure, or from the force of tradition?

7. Conduct (perhaps with one or more classmates) your own analysis of a set of contemporary advertisements. Select a single issue of a particular magazine, such as *Time* or the *New Yorker*. Review all of the full-page ads, classifying each according to Fowles's categories. An ad may make more than one appeal (as Fowles points out in ¶ 89), but generally one will be primary. What do your findings show? Which appeals are the most frequent? The least frequent? Which are most effective? Why? You may find it interesting to compare the appeals of advertising in different magazines aimed at different audiences—for example, a general-interest magazine, such as *Newsweek*, compared with a more specialized magazine, such as the *New Republic*, or *People*, or *Glamour*, or *Guns and Ammo*. To what extent do the types of appeals shift with the gender or interests of the target audience?

MAKING THE PITCH IN PRINT ADVERTISING

*Courtland L. Bovée, John V. Thill,
George P. Dovel, and Marian Burk Wood*

No two ads are identical, but the vast majority employ a common set of textual features: headlines, body copy, and slogans. In the following selection, the authors discuss each of these features in turn, explaining their importance in attracting the potential customer's attention and selling the virtues of the product or service offered. You will find this discussion useful in making your own analyses of advertisements.

Courtland L. Bovée is the C. Allen Paul Distinguished Chair at Grossmont College. John V. Thill is CEO of Communication Specialists of America. George P. Dovel is president of the Dovel Group. Marian Burk Wood is president of Wood and Wood Advertising. This passage originally appeared in the authors' textbook *Advertising Excellence* (McGraw-Hill, 1995).

Copywriters and Copywriting

Given the importance of copy, it comes as no surprise that copywriters are key players in the advertising process. In fact, many of the most notable leaders and voices in the industry began their careers as copywriters, including Jane Maas, David Ogilvy, Rosser Reeves, Leo Burnett, and William Bernbach. As a profession, copywriting is somewhat unusual because so many of its top practitioners have been in their jobs for years, even decades (rather than moving up the management ranks as is usual in many professions). Copywriters can either work for agencies or set themselves up as free-lancers, selling their services to agencies and advertisers. Because it presents endless opportunities to be creative, copywriting is one of those rare jobs that can be fresh and challenging year after year.

Although successful copywriters share a love of language with novelists, poets, and other writers, copywriting is first and foremost a business function, not an artistic endeavor. The challenge isn't to create works of literary merit, but to meet advertising objectives. This doesn't mean that copywriting isn't an art, however; it's simply art in pursuit of a business goal. Nor is it easy. Such noted literary writers as Stephen Vincent Benét, George Bernard Shaw, and Ernest Hemingway tried to write ad copy and found themselves unable to do it effectively. It's the combined requirements of language skills, business acumen, and an ability to create under the pressure of tight deadlines and format restrictions (such as the limited number of words you have to work with) that make copywriting so challenging—and so endlessly rewarding.

Copywriters have many styles and approaches to writing, but most agree on one thing: copywriting is hard work. It can involve a great deal of planning and coordinating with clients, legal staffers, account executives, researchers, and art directors. In addition, it usually entails hammering away at your copy until it's as good as it can be. David Ogilvy talked about doing 19 drafts of a single piece of copy and writing 37 headlines for a Sears ad in order to get 3 possibilities to show to the client. Actually, the chance to write and rewrite that many times is a luxury that most copywriters don't have; they often must produce copy on tight schedules with unforgiving deadlines (such as magazine publication deadlines).

The task of copywriting is most often associated with the headlines and copy you see in an ad, but copywriters actually develop a wide variety of other materials, from posters to catalogs to press releases, as well as the words you hear in radio and television commercials.

Print Copy

5 Copywriters are responsible for every word you see in print ads, whether the words are in a catchy headline or in the fine print at the bottom of the page. The three major categories of copy are headlines, body copy, and slogans.

Headlines

The *headline*, also called a *heading* or a *head*, constitutes the dominant line or lines of copy in an ad. Headlines are typically set in larger type and appear at the top of the ad, although there are no hard-and-fast rules on headline layout. *Subheads* are secondary headlines, often written to move the reader from the main headline to the body copy. Even if there is a pageful of body copy and only a few words in the headline, the headline is the most important piece of copy for two reasons: First, it serves as the "come-on" to get people to stop turning the page and check out your ad. Second, as much as 80 percent of your audience may not bother to read the body copy, so whatever message these nonreaders carry away from the ad will have to come from the headline.

Copywriters can choose from a variety of headline types, each of which performs a particular function.

- *News headlines.* News headlines present information that's new to the audience, such as announcing a new store location, a new product, or lower prices. This approach is common because potential customers are often looking for new solutions, lower prices, and other relevant changes in the marketplace. For example, a newspaper ad from the Silo home electronics chain announced a recent sale using a news headline: "Everything on Sale! 4 Days Only! 5–20% Off Everything!" Headlines like this are typical in local newspaper advertising.

- *Emotional headlines.* The emotional appeal...is represented by emotional headlines. The quotation headline "I'm sick of her ruining our lives" was used in an ad for the American Mental Health Fund to echo the frustration some parents feel when they can't understand their teenagers' behavior. Combined with a photo of a sad and withdrawn teenage girl, the headline grabs any parent who has felt such frustration, and the body copy goes on to explain that families shouldn't get mad at people with mental illnesses but should help them get treatment for their conditions.

- *Benefit headlines.* The benefit headline is a statement of the key customer benefit. An ad for Quicken personal finance software used the question-form headline: "How do you know exactly where your money goes and how much you have?" followed by "It's this simple" above a photograph of the product package. The customer benefit is keeping better track of your money, and Quicken is the solution offered.

- *Directive headlines.* Headlines that direct the reader to do something, or at least suggest the reader do something, can motivate consumer action. Such headlines can be a hard sell, such as "Come in now and save," or they can be something more subtle, such as "Just feel the color in these black and whites," the headline in an ad for Ensoniq keyboards.

- *Offbeat and curiosity headlines.* Humor, wordplay, and mystery can be effective ways to draw readers into an ad. An ad promoting vacation travel to Spain used the headline "Si in the dark," with a photo of a lively nighttime scene. The word *Si* is catchy because it first looks like an error, until the reader reads the body copy to learn that the ad is talking about Spain (*si* is Spanish for "yes").

- *Hornblowing headlines.* The hornblowing headline, called "Brag and Boast" heads by the Gallup & Robinson research organization, should be used with care. Customers have seen it all and heard it all, and "We're the greatest" headlines tend to sound arrogant and self-centered. This isn't to say that you can't stress superiority; you just need to do it in a way that takes the customer's needs into account, and the headline must be honest. The headline "Neuberger & Berman Guardian Fund" followed by the subhead "#1 Performing Growth and Income Fund" blows the company's own horn but also conveys an important product benefit. Since investors look for top-performing mutual funds, the information about being number one is relevant.

- *Slogan, label, or logo headlines.* Some headlines show a company's slogan, a product label, or the organization's logo. Powerful slogans like Hallmark's "When you care enough to send the very best" can make great headlines because they click with the reader's emotions. Label and logo headlines can build product and company awareness, but they must be used with care. If the label or logo doesn't make some emotional or logical connection with the reader, the ad probably won't succeed.

Headlines often have maximum impact when coupled with a well-chosen graphic element, rather than trying to carry the message with words alone. In fact, the careful combination of the two can increase the audience's involvement with the ad, especially if one of the two says something ironic or unexpected that has to be resolved by considering the other element. A magazine ad for Easter Seals had the headline "After all we did for Pete, he walked out on us." At first, you think the birth-defects organization is complaining. Then you see a photo of Pete with new artificial legs, walking away from a medical facility. It's a powerful combination that makes the reader feel good about the things Easter Seals can do for people.

Body Copy

The second major category of copy is the *body copy*, which constitutes the words in the main body of the ad, apart from headlines, photo captions, and other blocks of text. The importance of body copy varies from ad to ad, and some ads have little or no body copy. Ads for easy-to-understand products, for instance, often rely on the headline and a visual such as a photograph to get their point across. In contrast, when the selling message needs a lot of supporting detail to be convincing, an ad can be packed full of body copy. Some advertisers have the impression that long body copy should be avoided, but that isn't always the case. The rule to apply here is to use the "right" number of words. You might not need many words in a perfume ad, but you might need a page or two to cover a complex industrial product.

CHECKLIST FOR PRODUCING EXCELLENT COPY

❑ A. Avoid clichés.
  • Create fresh, original phrases that vividly convey your message.
  • Remember that clever wordplay based on clichés can be quite effective.

❑ B. Watch out for borrowed interest.
  • Make sure you don't use inappropriate copy or graphics since they can steal the show from your basic sales message.
  • Be sure nothing draws attention from the message.

❑ C. Don't boast.
  • Be sure the ad's purpose isn't merely to pat the advertiser on the back.
  • Tout success when you must convince nonbuyers that lots of people just like them have purchased your product; this isn't the same as shouting "We're the best!"

❑ D. Make it personal, informal, and relevant.
  • Connect with the audience in a way that is personal and comfortable. Pompous, stiff, and overly "businesslike" tends to turn people away.
  • Avoid copy that sounds like it belongs in an ad, with too many overblown adjectives and unsupported claims of superiority.

❑ E. Keep it simple, specific, and concise.
  • Make your case quickly and stick to the point. This will help you get past all the barriers and filters that people put up to help them select which things they'll pay attention to and which they'll ignore.
  • Avoid copy that's confusing, meandering, too long, or too detailed.

❑ F. Give the audience a reason to read, listen, or watch.
  • Offer a solution to your audience's problems.
  • Entertain your audience.
  • Consider any means possible to get your audience to pay attention long enough to get your sales message across.

10   As with headlines, body copy can be built around several different formats. *Straight-line copy* is copy that takes off from the headline and develops
the selling points for the product. *Narrative copy*, in contrast, tells a story as it
persuades; the same selling points may be covered, but in a different context.
Dialog/monolog copy lets one or two characters in the ad do the selling through
what they are saying. *Picture-and-caption copy* relies on photographs or illustrations to tell the story, with support from their accompanying captions.

Slogans

The third major category of copy includes *slogans*, or *tag lines*, memorable sayings
that convey a selling message. Over the years, Coca-Cola has used such slogans
as "Coke is it," "It's the real thing," and "Always Coca-Cola." Slogans are
sometimes used as headlines, but not always. Their importance lies in the fact
they often become the most memorable result of an advertising campaign.
You've probably got a few slogans stuck in your head. Ever heard of "Quality
is job number 1," "Don't leave home without it," or "Melts in your mouth,
not in your hand"?

The Korean automaker Hyundai recently switched back to the slogan
"Cars that make sense," which is a great way of expressing its desired po-
sitioning as a lower-cost but still reliable alternative to Japanese and U.S.
cars. For several years, the company had used "Hyundai. Yes, Hyundai,"
but "Cars that make sense" has proved to be a much more effective way to
define the value it offers consumers.

 Review Questions

1. What are the particular challenges of copywriting, as opposed to other
   types of writing?

2. How do the authors classify the main types of ad headlines?

3. What are the main types of body copy styles, according to the authors?

Discussion and Writing Suggestions

1. Apply the authors' criteria for effective headlines to three or four of the
   print ads in the portfolio (pp. 362–377)—or to three or four ads of your
   own choosing. To what extent do these headlines succeed in attracting
   attention, engaging the audience, and fulfilling the other requirements of
   effective headlines?

2. Imagine that you are a copywriter who has been assigned the account
   for a particular product (your choice). Develop three possible headlines

for an advertisement for this product. Incorporate as many as possible of the criteria for effective headlines discussed by the authors (¶s 6–8).

3. Classify the *types* of headlines in a given product category in the print ad portfolio (pp. 362–377). Or classify the types of headlines in full-page ads in a single current magazine. Which type of headline appears to be the most common? Which type appears to be the most effective in gaining your attention and making you want to read the body copy?

4. Classify the *types* of body copy styles in a given product category in the ad portfolio. Or classify the types of body copy styles in full-page ads in a single current magazine. How effective is the copy in selling the virtues of the product or the institution or organization behind the product?

5. Assess the effectiveness of a given ad either in the ad portfolio or in a recent magazine or newspaper. Apply the criteria discussed by the authors in the box labeled "Checklist for Producing Excellent Copy." For example, to what extent is the copy fresh and original? To what extent does the copy make the message "personal, informal, and relevant" to the target audience? To what extent is the message "simple, specific, and concise"?

6. Write your own ad for a product that you like and use frequently. In composing the ad, apply the principles of effective headlines, subheads, body copy, and slogans discussed by the authors. Apply also the principles of "Checklist for Producing Excellent Copy." You will also need to think of (though not necessarily create) an effective graphic for the ad.

SELLING HAPPINESS: TWO PITCHES FROM MAD MEN

One of the surprise TV hits of 2007 was *Mad Men*, an original series about the advertising business, created by writer/producer Matt Weiner for the American Movie Classics (AMC) network. *Mad Men*—short for Madison Avenue men—follows Don Draper, creative director of Sterling Cooper, a medium-size New York ad agency, along with his colleagues and his family (and his mistresses), as he maneuvers his way through the ruthlessly competitive world of advertising during the early 1960s. The show won Golden Globe Awards for best TV dramatic series for two consecutive seasons. With high-quality writing (creator Matt Weiner was also a writer and producer for *The Sopranos*), top-flight acting, and spot-on production design and period costumes, *Mad Men* became instant classic, must-see television.

Two segments from the first season depict a time-honored business ritual, the "pitch," in which one or more creative/business people attempt to sell their idea to a client in hopes of securing a lucrative contract. (In Hollywood, writers or directors pitch their ideas for films to the studio or to potential financial backers.) As the "Carousel" segment begins, Don Draper (portrayed by Jon Hamm) and his colleagues (accounts director Herman ["Duck"] Phillips [Mark Moses], copywriter Harry Crane [in glasses; Rich Sommer], and art director Salvatore Romano [Bryan Batt]) make a pitch to a couple of clients from Eastman Kodak. The Kodak engineers have just come up with a turning "wheel" to house the slides for its new projector, and the Kodak business execs are making the rounds of New York ad agencies to hear them pitch campaigns to sell this new product. In "It's Toasted," Draper attempts to explain to the clients that despite the federal government's recent lawsuits against cigarette manufacturers for making false health claims about their products, and despite the fact that "[w]e have six identical companies making six identical products," the company can still reassure customers about the safety of its particular brand of cigarettes.

Go to: YouTube.com

Search terms: "mad men carousel"
                   "mad men it's toasted"

Select the longer versions of each of the two scenes.

 ## Discussion and Writing Suggestions

1. What do these scenes say about the way that advertising people sell consumer products to the public? What other examples come to mind of items of hardware sold in a manner similar to how Draper and his creative team propose to sell the "Carousel"?

2. Study Don's reaction as he shows the slides of his family. What do you think is passing through his mind during the presentation? Does he appear to believe what he is saying? Does the writer of this scene suggest that advertising is nothing but fakery? Explain.

3. Relate the "Carousel" scene to Jib Fowles' "Fifteen Basic Appeals" of advertising. Which appeals are most at work during the presentation of the "Carousel"? Once you have analyzed "Carousel" with respect to one or more motivations reviewed by Fowles, comment on the emotional pull of the "Carousel" pitch as Draper develops it. Even though you understand how Draper's appeal may work psychologically (according to Fowles), can you still be emotionally vulnerable to the pitch? Did you find Draper's presentation moving? Discuss.

4. At one point during the Lucky Strike "It's Toasted" pitch (immediately before the first line in the clip), Don notes: "We have six identical companies making six identical products." How does his solution for making this particular client's "identical" product "distinctive" (in this case, making it "safe") bring to mind other successful advertising campaigns that have created distinctiveness through words alone?

5. The sales pitch depicted in these meetings were set in an era some fifty years ago. To what extent do you think advertising for high-tech products has become more or less sophisticated than advertising was during the early 1960s? (You may wish to refer not only to this scene, but also to print ads of the same period, as exemplified in the "Portfolio.") To what extent—if at all—

might today's consumers be less apt to be captivated and sold by the kind of appeals dramatized in this scene? Cite particular examples of contemporary advertising, both print and TV.

A PORTFOLIO OF PRINT ADVERTISEMENTS

The following portfolio offers for your consideration and analysis a selection of sixteen full-page advertisements that appeared in American and British magazines between 1945 (shortly after the end of World War II) and 2003. In terms of products represented, the ads fall into several categories—cigarettes, alcohol (beer and liquor), automobiles, household cleaners, lotions, and perfumes. The portfolio also includes a few miscellaneous ads for such diverse products as men's hats, telephones, and airlines. These ads originally appeared in such magazines as *Time, Newsweek, U.S. News and World Report, Sports Illustrated, Ladies Home Journal, Ebony,* and *Ms.* A number of the ads were researched in the Advertising Archive, an online (and subscription) collection maintained by The Picture Desk.

The advertisements in this portfolio are *not* representative of all ads that appeared during the past sixty years. We made our selection largely on the basis of how interesting, striking, provocative, and unusual these particular ads appeared to us. Admittedly, the selection process was biased. That said, the ads in this portfolio offer rich possibilities for analysis. With practice, and by applying principles for analysis that you will find in the earlier selections in this chapter, you will be able to "read" into these ads numerous messages about cultural attitudes toward gender relations, romance, smoking, and automobiles. The ads will prompt you to consider why we buy products that we may not need or why we prefer one product over another when the two products are essentially identical. Each advertisement is a window into the culture. Through careful analysis, you will gain insights not only into the era in which the ads were produced, but also into shifting cultural attitudes over the past sixty years.

Following the portfolio, we provide two or three specific questions for each ad (pp. 378–382), questions designed to stimulate your thinking about the particular ways in which the graphics and text are intended to work. As you review the ads, however, you may want to think about the more general questions about advertisements raised by the readings in this chapter:

1. What appears to be the target audience for the ad? If this ad was produced more than two decades ago, does its same target audience exist today? If so, how would this audience likely react today to the ad?
2. What is the primary appeal made by the ad, in terms of Fowles's categories? What, if any, are the secondary appeals?
3. What assumptions do the ad's sponsors make about such matters as (1) commonly accepted roles of women and men; (2) the relationship between the sexes; (3) the priorities of men and women?
4. What is the chief attention-getting device in the ad?
5. How does the headline and body text communicate the ad's essential appeals?

6. How do the ad's graphics communicate the ad's essential appeals?

7. How do the expressions, clothing, and postures of the models, as well as the physical objects in the illustration, help communicate the ad's message?

8. How do the graphic qualities of balance, proportion, movement, unity, clarity and simplicity, and emphasis help communicate the ad's message?

Consider, also, the following evaluative questions[1]:

- Is it a good ad? Why?
- What do you like most about it? Why?
- What do you dislike the most? Why?
- Do you think it "works"? Why or why not?
- How could the ad be improved?
- Could the sender have conveyed the same message using other strategies, other persuasive means? If so, explain.
- Even if you don't believe that this particular ad works or persuades you, is there anything in the ad that still affects you or persuades you indirectly?
- Does the ad have effects on you perhaps not intended by its creators?

---

[1]Lars Thoger Christensen, "How to Analyze an Advertisement." University of Southern Denmark—Odense. Jan. 2004. http://wms-soros.mngt.waikato.ac.nz/NR/rdonlyres/ebabz4jhzmg5fr5p45ypc-53mdvuxva5wxhe7323onb4ylelbaq3se5xjrslfc4mi3qgk6dmsx5dqbp/Advertisinganalysis.doc

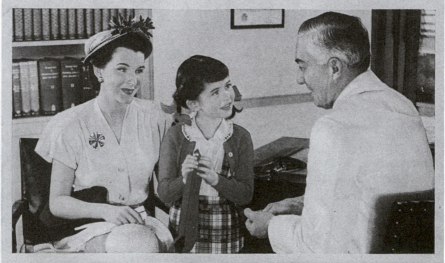

"I'm going to grow a hundred years old!"

...and possibly she may—for the amazing strides of medical science have added years to life expectancy

● It's a fact—a warm and wonderful fact—that this five-year-old child, or your own child, has a life expectancy almost a whole decade longer than was her mother's, and a good 18 to 20 years longer than that of her grandmother. Not only the expectation

of a longer life, but of a life by far healthier. Thank medical science for that. Thank your doctor and thousands like him...toiling ceaselessly, often with little or no public recognition...that you and yours may enjoy a longer, better life.

According to a recent Nationwide survey:

More Doctors smoke Camels
than any other cigarette!

NOT ONE but three outstanding independent research organizations conducted this survey. And they asked not just a few thousand, but 113,597, doctors from coast to coast to name the cigarette they themselves preferred to smoke.

The answers came in by the thousands...from general physicians, diagnosticians, surgeons—yes, and nose and throat specialists too. The most-named brand was Camel.

If you are not now smoking Camels, try them. Compare them critically. See how the full, rich flavor of Camel's costlier tobaccos suits your taste. See how the cool mildness of a Camel suits your throat. Let your "T-Zone" tell you *(see right)*.

THE "T-ZONE" TEST WILL TELL YOU

The "T-Zone"—T for taste and T for throat—is your own proving ground for any cigarette. Only your taste and throat can decide which cigarette tastes best to you... how it affects your throat. On the basis of the experience of many, many millions of smokers, we believe Camels will suit your "T-Zone" to a "T."

R. J. Reynolds Tobacco Co.
Winston-Salem, N. C.

CAMEL
TURKISH & DOMESTIC BLEND CIGARETTES
CHOICE QUALITY

CAMELS *Costlier Tobaccos*

Camels, 1940s

Marlboro, 1970s

19 mg. "tar", 1.3 mg. nicotine av. per cigarette, FTC Report MAY '78.
Satisfaction, Camel Filters style.
Some men taste it all: Rich warm flavor. Smooth even taste. Solid satisfaction.
Only from the Camel Filters blend of Turkish and domestic tobaccos.
Warning: The Surgeon General Has Determined That Cigarette Smoking Is Dangerous to Your Health.
CAMEL
FILTERS
Famous Camel Quality!

Camels, 1979

Cancer Patients Aid Association (Mumbai, India)

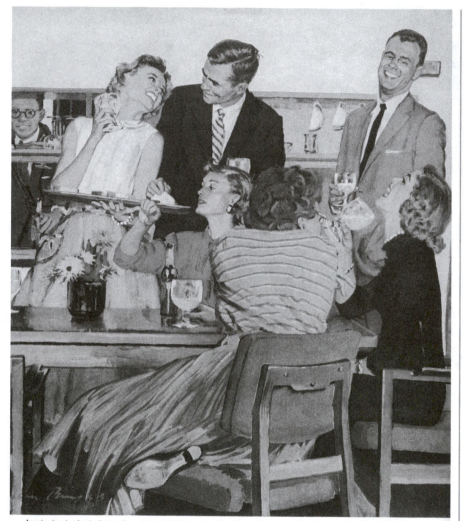

America is returning to the genuine — in foods, fashions and tastes. Today's trend to Ballantine light Ale fits right into this modern picture. In all the world, no other beverage brewed has such extra excellence brewed into it. And "Brewer's Gold" is one big reason for Ballantine Ale's deep, rich, genuine flavor.

They all ask for ale **Ballantine** LIGHT **Ale** !

Ballantine Ale, 1950s

AT THE PULITZER FOUNTAIN, N.Y.C.

In Fine Whiskey...

FLEISCHMANN'S
is the **BIG** buy!

The First Taste will tell you why!

Established 1870

BLENDED WHISKEY • 86 AND 90 PROOF • 65% GRAIN NEUTRAL SPIRITS
THE FLEISCHMANN DISTILLING CORPORATION, NEW YORK CITY

Fleischmann's Whiskey, 1964

Hennessy Cognac, 1968

Of all the De Soto cars ever built, 7 out of 10 are still running

8 out of 10 owners say, "De Soto is the most satisfactory car I ever owned"*

*FROM A MAIL SURVEY AMONG THOUSANDS OF OWNERS OF 1941 AND 1942 DE SOTO CARS

DE SOTO DIVISION OF CHRYSLER CORPORATION

De Soto
DESIGNED TO ENDURE

De Soto, 1947

"Ford's out Front from a Woman's Angle"

1. "**I don't know** synthetic enamel from a box of my children's paints... but if synthetic enamel is what it takes to make that beautiful, shiny Ford finish, I'm all for it!

2. "**My husband says** the brakes are self-centering and hydraulic— whatever that means! All I know is they're so easy that I can taxi the children all day without tiring out!

3. "Peter, he's my teen-age son, tells me that 'Ford is the only car in its price class with a choice of a 100-horsepower V-8 engine or a brilliant new Six.' He says no matter which engine people pick, they're out front with Ford!

4. "**The interior** of our Ford is strictly *my* department! It's tailored with the dreamiest broadcloth. Such a perfect fit! Mary Jane says women help design Ford interiors. There's certainly a woman's touch there!

5. "**Do you like** lovely silver, beautifully simple and chaste looking? That's what I always think of when I touch those smart Ford door handles and window openers.

6. "**Now here's another thing** women like and that's a blissfully comfortable ride—one that isn't bumpity-bump even on some of our completely forgotten roads."

Listen to the Ford Show starring Dinah Shore on Columbia Network Stations Wednesday Evenings.

There's a *Ford* in your future

Ford, 1947

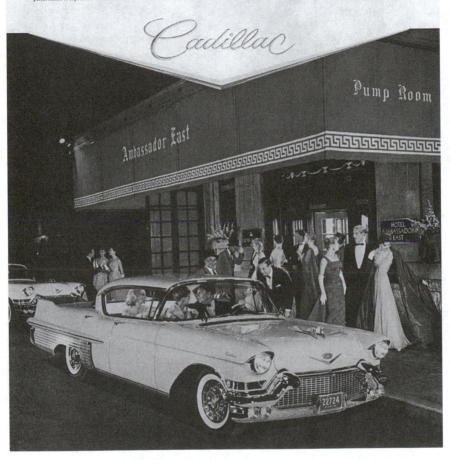

There Are Some Secrets a Man Can't Keep ...

Elizabeth Arden gowns by Count Sarmi

... when he is seen in the driver's seat of a new 1957 Cadillac. And not the least among these is the fact that he is a man of unusual practical wisdom. For it is widely recognized that when a motorist selects the "car of cars", he selects one of the soundest of all motor car purchases. The original cost of a new Cadillac, for instance, is remarkably modest—in view of the great beauty and luxury and performance it represents. Cadillac's marvelous economy of operation and its extraordinary dependability are without counterpart on the world's highways. And Cadillac's unsurpassed resale value assures its owner a greater return on his investment than any other automobile in the land. If you would like to enjoy these many practical benefits in *your* next motor car—then you are looking for Cadillac! The car is waiting for you in your dealer's showroom—and this is the perfect moment to make the move quickly and economically.

CADILLAC MOTOR CAR DIVISION • GENERAL MOTORS CORPORATION

Cadillac, 1950s

Corvette Sting Ray Sport Coupe with eight standard safety features, including outside rearview mirror. Use it always before passing.

The day she flew the coupe

What manner of woman is this, you ask, who stands in the midst of a mountain stream eating a peach?

Actually she's a normal everyday girl except that she and her husband own the Corvette Coupe in the background. (He's at work right now, wondering where he misplaced his car keys.)

The temptation, you see, was over-powering. They'd had the car a whole week now, and not once had he offered to let her drive. His excuse was that this, uh, was a big hairy sports car. Too much for a woman to handle: the trigger-quick steering, the independent rear suspension, the disc brakes—plus the 4-speed transmission and that 425-hp engine they had ordered—egad! He would teach her to drive it some weekend. So he said.

That's why she hid the keys, forcing him to seek public transportation. Sure of his departure, she went to the garage, started the Corvette, and was off for the hills, soon upshifting and downshifting as smoothly as he. His car. Hard to drive. What propaganda!

'66 CORVETTE BY CHEVROLET
Chevrolet Division of General Motors, Detroit, Michigan

Corvette, 1966

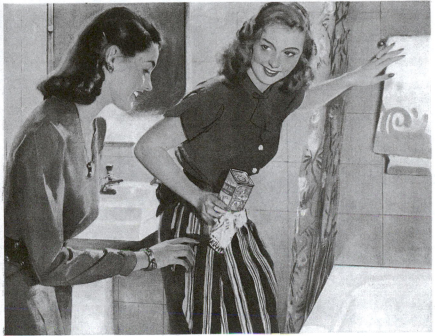

MAY: # Heavens, Ann —
wish I could clean up quick as that!

ANN: You could, hon! Just use a cleanser that doesn't leave dirt-catching scratches.

MAY: Goodness! What in the world do scratches have to do with it?

ANN: A lot, silly! Those tiny scratches you get from gritty cleansers hold onto dirt and double your cleaning time.

MAY: Well, you old smartie! I'd never thought of *that* before.

ANN: I hadn't thought of it either—till I discovered Bon Ami! See how fine-textured and white it is. It just *slides* dirt off—and when you rinse it away, it doesn't leave any of that horrid grit in the tub.

MAY: Say no more, darling! From now on there's going to be a new cleaning team in our house —me and Bon Ami!

EASY ON YOUR HANDS, Bon Ami *Powder* is the ideal cleanser for kitchen sinks, as well as bathtubs. Also try Bon Ami *Cake* for cleaner windows, mirrors and windshields.

 THE **SPEEDY CLEANSER** *that* "*hasn't scratched yet!*"

Bon Ami, 1947

Mrs. Dorian Mehle of Morrisville, Pa., is all three: a housewife, a mother, and a very lovely lady.

"I wash 22,000 dishes a year... but I'm proud of my pretty hands!"

You and Dorian Mehle have something in common. Every year, you wash a stack of dishes a quarter-mile high!

Detergents make your job so much easier .They cut right into grease and grime. They get you through dishwashing in much less time, but while they dissolve grease, they also take away the natural oils and youthful softness of your hands!

Although Dorian hasn't given up detergents her hands are as soft, as smooth, as young-looking as a teenager's. Her secret is no secret at all. It's the world's best-known beauty routine. It's pure, white Jergens Lotion, after every chore.

When you smooth on Jergens Lotion, this liquid formula doesn't just "coat" your hands. It penetrates right away, to help *replace* that softening moisture your skin needs.

Jergens Lotion has two ingredients doctors recommend for softening. Women must be recommending it, too, for more women use it than any other hand care in the world. Dorian's husband is the best testimonial to Jergens Lotion care. Even after years of married life, he still loves to hold her pretty hands!

Use Jergens Lotion like a prescription: three times a day, after every meal!

Now—lotion dispenser FREE of extra cost with $1.00 size. Supply limited.

Use JERGENS LOTION – avoid detergent hands

Jergens Lotion, 1954

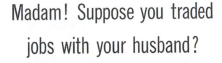

Madam! Suppose you traded jobs with your husband?

You can just bet the first thing he'd ask for would be a telephone in the kitchen.

You wouldn't catch him dashing to another room every time the telephone rang, or he had to make a call.

He doesn't have to do it in his office in town. It would be mighty helpful if you didn't have to do it in your "office" at home.

That's in the kitchen where you do so much of your work. And it's right there that an additional telephone comes in so handy for so many things.

Along with a lot of convenience is that nice feeling of pride in having the best of everything—especially if it is one of those attractive new telephones in color.

 P.S. *Additional telephones in kitchen, bedroom and other convenient places around the house cost little. The service charge is just pennies a day.*

Bell Telephone System

Bell Telephone, 1956

The phone company wants more installers like Alana MacFarlane.

Alana MacFarlane is a 20-year-old from San Rafael, California. She's one of our first women telephone installers. She won't be the last.

We also have several hundred male telephone operators. And a policy that there are no all-male or all-female jobs at the phone company.

We want the men and women of the telephone company to do what they want to do, and do best.

For example, Alana likes working outdoors. "I don't go for office routine," she said. "But as an installer, I get plenty of variety and a chance to move around."

Some people like to work with their hands, or, like Alana, get a kick out of working 20 feet up in the air.

Others like to drive trucks. Some we're helping to develop into good managers.

Today, when openings exist, local Bell Companies are offering applicants and present employees some jobs they may never have thought about before. We want to help all advance to the best of their abilities.

AT&T and your local Bell Company are equal opportunity employers.

Bell Telephone, 1974

A hard man is good to find.

Ken Norton : Pugilist/Thespian

To unlock your body's potential, we proudly offer Soloflex. Twenty-four old-fashioned iron pumping exercises, each correct in form and balance. All on a simple machine that fits in a corner of your home.

For a free Soloflex brochure, call anytime **1-800-453-9000.** In Canada, **1-800-543-1005.**

SOLOFLEX®
Weightlifting, Pure and Simple.

VHS Video Brochure™ available upon request.   © 1985, Soloflex, Inc. Hillsboro, Oregon 97124

Soloflex, 1985

● Discussion and Writing Suggestions

TOBACCO

Camels, 1947 (p. 362)

1. How does the intended appeal of this ad differ most dramatically from a comparable ad today?

2. What kind of psychological appeals are made by the picture in the top half of this ad and the text accompanying it? How does the image of a doctor seeing a five-year old girl and her mother in his book-lined office tie in with the "life expectancy" message of the text and the "More Doctors Smoke Camels" campaign?

Marlboro, 1970s (p. 363)

1. The Marlboro Man has become one of the most famous—and successful—icons of American advertising. What elements of the Marlboro Man (and his setting, Marlboro Country) do you notice, and what role do these elements play in the appeal being made by this ad?

2. This ad appeared during the 1970s (the popularity of the Marlboro Man extended into the 1980s, however). To what extent do you think it would have the same appeal today?

3. Comment on the elements of graphic design (balance, proportion, movement, unity, clarity and simplicity, emphasis) that help make this ad effective. Focus particularly on the element of movement.

Camels, 1979 (p. 364)

1. What do the relative positions and postures of the man and the woman in the ad indicate about the ad's basic appeal?

2. What roles do the props—particularly, the motorcycle and the models' outfits—and the setting play in helping to sell the product?

3. How do the design elements in the ad emphasize the product?

4. Compare the graphic elements of this ad to those of the Fleischmann's Whiskey ad (p. 367).

5. Compare and contrast the two Camels ads presented in this section of the portfolio. Focus on the psychological appeals, the cultural values implied in the ads, and the graphic and textual means used to persuade the buyer to smoke Camels.

Cancer Patients Aid Association, 2012 (p. 365)

1. How does the circle of onlookers help create or enhance the message of this advertisement?

2. In what way does the camera angle create meaning and affect the tone of the ad?

3. This advertisement doesn't aim to sell the viewer a product but, rather, to change behavior. Do you think that it's likely to be effective at that task—in particular, in persuading smokers to stop smoking? Explain.

BEER AND LIQUOR

Ballantine Ale, 1950s (p. 366)

1. This illustration, reminiscent of some of Norman Rockwell's paintings, is typical of many beer and ale ads in the 1950s, which depict a group of well-dressed young adults enjoying their brew at a social event. Comment on the distinctive graphic elements in this ad, and speculate as to why these elements are seldom employed in contemporary advertisements for beer and ale. Why, in other words, does this ad seem old-fashioned?

2. Contrast the appeal and graphics of this ad with the ads for Miller and Budweiser later in this portfolio.

3. Identify the adjectives in the body text, and attempt to correlate them to the graphic in helping to construct the message of the ad.

Fleischmann's Whiskey, 1964 (p. 367)

1. Comment on (1) the significance of the extra-large bottle of whiskey; (2) the stances of the two models in the ad; (3) the way the headline contributes to the ad's meaning.

2. Compare and contrast the graphic in this ad with that of the 1979 Camels ad earlier in this portfolio (the man on the motorcycle).

Hennessy Cognac, 1968 (p. 368)

1. What is the primary appeal of this ad? How do the woman, the horse, and the headline work to create and reinforce this appeal?

2. Compare and contrast this ad to the Cadillac, 1950s ad in terms of their appeal and their graphics.

Automobiles

De Soto, 1947 (p. 369)

1. How does the scene portrayed in the illustration help create the basic appeal of this ad? Focus on as many significant individual elements of the illustration as you can.

2. To what extent does the caption (in the illustration) and the headline support the message communicated by the graphic?

3. Explain why both this ad and the preceding Cadillac ad are products of their particular times.

Ford, 1947 (p. 370)

1. Cite and discuss those textual elements in the ad that reflect a traditional conception of the American woman.

2. How do the visual elements of the ad reinforce the assumptions about traditional gender roles reflected in the ad?

Cadillac, 1950s (p. 371)

1. What is the particular marketing strategy behind this ad? Based on the ad's text, compose a memo from the head of marketing to the chief copywriter, proposing this particular ad and focusing on the strategy. The memo doesn't have to be cynical or to insult the prospective Cadillac buyers; it should just be straightforward and direct.

2. How do the ad's graphics reinforce the message in the text? For example, what is the significance of the "motor car" being parked in front of the entryway to the Ambassador East Hotel? Of the way the people in the ad are dressed?

3. How is this ad designed to appeal buyers seeking both prestige and practicality?

Corvette, 1966 (p. 372)

1. How do the graphic elements reinforce the message developed in the text of this ad?

2. Comment on the dress and the posture of the model, as these relate to the ad's essential appeal. What's the significance of the woman eating a peach in a mountain stream?

3. The body text in this ad tells a story. What kind of husband–wife dynamic is implied by this story? To what extent do you find similarities between the implied gender roles in this ad and those in the 1947 Ford ad ("Ford's out Front from a Woman's Angle," p. 370)? To what extent do you find differences, ones that may be attributable to the 20 years between the two ads?

CLEANSERS, BEAUTY PRODUCTS, AND OTHER

Bon Ami, 1947 (p. 373)

1. How do the text and graphics of this ad illustrate a bygone cultural attitude toward gender roles? Notice, in particular, the dress, postures, and expressions of the women pictured, as well as the style of the illustration. Focus also on the wording of the text.

2. In terms of Jib Fowles's categories, what kind of appeal is being made by the Bon Ami ad?

Jergens Lotion, 1954 (p. 374)

1. Compare and contrast the appeals and the strategies of this Jergens Lotion ad and the Bon Ami ad preceding it. Are the ads intended to appeal to the same target audiences? To what extent are the psychological appeals of the two ads similar? Compare the illustrations of the ads. How do they differ in basic strategy?

2. The model in the Jergens Lotion ad is immaculately dressed and groomed, and she is sitting among stacks of fine china (as opposed to everyday dishware). What do you think is the marketing strategy behind these graphic choices?

Bell Telephone, 1956 (p. 375)

1. Discuss the attitude toward gender roles implicit in the 1956 Bell ad. How do the graphics, the headline, and the body text reinforce this attitude? What is the significance of the quotation marks around "office" in the final sentence of the third paragraph?

2. Notice that the woman at the desk seems a lot more comfortable and at ease than the man holding the crying baby and the dishes. What does this fact tell us about the attitudes toward gender roles of those who created this ad?

Bell Telephone, 1974 (p. 376)

1. Compare and contrast the 1956 Bell ad with the 1974 Bell ad, in terms of their attitudes toward gender roles. How do the text and graphics reinforce the essential differences?

2. The 1956 Bell ad pictures a woman at a desk (a white-collar job); the 1974 ad pictures a woman working at a telephone pole (a blue-collar job). Would the 1974 ad have the same impact if "Alana MacFarlane" had, like her 1956 counterpart, been pictured at a desk?

3. Like the 1950s Cadillac ad (p. 371), the 1974 Bell ad seems more of a public service announcement than a conventional advertisement. Compare and contrast these ads in terms of their messages to readers.

Soloflex, 1985 (p. 377)

1. How does the illustration in this ad reinforce the basic appeal of the headline?

2. Ads are frequently criticized for the incongruity between illustration and product being advertised—for example, a scantily clad woman posed

provocatively in front of a pickup truck. To what extent does the Soloflex ad present an appropriate fit between graphic and product advertised?

A PORTFOLIO OF TV COMMERCIALS

The world's first television commercial was a ten-second Bulova watch ad broadcast in 1941. But it wasn't until the 1950s, when TV became a mass medium, that the commercial became a ubiquitous feature of popular culture. Before viewers had the technology to fast-forward through commercials, many probably regarded TV ads as annoying, occasionally informative or entertaining, but generally unnecessary accompaniments to their television experience. But of course the commercial is not simply an extraneous byproduct of TV programming. It is television's very reason for existence. Before the age of public TV and of cable and satellite providers, television programs were financed entirely by the companies that created the commercials and that paid networks and local stations to broadcast them. Viewed from a marketing angle, the only purpose of commercial television is to provide a medium for advertising. The news, comedy, drama, game, and variety shows offered by TV are simply ways of luring viewers to watch the commercials.

Still, the unceasing deluge of commercials of every type means that advertisers have to figure out ways of making their messages stand out by being unusually creative, funny, surprising, or otherwise noteworthy. The standard jingles, primitive animation, catchphrases ("Winston tastes good like a cigarette should"), and problem-solution minidramas of TV commercials work for a while but are quickly forgotten in the onslaught of new messages. It becomes the job of advertising agencies (of the type represented in *Mad Men*) that create both print and TV ads to make their clients' products stand out by ever more-ingenious and striking ways of delivering their messages. To do this, these agencies rely not just on information about the product and clever audiovisual techniques; they attempt to respond to what they believe consumers crave, deep down. TV commercials, no less than print ads, rely on psychological appeals of the type discussed by Jib Fowles in his "Advertising's Fifteen Basic Appeals."

The following portfolio includes some of the most noteworthy and successful TV commercials of the past sixty years. Many (though not all) of these commercials are featured in Bernice Kanner's *The 100 Best TV Commercials...and Why They Worked* (1999), where you will find additional description and commentary. To access the commercials, go to YouTube (YouTube.com), and enter the search terms provided under the commercial's title into the search box. In some cases, additional information is presented, in brackets, to help you navigate to the commercial. In cases where multiple versions of the same commercial are available, you may have to experiment to determine which one offers the best video and audio quality. In a few cases, uploaded commercials have been truncated, so you should generally select the longest version. In some cases, the indicated commercials may have been removed from the YouTube Web site. No matter; thousands more remain available for your observation and consideration.

As with the print ads, we provide two or three sets of specific questions for each TV commercial. These questions are intended to stimulate your thinking and writing process about the particular ways in which the audio and visuals are intended to work. As you review these commercials, however, you might be thinking of the more general questions about advertisements raised by the preceding readings in the chapter. Here are some of those general questions:

1. What appears to be the target audience for this TV commercial? If it was produced more than two decades ago, how would this target audience likely react today to the ad?

2. What is the primary appeal made by the ad, in terms of Fowles's categories? What, if any, are the secondary appeals?

3. What is the chief attention-getting technique in the commercial?

4. How does the commercial make use of such tools as humor, surprise, fantasy, wonder, human interest, or social concern to achieve its goals?

5. What is the relationship between the visuals and the audio track? How do audio and video work together—or in contrast—to achieve the sponsor's purpose?

6. How do the commercial's visual techniques work to convey the message? Consider camera movement (or the lack of camera movement); the style and pace of editing (the juxtaposition of individual shots); and visual composition (the framing of the people and/or objects within the shot).

7. How do the expressions, the clothing, the postures of the person or people, and the physical objects in the shots help communicate the ad's message?

8. How do the words used by the actor(s) or by the voice-over narrator work to communicate the message of the commercial?

Consider, also, the following evaluative questions[2]:

- Is it a good ad? Why?
- What do you like most about it? Why?
- What do you dislike the most? Why?
- Do you think it "works"? Why or why not?
- How could the ad be improved?
- Could the sender have conveyed the same message using other strategies, other persuasive means? If so, explain.
- Even if you don't believe that this particular ad works or persuades you, is there anything in the ad that still affects you or persuades you indirectly?
- Does the ad have effects on you perhaps not intended by its creators?

---

[2]Lars Thoger Christensen, "How to Analyze an Advertisement." University of Southern Denmark—Odense. Jan. 2004. http://wms-soros.mngt.waikato.ac.nz/NR/rdonlyres/ebabz4jhzmg5fr5p45ypc53mdvuxva5wxhe7323onb4ylelbaq3se5xjrslfc4mi3qgk6dmsx5dqbp/Advertisinganalysis.doc

● Discussion and Writing Suggestions

Note: Because Web content frequently changes without warning, not all of the listed videos may be available when you attempt to access them. It is possible that errant searches may lead to other videos with objectionable content. Such videos, as well as user-submitted comments under the specified videos below, do not reflect the views of the authors or of Pearson Publishing.

COMMERCIALS OF THE 1960s

Volkswagen: Snowplow

YouTube Search Terms: vw snow plow commercial [select black and white version]

1. In the 1960s, Volkswagen became famous in the United States not only for its funny-looking cars—so different in style from Detroit's massive passenger vehicles—but also for its "soft-sell" approach to print ads and TV commercials. How does that soft-sell approach work in this ad? What is the sales strategy, as embodied in the relatively primitive visuals and the voice-over track? What exactly is being sold?

2. The closing shot of this commercial shows a snowplow driving past a Volkswagen. How does this image encapsulate the message of the ad? Write a sentence that expresses the message Volkswagen wants to communicate, without regard to the particular visuals of the ad.

Alka Seltzer: Spicy Meatball

YouTube Search Terms: alka seltzer meatball

1. Some TV commercials employ a "fake-out" strategy, based partially on our knowledge of other commercials. How does this approach work in the Alka Seltzer ad? Do you think it is likely to succeed in persuading viewers to buy the product?

2. Like many successful TV commercials, this one relies on humor, grounded in human foibles and imperfections, and based on our experience that if things can go wrong, they generally will. How do the visuals and the audio track of the Alka Selzter ad employ this kind of humor as a sales strategy?

COMMERCIALS OF THE 1970s

Quaker Oats: Mikey

YouTube Search Terms: quaker oats mikey

1. Why don't the older kids want to try Life cereal? How does reluctance tie into Quaker Oats's larger marketing problem with the product? How does the commercial attempt to deal with this problem?

2. Many viewers came to hate this commercial because it was shown repeatedly and because it lasted so many years. Still, it endured because
   many other viewers found it endearing—and it did the job of publicizing
   the product. Do you think a commercial such as this one would work
   today? Explain.

Coca-Cola: Mean Joe Green

YouTube Search Terms: coca cola joe green

1. This commercial is a study in contrasts. Identify some of these contrasts
   (both visual and aural), and explain how they work as part of the sales
   strategy.

2. To what emotions does this commercial attempt to appeal? Did you find
   this appeal successful?

3. Like many commercials, this one is presented as a minidrama, complete
   with plot, character, setting, theme, and other elements found in longer
   dramas. Explain the way that the drama functions in this ad, particularly
   as it concerns the characterization of the two actors.

COMMERCIALS OF THE 1980s

Federal Express (FedEx): Fast-Paced World [with John Moschitta]

YouTube Search Terms: federal express fast talker

1. The actor in this commercial, John Moschitta, was for many years celebrated in the *Guinness Book of World Records* as the world's fastest
   talker (he was clocked at 586 words per minute). How does Moschitta's
   unique skill make him an ideal spokesperson for Federal Express?

2. There is always a danger that particularly striking ads may be counterproductive, in that they draw attention to their own cleverness or
   unusual stylistic qualities, rather than to the product being sold. Put
   yourself in the position of a Federal Express executive. To what extent
   might you be concerned that this commercial, clever as it is, would not
   succeed in making more people select Federal Express as their express
   delivery service? On the other hand, might any striking commercial for
   Federal Express be successful if it heightened public recognition of the
   brand?

Pepsi-Cola: Archaeology

YouTube Search Terms: pepsi cola archaeology

1. Summarize the main selling point of this commercial. How does this
   selling point relate to (1) the basic situation presented in the commercial
   and (2) Pepsi's slogan, as it appears at the end?

2. Pepsi-Cola and Coca-Cola have been engaged in fierce rivalry for more than a century. How does this commercial exploit that rivalry to humorous effect? How is each product visually represented in the ad?

3. As contrasted with the Volkswagen "Snowplow" ad or the Quaker Oats "Mikey" ad, this ad features lavish production values and is presented as if it were a science fiction film. How do the sets, costumes, props, and special effects help support the overall sales strategy of the ad?

COMMERCIALS OF THE 1990S

Jeep: Snow Covered

YouTube Search Terms: jeep snow covered

I. "This may have been the most arrogant commercial ever made," declared the creative director of the agency that produced it. In what way might this be so? Possible arrogance aside, is this an effective advertisement for Jeep? Explain.

2. How do the visuals support the message of the ad? What *is* that message?

3. Which appeals are most evident in this commercial?

Energizer: Darth Vader

YouTube Search Terms: energizer darth vader

I. The Energizer bunny was featured in numerous commercials of the 1990s, generally in settings where its sudden appearance was totally unexpected. How do the creators of this add draw upon the *Star Wars* mythology to support their sales pitch? In what way is the strategy of this ad similar to that of Alka Seltzer's "Spicy Meatball"?

2. In a sentence, summarize the message of this ad—without mentioning *Star Wars* or Darth Vader.

Got Milk? (California Milk Processor Board): Aaron Burr [original Got Milk? Commercial]

YouTube Search Terms: got milk burr

I. The opening of this commercial is intended to convey a sense of culture and sophistication. How do the images and the soundtrack do this? Why is this "setup" necessary in terms of the ad's message? What is that message?

2. In the latter half of the commercial, how does the accelerated pace of the editing and camera work—and of the soundtrack—contribute to the ad's overall impact?

COMMERCIALS OF THE 2000s

Honda: Physics

YouTube Search Terms: honda physics

1. Put yourself in the position of the ad agency copywriters for Honda *before* they conceived of this particular ad. What is your main selling point? Express, in a sentence, what you want to communicate to the public about Honda automobiles and engineering.

2. This commercial involves no computer graphics or digital tricks; everything that happens is real. All the components we see came from the disassembling of two Honda Accords. The voice is that of *Lake Woebegon Days* author Garrison Keillor. According to Honda, this single continuous shot required 606 takes—meaning that for the first 605 takes, something, usually minor, went wrong, and the recording team had to install the setup again and again. There is always a danger (for the client) that memorable commercials such as this one will amaze and impress viewers but will also fail to implant brand identification in their minds. Do you think there may be such a problem with this commercial? To what extent are viewers who have seen it likely, days or weeks later, to identify it with Honda and to associate whatever message (if any) they draw from the commercial with the particular qualities of Honda automobiles?

Dove: Onslaught

YouTube Search Terms: dove onslaught

1. What is the message of this ad? How does the cinematic style of the visuals reinforce that message? Focus, in particular, on the contrasting visual styles used for the child and (later in the ad) her classmates, on the one hand, and the rest of the images, on the other. Consider, for example, how long the first image remains on screen, compared to those that follow.

2. How many of Jib Fowles's fifteen basic appeals do you detect at work in this ad? How do these appeals work to convey the essential contrast of values underlying the ad?

Tide to Go: Interview

YouTube Search Terms: tide to go interview

1. What is the message of this ad? How do the simple visuals and the more complex soundtrack work together (and against one another) to support that idea? How does that idea relate to one or more of Fowles's fifteen basic appeals?

2. Like many contemporary TV ads, this one relies on humor. To what extent do you find humor used effectively here? What is the source of the humor? How do the two actors help create that humor? How is this humor rooted in common concerns and fears that we all share?

Planters Peanuts: Perfume

YouTube Search Terms: planters perfume

1. Many of the elements in this ad are also found in perfume commercials. How are these elements used here to comic effect? Of what other commercials does this one remind you? Why?

2. The Planters ad relies on the visual motif of comic mayhem. Do you think such visuals are an effective way of selling the product? Explain.

VW, "The Force"

YouTube Search Terms: volkswagen the force

1. How does this commercial play against the Darth Vader image and mythology for the purpose of selling cars?

2. This commercial became a cultural phenomenon, with the child star even appearing on *Today* for an interview. Why do you think it became so popular? Consider the style, the storyline, the images and sound, and the message.

DirecTV, "Dog Collar"

YouTube Search Terms: directv dog collar

1. Many commercials rely on humor to help convey the advertiser's message. Among such ads represented in this portfolio: Alka Seltzer, "Spicy Meatball"; Quaker Oats, "Mikey"; FedEx, "Fast-Paced World"; Pepsi Cola, "Archaeology"; Energizer, "Darth Vader" (and another Darth Vader ad, VW, "The Force"); Got Milk? "Aaron Burr"; and Tide to Go, "Interview." How does the humor in DirecTV's commercial compare and contrast to the humor in some of these other funny commercials? Consider, for example, the consumer need (in Jib Fowles' scheme) to which this commercial claims to be appealing—as opposed to the need to which it is actually appealing. Consider, also, what it is we're actually smiling at when we view these commercials.

2. Would this commercial help persuade you (by its ironclad chain of reasoning) to switch from cable to DirecTV? If not, why do you think the company decided to create and air it?

3. The "Dog Collar" spot was one of a series of three similarly themed commercials created by DirecTV in 2012. Among the others in the

series: "Don't Wake Up in a Roadside Ditch" and "Stop Taking in Stray Animals." Here's your chance to be a famous copywriter: Create another 30-second spot in this series. Describe the visuals, and write the script for the voice-over.

ADDITIONAL TV COMMERCIALS

Note: Unless otherwise indicated, all commercials listed were produced in the United States.

Democratic National Committee: "Daisy Girl" (1964)

YouTube search terms: democratic daisy ad

American Tourister Luggage: Gorilla (1969)

YouTube search terms: luggage gorilla

Chevrolet: "Baseball, Hot Dogs, Apple Pie" (1969)

YouTube search terms: america baseball hotdogs

Keep America Beautiful: "Crying Indian" (1970)

YouTube search terms: america crying indian

Coca Cola: "Hilltop" ("I'd Like to Buy the World a Coke") (1971)

YouTube search terms: buy world coke 1971

Hovis: "Bike Ride" (UK, 1973) [shot by Ridley Scott]

YouTube search terms: hovis bike

Xerox: "Monks" (1975)

YouTube search terms: xerox monks

Hebrew National: "Higher Authority" (1975)

YouTube search terms: hebrew national higher

BASF: "Dear John" (New Zealand, 1979)

YouTube search terms: basf dear john

Lego: "Kipper" (UK, 1980)

YouTube search terms: lego kipper

Apple: Macintosh (1984)

YouTube search terms: apple macintosh

Sony Trinitron: "Lifespan" (UK, 1984)

YouTube search terms: sony trinitron advert

American Express: "Stephen King: (1984)

YouTube search terms: american express king

The Guardian: "Points of View" (UK, 1987)

YouTube search terms: guardian points of view

Volkswagen: "Changes" (UK, 1988)

YouTube Search Terms: vw changes

Energizer: "Bunny Introduction" (1989)

YouTube search terms: energizer bunny introduction 1989

Dunlop: "Tested for the Unexpected" (1993)

YouTube search terms: dunlop tested unexpected

Swedish Televerket: "Noxin" (Sweden, 1993)

YouTube Search Terms: Noxin

Little Caesar's Pizza: "Training Camp" (1994)

YouTube search terms: caesar's training camp

Campbell's Soup: Winter Commercial (1995)

YouTube search terms: campbell's soup winter

California Milk Processor Board: "Got Milk? Heaven" (1996)

YouTube search terms: got milk heaven

Ameriquest Mortgage: "Plane Ride" (2008)

YouTube search terms: ameriquest plane ride

Audi: "Oil Parade" (2009)

YouTube search terms: audi oil parade

Jack in the Box: "Junk in the Box" (2009)

YouTube search terms: jack in the box junk in the box

Synthesis Activities

1. Select one *category* of advertisements (cigarettes, alcohol, etc.) represented in the ad portfolio. Compare and contrast the types of appeals underlying these ads, as discussed by Fowles. To what extent do you notice significant shifts of appeal from the 1940s to the present? Which types of appeal seem to you most effective with particular product categories? Is it more likely, for example, that people will buy cigarettes because they want to feel autonomous or because the cigarettes will make them more attractive to the opposite sex?

2. Select a series of ads in different product categories that all appear to rely on the same primary appeal—perhaps the appeal to sex or the appeal to affiliation. Compare and contrast the overall strategies of these ads. Draw upon Fowles and other authors represented in this chapter to develop your ideas. To what extent do your analyses support arguments often made by social critics (and advertising people) that what people are really buying is the image, rather than the product?

3. Discuss how a selection of ads reveals shifting cultural attitudes over the past six decades toward either (a) gender relations; (b) romance between

men and women; (c) smoking; or (d) automobiles. In the case of *a* or *b*, the ads don't have to be for the same category of product. In terms of their underlying appeal, in terms of the implicit or explicit messages embodied both in the text and the graphics, how and to what extent do the ads reveal that attitudes of the target audiences have changed over the years?

4. Select a TV commercial or a TV ad campaign (for example, for Sprint phone service) and analyze the commercial(s) in terms of Fowles's categories, as well as the discussions of Bovée et al. in this chapter. To what extent do the principles discussed by these authors apply to broadcast, as well as to print ads? What are the special requirements of TV advertising?

5. Find a small group of ads that rely upon little or no body copy—just a graphic, perhaps a headline, and the product name. What common features underlie the marketing strategies of such ads? What kinds of appeals do they make? How do their graphic aspects compare? What makes the need for text superfluous?

6. As indicated in the introduction to this chapter, social critics have charged advertising with numerous offenses: "It fosters materialism, it psychologically manipulates people to buy things they don't need, it perpetuates gender and racial stereotypes (particularly in its illustrations), it is deceptive, it is offensive, it debases the language . . ." To what extent do some of the advertisements presented in the ad portfolio (and perhaps others of your own choosing) demonstrate the truth of one or more of these charges? In developing your response, draw upon some of the ads in the portfolio (or elsewhere).

7. Read the textual content (headlines and body text) of several ads *without* paying attention (if possible) to the graphics. Compare the effectiveness of the headline and body text by themselves with the effectiveness of the ads, *including* the graphic elements. Focusing on a group of related ads (related by product category, by appeal, by decade, etc.), devise an explanation of how graphics work to effectively communicate the appeal and meaning of the products advertised.

8. Many ads employ humor—in the graphics, in the body copy, or both—to sell a product. Examine a group of advertisements that rely on humor to make their appeal, and explain how they work. For example, do they play off an incongruity between one element of the ad and another (such as between the headline and the graphic), or between one element of the ad (or the basic message of the ad) and what we know or assume to be the case in the "real world"? Do they employ wordplay or irony? Do they picture people doing funny things (funny because inappropriate or unrealistic)? What appeal underlies the humor? Aggression? Sex? Nurturing? Based on your examination and analyses, what appear to be some of the more effective ways of employing humor?

9. Think of a new product that you have just invented. This product, in your opinion, will revolutionize the world of (fill in the blank). Devise an advertisement to announce this product to the world. Consider (or reject) using a celebrity to help sell your product. Select the basic appeal of your product (see Fowles). Then, applying concepts and principles discussed by Bovée et al. in this chapter, write the headline, subhead, and body copy for the product. Sketch out (or at least describe) the graphic that will accompany the text. Show your proposed ad to one or more of your classmates, get reactions, and then revise the ad, taking into account your market feedback.

10. Imagine that you own a small business—perhaps an independent coffee shop (not Starbucks, Peet's, or Coffee Bean), a video game company, or a pedicab service that conveys tourists around a chic beach town. Devise an ad that announces your services and extols its benefits. Apply the principles discussed by Fowles and the other writers in this chapter.

11. Write a parody ad—one that would never ordinarily be written— applying the selling principles discussed by Fowles and Bovée et al. in this chapter. For example, imagine you are the manager of the Globe Theatre in Elizabethan England and want to sell season tickets to this season's plays, including a couple of new tragedies by your playwright-in-residence, Will Shakespeare. Or imagine that you are trying to sell Remington typewriters in the age of computers (no software glitches!). Or—as long as people are selling bottled water—you have found a way to package and sell air. Advertisers can reportedly sell anything with the right message. Give it your best shot.

12. Based on the reading you have done in this chapter, discuss the extent to which you believe advertisements create needs in consumers, reflect existing needs, or some combination of both. In developing your paper, draw on both particular advertisements and on the more theoretical overviews of advertising developed in the chapter.

13. Select one advertisement and conduct two analyses of it, using two different analytical principles—perhaps one from Fowles's list of fifteen emotional appeals and one from Bovée's "Checklist for Producing Excellent Copy" (p. 356). Having conducted your analyses and developed your insights, compare and contrast the strengths and weaknesses of the analytical principles you've employed. Conclude more broadly with a discussion of how a single analytical principle can close down, as well as open up, understanding of an object under study.

14. As you have seen, advertisements change over time, both across product categories and within categories. And yet the advertisements remain a constant, their presence built on the assumption that consumers can be swayed both overtly and covertly in making purchasing decisions. In a paper drawing on the selections in this chapter, develop

a theory on why ads change over time. Is it because people's needs have changed and, therefore, new ads are required? (Do the older ads appeal to the same needs as newer ads?) In developing your discussion, you might track the changes over time in one product category.

Research Activities

1. Drawing upon contemporary magazines (or magazines from a given period), select a set of advertisements in a particular product category. Analyze these advertisements according to Fowles's categories, and assess their effectiveness in terms of the discussions of Bovée et al. in this chapter.

2. Select a particular product that has been selling for at least twenty-five years (e.g., Bayer aspirin, Tide detergent, IBM computers, Oldsmobile—as in "This is not your father's Oldsmobile") and trace the history of print advertising for this product over the years. To what extent has the advertising changed over the years? To what extent has the essential sales appeal remained the same? In addition to examining the ads themselves, you may want to research the company and its marketing practices. You will find two business databases particularly useful: ABI/INFORM and the academic version of LexisNexis.

3. One of the landmark campaigns in American advertising was Doyle Dane Bernbach's series of ads for the Volkswagen Beetle in the 1960s. In effect a rebellion against standard auto advertising, the VW ads' Unique Selling Proposition was that ugly is beautiful—an appeal that was overwhelmingly successful. Research the VW ad campaign for this period, setting it in the context of the agency's overall marketing strategy.

4. Among the great marketing debacles of recent decades was Coca-Cola's development in 1985 of a new formula for its soft drink that (at least temporarily) replaced the much-beloved old formula. Research this major development in soft drink history, focusing on the marketing of New Coke and the attempt of the Atlanta-based Coca-Coca Company to deal with the public reception of its new product.

5. Advertising agencies are hired not only by manufacturers and by service industries; they are also hired by political candidates. In fact, one of the common complaints about American politics is that candidates for public office are marketed just as if they were bars of soap. Select a particular presidential or gubernatorial election and research the print and broadcast advertising used by the rival candidates. You may want to examine the ads not only of the candidates of the major parties, but also the candidates of the smaller parties, such as the Green and the Libertarian

parties. How do the appeals and strategies used by product ads compare and contrast with those used in ads for political candidates?

6. Public service ads comprise another major category of advertising (in addition to product and service advertising and political advertising). Such ads have been used to recruit people to military service, to get citizens to buy war bonds, to obtain contributions for charitable causes, to get people to support or oppose strikes, to persuade people to stop using (or not to start using) drugs, to prevent drunk driving, etc. Locate a group of public service ads, describe them, and assess their effectiveness. Draw upon Fowles and Bovée et al. in developing your conclusions.

7. Research advertising in American magazines and newspapers before World War II. Focus on a limited number of product lines—for example, soft drinks, soap and beauty products, health-related products. What kind of differences do you see between ads in the first part of the twentieth century and more recent or contemporary advertising for the same types of products? In general, how have the predominant types of appeals used to sell products in the past changed (if they have) with the times? How are the graphics of early ads different from preferred graphics today? How has the body copy changed? (Hint: You may want to be on the alert for ads that make primarily negative appeals—i.e., what may happen to you if you don't use the product advertised.)

Video Links

Following is a list of online videos that we hope will enhance your understanding and enjoyment of the subjects treated in this book. Most, if not all, of these videos are available on YouTube <YouTube.com>. Using the indicated search terms on YouTube (or Google or Bing, if the videos are located elsewhere on the Web) will allow you to access these and, in many cases, numerous related videos. Note: In YouTube you may need to skip over the "Featured Videos" that sometimes appear first on the list of "hits" in order to get to the target video.

Note: Because Web content frequently changes without warning, not all of the listed videos may be available when you attempt to access them. It is possible that errant searches may lead to other videos with objectionable content. Such videos, as well as user-submitted comments under videos do not reflect the views of the authors or of Pearson Publishing.

To cite these videos in a paper, use the format for online videos. Thus:

"Climate Change." *American Association for the Advancement of Science.* YouTube, n.d. Web. 26 Jan. 2008.

Chapter 1: Summary

Alan Blinder on Free Trade and Outsourcing
YouTube search terms: "blinder outsourcing"

Chapter 2: Critical Reading and Critique

Save Constellation: Let's Go to the Moon, Mars, and Beyond!
YouTube search terms: "save constellation moon"
Obama Ends Space Flight for a Decade
YouTube search terms: "obama ends space flight"
Preserving Human Space Travel and Colorado Jobs (Senator Mark Udall)
YouTube search terms: "preserving space travel udall"

Chapter 3: Synthesis

Virginia Tech Shooting
YouTube search terms: "virginia tech shooting footage"; "virginia tech shooting confession"

Chapter 5: The Roar of the Tiger Mom

Amy Chua: "Didn't Expect This Level of Intensity"
YouTube search terms: "amy chua interview"
Child of Tiger Mom Speaks Out
YouTube search terms: "child tiger mom speaks"
Tiger Mom Responds to Uproar (PBS)
YouTube search terms: "amy chua responds uproar"
Amy Chua Promotes *Battle Hymn of the Tiger Mother*
YouTube search terms: "battle hymn tiger mother" (2:55 clip)
Amy Chua on "Today" Show
YouTube search terms: "amy chua today" (5:11 clip)
The Myth of China's Tiger Mothers
YouTube search terms: "tiger mothers myth"

Chapter 6: The Changing Landscape of Work in the Twenty-first Century

The New World of Work (statistics set to music)
YouTube search terms: "the new world of work"
Three Eras of Globalization
YouTube search terms: "thomas friedman's three eras of globalization"
The Virtual Office (ABC News Report)
YouTube search terms: "abc future workplace no office"
Generation Next in the Workplace
YouTube search terms: "generation next the workplace"
ABC News: Myth: Outsourcing Bad for America—Busted
YouTube search terms: "abc 20/20 outsourcing bad"
Outsource This (skit with Jason Alexander)
YouTube search terms: "outsource this jason alexander"
People in China Starving for Your Job
YouTube search terms: "tom peters: people in china starving for your job"
Educate for a Creative Society
YouTube search terms: "tom peters educate creative"

Chapter 7: Have You Heard This? The Latest on Rumor

Norman Rockwell's "The Gossips" (music: African Head Charge—"Off the Beaten
Track") *YouTube search terms: "gossips rockwell"*
A Conversation with Nicholos diFonzo on Rumor Psychology
YouTube search terms: "difonzo rumor"
How to Spread a Rumor
YouTube search terms: "how to spread rumor"
Paul is Dead? (Beatles rumor)
YouTube search terms: "paul is dead" (multiple videos)
Celebrity Death Rumors
YouTube search terms: "celebrity death rumors"
WWII: Private SNAFU Rumors
YouTube search terms: "world war 2 rumors"

Gang Members Killing Motorists in L.A.?
  YouTube search terms: "gang headlights rumor"
Alligators in the Sewers? (MonsterQuest series)
  YouTube search terms: "gators sewers" (multiple videos)
Is Obama a Muslim?
  YouTube search terms: "obama muslim debate"
Obama Dispels "Outlandish" Health Care Rumors
  YouTube search terms: "obama outlandish health care rumors"

Chapter 8: Green Power

Climate Change

Climate Change
  YouTube search terms: "aaas climate change"
Frontline: "Heat" [trailer for PBS program on climate change]
  YouTube search terms: "frontline heat pbs"
Climate Change (YouTube) [British perspective]
  YouTube search terms: "climate challenge greenhouse effect"
Al Gore Goes Green for "An Inconvenient Truth" (Speech at Constitution Hall, Washington, DC, July 17, 2008)
  YouTube search terms: "gore green inconvenient"
Trailer for *An Inconvenient Truth*
  YouTube search terms: "gore goes green inconvenient truth"

Nuclear Power

Nuclear Power: How it Works
  YouTube search terms: "nuclear reactor how it works"
Nuclear Power Station (animated graphic)
  YouTube search terms: "nuclear power station"
Nuclear Power Generator (live action and animation)
  YouTube search terms: "nuclear power generator"
YouTube Debate (Democratic Presidential Candidates): Nuclear Power?
  YouTube search terms: "youtube debate nuclear"
Fukushima Nuclear Disaster
  YouTube search terms: "fukushima" (multiple videos)

Wind Power

How Do Wind Turbines Work? (3D animation)
  YouTube search terms: "how do wind turbines work 3d"
Energy 101: Wind Turbines
  YouTube search terms: "energy 101 wind"
National Renewable Energy Laboratory's (NREL's) National Wind Power Technology Center
  YouTube search terms: "windpower national"
Rooftop Wind Turbine
  YouTube search terms: "wind power rooftop" (multiple videos)

Solar Power

Energy 101: Solar
YouTube search terms: "energy 101 solar power"
How Does Solar Energy Work? (EnfinityChannel animation)
YouTube Search terms: "how does solar energy work"
Solar Power 101: How Does Sunlight Turn into Electricity? (Sierra Solar Systems)
YouTube Search terms: "solar power 101"
Solar Energy Breakthrough in Negev Desert, Israel
YouTube search terms: "solar power breakthrough negev"

Chapter 9: New and Improved: Six Decades of Advertising

A Conversation about Advertising with David Ogilvy (celebrated ad man inter-
viewed by John Crichton, 1977)
YouTube search terms: "conversation advertising ogilvy"
David Ogilvy: Essentials (the great campaigns of legendary ad man)
YouTube search terms: "ogilvy essentials"
Mad Men trailer
YouTube search terms: "mad men meet don draper"
Psychology and Advertising
YouTube search terms: "psychology and advertising"
Psychological Advertising
YouTube search terms: "psychological advertising"
What Psychological Tricks Do They Use?"
YouTube search terms: "advertising psychological tricks"
How to be Creative in Advertising
YouTube search terms: "creative advertising"

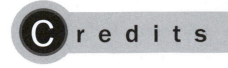
Credits

CHAPTER 1

Page 8: Reprinted with permission from Alan S. Blinder, "Outsourcing: Bigger Than You Thought," The American Prospect: October 2006. Volume 17, Issue 11, http:// www.prospect.org. The American Prospect, 1710 Rhode Island Avenue, NW, 12th Floor, Washington, DC 20036. All rights reserved.

CHAPTER 3

Page 63: "Why a GM Freeze?" GM Freeze, © September 9, 2009. http://www. gmfreeze.org. Reprinted with permission from GM Freeze. **Page 70:** "Summary of Key Findings" from "Mass Shootings at Virginia Tech, April 17, 2007: Report of the Review Panel Presented to Governor Kaine, Commonwealth of Virginia, August 2007. Used with permission. **Page 73:** "Colleges are Watching Troubled Students" by Jeffrey McMurray. From The Associated Press, March 28, 2008. Used with permission of The YGS Group on behalf of The Associated Press. All rights reserved.

CHAPTER 4

Page 115: "Cookies or Heroin?", from THE PLUG-IN DRUG, REVISED AND UPDATED-25TH ANNIVERSARY EDITION by Marie Winn, copyright © 1977, 1985, 2002 by Marie Winn Miller. Used by permission of Viking Penguin, division of Penguin Group (USA) Inc. **Page 126:** "The Satisfaction of Housewifery and Motherhood in 'An Age of Do-Your-Own-Thing,'" by Terry Martin Hekker from The New York Times, Dec. 20, 1977, copyright © 1977 The New York Times. Reprinted by permission of the author.

CHAPTER 5

Page 152: "Eye of the Tiger" by Meghan Daum from The Los Angeles Times, January 20, 2011. Meghan Daum has been a columnist at The Los Angeles Times since 2005. Reprinted with permission of the author. **Page 154:** Patrick Goldstein, "Tiger Mom vs. Tiger Mailroom," from the Los Angeles Times, Feb. 6, 2011. Copyright © 2011 Los Angeles Times. Reprinted with permission. **Page 156:** "America's Top Parent" by Elizabeth Kolbert from The New Yorker, January 31, 2011. Reprinted with permission. **Page 161:** "In Defense of Being a Kid" by James Bernard Murphy, February 9, 2011. Reprinted with permission from The Wall Street Journal © 2011 Dow Jones & Company and the author. All rights reserved.

CHAPTER 6

Page 174: Jenna Brager. **Page 177:** Johnson, Lacey. "Job Outlook for College Graduates Slowly Improving" from The Chronicle of Higher Education. The Chronicle of Higher Education by Editorial Projects for Education, Inc. Copyright © 2011. Reproduced with permission of Chronicle of Higher of Education, Inc. in the format Textbook via Copyright Clearance Center. **Page 179:** Carnevale, Anthony, Ban Cheah, and Jeff Strohl, "Not All College Degrees are Created Equal" from Georgetown University Center for Education and the Workforce, January 4,

2012. Reprinted with permission. **Page 190:** "Drift" from The Corrosion of Character: The Personal Consequences of Work in the New Capitalism by Richard Sennett. Copyright © 1998 by Richard Sennett. Used by permission of W. W. Norton & Company, Inc. **Page 203:** "Is Your Job an Endangered Species?" by Andy Kessler, from The Wall Street Journal, Feb. 17, 2011. Reprinted by permission from The Wall Street Journal © 2011 Dow Jones & Company. All rights reserved.

CHAPTER 7

Page 217: Printed by permission of the Norman Rockwell Family Agency, Copyright © 1948 The Norman Rockwell Family Entities. Photo: Curtis Licensing. **Page 220:** "Truth Is in the Ear of the Beholder" by Gregory Rodriguez, in The Los Angeles Times, Sept. 28, 2009. Gregory Rodriguez is the Founder and Executive Director of the Center for Social Cohesion at Arizona State University. **Page 223:** Salmans, Sandra, "Fighting That Old Devil Rumor" from The Saturday Evening Post, October 1982. Reprinted by permission. **Page 231:** "Paul is Dead!" by Alan Glenn, in Michigan Today, Nov. 11, 2009, michigantoday.umich.edu. Reprinted with permission. **Page 233:** Express Newspapers/AP Images. **Page 240:** "It's Clear That It's Unclear," from The Watercooler Effect by Nicholas DiFonzo, copyright © 2008 by Nicholas DiFonzo. Used by permission of Avery Publishing, an imprint of Penguin Group (USA) Inc. **Page 255:** Sunstein, Cass. From On Rumors: How Falsehoods Spread, Why We Believe Them, What Can Be Done, Farrar, Straus, and Giroux, 2009. **Page 265:** Reputation Management: The Key to Successful Public Relations and Corporate Communication by Doorley, John. Copyright 2007. Reproduced with permission of Taylor and Francis Group LLC-Books in the format Textbook via Copyright Clearance Center.

CHAPTER 8

Page 283: Copyright © 2009 Robert Bryce, Reprinted by permission of PublicAffairs, a member of the Perseus Books Group. **Page 296:** "Why I Still Support Nuclear Power, Even After Fukushima" by William Tucker from The Wall Street Journal, April 23, 2011. Reprinted with permission of the author. **Page 302:** Maria Dickerson. "State Solar Power Plans are as Big as all Outdoors" from The Los Angeles Times, December 3, 2008. Copyright © 2008 Los Angeles Times. Reprinted with permission. **Page 303:** "How Solar Energy Works", Illustration by Maury Aaseng. Reprinted with permission. **Page 307:** Plumer, Brad. "Solar Is Getting Cheaper, But How Far Can it Go?" from The Washington Post, November 7, 2011. Reprinted with permission of the author. **Page 311:** "The Island in the Wind" by Elizabeth Kolbert, originally published in The New Yorker, July 7, 2008. Reprinted by permission of the author. **Page xxx:** Stevens, Doug. "Catching the Wind" from the Los Angeles Times, March 1, 2009. Copyright © 2009 Los Angeles Times. Reprinted with permission. **Page 318:** "Wind Power Puffery" by H. Sterling Burnett, published in The Washington Times, Feb 4, 2004. Reprinted by permission of the author.

CHAPTER 9

Page 333: Jib Fowles, "Advertising's Fifteen Basic Appeals," in Advertising and Popular Culture. Et Cetera: A Review of General Semantics, Vol. 39, Number 3. July, 1982. Institute of General Semantics. Used by permission. **Page 352:** Bovee, Courtland, John Thill, George Dovel, Marian Burk Wood. From "Advertising Excellence." Used by permission. **Pages 362–364:** Images courtesy of the Advertising Archives. **Page 365:** Courtesy of the Cancer Patients Aid Association (CPAA) www.cancer.org.in. **Pages 366–377:** Images courtesy of the Advertising Archives.

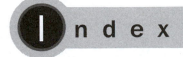

ndex

QUICK INDEX: APA DOCUMENTATION BASICS

APA In-Text Citations in Brief

When quoting or paraphrasing, place a parenthetical citation in your sentence that includes the author, publication year, and page or paragraph number.

Direct quotation, author and publication year not mentioned in sentence

> Research suggests that punishing a child "promotes only momentary compliance" (Berk & Ellis, 2002, p. 383).

Paraphrase, author and year mentioned in the sentence

> Berk and Ellis (2002) suggest that punishment may be ineffective (p. 383).

Direct quotation from Internet source

> Others have noted a rise in "problems that mimic dysfunctional behaviors" (Spivek, Jones, & Connelly, 2006, Introduction section, para. 3).

APA References List in Brief

On a separate, concluding page titled "References," alphabetize sources by author, providing full bibliographic information for each.

Article from a Journal

Conclude your entry with the digital object identifier—the article's unique reference number. When a DOI is not available and you have located the article on the Web, conclude with *Retrieved from* and the URL of the home page. For articles located through a database such as *LexisNexis*, do not list the database in your entry.

Article (with volume and issue numbers) located via print or database

> Ivanenko, A., & Massie, C. (2006). Assessment and management of sleep disorders in children. *Psychiatric Times, 23*(11), 90–95.

Article (with DOI and volume number) located via print or database

> Jones, K. L. (1986). Fetal alcohol syndrome. *Pediatrics in Review, 8,* 122–126. doi:10.1542/10.1542/pir.8-4-122

Article located via Web

> Ivanenko, A., & Massie, C. (2006). Assessment and management of sleep disorders in children. *Psychiatric Times, 23*(11), 90–95. Retrieved from http://www.psychiatrictimes.com

Article from a Magazine

Article (with volume and issue numbers) located via print or database

> Landi, A. (2010, January). Is beauty in the brain of the beholder? *ARTnews, 109*(1), 19–21.

Article located via Web

> Landi, A. (2010, January). Is beauty in the brain of the beholder? *ARTnews, 109*(1). Retrieved from http://www.artnews.com

Article from a Newspaper

Article located via print or database

> Wakabayashi, D. (2010, January 7). Sony pins future on a 3-D revival. *The Wall Street Journal*, pp. A1, A14.

Article located via Web

> Wakabayashi, D. (2010, January 7). Sony pins future on a 3-D revival. *The Wall Street Journal*. Retrieved from http://www.wsj.com

Book

Book located via print

> Mansfield, R. S., & Busse, T. V. (1981). *The psychology of creativity and discovery: Scientists and their work.* Chicago, IL: Nelson-Hall.

Book located via Web

> Freud, S. (1920). *Dream psychology: Psychoanalysis for beginners* (M. D. Elder, Trans.). Retrieved from http://www.gutenberg.org

Selection from an edited book

> Halberstam, D. (2002). Who we are. In S. J. Gould (Ed.), *The best American essays 2002* (pp. 124–136). New York, NY: Houghton Mifflin.

Later edition

> Samuelson, P., & Nordhaus, W. D. (2005). *Economics* (18th ed.). Boston, MA: McGraw-Hill Irwin.

QUICK INDEX: MLA DOCUMENTATION BASICS

MLA In-text Citations in Brief

When referring to a source, use parentheses to enclose a page number reference. Include the author's name if you do not mention it in your sentence.

> From the beginning, the AIDS test has been "mired in controversy" (Bayer 101).

Or, if you name the author in the sentence:

> Bayer claims the AIDS test has been "mired in controversy" (101).

MLA Works Cited List in Brief

At the end of the paper, on a separate page titled "Works Cited," alphabetize each cited source by author's last name. Provide full bibliographic information, as shown. State how you accessed the source, via print, Web, or downloaded digital file. As appropriate, precede "Web" with a database name (e.g., *LexisNexis*) or the title of a Web site and a publisher. Follow "Web" with your date of access. Note the use of punctuation and italics.

In MLA style, the medium by which you access a source (print, Web, database, download) determines its Works Cited format.

Magazine or Newspaper Article
Article accessed via print magazine or newspaper

> Packer, George. "The Choice." *New Yorker* 28 Jan. 2008: 28-35. Print.

> Warner, Judith. "Goodbye to All This." *New York Times* 18 Dec. 2009, late ed.: A27. Print.

Article (version exists in print) accessed via downloaded file

> Packer, George. "The Choice." *New Yorker* 28 Jan. 2008: 28-35. AZW file.

> Warner, Judith. "Goodbye to All This." *New York Times* 18 Dec. 2009, late ed.: A27. PDF file.

Article (version exists in print) accessed via database

> Packer, George. "The Choice." *New Yorker* 28 Jan. 2008: 28-35. *Academic Search Premier*. Web. 12 Mar. 2010.

> Warner, Judith. "Goodbye to All This." *New York Times* 18 Dec. 2009, late ed.: A27. *LexisNexis*. Web. 14 Jan. 2010.

Article (version exists in print) accessed via Web

Packer, George. "The Choice." *New Yorker.com*. CondéNet, 28 Jan. 2008. Web. 12 Mar. 2010.

Warner, Judith. "Goodbye to All This." *New York Times*. New York Times, 18 Dec. 2009. Web. 14 Jan. 2010.

Scholarly Article

Scholarly article accessed via print journal

Ivanenko, Anna, and Clifford Massie. "Assessment and Management of Sleep Disorders in Children." *Psychiatric Times* 23.11 (2006): 90-95. Print.

Scholarly article (version exists in print) accessed via downloaded file

Ivanenko, Anna, and Clifford Massie. "Assessment and Management of Sleep Disorders in Children." *Psychiatric Times* 23.11 (2006): 90-95. PDF file.

Scholarly article (version exists in print) accessed via database

Ivanenko, Anna, and Clifford Massie. "Assessment and Management of Sleep Disorders in Children." *Psychiatric Times* 23.11 (2006): 90-95. *Academic OneFile*. Web. 3 Nov. 2010.

Scholarly article (version exists in print) accessed via Web

Ivanenko, Anna, and Clifford Massie. "Assessment and Management of Sleep Disorders in Children." *Psychiatric Times*. United Business Media, 1 Oct. 2006. Web. 3 Nov. 2010.

Scholarly article from an e-journal that has no print equivalent

Blackwood, Jothany. "Coaching Educational Leaders." *Academic Leadership: The Online Journal* 7.3 (2009): n. pag. Web. 2 Feb. 2010.

Book

Book accessed via print

James, William. *The Varieties of Religious Experience: A Study in Human Nature; Being the Gifford Lectures on Natural Religion Delivered at Edinburgh in 1901–1902*. New York: Longmans, 1902. Print.

Book (version exists in print) accessed via downloaded file

James, William. *The Varieties of Religious Experience: A Study in Human Nature; Being the Gifford Lectures on Natural Religion Delivered at Edinburgh in 1901–1902*. New York: Longmans, 1902. MOBI file.

Book (version exists in print) accessed via Web or database

James, William. *The Varieties of Religious Experience: A Study in Human Nature; Being the Gifford Lectures on Natural Religion Delivered at Edinburgh in 1901–1902*. New York: Longmans, 1902. *U. of Virginia Etext Center*. Web. 12 Jan. 2010.

James, William. *The Varieties of Religious Experience: A Study in Human Nature; Being the Gifford Lectures on Natural Religion Delivered at Edinburgh in 1901–1902*. New York: Longmans, 1902. *ACLS Humanities E-Book*. Web. 12 Mar. 2010.

Online book that has no print equivalent

Langer, Maria. *Mastering Microsoft Word. Designprovideo.com*. Nonlinear Educating, 2009. Web. 23 Jan. 2010.

Web-Only Publication (Content Created for and Published on the Web)

Home page

Boucher, Marc, ed. Home page. *The Space Elevator Reference. Spaceelevator.com*. SpaceRef Interactive, 2009. Web. 17 Dec. 2009.

Web-based article on a larger site

Landau, Elizabeth. "Stem Cell Therapies for Hearts Inching Closer to Wide Use." *CNN.com*. Cable News Network, 18 Dec. 2009. Web. 14 Jan. 2010.

White, Veronica. "Gian Lorenzo Bernini." *Heilbrunn Timeline of Art History*. Metropolitan Museum of Art, New York, 2009. Web. 18 Mar. 2010.

Blog

Lubber, Mindy. "The Climate Treaty Announcement." *Climate Experts' Forum—Copenhagen*. Financial Times, 19 Dec. 2009. Web. 22 Dec. 2009.

CHECKLIST FOR WRITING SUMMARIES

- **Read the passage carefully.** Determine its structure. Identify the author's purpose in writing.
- **Reread.** *Label* each section or stage of thought. *Highlight* key ideas and terms.
- **Write one-sentence summaries** of each stage of thought.
- **Write a thesis:** a one- or two-sentence summary of the entire passage.
- **Write the first draft** of your summary.
- **Check your summary** against the original passage.
- **Revise** your summary.

CHECKLIST FOR WRITING CRITIQUES

- **Introduce** both the passage being critiqued and the author.
- **Summarize** the author's main points, making sure to state the author's purpose for writing.
- **Evaluate** the validity of the presentation.
- **Respond** to the presentation: agree and/or disagree.
- **Conclude** with your overall assessment.